W9-ACY-758

CHINA'S NATIONAL MINORITY EDUCATION

REFERENCE BOOKS IN INTERNATIONAL EDUCATION
VOLUME 42
GARLAND REFERENCE LIBRARY OF SOCIAL SCIENCE
VOLUME 1090

CHINA'S NATIONAL MINORITY EDUCATION
CULTURE, SCHOOLING, AND DEVELOPMENT

EDITED BY
GERARD A. POSTIGLIONE

FALMER PRESS
A MEMBER OF THE TAYLOR & FRANCIS GROUP
NEW YORK AND LONDON
1999

Library of Congress Cataloging-in-Publication Data is available from the Library
of Congress.

China's national minority education: culture, schooling, and development
/ edited by Gerard A. Postiglione.

ISBN 0–8153-2223-2 (alk. paper)

Printed on acid-free, 250-year-life paper
Manufactured in the United States of America

Contents

List of Appendices

List of Figures

List of Tables

Series Editor's Foreword

This series of scholarly works in comparative and international education has grown well beyond the initial conception of a collection of reference books. Although retaining its original purpose of providing a resource to scholars, students, and a variety of other professionals who need to understand the role played by education in various societies or world regions, it also strives to provide accurate, relevant, and up-to-date information on a wide variety of selected educational issues, problems, and experiments within an international context.

Contributors to this series are well-known scholars who have devoted their professional lives to the study of their specializations. Without exception these men and women possess an intimate understanding of the subject of their research and writing. Without exception they have studied their subject not only in dusty archives, but have lived and traveled widely in their quest for knowledge. In short, they are "experts" in the best sense of that often overused word.

In our increasingly interdependent world, it is now widely understood that it is a matter of military, economic, and environmental survival that we understand better not only what makes other societies tick, but also how others, be they Japanese, Hungarian, South African, or Chilean, attempt to solve the same kinds of educational problems that we face in North America. As the late George Z. F. Bereday wrote more than three decades ago: "[E]ducation is a mirror held against the face of a people. Nations may put on blustering shows of strength to conceal public weakness, erect grand façades to conceal shabby backyards, and profess peace while secretly arming for conquest, but how they take care of their children tells unerringly who they are" (*Comparative Methods in Education*, New York: Holt, Rinehart and Winston, 1964, p. 5).

Perhaps equally important, however, is the valuable perspective that studying another education system (or its problems) provides us in understanding our own system (or its problems). When we step beyond our own limited experience and our commonly held assumptions about schools and learning in order to look back at our system in contrast to another, we see it in a very different light. To learn, for example, how China or Belgium handles the education of a multilingual society; how the French provide for the funding of public education; or how the Japanese control access to their universities enables us to better understand that there are reasonable alternatives to our own familiar way of doing things. Not that we can *borrow* directly from other societies. Indeed, educational arrangements are inevitably a reflection of deeply embedded political, economic, and cultural factors that are unique to a particular society. But a conscious recognition that there are other ways of doing things can serve to open our minds and provoke our imaginations in ways that can result in new experiments or approaches that we may not have otherwise considered.

Since this series is intended to be a useful research tool, the editor and contributors welcome suggestions for future volumes, as well as ways in which this series can be improved.

Edward R. Beauchamp
University of Hawaii

CHINA'S NATIONAL
MINORITY EDUCATION

Introduction
State Schooling and Ethnicity in China
Gerard A. Postiglione

Most countries in the world are multiethnic and thus face a similar educational challenge.[1] They must convince their citizens, as well as the global community, that state-sponsored schooling ensures equal opportunities for all ethnic groups, promotes the economic development of poor ethnic minority regions, permits ethnic groups to practice cultural autonomy and builds inter-ethnic unity.[2] Educational systems expand in reaction to a market of demands. Individuals and employers demand practical skills, social groups demand status culture, and the state demands national unity and social control.[3] Representations of ethnic culture in school curricula are greatly affected by the market of demands. Within China, the market is heavily influenced by the state. Though the demand of ethnic minorities for schools to elevate the status of their culture within the national framework is ubiquitous, the actual content of schooling reflects the state's view of ethnic inter-group processes. Hence, a great deal can be learned about the People's Republic of China by studying how it schools its many ethnic groups, represents their heritage, socializes them into a national identity, structures their educational opportunities and links their schooling to economic development.

Social context is a profound determinant of the form and content of schooling and state schooling serves a conservative function by defining and reproducing a national culture that bolsters dominant social structures.[4] China's state schools conserve a particular brand of national culture *(zhonghua minzu wenhua)*, and are supervised by an authoritarian state wary of outside cultural influences, especially from the West.[5] State schooling is also charged with the responsibility to conserve ethnic cultures within a national context that places a premium on Han Chinese cultural capital.[6]

While many aspects of China's ethnic minority education remain highly centralized, the national move to a market economy, administrative decentralization and local elections could begin to have a profound effect on ethnic minority schooling. Yet the notion of ethnic pluralism remains carefully proscribed, and multiethnic education is still a sensitive issue. Discussion of multiculturalism is found in academic discourse, but much less so in policy and practice.[7] To what extent do schools in China create an atmosphere that has positive institutional norms toward diverse cultural groups within the nation state?[8] To what degree do schools in China modify their total environment to make it more reflective of the ethnic diversity in the society? State policy accords importance to the special cultural characteristics of ethnic minority regions; however, not enough is known about actual practice to provide detailed answers to such questions.[9] In-depth study of the schooling in particular ethnic communities is needed to measure the gap between the policy and practice of ethnic minority regional autonomy in education, and to understand the manner in which ethnic communities innovate in their adjustment to state schooling. With this purpose in mind, this volume aims at providing grounded field research, quantitative surveys, and thoughtful analysis regarding how the Chinese state in general, and Han China in particular, deals with the problem of ethnicity and schooling.

The Rise or Demise of Multiculturalism?

The chapters in this volume examine ethnic minority education in China and address issues that relate to culture, schooling, and development. The issues include the degree to which ethnic groups are drawn away from traditional religious institutions and toward modern schooling, the manner in which state schooling represents ethnic cultures, the effect of state schooling on the conservation of ethnic group languages, the scope of basic education across ethnic minority regions, the results of preferential policies to admit ethnic minorities to higher education and the results of state schooling's attempt to ensure equal educational opportunities, reproduce national culture, and foster inter-ethnic unity. In general, chapters work toward addressing the question of what state schooling does to ethnicity and development. Taken together, the chapters of this book question claims that ethnic minority schools adequately represent ethnic minority culture. Furthermore, the authors operate on the assumption that a multicultural education can further improve understanding between Han Chinese and other ethnic groups, even to the extent that the latter will increase their participation in state schooling, thereby raising their potential to reap equal rewards in terms of social and economic development. The chapters are divided into three parts: cultural challenges to state schooling, educational disparities and case studies of ethnic minority schooling. The first part focuses on religion and language, both of which usually encapsulate the core of ethnic minority cultural heritage.

Cultural Challenges to State Schooling: Religion and Language

Part One begins with religion because it pervades the culture of most of China's minorities and they are generally more committed to it than the Han Chinese majority. Religion has traditionally been the main form of organized education outside of the family. As a challenge to state schooling, the government is more concerned about minority religions than about minority languages. Moreover, state schools must often compete with religious education for attendance rates, as well as financial contributions and support from families.

The main religions of China's minorities are Islam, Buddhism and Lamaism, but others also have a following. Most of China's minorities have a strong religious tradition. For some, like the Muslim Hui, religion is the main attribute of their identity as an ethnic minority. Members of the Hui, Uygur, Kazak, Kirgiz, Tatar, Uzbek, Tajik, Dongxiang, Salar and Bonan groups are adherents of the Islamic faith. The Tibetan, Mongol, Yugur and Tu groups are adherents of Lamaism. The Dai, Bulang and Benglong are adherents of Hinayana Buddhism. Shamanism is practiced by Oroqen, Daur and Ewenki. The Drung, Nu, Wa, Jingpo and Gaoshan practice polytheism as well as totemism and ancestor worship. A small group of adherents to Christianity can be found among the Koreans, Miao, Lahu, and Yi.

After the founding of the People's Republic of China, freedom of religion was guaranteed in the new constitution. During the early years of communist rule, Mao Zedong argued that religion should not be prohibited, only restricted. Religion was viewed as a historical product that could only be abolished under certain socioeconomic conditions. Thus, the practice of religion has come to be viewed as something that must be permitted to a certain extent. Also, religion shares certain social concerns with communism that permit mutual cooperation in some circumstances. For example, religious leaders have joined educators and officials in efforts to eradicate illiteracy.[10] Nevertheless, only state-sponsored religious organizations are permitted; all others are severely suppressed. The official policy, however, is that government authorities are not to interfere in religious affairs of minorities unless affairs of the state are affected. Ethnic minority cadres are not supposed to be dismissed because they have religious beliefs, but rather be persuaded of the advantages of shedding their religious views, as cooperation between religious leaders and communists is still viewed as valuable.

Of all of the ways that the government has attempted to win back support lost during the Cultural Revolution, granting autonomy in the area of culture, especially religion, has been central. Nevertheless, religious autonomy in the context of a communist authoritarian government has been a matter of degree more than anything else. Ethnic minority religion has been increasingly tolerated, and even encouraged when it helps tourism, yet severely limited when it threatens national sovereignty.

Colin Mackerras, in Chapter Two, outlines the basic situation regarding the many religions of China's minorities, with particular emphasis on Islam and Buddhism. He divides his analysis into pre- and post-1949 periods, and within the latter describes three phases regarding how religion survived after the communist revolution. His emphasis throughout is on how monasteries, mosques and churches, which predated state schooling, remain repositories of traditional culture and learning, continue to flourish in one form or another. In examining state schooling he makes clear that the "state school system generally adheres strictly to the principle of secularity" (page 39, this volume). For example, clerics do little inside of schools, and there are no religious representations, and students are prohibited from reading religious books or praying in schools. The few clergy that teach in schools usually teach language courses rather than religious material. Moreover, such clerics would have to dress in secular clothes while in school.

Mackerras also notes that state schooling has expanded at the same time that minorities are experiencing a religious revival. Thus, the question: is state schooling responsible for this religious resurgence? "It is possible that in some minority areas this religious revival is in part directly related to the secularization" (page 47, this volume). As signs of the religious revival, he points to the large number of Tibetan boys entering monasteries and Muslim boys reading the Koran in mosques. Moreover, while religion is still kept apart from secular education, state education and religious education are not positional, and sometimes graduates of state schools go on to mosques.

The expansion of state schooling is having a profound affect on ethnicity, even to the extent that schools actually make and remake ethnic nationalities. In Chapter Three, Dru Gladney critically examines these processes in his study of Chinese Muslims, and notes how religious education and state education do very different things. In fact, state schooling runs counter to religious teaching, so China's Muslims must initiate a process of negotiation to deal with conflicting sets of norms. Furthermore, Han Chinese often view minority cultures as backward and their religious education as being of little value, as Gladney illustrates with the case of the Hui Hajji he met in China who said he "had no culture," though he had lived for 12 years in the Middle East, and was fluent in Persian and Arabic and was a master of Islamic Natural Sciences.

What is state schooling doing to ethnic minority culture? From Gladney's perspective, representations of ethnic minority culture are unbalanced. " For most Han Chinese, who have never darkened the door of a mosque and learn little about Islam in public schools, this representation in the 'public sphere' is their only exposure to knowledge about Islam in China or Muslim identities" (page 64, this volume). Muslims in China have a very different representation of themselves than that given to them by mainstream culture. Moreover, they are not only members of an ethnic minority but members of a long religious and scholarly tradition that has contributed to Chinese culture and society. Yet, in some cases, state schooling actually marginalizes Muslim minorities. Because many score lower in state schooling, they also become represented as failures.

The Chinese Muslim experience in state education is not monolithic. Even though the Hui do not excel in school measures of achievement, the Tatars and Uzbeks do extremely well. Other Muslims approach the national average as a group. Gladney attributes this either to assimilating to mainstream culture and not rejecting the images represented by the state, or more likely, viewing schooling as merely a tool and resisting the images of their ethnicity represented there. As Chinese Muslims move up the school ladder, they will come to exert an influence on the images and representations that the state assigns to their culture.

Education for Muslims, in sum, seems to result in parallel streams, one in which the state represents Muslim culture and the other in which Muslims represent their own culture. This will not change as long as state education does not incorporate more information about Muslim life. As Gladney states: "The lack of nationality content and Muslim world history may be forcing Muslims interested in their people's history to go to the mosque rather than the public schools and libraries for such 'religious' knowledge" (page 78, this volume).

A second major challenge relating to ethnic minority culture and schooling is language. With the exception of the Hui and Manchu who use the Chinese language (*Hanyü*), all of China's minorities have their own language, with some minority groups having more than one. Most of the languages belong to the Sino-Tibetan and Altaic families, while some belong to the South Asian, Austronesian and Indo-European families. Before 1949, only 20 minorities had their own written language. Those in most common use were Mongol, Tibetan, Uygur, Kazak, Korean, Xibe, Dai, Uzbek, Kirgiz, Tatar and Russian. Others included Yi, Miao, Naxi, Jingpo, Lisu, Lahu and Wa. Since 1949, the communist government helped to derive a written script for nine national minorities formerly without one. Still, many minorities are without a written script. While most of the Manchu have long since abandoned their script and now use the Han language, others groups such as the Jingpo speak a variety of different languages, some of which are totally unlike each other. Other groups are trilingual, speaking their native tongue, the language of the nationality in closest proximity and Chinese.

Since the beginning of the Four Modernization period, national minority languages have been increasingly emphasized. Nevertheless, there is a strong call for Chinese as the main medium of instruction. This is being justified by pointing out that there are few scientific materials published in national minority languages, therefore, the Han Chinese language, which is "international," should be the main education language and medium of instruction. According to one Chinese scholar, this is further supported by "the Chinese language craze that is sweeping the world."[11] The case of Xinjiang, with a 62 percent minority population, is illustrative. The Uygur, Kazak, Mongol, Kirgiz, Xibe and Russian groups have their own written language, while the Hui and the Manchu use the Han language system. Moreover, certain groups have dual or multiple languages, such as the Uygurs, Kazaks and Xibe, some of whom use each other's language as well as their own. And some groups who do not have a written language may take school examinations in the language of another ethnic minority.

As a result of the many languages in use, students from different ethnic minorities attend different schools; thus, ethnic segregation is common. This trend has many educators very concerned, and in turn has led to a call for school desegregation. As one educator, almost echoing the 1954 *Brown v. the Board of Education* Supreme Court decision in the United States, stated: "My understanding is that separate schools are detrimental to the development and improvement of ethnic minority populations."[12] Among the cited advantages of desegregated schools are allowing for a more healthy competition among ethnic minorities, a concentration of educational resources and an increased possibility for teachers to become more specialized. Also, it is argued that integrated schools encourage mutual understandings and friendly relations, and help to cement unity among the nationalities. Ethnic minority students would "get a correct understanding of the strong and weak points of their own and of other nationalities . . . for stimulating proper ideas."[13]

Language is the medium for the communication of culture. Therefore, the manner in which the state permits ethnic minority languages to be used in school is crucial for the form of ethnicity that schools reproduce. Unlike religion, language is essential for achieving the goals of state schooling. The implementation of minority languages as a medium of instruction can increase attendance rates and strengthen socialization into national ideologies. As Regie Stites notes in chapter four: "What the Chinese party/state wants and needs is a bilingual education system capable of producing people who are both 'ethnic and expert'" (page 124, this volume). Stites maps out the complex linguistic diversity of China and examines language policies and the literature on bilingual education in China. A great many permutations are evident in the manner in which minority and Chinese languages and scripts are organized as part of the curriculum within state schools. Four minority languages, Zhuang, Yi, Uygur and Tibetan, are taken as examples to examine China's efforts to develop a viable bilingual system of education. Most of those in these four language groups will spend their lives within a linguistic environment different from that of the Han Chinese majority. The Chinese state has recognized this and gone through a long historical process that taught many lessons. Stites points out both successes and mistakes. Still, the Chinese state has gone to great lengths to accommodate minority languages. Minority language textbooks and teaching materials are available, more so than in the United States. Nevertheless, success in bilingual and literacy education for minorities will be shaped to a large extent by the politics of ethnic identity.

Educational Disparities: Literacy Levels and Access to Higher Education

Part Two takes a closer look at the basic situation with regard to ethnic minority education at different levels and across various regions. Although the provision of education for ethnic minorities at all levels has been increasing, most minorities are below the national average at all levels; this is especially the case with minority women. Nevertheless, national policies have attempted to correct this situation and have met with varying levels of success.

In his work that conceptualizes the developmental process with respect to minority education in different regions, Jacques Lamontagne (in Chapter Five) introduces a model in which phases of the developmental process can be considered separately. His research highlights the educational disparities across regions and ethnic minorities, and then compares the patterns of increase and decrease over time. In this way, he can identify factors which facilitate or hinder the development of education in these regions. As key indicators, he chooses levels of literacy, across regions, as well as across ethnic groups and genders. His model not only permits him to identify the most literate provinces, counties, ethnic minorities and genders, but also their trajectories over time. Lamontagne is able to classify selected groups as being in either one of four phases: the Low-slow phase (Salar, Tibetan Bonan, Dongxiang), Low-fast phase (Achang Jingpo), High-fast phase (Jing and Mulao), and High-slow phase (Tartar,

Korean, Xibe). This model of development provides rich avenues for further research.

The gap between minority and Han achievement in education has been especially apparent in higher education. In order to ensure national integration, ethnic minority participation at the highest levels of the education system will have to be increased. Since 1980, measures have been taken to accelerate the expansion of higher education for ethnic minorities. Preferential policies in family planning, housing and jobs play a major role. The most important preferential policy dealing with education concerns admission into institutions of higher education. Although these policies have generated some resentment, as they have in other countries, they are viewed as necessary in order to bring minorities into the mainstream. As Barry Sautman points out in Chapter Six, China is ahead of most countries in the policies and practices of preferential treatment in higher education: "The PRC has one of the oldest and largest programs of state sponsored preferential polices (*youhui zhengce*) for ethnic minorities" (page 173, this volume). Sautman believes that preferential policies have led to a misplaced sense of identity, and points out that from 1982 to 1990 some 14 million minority people who had previously elected to be classified as Han Chinese had themselves reclassified as minority group members.

A variety of measures have been taken to increase enrolment in higher education. Nationality institutes, which mainly serve the function of training minority cadres, admit the largest proportion of ethnic minority students. Teacher training institutions have high rates of minority enrolment since they are considered essential institutions to increase the low minority student participation rates in elementary and secondary schools. In order to increase success rates in higher education, minorities may opt to take the university entrance examinations in their own language (*min kao min*). Taking the examination in standard Chinese (*min kao han*) is usually accompanied by the addition of bonus points (*jia fen*). For those ethnic minorities that do gain admission to a university, preparatory classes (*yuke ban*) are often provided during the first year, especially at prestigious institutions. The system of preferential treatment is complex and dynamic. Sautman's research provides a comprehensive analysis of this massive system of preferential treatment for minorities in China's universities. A major aim of this policy is also to increase the number of trained personnel in minority regions; however, many minorities do not return to their home regions after graduation from universities. This pattern is on the rise as universities begin to charge tuition and do away with the job allocation system that was used in the past to ensure that students would return home after graduation.

Case Studies of Ethnic Minority Schooling

Case studies have greatly improved our understanding of important processes at work in the field of ethnic minority education. Compared with previous decades, the 1990s have seen a massive increase in the amount of quantitative data available on minority education in China. While this information has been useful in understanding the general situation, establishing patterns over time and making comparisons between groups, it has limited use in providing explanations of the processes at work in minority education. Quantitative research has not been able to capture detailed processes at work as ethnic minority communities adjust to state schooling, nor permit us to understand the manner in which minority students and their families come to construct the meaning of schooling within their own communities. Only by using ethnographic methods can answers be found to the question of why minority children have higher dropout rates than Han students. While the available literature describes the problems of economic development in minority regions, ethnographic methods show how locality, culture and the perceived value of schooling play a determining role in the willingness of parents to make the financial sacrifice necessary to pay schools fees, and at what point they would consider supporting the decision to discontinue the schooling of a child. Ethnographic methods can also provide a way of understanding where schooling fits in the constellation of ethnic minority culture; in what respects it is a support or a threat to the preservation of minority heritage and under what conditions support for school attendance would diminish. Finally, ethnographic methods are essential for gaining an understanding of the ways in which members of ethnic minorities deal with the identity conflicts that result from their semi-sinicization through national institutions. National integration has little chance of succeeding without high rates of school attendance. The manner in which the state uses schooling for political socialization, especially within the classroom, can be studied ethnographically. [14]

Part Three of this volume contains case studies of minority education in four provinces that are ethnographic in character. In Chapter Seven, Stevan Harrell and Ma Erzi begin by examining the relevance of the cultural discontinuity hypothesis for ethnic minority education in China: "the idea that linguistic and cultural boundaries or differences between the home environment of a minority group and the school environment in which they are expected to learn the values of the dominant majority were the primary cause for the poor performance by minorities" (page 213, this volume). Finding this inadequate to explain the success of some (especially involuntary) minorities, they employ John Ogbu's notion of folk theories of success: "if members of a minority hold the view that they can use education to achieve success, they devise ways to surmount the obstacles posed by cultural divergence. If they hold, on the other hand, that the education system will merely strip them of their own culture and identity without giving them equal opportunity in the wider society, they will respond with resistance." (page 214, this volume). Harrell and Ma contend that most involuntary minorities hold the oppositional folk theory of success, and most voluntary minorities hold the positive folk theory. These folk theories of success, developed on the basis of perceived chances for success, permit minorities to submit themselves to state schooling for the purposes of achieving social mobility but do not necessarily validate the state's aim of making them into compliant and subordinate citizens. From their research in Baiwu township of Sichuan province, where 92 percent of the population is Yi (Nuoso), they conclude that status is more important than ideology, and that ethnic subgroups, in this case subgroups of the Yi, have distinct differences that explain differential success in school. The success of the Mgebbu, a Yi clan, is highly attributed to their folk theories of success. Differential school success in Baiwu cannot be explained fully in terms of cultural and linguistic difference, however, mother tongue teaching did matter greatly for Yi girls.

While folk theories of success are shown to be important determinants of an ethnic minority's success in school, the state advances its own folk theory that Han perform better in school due to the "backwardness" (*luohou*) of the minorities. The prevalence of this notion is shown through the ethnographic research of Mette Halskov Hansen in her examination of the Tai of Sipsong Panna in Yunnan Province. Using Stevan Harrell's notion of "civilizing project," she traces the history of the Tai, including the central role played by Buddhism and Buddhist temples. She notes in Chapter Eight that "several monasteries have started to extend education to include mathematics, Thai language (standard Thai of Thailand) and, more rarely, Chinese" (page 250, this volume). This is significant in that ethnic minority attendance rates in state schools are still low, and parents often support religious institutions more than schools. If formal education is the aim, it may very well be in the interest of the state to permit formal education that combines religion with "modern education." Moreover, the state could benefit from having religious groups run schools because of their ability to raise funds for schools. The problem, Hansen points out, is that "Most Han Chinese cadres, teachers, and researchers in and outside Sipsong Panna continue to express negative views on the influence of Buddhist education among the Tai" (page 251, this volume). There is also a fear that "because the Tai are concerned about learning their own script they run the risk of becoming 'more backward' than the minorities from the mountains who have always been considered the most backward" (page 257, this volume). A key issue, then, concerns what the school does to minority culture, through representations, textbooks and notions of backwardness. The need for multicultural education, or at least more content about a group's cultural heritage, may be essential to foster an attachment to its schools. As Hansen remarks, "All the Tai students I have talked to are (sometimes painfully) aware that they belong to what is considered a backward minority group" (page 258, this volume). Chapter Eight represents only part of Hansen's extensive work in Sipsong Panna, which also focuses on other ethnic minorities.[15]

Although access to Tibetan regions remains an obstacle to research, Tibetan education is particularly illustrative of the dilemma of ethnic education in China, as shown by Janet Upton's research. Her fieldwork in the Abba region of Sichuan provides insight into school-based Tibetan language education. The Chinese government is doing much to support mother tongue education for Tibetans, which may seem surprising given the view that it obstructs national unity. Nevertheless, though China has done well in certain respects in the way it has handled minority language issues, it is not as well as most Tibetans want or expect. Very few Tibetans, however, advocate learning no Chinese. An increasing number of Tibetans want to learn Chinese fluently because their day to day survival, as well as access to broader occupational opportunities, depend upon it. Moreover, some would like to study as much English in school as do Han Chinese students.

In Tibetan areas of China, dual track education (Tibetan and Chinese) is generally available in the urban areas, but after the third grade most courses are taught in Chinese with only language and some Tibetan "culture" courses taught in the Tibetan language. However, there are many variations. In the Kangding area of Sichuan, for example, there are opportunities to learn all courses (science, math, history, etc.) in Tibetan up through senior middle school. Some schools offer instruction solely in the Chinese language and some offer all courses in Tibetan. There are also experimental programs that use Tibetan as the language of instruction for all the science and math subjects. These reforms began in Qinghai Province. Tibetans advocating the trial programs want to make Tibetan a language of science and modernity and a language of employment so that Tibetans can use their own language as the main form of communication, as well as increasing their opportunities to go into higher education since they will learn better and thus perform better on the college entrance examinations. This same argument is used by those who advocate introducing Chinese in the early years, because that, too, will enable children to do better on the standardized tests. Most rural children have no chance to learn Chinese until the third or fourth grade, and their Chinese is often too poor to pass examinations. Thus, the dropout rate is high and the incentive to work hard is diminished. The trial programs have proven that the participating students do much better on tests than those who are not participating. Nevertheless, problems remain, including a lack of qualified teachers.

To provide a better understanding of the language issue, in Chapter Nine Upton traces the history of Tibetan modern language education since 1949 though periods of development and change, including the Cultural Revolution. Her research is focused on Songpan County of Aba Prefecture, about which she provides a very detailed account of its local Tibetan language school. This account demonstrates how the school had a major influence on the surrounding community in its role as a training ground for the elite of Songpan. Regarding school text-books, she observes: "Contrary to the rhetoric that often surfaces in Western and Tibetan-exile reports about the Tibetan language curriculum in the PRC, the textbooks in use do contain a fair amount of material drawn from Tibetan sources and relevant to Tibetan cultural life in the broad sense" (page 307, this volume). Nevertheless, she asserts that the "view of Tibetan history that is presented in the formal curriculum under the current political and cultural regime is far removed from the 'real history' that so many Tibetans at home and abroad currently crave" (pages 307, this volume). Her research highlights an important point about multicultural and multethnic content in school lessons: "But what may come as a surprise to some readers, as it did to me, is that some of the most forceful lessons about the value of Tibetan culture can be taught to students through lessons that derive from works that are historically and culturally distant" (pages 309–310, this volume). The implications for this mode of teaching in ethnic minority schools is an important topic for further research.

The impact of schooling on ethnic identity depends on what is taught, how it is taught, and how it is evaluated. Yet ethnic identity in China is still also officially defined and there are some groups that are not recognized for what they consider themselves to be. The Minhe Monguor are not one of the official 55 minorities, except insofar as they are considered by the government to be part of the Tu ethnic group. Perhaps because of their characterization as Tu, the Monguor do not benefit from the kind of bilingual education that the Tibetans do. In Chapter Ten, Zhu Yongzhang and Kevin Stuart point to the artificiality of the educational experience: " . . . a school in the area decreed that teachers and students must not speak Monguor, but were instead to speak only Chinese" (pages 372, this volume). Stuart and Zhu propose that students would greatly benefit from Monguor textbooks. "There is nothing in the curriculum that reinforces this sense of ethnic identity for texts are the standard Chinese language curricula," (page 374, this volume). This point is echoed by the Tibetan scholar Baden Nima:

> For a long time we have held the misconception that the majority nationality is the main fountainhead for school curriculum. We have also believed that technological knowledge is an outcome of the majority nationality's social development. Such reasoning creates problems for minority peoples. One is that minority nationality children become very self-abased when they find no reference to their own culture or history in school materials. When they find there is no

content which can make them feel proud of being a person of their own nationality, they lose self-esteem and interest in schooling. This is reflected in the high dropout rates of minority children.[16]

Taken together, the chapters of this volume argue that despite the authoritarian character of state schooling in China, a great deal of diversity continues to exist. This diversity derives from the vast variety of cultural traditions and practices, especially in religion and language, that continue to flourish. Yet, the diversity that exists among China's ethnic minority population does not appear to be fully reflected in the content of schooling, even though minority languages are emphasized in many regions.[17] School curriculum in predominantly Han Chinese schools has even less of a multicultural emphasis.[18] As the market economy leads to more Han population floating into ethnic minority regions, the chances of cultural misunderstandings will grow unless schools do more to foster a sensitivity to minority cultures. School curricula that more accurately reflect the cultural diversity that characterizes China's ethnic minorities might not only increase understanding among ethnic groups and conserve their cultures within the process of economic modernization, but also make state schools much more attractive to ethnic communities, thereby strengthening their identities within the national community.

NOTES

1. See Gerard Postiglione "National Minorities and Nationalities Policy in China, in Berch Berberoglu (ed.) *The National Question*, Philadelphia: Temple University Press, 1995, pp. 259-279. Douglas Ray and Deo Poonwassie (eds.), *Education and Cultural Differences: New Perspectives* (New York: Garland Publishing, 1992); Center for Educational Research and Innovation (ed.), *The Education of Minority Groups: An Enquiry into the Practices of 15 Countries* (Hampshire: Avebury, 1984).

2. See, for example, John W. Meyer, "The Functions of Education as an Institution," in *American Journal of Sociology*, No. 83 (September 1977), pp. 340-363; Francisco O. Ramirez and John W. Meyer, "Comparative Education: The Social Construction of the Modern World System," in *Annual Review of Sociology*, No. 6 (1980), pp. 369-399.

3. Randall Collins, "Some Comparative Principles of Educational Stratification," in *Harvard Educational Review*, No. 47 (1977), pp. 1-27.

4. See, for example, Raymond A. Morrow and Carlos Torres, *Social Theory and Education: A Critique of Theories of Social and Cultural Reproduction* (Albany: State University of New York Press, 1995); Martin Carnoy and Henry M. Levin, *Schooling and Work in the Democratic State* (Stanford: Stanford University Press, 1985); Randall Collins, *The Credential Society* (New York: Academic Press, 1979); Gerard A. Postiglione (ed.), *Education and Society in Hong Kong: Toward One Country and Two Systems* (New York: M.E. Sharpe, 1991); Gerard A. Postiglione and Wing On Lee (eds.), *Schooling in Hong Kong: Organization, Teaching and Social Context* (Hong Kong: Hong Kong University Press, 1997).

5. Frank Dikotter, *The Discourse of Race in Modern China* (Hong Kong: Hong Kong University Press, 1992); Frank Dikotter (ed.), *The Construction of Racial Identities in China and Japan* (Hong Kong: Hong Kong University Press, 1997).

6. Tao Tao Liu and David Faure (eds.), *Unity and Diversity: Local Cultures and Identities in China* (Hong Kong: Hong Kong University Press, 1996); Melissa J. Brown (ed.), *Negotiating Ethnicities in China and Taiwan* (Berkeley: Institute of East Asian Studies, University of California, 1996).

7. See *Minzu jiaoyu yanjiu* (Nationality Education Research), the journal of the Institute of Ethnic Minority Education of the Central University of Nationalities.

8. James Banks, *Multiethnic Education*, third edition (Boston: Allyn and Bacon, 1994).

9. *Zhonghua renmin gongheguo guojia jiaowei weiyuanhui minzu diqu jiaoyusi* (People's Republic of China State Education Commission Department of Ethnic Region Minority Education), *Shaoshu minzu jiaoyu gongzuo wenjian xuanpian 1949-1988 (A Selection of National Minority Education Work Documents 1949-1988)* (Hohot: Neienggu jiaoyu chubanshe, 1991).

10. Teng Xing, "Woguo shaoshu minzu diqu jiaoyu zhengti gaige guanjian" ("The Crux of Overall Educational Reform in China's Minority Regions"), in *Qiushi*, No. 7 (April 1989), pp. 19-22.

11. Muhate'erer, "Jixu gaige minzu jiaoyu" ("Continue to Reform Nationality Education") in *Xinjiang shehui kexue (Xinjiang Social Sciences)* No. 3 (June 15, 1989), pp. 53-57.

12. Ibid.

13. Ibid.

14. See Gerard A. Postiglione, "National Minority Regions: Studying School Discontinuation," in Judith Liu (ed.), *The Ethnographic Eye: Education in the People's Republic of China* (New York: Garland Publishing, 1999);

Gerard A. Postiglione, Teng Xing and Ai Yiping, "Basic Education and School Discontinuation in National Minority Regions of China," in Gerard A. Postiglione and Wing On Lee, *Social Change and Educational Development in Mainland China, Taiwan and Hong Kong* (Hong Kong: Centre of Asian Studies Press, 1995), pp. 186-206.

15. Mette Halskow Hansen, *Lessons in Being Chinese: Minority Education and Ethnic Identity in Southwest China* (Seattle: University of Washington Press, 1999).

16. Baden Nima, "The School Curriculum From a Multicultural Perspective: Building a Common Spirit for Peace and Development," unpublished manuscript, 1996. See also Baden Nima, "Zangzu jiaoyu de chulu" ("The Way Out for Tibetan Education"), *Xizang yanjiu (Tibetan Studies)*, No. 3 (1994), pp. 44-50.

17. Two books have been published for school children in 1997 that focus on China's multiethnic and multicultural characteristics, however, they are intended as reference books rather than as part of the school curriculum. The first book is for elementary school students and is entitled *Wushiliu ge minzu, wushiliu ge wenhua (56 nationalities, 56 cultures)* and the second, for high school students, is entitled *Duocai de minzu huajuan (A Painted Scroll of Colorful Nationalities)*. Both books were produced by Zhao Shaomin and published by Yunnan Education Press in 1997.

18. The Department of Ethnic Minority Education of the State Ministry of Education is piloting a limited multicultural education program in selected schools of five eastern cities where the population is largely Han Chinese.

PART I

Cultural Challenges to State Schooling: Religion and Language

CHAPTER 2

Religion and the Education of China's Minorities

Colin Mackerras

In general, the minorities of China are much more committed to religious belief than are the Han people. There are, of course, exceptions to this generalization, among which the Koreans with their strongly Confucian tradition and secular outlook are a good example. The peoples with the greatest dedication to religion are those who believe in faiths with strong clergies and important buildings and texts. For China's minorities, the most important such faiths, at least in terms of scale, are Islam and Tibetan Buddhism.

Among the most committed and populous Islamic nationalities are the Hui, or Chinese Muslims, who are spread over many parts of China. And the Uygurs and Kazaks of Xinjiang, both of which are Turkic peoples. The Kazaks are nomadic, and from early times both their attendance at prayer in the mosque and their practice of Islamic customs has been less strict than among the Uygurs. The less populous Islamic minorities include the Dongxiang, Bonan and Salars of Qinghai and Gansu, and the Kirgiz, Uzbeks, Tatars and Tajiks of Xinjiang. The Tajiks, although not numerous in China, are distinguished by being the only minority in the state to speak an Iranian language.

The main believers in Tibetan Buddhism are of course the Tibetans. However, the Mongols were converted to Tibetan Buddhism in the sixteenth century and their people have believed in that religion ever since, although with very much less dedication than the Tibetans in this century. Other minorities adhering to Tibetan Buddhism include the Tu of Qinghai, the Yugur of Gansu, the Monba of Tibet, the Prmi and Nosuo of Yunnan,[1] and part of the Xibe of Xinjiang.

Another branch of Buddhism of some importance is Theravada (or Hinayana) Buddhism, to which the Dai of Yunnan are strongly committed. Very similar culturally to the Thais of Thailand and the Shan people of Burma, the Dai have a long tradition of adherence to Buddhism so widespread in Southeast Asia.

Christian missionaries from the West, especially Britain, France and the United States, tried to convert the minority peoples in the late nineteenth and first half of the twentieth centuries. However, it should be noted that on the whole their efforts were generally far stronger in the Han area than in the minority areas. Moreover, when they tried to spread Christianity among the minorities, they were not very successful. The Islamic and Buddhist nationalities resisted the influence of Christianity very strongly.

Christian impact was a bit more substantial among a few of the minority groups with weaker commitment to their traditional religions, such as the Koreans and the Miao. A particularly well-known missionary was Samuel Pollard of the United Methodist Church Mission, who lived in China's Southwest from 1887 until his death in 1915. According to one notable account of the Christian missionaries in China, between 1904 and 1910 he "witnessed what was almost a mass movement into the Church" among the Miao, devising a specific Miao script and preparing literature in it.[2] Of the Christian communities created under Pollard's leadership, the one with the greatest long-term success was that in Shimenkan in Weining County, western Guizhou province.[3]

It is the aim of this chapter to analyze the relationship between religion and education, and specifically the impact of religion on the education system of the minorities in China. The focus will be on those minorities among whom religion is most pervasive in its influence, but will not exclude the others altogether. The period of focus is the People's Republic of China PRC since 1949, and more specifically, the period of reform from the end of 1978 to the present. However, in discussing religion, it is quite impossible to ignore the past, therefore I will begin with discussion of the pre-PRC period.

BACKGROUND OF THE RELATIONSHIP BETWEEN RELIGION AND EDUCATION

In general, Han Chinese culture is determinedly secular. Its education system was historically dominated by Confucianism, a secular ideology which on the whole expressed itself in non-religious ways. The Confucian examination system, which was for centuries the most important way of selecting officials, did not concern itself with religious matters. Buddhist and Taoist priests were generally kept out of the education system and in only very few periods of Chinese history did they operate schools. Religion was influential in society, but as a noted scholar points out, it "had no organized authority to enforce social morality," and its function lay above all "in providing sanction for ethical values that stemmed mainly from secular sources."[4] The same situation applied among the minorities most heavily influenced by Confucianism, among which the Koreans are the most populous.

However, the situation was very different indeed among the minorities who were dedicated to religion. The Tibetans are a good case in point. For centuries, the great monasteries of Tibet and other Tibetan areas of China functioned as the intellectual repositories of the Tibetan people. In this sense they were much like universities. It was there that academic debate on religion was pursued and that the community's libraries and printing presses were housed. They were not only religious centers, but were cultural centers in the broadest sense of the term.

Formal education was wholly organized at the monasteries. Any boy who wanted to learn that kind of knowledge respected by Tibetan society would certainly go into one of the monasteries. The influence of religion on education was very profound indeed. One contemporary PRC writer has written the following regarding the monasteries:

> Apart from Buddhist learning, it was possible to study Tibetan language and medicine, astronomy, calendar calculation, painting and other branches of knowledge. Because of this, there was the abnormal phenomenon that "temples were schools, and religion was equivalent to education." Tibetan education was controlled by the monasteries and monks were society's intellectuals.[5]

In emphasizing the function of the monasteries in education, it is important not to overlook education that was outside of their jurisdiction. There was a secular education aimed at training government officials and a few private schools for the aristocracy. The courses given in these private schools included both secular and religious material, such as chanting the sutras by heart. What this meant was that even in the non-monastic schools, boys learned religious curricula. Attempts by the thirteenth Dalai Lama to begin the modernization of Tibetan education, for example by extending non-religious material, ended up in failure amidst the virulent opposition of the great monasteries of the Yellow Hat sect of Tibetan Buddhism.[6]

Apart from the Hui, the Islamic nationalities also regarded education as more or less equivalent to training in their religion. The Quran, as well as Islamic doctrines, practices and history automatically dominated the curriculum. Moreover, the site for education was the mosque and the main aim was to train religious leaders.

The situation with Hui education was somewhat more complicated, because they accepted Confucian and hence Han influence to a far greater extent than did the Turkic nationalities or the Tajiks. During the Ming (1368-1644) and succeeding Qing (1644-1911) dynasties, there were special government schools for the Hui, which taught the Confucian classics and ethics; and in addition, some Hui opened their own private academies. There were also Quranic schools at the Hui mosques. In the early Ming period, the tendency was for the Hui to adopt Chinese as their own language, and consequently give up speaking Arabic and Persian. In order to remedy this situation, the Hui Muslim clergy began to set up Arabic and Persian Quranic schools called Hui-language great schools (*Huiwen daxue*). By the sixteenth century, there was a whole system of these mosque schools, the aim of which was to teach Arabic, Persian, the Quran and Islamic doctrine to selected men in order to train them as Muslim teachers and clergy. Later, a very limited number of similar schools were founded for women, an important example of which was the Muslim women's school (*Qingzhen nüxue*) that was established in Kaifeng, Henan Province, during the Jiaqing period (1796-1820).[7]

The reform of the Islamic education system began in the late nineteenth century, and gathered some momentum in the first half of the twentieth. In Xinjiang a new education system began to make itself felt as early as the late nineteenth century; one of its features was a reduction in Islamic content and a strengthening of modern scientific ideas. A striking feature of education in Xinjiang was the influence of

Turkey, which was itself in the last days of the great Ottoman Empire, which finally collapsed with the establishment of the republic of Turkey in 1923. Since the great majority of the Muslims of Xinjiang were Turkish both ethnically and culturally, Ottoman influence there is not too surprising. For a period in the early years of the Chinese Republic, an Ottoman subject set up a school in Kaxgar, southern Xinjiang, where the curricula followed a Turkish model and the children were encouraged to recognize the sultan of Turkey as their spiritual and temporal leader. The Chinese leader of Xinjiang, Yang Zengxin, had the school banned as subversive and, although he later allowed its reopening, did so only on the condition that all vestiges of subordination to Turkey be removed. With Turkey's defeat in World War I, its impact in Xinjiang declined greatly.[8]

Ottoman influence, although slightly diminished in Xinjiang, had been visible also in the activities of Wang Kuan (1848-1916), the most important of the Hui reformers, including in the field of education. When Wang returned to China in circa 1908 after extensive study in Islamic countries, he brought two Turkish scholars with him, under whose influence he moved to include more secular material in the curriculum while preserving the emphasis on Arabic, the Quran and Islamic doctrine. He set up a Muslim teacher training school in Beijing that taught general subjects as well as Islamic doctrine and used both Chinese and Arabic languages. Shortly afterwards, he founded an elementary school especially for Muslim children. One writer has described Wang's moves as "epoch-making" because of the use of Chinese in Muslim teaching, the extension of purely Muslim to more general content in the curriculum and the moving beyond training people for the clergy to a form of more widespread education.[9]

In Xinjiang, the Soviet-influenced government of Sheng Shicai that lasted from 1933 to 1944 actively promoted secular education and did its best to undermine Islamic influence in the schools. This brought down on Sheng Shicai the undying hatred of the Islamic clergy, among others. Even now, very few Uygurs have anything positive to say about Sheng and his rule. Yet Sheng does deserve credit for the beginnings of secular education in Xinjiang. Moreover, although the Guomindang government that ruled China at the time began the establishment of a national secular system of education in the minority areas, including those of the religious minorities, it had not gone far at all in this endeavor by the time it fell. Not only was Sheng Shicai's the first secular education system in Xinjiang, but it was also the most far-reaching of any of those in the areas of the religiously committed minorities.[10]

Reformed Muslim education spread gradually in other parts of China. In 1936 there were eleven Islamic secondary schools in various parts of China other than Xinjiang, of which three were for religious education and the remainder for general education, four of them teacher training schools. In addition, there were quite a few elementary schools. In 1945, the Islamic Theological College was opened at the main mosque in Chongqing.[11]

This was also the period when the first Muslim schools for girls were set up in China. In Qinghai, the first such school was established in 1930, but did not last long due to lack of leadership and funds. In 1945 three Hui girls' schools were established in Qinghai with some 500 students aged between 8 and 15. The curriculum included a substantial emphasis on Arabic, with the aim of being able to read the Quran.[12]

Despite their general failure to win converts among China's minorities, the Christian missionaries were very active in the field of education. Their role as educational innovators was their chief accomplishment, especially in the first half of the twentieth century. They set up substantial numbers of schools providing education that was both more modern and more progressive than anything minority populations had seen up to that time. In many minority areas these schools were also much more generally available than schools of traditional education.

Although the primary purpose of the Western missionary schools was the spread of Christianity, the education they provided was not only religious but general as well. The curriculum varied according to the country of origin of the missionaries; for example, it was much more likely to include Latin if the missionaries were French than if they were American. But it was virtually certain to include one or more European languages, Chinese, mathematics, history and geography and science, as well as the bible and Christian knowledge. Because the curriculum tended to follow that of the missionaries' home country, many people, including the missionaries themselves, complained that the missionary education was so "poorly adjusted to the local environment" that it "tended to denationalize its product."[13]

Initially, the missionary schools were staffed by missionaries themselves. However, in the course of time and with pressure from nationalists and the Chinese governments and nationalists, the balance shifted in favor of local people, including members of the minorities. Government rules introduced in 1925 and later revised several times placed heavy restrictions on missionary schools, included a ban on inducing, let alone compelling, students to attend religious classes.[14]

A major area of contribution by the missionary schools in China, including in the minority areas, was the education of girls. In this respect the Catholics were ahead of the Protestants; a government publication acknowledged that "in the education of girls the Catholic schools have done valuable pioneering work in China." In many of the rural areas, the Catholic schools were "the first to cater specially for girl students,"[15] and these places included some inhabited by minorities.

One place where a missionary was the first to open *any* school, let alone one especially for girls, was among the Miao people of Weining County, Guizhou. The British missionary Samuel Pollard set up the first church and school in Shimenkan in 1905, with 24 elementary schools, and one at secondary level following. The local population supported the system enthusiastically, despite its complete novelty, and it produced a high rate of education among the Miao population of Weining. Thanks to the missionary schools, the Miao of Weining had, for the minorities during that time, an unusually high rate of university graduates in a range of fields, including modern medicine. Among the most notable of the system's products was the Miao teacher Zhu Huanzhang, who was one of the leaders of the Shimenkan Secondary School. Although Chinese accounts, especially those of the PRC period, tend to emphasize very strongly the imperialist nature of the missionaries, painting their education as indoctrination for sinister power motives, they speak with some pride of these schools in Weining. An officially written survey of Weining County, noting who set up the schools but making no attempt to criticize the British, emphasizes that the Miao intellectuals produced by this missionary system "did everything they could to reinvigorate their own nationality, winning the respect of all nationalities" in China.[16] The implication is that, no matter what their motives, the British missionaries actually did good for the Miao, for Miao education, for Miao nationalism and for Miao identity.[17]

RELIGION IN THE PEOPLE'S REPUBLIC OF CHINA

The policy of the Chinese Communist Party (CCP) toward religion can be divided essentially into three periods: from 1949 until the Cultural Revolution started in 1966; the Cultural Revolution period itself, 1966-1976; and the period since then. There are similarities between the first and third periods, but also significant differences.

In all three periods, the state has set up its own official bodies subordinate to itself with the aim of trying to control religious activity. However, the intensity of the attempts at control and their degree of success has varied considerably over the years, being greatest during the Cultural Revolution and slightest in the 1980s and 1990s. In all three periods, religion has in theory been free, but again the reality has varied, with freedom being greatest in the 1980s and 1990s, and slightest during the Cultural Revolution.

During the 1950s, the CCP laid down some essentials which still apply in China in the 1990s. The first is that everybody should be free to believe in, or not to believe in, any religion. Although religious practice should also be free, it may never be directly anti-socialist or anti-patriotic. Exploitation and feudal practices carried out under the cloak of religion are banned. The use of religion by counterrevolutionaries bent on restoring lost power or imperialists determined to incite secession and split the unity of China are considered to be bad as well. In essence, religious practice is free only insofar as it poses no threat to the Chinese state.[18]

In the 1950s and 1960s, China was very active in forming diplomatic links, sometimes strong ones, on the grounds of opposition to imperialism, whether or not the target country advocated socialism or was ruled by a Marxist-Leninist party. This policy had several implications. It meant that, for the sake of its relations with anti-imperialist, Islamic countries, China was very tolerant of Islam within its own borders. But on the other hand, Christianity was a religion under strong suspicion because of its links with Western countries, which the Chinese government regarded as imperialist.

Among the minority regions, the one that was of the greatest trouble to China for its religion was Tibet. In March 1959, there was a full-scale rebellion in Lhasa, resulting in the Dalai Lama fleeing to India. While the Dalai Lama and his supporters charged that the Chinese had tried to suppress Tibetan religion and culture, the Chinese government's reaction and interpretation brought out the issues that they saw as related to the sorts of threats religion could potentially pose for the state.

In a joint speech made by five Protestant Christian leaders at the first session of the third People's Political Consultative Conference on May 11, 1959, the government view comes through with crystal clarity concerning the rebellion that had just occurred two months before in Tibet:

> Under the instigation of the imperialists, the Indian expansionists and the reactionaries of the Chiang Kai-shek clique, a small group of thoroughly reactionary masters of the farmer slaves in our country's territory, Tibet, have recently seized the Dalai Lama and staged an open rebellion. Thus they have attempted to destroy the unification of the fatherland, rend the unity of the various nationalities of our nation and restore the imperialists' enslavement of our people in Tibet so that the special privileges and position of these reactionary leaders of continuously exploiting and oppressing the Tibetan people may be maintained.[19]

In theory, the Cultural Revolution decade of 1966-1976 retained freedom of religion. Indeed, the 1975 Constitution that came out of the upheavals of that period included the statement that citizens of China "enjoy freedom to believe in religion and freedom not to believe in religion and to propagate atheism."[20] The wording may express some misgivings about freedom of religion, but does indeed enshrine that concept in so many words.

The reality of that period, however, was quite different. The Red Guards, whose activities ravaged China from August 1966 until the summer of 1968, had religious buildings closed down and, in many cases, destroyed. They humiliated clerics of all kinds and sent them out of their monasteries, mosques or churches for manual labor. Many monks of celibate orders, such as the Yellow Hat sect of Tibetan Buddhism, were forced to marry. Islam was also targeted as backward and reactionary. A poster seen in Beijing in the autumn of 1966 urged that authorities should:

> Close all mosques;
> Disperse [religious] associations;

Abolish Quranic study;
Abolish marriage within the faith;
Abolish circumcision.[21]

In extensive conversations with clergy of various religions throughout China in the 1980s and 1990s, this writer found not a single person who was prepared to say that the 1975 constitution's requirement for religious freedom was upheld. There may be a political side to what Chinese will say to foreigners at any time, but the degree of condemnation was savage and uncompromising. In the great Wudang Monastery of Tibetan Buddhism, in Inner Mongolia not far from Baotou, one old Mongol monk told me during a visit in 1992 that for him and others like him life under the Japanese occupation had been greatly preferable to that during the Cultural Revolution. Considering that the Japanese occupation is more or less synonymous with brutality and cruelty in China, his judgment on the Cultural Revolution could scarcely have been harsher.

Since the period of reform begun in the late 1970s, policy toward religion, and its condition in China, have changed drastically. In essence, policy has reemphasized freedom of religion, within certain specific parameters, while in practice there has been a very substantial religious revival which, as of the mid-1990s, shows very few signs of abating.

There are two basic documents concerning policy. These are the Constitution of December 1982 and an official document issued by the central committee of the CCP in the same year entitled Concerning the Basic Viewpoint and Policy toward the Question of Religion during China's Socialist Period. Both lay down freedom of religion. The Constitution specifically forbids any person or organization to "discriminate against citizens who believe in, or do not believe in, any religion."[22]

Yet according to CCP policy, all freedoms are relative and "limited by objective circumstances,"[23] which means that freedom of religion is not total and nobody should expect it to be so. The first of the restrictions carries fairly comprehensive importance and substantial implications for the minorities: "religious believers, like the people of all nationalities, must support the leadership of the Communist Party, support the socialist system, love their country, maintain the unity of the nation and solidarity of the nationalities . . . and do good deeds for socialism."[24] The restrictions outlined here are actually fairly wide-ranging, since a Buddhist monk or Islamic ahong might well have reservations about supporting the leadership of a party such as the CCP, which is so overtly atheist. But in practice, as long as such a cleric took no action demonstrating his opposition to the leadership of the CCP, few questions would be raised.

But the issue of "maintaining the unity of the nation and solidarity of the nationalities" is another matter. What this means is that to use religion as a cloak for secessionist activities is totally banned. Equally discouraged is any attempt by foreign countries to link up with religious devotees to try and upset or overthrow the Chinese state, and specifically the Chinese Communist Party.

Just as in the 1950s, there are some very prominent examples today to show that the Chinese state will suppress firmly any attempt to secede, and does not see such suppression as hostile to freedom of religion. From 1987-1989, there were quite a few demonstrations in favor of independence in Lhasa and other parts of Tibet, in most of which monks were leaders.[25] These were put down by the Chinese authorities; monks were beaten up and imprisoned. Although many in the West denounced the Chinese authorities for such abuses of human rights as attacks on freedom of religion, Chinese government spokesmen countered with the argument that being free to practice any religion was not the same as freedom to use religion in order to split the unity of China. There have also been similar, although far less publicized, uprisings by Muslims in Xinjiang. In April 1990, the Islamic Party of East Turkestan led an uprising in Akto, Kashgar, which the Chinese military quickly suppressed.[26] In May 1996, Xinjiang authorities again cracked down on separatists after nine armed Muslim activists were killed in a clash with authorities in Kuqa late in April, with large-scale arrests and some executions following.[27]

Yet my experiences in a range of minority areas suggest to me most strongly that the claims of religious freedom are very much more than a facade. In the Tibetan areas there are numerous signs of religious worship and practices of various kinds. Not only are monasteries functioning actively, but all ordinary houses that I have visited have their own shrines. Prayer flags flutter above virtually all Tibetan houses, while pilgrims are numerous not only in the great monasteries but also in the smaller ones. In towns such as the prefectural capital of Qinghai province's Huangnan Tibetan Autonomous Prefecture,

Tongren, monks are numerous and very noticeable on the streets, with their saffron robes. Even among the Mongols of China, whose Tibetan Buddhist religion has weakened very much more in the twentieth century than that of the Tibetans, there are numerous signs of surviving religious practice, especially in the rural areas.

During a visit to Qinghai in July 1995, I visited Huzhu, a Tu area not very far from the capital Xining. The Tu people speak their own language, which is quite different from Tibetan, but they are similar in many respects to the Tibetans, especially with regard to their belief in Tibetan Buddhism. In a Tu village in Huzhu I came by chance upon a Buddhist religious ritual. Many of the villagers had crowded into the very small village temple, dressed in elaborate traditional clothing, especially the women. Numerous people were prostrating themselves in front of the main hall of the temple, while lamas conducted a ceremony inside.

The main object of the ceremony was to celebrate a 16-day fast aimed at cleansing the body. Those men and women of the village over age 50 were living at the temple for 16 days reading sutras and attending such ceremonies. They were going completely without food and drink every alternate day. On the other days they were allowed lunch, including fluids, but no meat and no other meals or drink at any other time of the day.

In the Islamic areas, religious activity is, if anything, even stronger than among the Tibetans. The number of mosques functioning and active is substantial and growing, numbering possibly 20,000 in Xinjiang alone.[28] Men go in large numbers to pray on Fridays, even young men. According to my informants, circumcision has again become very widespread or even universal among most of the Muslim minorities of China's northwest.

The division into the Old and New Sects remains important. The difference is that the Old Sect adheres rigidly to the original interpretation of the Quran, but the New Sect is more reformed, being more flexible in its doctrinal explanations and simpler in its rituals, but stricter than the Old Sect in the application of rules.[29] The conflict between the two sects of Islam remained intense enough to have caused rioting in Ningxia in the early 1990s.[30] However, in general the two are very similar to each other in teachings and practice. In most parts of China it is the Old Sect which remains dominant.

The issue of relations with foreign countries remains relevant in the period of reform since 1978. In essence, China is still very concerned about its relations with Islamic countries and generally sees them as important actual or potential allies. Although China is even more concerned about its relations with Western nations, it still sees them as willing to interfere in Chinese affairs for their own advantage, and consequently with vestiges of imperialism. It is for this reason that China allows Muslim influence on its Islamic minorities from Muslim international organizations of a kind that it would not tolerate from the West.

It is CCP policy to regard Islam as favorable to modernization. It also sees many areas of convergence of ideas advocated by Muslims and communists. Examples include hard work, commitment to the poor and to society as a whole, respect for the old, filial piety and abstention from harmful substances. As consumerism has taken an increasing hold of Chinese society in the 1980s and 1990s, drunkenness and even drug abuse among its people has become a more and more serious problem. These are practices which the Quran condemns in very strong terms.

The following question inevitably arises: do young Muslim men drink any less than non-Muslim counterparts? I have asked numerous Muslim clerics and laity about this matter and, although the consensus is that young people are not nearly as strict as clerics think they ought to be, the extent of confidence in China's Muslim youth varies somewhat. Some say that the young are strong in faith but in practice weak against alcohol, others that for all their shortcomings they are indeed more abstinent than non-Muslims. In such matters, it is extremely difficult to desegregate ideals from the reality, and the Muslim clerics are not necessarily in a very good position to know about the behavior of youth anyway.

In the early 1980s, the Center for Religious Research at the Xinjiang Social Studies Institute carried out surveys in two Uygur villages in Kangaroo, southern Xinjiang, and two Kazak places in Yili, in the north of Xinjiang. The results were unequivocal: less than 1 percent of male adults in the Uygur villages drank alcoholic beverages, while among the Kazaks surveyed in Yili the figure was about 12 percent. Both figures are very much less than normal in China nowadays.[31] What appears to follow from this is that the influence of Islam is still strong enough in the personal lives of its adherents to make a significant difference in their private behavior.

An issue of some interest in the revival of Islam is the role of women. This is because in world forums Islam has adopted stances distinctly hostile to many Western feminist causes. Muslims are very insistent that Islam is not anti-women, in part because of the strong support for women as mothers in the Quran.[32]

In northwestern China it appears to me that Islam is indeed still strongly male-dominated. In Xinjiang women are not allowed to enter mosques, and in Kashgar one can still see many women in public places wearing veils that cover the whole head, even including the eyes. In Ningxia, women are allowed to enter the main mosques, but must sit at the back and to the side. In Ningxia and Gansu there is a limited number of mosques specially for women, from which men are generally excluded. What became obvious from the two I visited, one in Wuzhong, Ningxia, and the other in the Gansu capital Lanzhou, is that they are not numerous and are very small by comparison with the ordinary mosques, obviously occupying a very low priority for the clergy. Among China's provinces, the one with the most active women's Islamic culture is Henan; for example, it boasts the largest number of women's mosques among all provinces in China.

Henan is also the province with the largest number of female ahongs, as well as the source of those in Gansu. There is also a small number of female ahongs (they are the clerics who dominate the women's mosques) in Ningxia. According to Dru Gladney, there are some female ahongs in Yunnan, where he found attitudes to be more liberal than those in the northwest.[33] On the other hand, in Xinjiang ahongs are all male. It is important to note, at least according to those I interviewed in Ningxia and Gansu, that female ahongs see their role as a social one—namely, to look after the religious life of girls and women—not as a theological or feminist one. Their ideas are identical to those of their male counterparts, and the notion that they might be representative of a Chinese Muslim feminism is anathema to them.[34]

Both Tibetan Buddhism and Islam are showing their greatest strength in China among peoples with a traditional adherence to these religions. There are, however, cases where the opposite is true; that is, the traditional faith is weak but a newer religion is showing vigor. A case in point is with the Koreans, among whom Buddhism is weak but Christianity retains some influence.

An official account of Christianity among the Koreans of Yanbian in Jilin and other parts of northeastern China presents a glowing picture of fervor and faith, with particular attention being paid to its distinctly Korean features. Examples of this are that most churches in the Korean districts were established and are run by the Koreans themselves, despite the earlier activities of American and other missionaries. Korean Christians use Korean-language bibles, and "they sit on the floor with men separated from the women, as is their custom."[35]

My own impressions of religion among the Koreans suggest that Christianity is by far the strongest faith among them. During two visits to Yanbian I searched in vain for any sign of surviving Buddhism, but instead found several new and active Christian churches, as well as some old ones. The priests and pastors I interviewed or of whom I became aware were mainly Koreans who gave sermons both in Korean and Chinese. It is also notable that the Christian churches appear to maintain active connections with the outside world, with money and personnel coming from South Korea and even the United States.

One major study of Chinese religion in the late 1970s and early 1980s acknowledges the great improvements that have taken place in terms of state policy for Chinese religious believers during that period, especially the increasing pragmatism of policy toward religion in China in the 1980s. The conclusion reached by Julian Pas is: "it testifies to the practical common sense of the Chinese people that theoretical contradictions can be somehow accommodated if that is the most practical solution toward co-existence and social harmony."[36] My own impressions concerning religion among minorities bears out this overall conclusion. Both the government and the CCP, and most ordinary people as well, go out of their way to avoid giving offense to minorities' religions. While there are plenty of cases of religious conflict, it generally occurs despite, rather than because of, official policy or Han provocation.

RELIGION AND EDUCATION IN THE PRC

Although the process of setting up a secular education system was certainly not totally new to the religiously committed minorities in 1949, it has gone very much further under the PRC than it ever did under the republic. The result is that, for the first time, China has a reasonably comprehensive and very widespread, though not completely universal, system of secular education among the minorities.

In theory all children, including those of minorities, should attend this secular state education system. Although there are variations in the extracurricular part of the system for minorities, which is discussed elsewhere in this volume, there is a common curriculum throughout the whole country, which every child must learn. For the purposes of this chapter, the main point to make about this common curriculum is that it is more or less entirely secular. Any part of its content relating to religion is likely to be negative; it certainly does not propagate religious belief or practice.

There are some minor exceptions to this principle. One is that in language schools the teaching of Arabic might use the Quran as material, especially for Islamic minorities, without criticizing its content. In the 1990s, English-language classes occasionally used the Bible in the same way as an illustration of foreign cultures. Such is the current practice at the Beijing Foreign Studies University's Arabic and English Departments. However, this must be carried out in such a way that it does not cross the borderline which separates an understanding of another culture from religious propaganda.

Tongxin, a strongly Islamic center in central Ningxia Hui Autonomous Region, is home to a government-recognized and sponsored school which aims to train Hui youth for professional careers. The Tongxin Arabic School was built in Arab architectural style, featuring a large mosque as a centerpiece, with a grant from the World Islamic Development Bank. About two-thirds of the students are men, their aim being to become diplomats in Islamic countries. The remaining one-third are female students who are most likely to enter the teaching profession. The state pays for the students from Ningxia, in fact the great majority, but those from other parts of China must pay fees.[37] Admission is through the state's unified examination system, and examination remains the central method of assessment in the school. The courses are solely in the humanities, including an emphasis on Arabic, the Quran, and Islamic doctrine and history. The students all live at the school, with boys and girls on separate floors of the dormitory wing. They are encouraged to pray regularly, reflecting perhaps the influence of the World Islamic Development Bank, but they are not compelled to do so, since China remains a secular state and this school is sponsored by the Chinese government. It is nonetheless very notable that the Chinese government allows a mosque in the state education system.

According to my explorations in minority areas of China, the state school system generally adheres strictly to the principle of secularity. Other than in the Tongxin Arabic School, I found no cases where religious representatives could be described as teaching religious content in the state system. Those clergy I interviewed, including Tibetan and Mongol incarnation lamas (in Chinese *huofo*, literally "living Buddha"), and Islamic ahongs and minority Christian priests or pastors, said that they were happy with, or at least accepted, this situation.

However, given the tradition among some of the minorities, it would not be surprising if there were actually far more opposition than appears on the surface. According to the official New China News Agency in July 1994, the Ningxia authorities felt called upon to issue strict regulations aimed at curbing the growing influence of Islamic religious leaders in regional affairs, one of the reasons being that "under the cover of religion," some clerics had been "unduly meddling in education."[38] An unofficial group of lay Muslims whom I interviewed at random in October 1994 in a mosque in Yili made no bones about their resentment that the government forbade teaching Islam and the Quran in the schools. They attacked the local *ahong* for being in the pocket of the government and for abandoning demands for giving the Quran a place in the curriculum. One member of the group nearly burst into tears with emotion at the thought that it was not possible to learn the traditional religion through the education system. "Only those young people who come to the mosque can really learn any culture," he said. "The others just end up drinking, going to brothels and taking drugs." It is certainly true that heroin has become a serious problem in Xinjiang in the 1990s, which even the government makes no attempt to deny. But the above-quoted Muslim's implication that reinstating the Quran in the education system would solve the problem is less obviously valid.

My inquiries among Tibetan monks and Uygur ahongs brought out no examples of clergy who teach in the secular school system. However, it is not actually forbidden to them, on the condition that they do not present themselves as clergy and that what they teach has no religious content. In Inner Mongolia, just north of the northern arm of the Yellow River, I met in late 1992 a Mongol incarnation lama who worked at two monasteries, the great Wudang Monastery and the nearby Guanghua or Lama Cave Monastery. He told me that he teaches

Mongolian at a secondary school near the Lama Cave. There is no religious content and he normally dresses in lay clothes, except when in the monastery. But he does make a small amount of money, and he is able to make a contribution to keep Mongolian culture alive among the young, a task he is finding increasingly difficult among the modernizing Mongol youth of today.[39]

The only other kind of religious teacher in the secular system is the foreigner who spreads knowledge of the Bible and advocates Christianity at the same time as teaching a subject such as English. Such teachers, mostly Americans, became fairly common in the 1980s all over China, including in the minority areas. According to the Chinese authorities, such covert proselytizing is forbidden. While in Yanbian in September and October 1990, I met several young Koreans who had been much influenced by them, and were thinking of converting to Christianity. In February 1994, the Chinese government adopted a law on religion, one part of which was to ban foreigners from using teaching positions to spread Christianity. In the regulations displayed for foreign faculty at their living quarters in the Beijing Foreign Studies University where I taught in 1995, one clause forbade using a class "to carry on religious activities."

Where religion remains important in Chinese minority education is not in the state secular system but in the monasteries, mosques and even churches. The fact is that, just as in the past, the great Tibetan monasteries are in some ways like religious universities. Mosques are still centers not only for religious education, but for the training of further Muslim clergy.

In some minority areas there are still parents who prefer to send their children for religious education in preference to the state secular system. In his account of Hui Muslim areas, Gladney found that in Liberation Township (*Jiefang xiang*) of Guyuan County, in the far south of Ningxia, only 12 of 104 school-age children were attending school in 1985, while 27 of those not in school were studying the Quran in the mosque.[40] What is implied here is that school-age children go to the mosque for religious education *instead of* going to the public state schools, with the result that attendance at religious institutions affects school attendance to some extent. Gladney also suggests that in particular quite a few girls, either do not go to the state schools, or leave them after a comparatively short time in favor of the mosque because their parents are not convinced of the value of learning Chinese or mathematics, but prefer them to learn the Quran, Arabic and Persian.[41]

In the 1980s and 1990s a similar situation is found in the Tibetan areas of China, especially in the Tibetan Autonomous Region itself. Authorities are very frank about the long-term influence of religion on the education system, and about the preference of some parents for traditional religious education over the contemporary secular state system. One writer, Peng Cunxuan, argues that the impact of religion is one of the "realities in Tibet" which all must address in trying to improve the public education system there. This is not to say that the cornerstone of PRC life, secularism, should be abandoned. Authorities must make greater efforts to spread a love of science and scientific thought. He goes on:

> Nowadays there are several views [about religion and education]. One is that conditions in the monasteries are better than in the schools; another that it is more appropriate to learn Tibetan spoken and written language in the monasteries than in the schools. And the third is that by learning the sutras in the monasteries you can learn many humane principles and general knowledge of natural science, so therefore there are quite a few family heads who send their children to become lamas. In direct opposition to such views we must, on the one hand, prudently but actively infuse further guidance, and on the other hand we must conscientiously improve conditions in the schools, strengthen school administration and raise the quality of schooling, in order to make even more family heads send their children to the schools.[42]

The major Tibetan monasteries, such as those of Lhasa, Gyaze and Xigaze, as well as the Kumbum of Qinghai province and the Labrang in Gansu province, are still the repositories of Tibetan traditional learning. They contain major libraries of traditional Buddhist learning, as well as printing presses. There are still institutes within them which teach such matters as religious philosophy, Tibetan language and literature, Tibetan religious astronomy and traditional religious arts, including painting and dance. The system of learning is still heavily influenced by traditional practices, including the recitation of the Buddhist sutras relevant to the particular branch of learning. Tibetan clergy still teach disciples in the traditional way and this has resulted in an increase in the number of clergy.

As the above quotation from Peng Cunxuan suggests, the number of novices entering the great monasteries as disciples of older monks or lamas is again rising and many of them are strikingly young. Indeed, some of them are clearly underage. According to CCP policy it is not permitted to put pressure on children under the age of 18 to enter the clerical order,[43] and to become a monk at all below that age is strongly discouraged. Yet in the great Kumbum Monastery of Qinghai Province and Labrang Monastery in Gansu, I found boys well below the age of 18 who were making no secret of the fact that they had been sent into the monastery by their parents. Reasons included both poverty and religious dedication. Poor Tibetan parents know that their son will have a much better life materially in a monastery than in ordinary lay life. It is their duty to send regular gifts to the boy's master, but this is not difficult, since they are supposed to support their religion materially anyway. With a son in the monastic life, they are relieved of paying for his upbringing.

Three additional comments are in order regarding this surprising remnant of the old days, when both Tibetan and Mongol families were expected to dedicate at least one son to the religious life. In the first place, my research suggests that, despite its revival, this practice is not nearly as widespread in the 1990s as it was before the accession of the CCP to power. There are trends here and there, but it certainly does not affect every family the way it used to do. Secondly, the boys I interviewed seemed quite cheerful about their lot. One, a boy of 17 who had been studying for the clerical order in the monastery for 4 years already, told me his parents had sent him without consulting him; but he also stressed that he was quite happy with his monastic student life. In theory, he can leave the monastery if he wants to, but in practice family pressure makes this extremely difficult and rare.

These boys will have no chance to meet girls and no doubt take it for granted that they will never marry. Whether the prospect of lifelong celibacy worries them is an interesting question which it is not possible to pursue here. Unlike the monks of the dominant Yellow Hat sect of Tibetan Buddhism, those of the minority Red Hat sect are allowed to marry. Since they too lack the opportunity to meet members of the opposite sex in the monastery, they find their wives in the traditional way-with the aid of their parents and a matchmaker.

My final comment goes to the response of the government to the apparently illegal behavior of sending boys to monasteries without their consent. The government basically turns a blind eye, for two reasons. The first is that it does not want to irritate minorities over a form of activity which, while no doubt highly undesirable from the government's point of view, does not appear to pose any immediate threat to its tenure of power. Secondly, CCP control over such day-to-day minority cultural affairs has weakened substantially in recent years and reasserting it is not easy. If secession is threatened, the CCP most certainly can, and will, tread on such opposition; but boy monks are unlikely to pose much of a threat to CCP power.

Like Tibetan Buddhism, Islam is supported by an educational system. There are two main types of Islamic schools in China. The first and most important type is those that aims to train further clergy. This category can itself be subdivided into the large Quranic or theological colleges (Jingxueyuan) and the smaller schools attached to mosques. The second type of Islamic school is that for teaching Muslim children Arabic, as well as Islamic doctrine and the Quran. All students in both of these types of Islamic schools should either be attending, or have already studied at, a state secular school. As noted above, however, there are some cases of infringement.

As of the mid-1990s, there were 7 Quranic colleges for religious instruction, compared with 12 state-run nationalities universities or institutes in 1991.[44] Two very large Quranic colleges are those in Yinchuan and Ürümqi, the capitals of Ningxia and Xinjiang, respectively, both of them built in the mid-1980s with substantial funds from the World Islamic Development Bank. Both include very fine mosques, built not in Chinese style, but in Arab style. Both take students primarily from their own region and nationality, Hui in the case of the Yinchuan College, and Uygurs in that of Ürümqi.

Only men are admitted to these colleges. Other than gender, the chief criteria for entry into them are dedication to Islam, knowledge of the Quran and general ability. Students are selected by examination, including both written and oral and competition for entry is very keen. At the Ürümqi College I was informed that only about one in five applicants are admitted.

The main part of the curriculum, taking up about 70 percent of allotted time, consists of Arabic language and Islam, with emphasis on the Quran, Islamic doctrine, the life of Muhammad and the history of

Islam, including Islam in China. The remaining 30 percent of the time is given over to learning Chinese language, history, law and contemporary policy on religion. These courses are focused on the Chinese experience as a whole rather than on Islam or the Islamic nationalities.

The inclusion of a course on law is particularly interesting. At the Yinchuan College it was explained to me that this course is offered because the ahong holds a high status and respect in society and often has to be involved, as arbiter, in conciliating between people. Since villages have no law courts, the ahong often finds himself acting in the place of the law. He must follow Chinese state law, not Islamic law; for instance, the former permits only one wife for each man even though four wives is expressly condoned by the Quran.

Courses at these Islamic colleges last 5 years, with one cohort only being trained at any one time. All assessment is through examination, either written or oral. Virtually all students eventually graduate, dropout rates being extremely low. Most work as ahong after graduation. However, the college leaves them to find work themselves and does not allocate them to a particular mosque or location.

Students pay no fees, since virtually all costs are borne by the local government. It is ironic that by the mid-1990s, the atheist government had already introduced tuition fees in many universities, while the Islamic colleges had not. Teachers in the latter graded and receive salaries commensurate with those at other educational institutions. As in other colleges in China, teachers and students live on campus. Married students must leave their wives at home, returning to see them only on Sundays.

Another type of Islamic theological school is that attached to the mosques. Large mosques I visited in the 1990s in Ningxia, Gansu, Qinghai and Xinjiang mostly featured these schools, the aim of which is to train Islamic clergy. In Xinjiang, I was informed at the great Idkah Mosque in Kashgar that the government allows only very small numbers of such schools, but that in fact illegal ones are quite prevalent, even in the villages. Although my informant expressed the view that the government does not know about these schools, he was making no attempt to hide their existence, and it appears to me more likely that the government chooses to turn a blind eye to them, except when it perceives a political threat to stability or to its own power.

In the various mosques, I found substantial differences in the amount of time students take to graduate, ranging from 2 to 10 years. What is consistent, however, is that the emphasis is on the Quran and Arabic, as well as on Islamic doctrine and history. In most cases, there is also some material in the curriculum covering general knowledge, including Chinese history and its legal system. The students that I became aware of had already graduated from the state system, and the mosque school courses were taken in addition to, not instead of, the standard secular education.

There were variations in the fees of those schools I visited, some requiring tuition fees, others money for accommodation and/or food, with still others gave their services entirely free, even if they accepted donations when they were offered. The students live at the mosque during the course of their students, and if married, they go to see their wife only on occasion. At most mosques, the number of students is severely constricted by the amount of accommodations available, exceeding 10 or so only at the largest ones. Yet because of the large and growing number of mosques in China in the 1990s, the cumulative importance of these schools is enormous, and the number of imams trained is bound to grow, making Islam potentially even stronger over the coming years than it is at present.

In the ordinary mosque schools, all students are male. However, the women's mosques also run their own schools and are already producing a few female ahongs. The curriculum is very similar to that found in the men's mosques, with feminist thinking regarded as very negative. The main teachers are currently female ahongs, but in the women's mosque in Lanzhou I met an old man who helps teach, the significance being that whereas it is totally impossible for women to teach in the ordinary mosques, the converse does not hold true. All students in the Lanzhou women's mosque school had already graduated from junior secondary school in the state system.

In addition to schools for the training of clergy, some mosques in certain Islamic areas have classes in Arabic and other Islamic subjects for Muslim children. In the county town of Guanghe in Linxia Hui Autonomous Prefecture, Gansu province, I happened upon such a class of around 100 children, all who were on holidays from their normal state education, and who were all sitting in the open courtyard in front of the main mosque hall. There were about an equal numbers of girls and boys, the girls sitting in the front rows. There was one senior teacher, the ahong, sitting in the middle of the courtyard, who did the actual teaching with some student teachers helping. All of them had straps, which was the first time I have ever seen such a thing in a school of any kind in China. The children generally seemed cheerful and enthusiastic, although one boy who was lightly strapped once in my presence was obviously distressed. The teachers at the class told me that this kind of Islamic instruction is widespread in Linxia, a very strong Hui Muslim area. However, I learned at a large mosque in the prefectural town of Linxia that it occurs only with the more rigid New Sect, and not in the more liberal Old Sect. What it does show is that some Muslims are still very insistent that their children be as dedicated to Islam as are they themselves.

A variation on this mosque school in Guanghe was one that I visited late in 1992 in Tongxin, central Ningxia. This was a girls-only school called the Chinese-Arabic Women's School (Zhonga nüzi xuexiao) attached to the West Mosque of Tongxin. At the time of my visit, it had over 30 students and 3 teachers, all of the latter with the status of female ahongs. The students, all girls, were age 14 to 18, and had already passed through the state education system. The school was organized on a full-time basis, with the course lasting 3 years in all. The content was chiefly religious; one of the classes I witnessed featured a lecture to a dozen veiled girls on the theme that Allah should be feared and respected. The reason why the girls attended this school, according to the male ahong from the West Mosque, was because they wanted to learn culture and become better people; they did not aspire to become ahongs. The teachers received a regular salary of 100 yuan per month each. Some of the students paid fees, but those whose parents could not afford the cost were allowed to attend free, since it was the faithful who attended the mosque who subsidized the school.

One interesting aspect of education in monasteries and mosques is its effect on literacy and the survival of minority scripts and written languages. In January 1996, I interviewed a young Nosuo novice in a monastery on an island in the middle of the Lugu Lake on the border between Yunnan and Sichuan. He told me that one of his major reasons for entering the monastery was to learn the Tibetan script, which he could do in the lamasery, but not outside it. I have found this to be a frequent pattern in many Tibetan areas. Many Dai boys spend time in temples in order to learn the traditional Dai script and written language. Moreover, the same may apply in Hui and other Islamic areas. For instance, the children attending mosque schools in Guanghe, Linxia, Gansu, are learning not only the Quran but Arabic as well. One female ahong I interviewed in Wuzhong, Ningxia, was illiterate in her own language Chinese but could read enough Arabic to read the Quran.

CONCLUSION

The signs suggest that authorities remain highly successful in keeping religion out of the secular education system among minority groups. However, the clergies of the minorities are experiencing great success in gaining recruits to their ranks and in finding educational and social ways of keeping religion alive in the minds of the next generation. This especially applies to the Islamic minorities and to some of the Tibetan Buddhist minorities, above all the Tibetans themselves.

How long will this religious revival continue? The answer to that question is of course unclear, since it lies in the future. However, Islam appears to be gaining in strength in many parts of the world, not just China. Moreover, religions such as Tibetan Buddhism are gaining in following not only in the Tibetan areas of China, but even in Western countries. Although the minority areas of China may not be at the head of the line to link up with the global information superhighway, they are more or less certain to be affected by it in the reasonably near future. What this suggests is that religious revival among at least some of China's minorities may continue for a while yet.

It is possible that in some minority areas this religious revival is in part directly related to the secularization of education. This conclusion is suggested by the fact that many parents prefer to send their sons to monasteries and mosques than to the secular education system. Clergies are quite consciously trying to use their own influence to spread their religion among their own and to other nationalities, and one of the reasons is in order to counter the anti- or at least non-religious impact of the secular system. For example, it has been pointed out that some Uygur Muslims bitterly resent the lack of Quranic study in the secular system.

Yet it is easy to exaggerate the extent to which the secular education system has been responsible for the religious revival. The secular education system and rising standard of living are beginning to produce substantial influences on minorities, especially among youth, including among the most religiously committed, such as the Tibetans and Uygurs. What this means is that secular attitudes and the wish to partake in modernization and the higher social status and living standards accorded to modern activities are increasing their hold among the young and among middle-aged minority people. So the religious revival is hardly likely to be completely permanent, any more than other such movements have been in the past. Just as religion is not as all-pervasive in its impact in the 1990s as it was in the 1940s, it may well be weaker in the 2040s than in the 1990s.

There is another aspect to this issue, too. For the Islamic and Tibetan Buddhist nationalities, the religious revival is closely related to the preservation of national cultures. By entering a monastery a Tibetan boy learns not only Tibetan but many aspects of traditional Tibetan culture which the secular system would either not wish or not be able to teach him. Religion is so central to the culture of Islamic nationalities that teaching the Quran in the mosques cannot fail to act as an incentive to the preservation of the national culture.

One of the global tendencies of recent times is increasing ethnic identity. Certainly this has applied in China as well as in other countries. I have argued elsewhere that religion is a major aspect of this rise in identity,[45] but it is certainly not the only one, as evidenced by the fact that it applies not only to religiously committed minorities such as the Tibetans and Uygurs, but also to the Koreans, who are not particularly interested in religion. It seems likely to me that this growing sense of ethnic consciousness will persist for some time.

This rise in ethnic identity cannot possibly favor the integration of China. However, it will not necessarily lead to the breakup of China, either. At present, secessionist movements are strong only in Tibet and Xinjiang. It is possible that these two regions could gain independence without splitting the rest of China. Yet to judge from history, any government of China, no matter what its political makeup, is likely to resist the secession of either Tibet or Xinjiang tooth and nail. China's long history as a unified and centralized state, combined with the numerical, political and cultural dominance of a single ethnicity, make the situation there very different from that in such recent multinational states as the Soviet Union or former Yugoslavia, or in longer deceased ones like the Austro-Hungarian Empire. What appears to follow is that while the secession of Tibet and Xinjiang, and indeed the breakup of China, are all possible, they are far from inevitable. If any or all of them do occur, religion must be accounted as a major contributing factor.

The success or lack of success of modernization may affect both the integration of China and how long the revival of religion persists there.[46] But the precise direction of modernization's impact on religion is by no means obvious. The late years of the twentieth century have seen religions reviving in some highly modern countries, especially the United States, and continuing to decline in others. So although modernization has indeed tended to weaken religious belief in many contexts, there is no guarantee at all that it must do so.

To me it appears highly likely that modernization will indeed continue in China's minority areas. Religion, which has proven itself so tenacious in some of them, notably the Tibetan and Islamic areas, may well weaken by comparison with today over the coming decades. But it would be very foolhardy to predict its demise, even in the long-term future.

NOTES

1. The Chinese state classifies the Mosuo as a branch of the Naxi people. However, it was my strong impression during a visit to the Mosuo community of the Lugu Lake, which forms a small part of the border between Yunnan and Sichuan, that many Mosuo people consider themselves a nationality separate from the Naxi. See also Charles F. McKhann, "The Naxi and the Nationalities Question," in Stevan Harrell (ed.), *Cultural Encounters on China's Ethnic Frontiers* (Seattle and London: University of Washington Press, 1995), pp. 39-62.

2. Kenneth Scott Latourette, *A History of Christian Missions in China* (London: Society for Promoting Christian Knowledge, 1929; Taipei: Ch'eng-wen Publishing Company, 1970), p. 589.

3. In addition to the ones discussed here, there is a range of religious beliefs among China's minorities, including shamanism and polytheism. For a brief rundown on this subject, see Colin Mackerras, *China's Minority Cultures: Identities and Integration Since 1912* (Melbourne: Longman Australia; New York: St Martin's Press, 1995), pp. 28-31.

4. Yang Chingkun, *Religion in Chinese Society: A Study of Contemporary Social Functions of Religion and Some of Their Historical Factors* (Berkeley, Los Angeles, London: University of California Press, 1961), p. 339.

5. Zhu Jielin, *Zangzu jinxiandai jiaoyu shilüe (A Record of Modern Tibetan Education)*(Xining: Qinghai renmin chubanshe, 1990), p. 2.

6. For more detail on Tibetan education in the first half of the twentieth century see Mackerras, *China's Minority Cultures*, pp. 40-43.

7. See Huang Tinghui, "Huizu wenhua shi"("A History of Hui Culture,") in Li Dezhu et. al. (eds.), *Zhongguo shaoshu minzu wenhua shi* (*A Cultural History of China's National Minorities*) (Shenyang: Liaoning renmin chubanshe, 1994), p. 344.

8. See the account of Andrew D. W. Forbes, *Warlords and Muslims in Chinese Central Asia: A Political History of Republican Sinkiang 1911–1949* (Cambridge: Cambridge University Press, 1986), p. 18.

9. Wing-tsit Chan, *Religious Trends in Modern China* (New York: Columbia University Press, 1953; New York Octagon Books, 1969), p. 199. See also Tinghui, "Huizu wenhua shi," p. 345.

10. See Mackerras, *China's Minority Cultures*, pp. 45-46.

11. Chan, *Religious Trends in Modern China*, pp. 200-201.

12. Ma Zhong, "Tantan Qinghai Huizu nüzi jiaoyu" ("On Girls' Education among the Hui of Qinghai,") in Jiang Huandong, Liu Wenpu, Ren Yugui, Liu Lihui, Wang Zhenling, Liu Wenzong (eds.), *Qinghai minzu nütong jiaoyu yanjiu* (*Studies on Education for Girls among the Nationalities of Qinghai*) (Xining: Qinghai People's Press, 1994), pp. 183-184.

13. Latourette, *A History of Christian Missions in China*, pp. 645-646.

14. See Colin Mackerras, "Education in the Guomindang Period, 1928-1949," in David Pong and Edmund S. K. Fung (eds.), *Ideal and Reality: Social and Political Change in Modern China, 1860-1949* (Lanham, New York, London: University Press of America, 1985), pp.164-165, 182.

15. *China Handbook 1937-1944: A Comprehensive Survey of Major Developments in China in Seven Years of War* (Chungking: Chinese Ministry of Information, 1944), p. 465.

16. Survey of the Weining Yi, Hui and Miao Autonomous County Compilation Group, *Weining Yizu Huizu Miaozu zizhi xian gaikuang* (*Survey of the Weining Yi, Hui and Miao Autonomous County*) (Guiyang: Guizhou People's Press, 1985), p. 204.

17. See also the verdict on Pollard and other missionaries among the Miao in a major study of minorities cultures published in China: "The missionaries were quite successful in the field of education, and one cannot make a one-sidedly negative evaluation of their interference in Miao traditional culture. For instance, we should commend their bans on drinking alcohol and on killing livestock to sacrifice to their ancestors, but their bans on singing and on free love did have the flavor of the destruction of traditional culture." Li Bingze,

"Miaozu wenhua shi," in Li Dezhu et. al. (eds.) *Zhongguo shaoshu minzu wenhua shi (A Cultural History of China's National Minorities)* p. 1452.

18. Documents concerning religious policy and the minority nationalities are collected in Donald E. MacInnis (ed.), *Religious Policy and Practice in Communist China: A Documentary History* (New York: Macmillan, 1972), pp. 119-131: those on religion and imperialism, pp. 133-156.

19. Ibid., p. 143.

20. Article 28, "The Constitution of the People's Republic of China," adopted January 17, 1975, *Peking Review*, Vol. 4, No.18, (January 24, 1975), p. 17.

21. Quoted from MacInnis (ed.), *Religious Policy and Practice in Communist China*, p. 292. Further documentation on religion and the Cultural Revolution can be found on pp. 284-306.

22. Article 36 of the "Constitution of the People's Republic of China" of 1982. See *Beijing Review*, Vol. 25, No. 52 (December 27, 1982), p. 16.

23. "The Policy of Freedom of Religious Belief," in Luo Zhufeng (ed.), trans. Donald E. MacInnis and Zheng Xi'an, with an introduction by Donald E. MacInnis, *Religion under Socialism in China* (Armonk, New York and London: M. E. Sharpe, 1991), p. 140.

24. Ibid., p. 141.

25. Young Tibetan nuns have also been active in demonstrations in Tibet since the autumn of 1987. See especially Hanna Havnevik, "The Role of Nuns in Contemporary Tibet," in Robert Barnett and Shirin Akiner (eds.), *Resistance and Reform in Tibet* (London; Hurst and Company, 1994), pp. 259-266.

26. For further discussion of these issues, see Colin Mackerras, *China's Minorities: Integration and Modernization in the Twentieth Century* (Hong Kong: Oxford University Press, 1994), pp. 186-190, 173-176.

27. *China News Digest, Global News*, No. GL96-075, June 5, 1996, News Briefs, Item 2.

28. In Xinjiang in the Fall of 1994, Muslim clergy gave me very conflicting figures for the number of mosques in the autonomous region. The Imam of the Tatar Mosque in Ürümqi gave a figure of 20,000, while two senior clerics at the great Idkah Mosque in Kashgar agreed on only about 6,000 for that region alone. An official figure announced in conjunction with the fortieth anniversary of the establishment of the Xinjiang Uygur Autonomous Region on October 1, 1995 specified the number of mosques in Kashgar Prefecture alone as exceeding 9,900 (see *China Daily*, September 29, 1995, p. 4), while the Chairman of the Xinjiang Government, Abulat Abdurixit, gave a figure of

30,000 "mosques and religious halls" for the whole of Xinjiang *("Xinjiang Unity Creates Better Life", China Daily*, 3 October 1995, p. 3).

29. The New Sect was founded by *Ma Mingxin* (1717-1781) of *Hezhou* in Gansu province as a reaction to the Old Sect. See Tinghui, "Huizu wenhua shi," p. 339.

30. In February 1994, a Ningxia court handed down stiff sentences to 20 people for organizing a spate of gang fights that had left 49 dead, 2 missing and up to 30 injured since 1992. Unconfirmed reports stated that 4 of those convicted were Muslim clerics battling to head the Old Sect. See "New Rules to Curb Moslem Influence in Northern China," Agence France Presse English Wire, July 17, 1994, carried in *China News Digest-Europe/Pacific Section* (CND-EP), Monday, August 1, 1994, Item 5. According to my private sources, the main issues causing this rioting were connected with inter-sect conflict.

31. He Yanji, "Adapting Islam to Chinese Socialist Practice in Xinjiang," in Luo (ed.), *Religion under Socialism in China* (Armonk, New York and London: M. E. Sharpe, pp. 230-231. See also Mackerras, *China's Minority Cultures*, p. 116.

32. In the Quran, Sura IV, entitled "Women," is mainly about women. Its first paragraph has the injunction to "reverence the wombs *that bare you*" (italics in original). See *The Koran* (Ivy Books; New York, 1993), p. 44. Paragraph 123 puts men and women on an equal basis in the reward of the next life: "But whose doth the things that are right, whether male or female, and he or she a believer,—these shall enter Paradise" (p. 57). On the other hand, the tenor of the chapter has overtones of women as possessions; and paragraph 38 opens: "Men are superior to women on account of the qualities with which God hath gifted the one above the other, and on account of the outlay they make from their substance for them" (p. 48).

33. Dru C. Gladney, *Muslim Chinese: Ethnic Nationalism in the People's Republic* (Cambridge, Mass.: Council on East Asian Studies, Harvard University, Harvard University Press, 1991), pp. 33, 237, 348.

34. For comments on women in Islam in Ningxia, see also Colin Mackerras, "Religion, Politics and the Economy in Inner Mongolia and Ningxia," in Edward H. Kaplan and Donald W. Whisenhunt (eds.), *Opuscula Altaica: Essays Presented in Honor of Henry Schwarz* (Bellingham, WA: Center for East Asian Studies, Western Washington University, 1994), pp. 449-450.

35. "The Church at the Foot of Changbai Mountain: A Survey of Christianity among the Korean People in the Northeastern Provinces," in Luo

(ed.), *Religion under Socialism in China* (Armonk, New York and London: M. E. Sharpe, 1991), p. 207.

36. Julian F. Pas, "Introduction: Chinese Religion in Transition," in Julian F. Pas (ed.), *The Turning of the Tide: Religion in China Today* (Hong Kong: Hong Kong Branch of the Royal Asiatic Society and Oxford University Press, 1989), p. 22.

37. According to a statement issued by the State Education Commission late in September 1995, over 200 of the more than 1,000 universities and colleges in China had abolished the free tuition system by the beginning of the 1995-1996 academic year. Most colleges and universities would introduce the new system by 1997, and all of them by the year 2000. See "Tuition: Public to Invest More Capital in Education," in *Beijing Review*, Vol. 38, No. 39 (September 25-October 1, 1995), p. 15.

38. CND-EP, August 1, 1994, Item 5.

39. For material on religious education in Inner Mongolia and Ningxia see also Mackerras, "Religion, Politics and the Economy in Inner Mongolia and Ningxia," in Edward H. Kaplan and Donald W. Whisenhunt (eds.), *I puscula Altaica: Essays presented in Honozoy Henry Schwartz,* Center for Asian Studies, Western Washington University, Bellingham WA, 1997, pp. 447-449.

40. Gladney, *Muslim Chinese,* p. 125.

41. See the comments about the Na Homestead place, ibid., p. 126.

42. Peng Cunxuan, "Cong xizang shiji chufa duanzheng banxue zhidao sixiang"("Make Upright the Guiding Thought for Establishing Education By Basing It on The Reality of The Situation in Tibet,") in Geng Jinsheng, Wang Xihong, (eds.), *Xizang jiaoyu yanjiu (Tibet Education Research)* (Beijing: Zhongyang minzu xueyuan chubanshe, 1989), pp. 85-86.

43. See Pas, "Introduction: Chinese Religion in Transition," in Julian F. Pas (ed.), *The Turning of the Tide,* p. 8.

44. These are listed, with their staff and student numbers, in State Nationalities Affairs Commission Economics Section and State Statistical Bureau Village Society Economic Investigation Team, comp., *Zhongguo minzu tongji (China's Ethnic Statistical Yearbook), 1992* (Beijing: Zhongguo tongji chubanshe,1993), p. 251. The one with the largest number of students was the Central Southern Nationalities Institute, with 2,952 students.

45. Mackerras, *China's Minority Cultures,* pp. 208-210.

46. I have argued in *China's Minorities: Integration and Modernization in the Twentieth Century,* (Hong Kong: Oxford University Press, 1994), especially p. 260, that modernization has tended to assist Chinese integration in the

twentieth century and that this process could gather momentum in the coming decades.

Making Muslims in China: Education, Islamicization and Representation

Dru Gladney

"We have made Italy, now we have to make Italians"

—Massimo d'Azeglio, at the first meeting of the
parliament of the newly united Italian Kingdom[1]

How are Muslims "made" in China? This chapter suggests that while they are born at home (or in hospitals in urban areas) they may very well be made in the school. There are at least two types of schools for Muslims in China: state-sponsored and mosque-sponsored (the latter which sometimes receive state funding). As yet, there are few if any non-Muslim private schools in China to which Muslims have access, with the exception of wealthier urban Muslims. Although I and others have written extensively about Muslim minority identity and identification in China, few have addressed in particular the role of education and the transmission of Islamic knowledge in the "making" of Muslims in China. School socialization is taking an increasing role in the making of Muslims, in that the socialization provided by the family (and the mosque) is no longer adequate for full participation in a Han-dominated society. State schooling provides that bridge between family and Chinese society, but in the process confronts Islamicization, raises contradictions, and at the present often runs counter to the foundations of socialization provided by home and mosque. While there are at least 10 official Muslim nationalities in China, with extremely divergent histories and diverse identities, this chapter suggests that through centralized, state-sponsored education and a tradition of fairly regularized Islamic education in China, the education of Muslims, both public and private or state-sponsored and Islamic-inspired, are fairly systematized. I would argue that the systematization of the transmission of knowledge to Muslims in China has played a privileged role in influencing Muslim identities.[2]

This chapter examines two sides of this transmission of knowledge about and among Muslims in China, involving both the state education of Muslims as members of China's 55 official minority nationalities, as well as Muslim education of their own populations. In this way, the chapter seeks to some extent to answer John R. Bowen's question, "How do people negotiate among competing and conflicting sets of norms and ideals?"[3] With respect to the Muslims in China, they do it through public and private systems of education.

As has been noted, given that there are 10 official Muslim nationalities in China (see Table 3.1), Muslim identities range widely, from Turkic to Indo-European, Central Asian to East Asian, northerner to southerner, rural to urban, religious to secular, and educated to illiterate. In addition to a shared Islamic heritage (much of which is forgotten by some, and denied to others), there are at least two main streams of educational training that brings these divergent Muslim nationalities together to a remarkable extent through a systematized fulcrum of socialization: state-sponsored education and traditionally maintained Islamic education. While both aspects of this educational socialization will vary for each of the 10 Muslim nationalities, I would argue that the similarities at least bind them closer together than the Han Chinese majority and the other 45 minority nationalities. One aspect of this is the representation of Muslims in China as members of minority nationalities, and specifically as Muslims. This other- and self-representation is perhaps the most public of the widespread transmission of knowledge about Islam in China and will be dealt with first. Corrections and confirmations of these representations will then be addressed in sections on China's education of minorities and then Muslims in China. I will only then turn my attention to traditional and contemporary Islamic educational trends in China. Finally, I will conclude with a discussion of public and private discourse regarding Islam in China.

Table 3.1. Muslim Nationality Populations in China, 1982-1990

Ethnonym	Location	Languages	1982 Census	1990 Census	Percent Growth
Hui (Dungan)	All China, esp. Gansu, Ningxia, Henan Xinjiang, Qinghai, Yunnan, Hebei, Shandong	Sino-Tibetan	7,219,352	8,602,978	19 percent
Uygur	Xinjiang	Altaic (Turkic)	5,957,112	7,214,431	21 percent
Kazak	Xinjiang, Gansu, Qinghai	Altaic (Turkic)	907,582	1,111,718	24 percent
Dongxiang	Gansu, Xinjiang	Altaic (Turkic)	279,397	373,872	34 percent
Kirgiz	Xinjiang, Heilongjiang	Altaic (Turkic)	113,999	141,549	24 percent
Salar	Qinghai, Gansu	Altaic (Turkic)	69,102	87,697	27 percent
Tajik	Xinjiang	Indo-European	26,503	33,538	27 percent
Uzbek	Xinjiang	Altaic (Turkic)	12,453	14,502	16 percent
Bonan	Gansu	Altaic (Mongolian)	9,027	12,212	35 percent
Tatar	Xinjiang	Altaic (Turkic)	4,127	4,873	18 percent
Total	Muslim minority populations		14,598,654	17,597,370	26 percent
Total	minority populations		67,295,217	91,200,314	35 percent
Total	Han majority populations		940,880,121	1,075,470,555	10 percent

Note: Name(s) of group based on most commonly used and Chinese *pinyin* transliterations.

Sources: Renmin Ribao, "Guanyu 1990 nian renkou pucha zhuyao de gongbao" [Report Regarding the 1990 Population Census' Primary Statistics], November 14, 1991, p. 3; Dru C. Gladney, *Muslim Chinese: Ethnic Nationalism in the People's Republic* (Cambridge: Harvard University Press, Council on East Asia, 1996), (pp. 20, 224). Note that Muslim population estimates in China are based on the official census nationality categories, which do not include religion. Non-Muslim nationalities, such as the Han, may include believers in Islam, just as the so-called "Muslim Nationalities" may include those who do not believe in or practice Islam.

EDUCATION AND CHINA'S CIVILIZING MISSION

Recent writing on China's minorities and national identification program have begun to focus on the "civilizing" or developmentalist efforts of China's policy toward its "backward minorities."[4] In state-sponsored media and publications and in public representations, the Han majority are represented as the most "modern" and, by implication, the most "educated." The Han are frequently represented as somewhere near the "modern" end of a Marxist historical trajectory upon which China's minorities must journey. Much of this derives from a continued commitment in Chinese social science to the study of minorities as "living fossils" indicating the origins of "primitive communism."[5] Matrilineality, communal living and property holding, and even extra-marital sexuality among the minorities all become "proofs" of how far the Han have come. Chinese Marxist social science has been heavily influenced by stage evolutionary theory, particularly as represented in the writings of the American anthropologist Lewis Henry Morgan.[6] In his famous 1878 treatise, *Ancient Society*, Morgan described in his first chapter, entitled the "Ethnical Period," the development of society from savagery, to barbarism, and then to civilization. Tong Enzheng, the Sichuanese anthropologist and musicologist, was one of the earliest to criticize publicly Chinese anthropology's heavy reliance on, and almost reverence for this theory of societal evolution, in which Morgan's work was "canonized, and for the past 30 years has been regarded as something not to be tampered with therefore, to cast any doubt on it would be to cast doubt on Marxism itself."[7]

The Han, as representative of those at the "higher" end of development, were thought to be more evolved, and were to lead the way for minorities to follow. While there are many nationalities in China, the Han are defined to be in the cultural and technical vanguard, leading the manifest destiny of all the minorities. While many younger scholars, like Tong Enzheng, are beginning to challenge the dominance of the Marxist-Stalinist-Morganian paradigm, it still heavily influences the popular discourse regarding the goal of education and Han superiority in China, as well as state policy.

Minorities, who are generally less educated in the Chinese school system than the Han majority, are thought to be somewhere behind the Han culturally, and education plays a privileged role in executing China's national integration.[8] This is reflected in popular discussion about education and "culture" in China. One of the most difficult questions I had to ask in China was one regarding education.[9] The way to pose the question in Chinese is, literally: "What is your cultural level?" (*nide wenhua chengdu duoshao*). "Culture" here refers only to learning in state-sponsored schools and literacy in Chinese characters. In the volume of "nationality statistics" recently published by the Department of Population Statistics of State Statistical Bureau and Economic Department of State Nationalities Affairs Commission, the educational sections are all listed under the category of "cultural levels" (*wenhua chengdu*) of the various minority nationalities as compared to the Han.[10] I still remember asking this question to an elderly Hui Hajji in Hezhou, who answered that he "had no culture." This Islamic scholar had spent 12 years living in the Middle East, and was fluent in Persian and, Arabic and a master of the Islamic natural sciences. Efforts to integrate "nationality general history" (*minzu changshi*) into the state school curriculum do not even begin to address this issue of pervasive Han chauvinism. It may be a strong factor that keeps Hui children from wanting to go to mainly Han schools.

Muslims, as minorities, are generally thought to be less educated and more backward than the majority, portrayed as exotic and even eroticized in the public media in similar fashion as other minorities, even though Muslims are generally much more conservative socially and morally.[11] This is quite remarkable given the long tradition of learning idealized by Muslims (the desire, as the prophet Muhammad said, to "seek knowledge, even unto China"), the proliferation of Muslim centers of learning in China, and the fact that at least two Muslim groups, the Tatars and Uzbeks, are considerably better educated than the general populace including the Han Chinese. This is not unusual, however, given the fact that the Korean minority in China is also popularly perceived as "backward" precisely because they are grouped as one of the "minorities," even though the Koreans in China possess the highest literacy and educational rates in the country, far surpassing the Han and other groups (with three times the proportional number of college students than any other nationality).[12] We must remember that in the Marxist-Leninist-Stalinist-inspired developmentalist policy of China, those groups clinging to their "religion" (such as the Muslims and Tibetans), and those clinging to their "nationality" (such as the Koreans, Manchu, etc.), are thought to be similar to those groups clinging to class difference (landlords, semibourgeoisie, and the like), and thus more backward than those more advanced, secularist groups with a developed class consciousness (such as the Han).

This may also reflects the long held view in China that education was the means to acculturation into Chinese society, which depended on literacy, or the learning of Chinese. Since ancient times, minorities and foreigners per force had less possibility of attaining such in-depth knowledge of Chinese and would therefore always be on the periphery. Yet, this knowledge was not limited to elites. Myron Cohen argues that interaction between elites and common people in China's educational system led to not just "a common culture in the sense of shared behavior, institutions and beliefs," but also to "a unified culture in that it provided standards according to which people identified themselves as Chinese."[13] As long as one maintained these standards, one was Chinese. Yet knowledge of those standards was communicated in Chinese, in state schools. In imperial China, exhortations and rituals articulating the standards set by those in power helped to extend beyond establishing a "tiny literate reef" in the midst of "illiterate oceans" of the general populace.[14] As David Johnson notes, "The values and beliefs of a dominant class take on the radiance of truth in the eyes of ordinary people."[15] Yet this top-down view often excludes those it fails to inspire, particularly groups like Muslims, Tibetans and Mongols, who follow different moralities according to different religious texts. Charles Stafford has argued that in Taiwan, school children are given strong moral instruction as early as the fourth grade, including being taught such virtues as "filial piety to relatives, repaying the nation" (*xiao qin bao guo*) and "sacrificing the body, repaying the nation" (*xian shen bao guo*).[16] The link here between nation, morality and education is altogether clear. In mainland China morality, culture and education are also linked to its nationalization program.

This is perhaps why culture (*wenhua*) in China is so tied to literacy, particularly literacy in Chinese. The Chinese term *wen,* translated as "literature, writing, inscription," is a central part of the idea of culture. To be "cultured" is to possess *wen* or "literateness," and to be transformed by such knowledge of *wen*. In contrast to Western notions of culture, implied by the noun "culture," which one might belong to or possess (i.e., Western "culture"), Chinese notions are more transformative, and *wenhua* might best be considered as a verb. "Enculturation" might be a better translation of the Chinese idea, or perhaps even better, "in-literaticization." Strassberg's work on inscribed landscapes emphasizes the transformative power of writing in traditional China that helps to incorporate the landscapes into the realm of Chinese culture.[17] By the same token, literacy inculcates not only Chinese language, but also Chinese culture, or wenhua, into those minorities who are to become Chinese. Literacy and education are thus central to China's nationalist project of integration.

In an earlier article, I argued that non-Chinese vocabularies regarding ethnicity and nationality (*minzu*), religion (*zongjiao*), superstition (*mixin*), entered China from Japan in the late nineteenth century at a time of enthusiastic adaptation of foreign terms and notions of society, both Japanese and Western, in order to assist China's transformation.[18] Early nationalists such as Liang Qichao, Kang Youwei, and Sun Yat-sen combined these derivative discourses, to use Partha Chatterjee's term, with traditional Chinese, generally Confucian ideas, into new notions of the ideal society and nation. I argued, therefore, that these ideas were not entirely "derived," as Chatterjee seems to suggest for Indian views of nationalism,[19] but were rather combined with Chinese notions of person, family, clan and state. This project may very well have included the same constellation of terms such as "culture" (*wenhua*) and "civilization" (*wenming*) that were reformulated by Western, Japanese and Chinese ideas of development, literacy and modernity. Literacy in Chinese then, was a crucial step in the staged, developmentalist process of nationalization and enculturation.

As Pamela Crossley has argued, belief in the tenets of Chinese classicism, including "a reverence for the imputedly inherent transformative power of civilization, a distaste for displays of military power, [and] a contempt for commerce and semiliterate or illiterate cultural values" contributed in the West to notions of the inevitability of sinicization and assimilation of minorities and other marginals.[20] In other words, to learn Chinese meant one became Chinese. This notion has been shared by both Chinese and Western scholars who adhere to a sinicization paradigm that links literacy and education with assimilation, the primary method of China's developmentalist project. As LaBelle and Verhine have theorized, access to education contributes to the nature of social stratification in many societies.[21] In China, Muslim minorities have increasing access to education, but as will be seen below, there seems to have been little progress in their educational development.

REPRESENTATION OF MUSLIMS AS MINORITY NATIONALITIES

Muslims are grouped and displayed as independent nationalities (*minzu*) in all of China's many nationality publications, including the state-sponsored magazines *Nationality Pictorial* (*Minzu Huabao*) and *United Nationalities* (*Minzu Tuanjie*), as well as various collections, such as *Chinese Nationalities* (1989), *China's Minorities* (1994), *and Nationality Style and Figures* (1985). A cursory examination of photographs and paintings of Muslims in these state-sponsored publications reveals no real difference from the usual portrayal of minorities in China as "exotic" and "erotic."[22]

These representations are important for self- and other-understanding in China. As Paul Rabinow has pointed out, representations become "social facts."[23] Representations are manifestations of and manifested in knowledge, values, beliefs and social hierarchies and their justifications in the wider society. Perceptive China scholars have noted the colorful portrayal of minorities in China as derogatory, colonial and useful to the hegemony of the Han,[24] but this extends from imperial times and is not particularly new.[25] Studies of modern Chinese art have also drawn attention to the important place of minorities in the formation of art history of the People's Republic of China PRC.[26] Elsewhere, I argued that this represented an active policy of "internal colonialism in China."[27] Rarely, however, have Muslims been distinguished from this corpus, since they are generally treated in similar ways as other minority subjects.

After the PRC was founded in 1949, the state embarked upon a monumental endeavor to identify and recognize as nationalities those groups that qualified among the hundreds applying for national minority status. The question of one's nationality, which is registered on one's passport and on all official documents, is determined by Stalinist and historical criteria that determine if one is a member of a group that was ever linguistically, economically, geographically, or "culturally" distinct from the so-called Han majority population.[28] This recognition may make a considerable difference in obtaining certain privileges accorded to minorities, in some cases including permission to have more than one child; having access to local political office, special economic assistance, tax relief programs; and, important for the educational focus of this chapter, priority and preference in higher education (with reduced entrance requirements, lower scores and even affirmative action quotas). Those who were recognized by the state are always portrayed in the state-sponsored media as happily accepting that objectivized identity, as the caption for a photograph of several minorities in traditional costume pictured in a brochure introducing the Nationalities Cultural Palace in Beijing reads, "The Happy People of Various Nationalities."[29] This reflects the commonly held view that minorities in the southwest are "soft," while those in the north and northwest are "hard."[30] Northern minorities, generally Muslim, Tibetan or Mongolian, are thought to be more harsh primitives, represented as more masculine, warlike, and resistant to Chinese acculturation.[31]

In one published painting, several minorities are portrayed on the Great Wall, happily proclaiming in the caption: "I love the Great Wall"[32]—though the Great Wall was primarily built to keep nomadic peoples out. It is also interesting to note that in this figure, clearly geared for school children, the figures on the Great Wall, with one exception, are clearly Muslim: the men wear Turkic and Hui (Muslim Chinese) Islamic hats, and the woman is veiled. The odd man out, strangely enough, is an African. Perhaps he is placed on the wall with the other minorities to represent their ethnic solidarity; more seriously, perhaps it is to emphasize their corporate "primitivity" (i.e., promoting the idea that China's minorities are like "primitive" Africans), which is key to understanding the position of the minorities in the Marxist-Maoist evolutionary scheme (see below). The point of this painting is that the Muslims fit right into this scheme of minority representation, a representation that generally focuses on the naturalness, primitivity, backwardness, sensuality and even sexuality of the minority subjects. A popular art school now known as the Yunnan Art School, which I have described elsewhere, frequently uses Muslim and "Silk Road" subjects, such as the Dunhuang Buddhist dancers and apsaras, etc., in its extraordinarily eroticized paintings.[33]

While one might be prepared to allow for the fact that southwestern minorities may have more "open" sexual practices than the Han in China today, they are not the only minorities portrayed as sensual and erotic. While Thai women did traditionally bathe in the nude (though many may fear to now), and some southwestern matrilineal groups may very well have allowed extramarital sexual practice at the matrilocal residence, the traditional culture of Uygurs and other Muslim peoples can hardly be said to be more publicly erotic or sensual than that of the Han.[34] Uygur women are widely known throughout China to traditionally cover themselves with purdah-like head scarves and wraps that envelope their entire faces and hair. Unlike the Middle Eastern purdah, where eyes and sometimes faces are exposed, Uygur veils cover the entire face. As Muslims, they are generally much more conservative than Han Chinese with regard to the public sexual sphere. Despite their protestations, these representations continue, underscoring the extraordinary contrast between the Han and minority portrayal in China. Muslims also protest publications about Islam that they find denigrating, as evidenced by the China "Salman Rushdie" protest, an encyclopedic portrayal of Islam as sensual and eroticized in a book entitled *Sexual Customs,*[35] a representation that has a long history in China. Despite the government's crackdown on such publications, these kinds of representations of Islam and Muslims continue. For most Han Chinese, who have never darkened the door of a mosque and have learned little about Islam in public schools, this representation in the "public sphere" is their only exposure to knowledge about Islam in China or Muslim identities.

Like many tourist hotels, the Sheng Tang ("Ascendant Tang") Hotel in northeast Beijing has a tile mural of a Tang dynasty minority dancer, with accentuated nude breasts, in the center of its main dining hall. On the opposite walls, erotic stylized murals from the Dunhuang Buddhist grottoes grace the dining room. Like many public places in China, the sensual "Flying Absarases" are an officially sanctioned art subject.[36] I once asked a group of Han scholars viewing this mural if they thought the dancers were minorities or Han, and they all said minorities, even though the theme is from the Buddhist caves of Dunhuang, supposedly the cradle of Chinese Buddhist religious tradition. While Buddhism became transformed into a "Chinese" religion, its sensual representation in art and absarases have apparently remained an attribute of foreigners and minorities, rather than of Han. In many state-sponsored representations, Uygur Muslim dances are directly linked to the eroticized, exoticized representations of the Dunhuang Buddhist caves. While many Uygur today believe their ancestors introduced Buddhism and Buddhist art to China, few would approve of their modern dances as being portrayed in such an eroticized fashion. Eight hundred years of Islam in the Tarim Basin has had some influence on Uygur aesthetic and moral sensibilities.

MUSLIM SELF-REPRESENTATION

As China does not yet have a free press, opportunities for Muslims to represent themselves in the public sphere entirely without state mediation is still not yet possible. Even recent popular novels such as Zhang Chengzhi's *A History of the Soul* (1991) and Huo Da's *Jade King* (1993) (or, in Chinese, *Muslim Funeral*, *(Musilin zangli)* 1992) which are written by Muslims about Muslim lives and conflicts have passed through state bodies of literary approval. Both of these works, though controversial in their own right, are remarkable in their serious and upright portrayal of Muslim society in general (despite internal conflicts), representing modern attempts to reveal a Muslim morality similar to earlier Muslim portrayals of Islam as "Confucian" (see below).

One earlier pictorial published for charity by the China Islamic Association, *A Collection of Painting and Calligraphy Solicited for Charity in Aid of the Disabled*, presents an entirely different view of Muslims than that found in Nationality Pictorial and the Yunnan Art School.[37] Here, Muslims are represented as studious, hardworking, devout and dedicated to the family and society. There is even a presentation of Chinese calligraphy by Muslim artists (and at least one Han artist who wrote calligraphy in praise of Islam!), reminiscent again of Muslim attempts to establish their literary and artistic credentials in the classic Chinese arts of painting and calligraphy (see below). The various publications by the China Islamic Association entitled *The Religious Life of Chinese Moslems* (1957, 1978, 1985) feature not only various mosques and prominent Muslims, but also a great deal of emphasis on education. The Muslim-sponsored pictorial, *Islamic in Beijing,*[38] contains not only fine examples of Islamic architecture, art and scholarship in Beijing, but also features photos of famous Muslim scholars and teachers. Similarly, the Xinjiang publication by the Uygurs Jori Kadir and Halik Dawut, *Examples of Uygur Architectural Art* (1983), contain not only fine examples of mosques and tombs dedicated to religious figures, but also tombs dedicated to Muslim scholars such as the poet Yusup Has Hajip and the lexicographer al-

Kashgari. Indeed, many of the Muslim tombs being quickly restored across China are dedicated to Muslim scholars as well as to religious personages, only some of whom were Sufis.[39]

A striking example of the usual mode of Muslim representation is contained in the interesting tourist collection, *Picture Album of Turpan Landscape and Custom.*[40] Here, out of 67 paintings and woodblock prints, only 5 paintings can be identified as produced by Uygurs according to their names (Imin, Kazi Amet, Aini, Kilim, Haz Aimitinote that the names are only given in Chinese character translations of the original Uygur). The 45 paintings by Han artists that can be identified presumably by their Chinese names (though a few might be Hui) present the usual figures of Uygur women dancing and playing musical instruments, scenes of ancient ruins and natural beauty, and of men leading camel caravans or preaching in the mosque.[41] Typical examples include the very first painting in the collection of colorful, enticing Uygur women dancing, by Huang Zhou, entitled *The Uygur dance;*[42] another similar dance scene by Ou Chujian, entitled *Turpan Impression-Girls There;*[43] and finally, the classic rendition by Gu Shengyue[44] of a Uygur musician playing the reed saz flute, with barebreasted Dunhuang-style Buddhist appsarasses whirling overhead, entitled *Ancient Music Playing on the Silk Road.*

Typical of this fascination with minority women is the painting by Liu Bingjiang,[45] entitled simply, *Uygur Girl.* Here, however, unlike another painting of a minority woman by Liu that I have discussed in a previous article,[46] the Uygur woman is clothed with a headscarf. Liu's other painting, entitled *Nude* was shown at the Oil Painting Research Association Exhibition in Beijing in 1979, which is surprisingly early in China's reform period for such a painting. The subject is a dark-skinned female, completely nude, and realistically portrayed in a kneeling position with her hands on the ground in a submissive pose, wearing nothing but her jewellery. Given the tapestry background, her jewellery and most importantly, the posture, the painting is one of the earliest works in the Yunnan School style. According to Cohen, her kneeling position is not within the officially sanctioned "academic painting repertoire" and thus suggests to Cohen a "South Asian" influence.[47] It is important to note that the bracelets she wears clearly resemble shackles, and combined with the posture, the painting evokes erotic subservience and submission. This contrasts with Liu's *Uygur Girl*, where the subject is clothed and scarved. Perhaps this is due to the fact that the Han artists were aware that nudes would not be appropriate in the Turpan Landscape collection, unless they were of ancient Buddhist motifs (such as the paintings by Gu Shengyue and Jiang Zhenhua). Indicative of this sensitivity to Muslim self-representations, there are three extraordinary paintings of women Muslims studying and reading while performing their daily chores. Zhao Zhongzao[48] presents a traditional woodblock entitled *After School Hours* in which three Muslim girls are huddled over their books, after school is out. Long Qinglian[49] in his painting *Harvesting Time of Grapes* has a Uygur woman sitting under a grape arbor, preoccupied with something she is writing. Wu Qifeng's[50] *A Teacher in the Countryside* is the most remarkable. Here a Uygur woman is sitting under a grape arbor, rocking a cradle, and entirely focused on what looks like a stack of exams she is grading. Each of these paintings reveal a sensitivity to and awareness of Muslim interest among women toward learning, which is belied by national images and statistics (see below).

These few examples reveal that Muslims have a very different view of themselves than that found in most state-sponsored public media. They are not only a minority nationality, but members of a long religious and scholarly tradition that has contributed to Chinese culture and society. The transmission of this image of Islam and Islamic knowledge in China is a difficult task for a population that occupies only 2 percent of the total, and one that has generally been stigmatized throughout much of Chinese history. Generally thought to be lower in "cultural level" than most Han Chinese and less "educated," their pride in their own tradition of Islamic learning is only now beginning to be communicated to non-Muslims. And, as will be seen below, for most Muslim nationalities in China, including the Hui, Uygur, Uzbek and Tatar, their general Chinese education equals or exceeds that of the Han. However, this is not the general perception in China, a fact that is changing only gradually.

CHINESE EDUCATION OF MUSLIMS

International travel and exposure for China's Muslims in this century has meant a rush to attain both Chinese and Islamic education in the hope of "modernizing" China's Muslim communities. In the early decades of the twentieth century, China was exposed to many new foreign ideas, and in the face of Japanese and Western imperialist encroachment sought a Chinese approach to governance. Intellectual and organizational activity by Chinese Muslims during this period was also intense. Increased contact with the Middle East led Chinese Muslims to reevaluate their traditional notions of Islam. Pickens records that from 1923 to 1934 there were 834 known Hui Muslims who made the *Hajj*, or pilgrimage, to Mecca.[51] In 1937, according to one observer, over 170 Hui pilgrims boarded a steamer in Shanghai bound for Mecca.[52] By 1939, at least 33 Hui Muslims had studied at Cairo's prestigious Al-Azhar University. While these numbers are not significant when compared with pilgrims on the *Hajj* from southeast Asian Muslim areas, the influence and prestige attached to these returning Hui *Hajji* was profound, particularly in isolated communities. In this respect, it appears that secluded and remote Muslim communities far from the main centers of Islamic cultural life in the Middle East, were more susceptible to those centers' most recent trends. [53]

As a result of political events and the influence of foreign Muslim ideas, numerous new Hui organizations emerged. In 1912, one year after Sun Yat-sen was inaugurated provisional president of the Chinese Republic in Nanjing, the Chinese Muslim Federation was also formed in that city. This was followed by the establishment of other Hui Muslim associations: the Chinese Muslim Mutual Progress Association (Beijing, 1912), the Chinese Muslim Educational Association (Shanghai, 1925), the Chinese Muslim Association (1925), the Chinese Muslim Young Students Association (Nanjing, 1931), the Society for the Promotion of Education Among Muslims (Nanjing, 1931), and the Chinese Muslim General Association (Jinan, 1934).

The Muslim periodical press flourished as never before. Although Lowenthal reports that circulation was low, there were over 100 known Muslim periodicals produced before the outbreak of the Sino-Japanese War in 1937.[54] Thirty journals were published between 1911 and 1937 in Beijing alone, prompting one author to suggest that while Chinese Islam's traditional religious center was still Linxia (Hezhou), its cultural center had shifted to Beijing.[55] This took place when many Hui intellectuals traveled to Japan, the Middle East and the West. Caught up in the nationalist fervor of the first half of this century, they published magazines and founded organizations, questioning their identity as never before in a process that one Hui historian, Ma Shouqian, has recently termed "The New Awakening of the Hui at the end of 19th and beginning of the 20th centuries."[56] As many of these Hui Hajji returned from their pilgrimages to the Middle East, they initiated several reforms, engaging themselves once again in the contested space between Islamic ideals and Chinese culture. This zeal for "modern" education led to the establishment of more modernist Islamic movements in China, including the Ikwan (known in China as the "Yihewani") and the Salafiyya. The Yihewani differ from the traditionalist and Sufi Muslim groups in China primarily with regard to ritual matters and their stress upon reform through Chinese education and modernism. Because of their emphasis on nationalist concerns, education, modernization and decentralized leadership, the order has attracted more urban intellectual Muslims. The Yihewani are also especially numerous in areas like Qinghai and Gansu where they proliferated during the republican period under the patronage of Hui warlords. Many of the large mosques and Islamic schools rebuilt with government funds throughout China in the late 1970s and early 1980s tend to be staffed by Yihewani Imam.

The spread of Islamic reform movements in China during the late nineteenth century saw Beijing's establishment as the "cultural center of Chinese Islam." These movements in many ways displaced central and western China (in places such as Hezhou, Yunnan, Kashgar and Zhengzhou) as the main sites for Muslim learning, shifting many of China's Muslims from traditionalist and Sufi Islamic associations to those of the modernist Yihewani. While Muslims in the northwest saw religious conservatism and revival as the answer to their social and cultural problems, the Muslims in many urban centers, especially Beijing, decided that education was the solution:

> [The decline of the Hui in Beijing] is associated with the following four things: 1) the degeneration of Islam among all religions, 2) the degeneration of China among the nations, 3) the degeneration of Beiping among the capitals, 4) the degeneration of Niujie where the Hui people are crowded together. In fact, it isn't the degeneration of the people but the backwardness of their education. . . . The relationship between education and living standard is one of cause and effect. Obviously, without education there would not be people of talent, without talented personnel there would be no better means of livelihood.[57]

The question of what kind of education was debated throughout the republican period, with various private Hui schools attempting different combinations of secular and religious education. By the early days of the People's Republic, these private schools became secularized and nationalized. Religious education now became the responsibility of the mosque and home, whereas secular education was the responsibility of the state. Shortly after the establishment of the PRC, the Beijing city government combined the Hui middle schools of Cheng Da Normal School, Northwest Middle School and Yanshan Middle School into the Hui Institute (Huimin Xueyuan). In 1963 the Hui Institute was changed to the Hui Middle School. In 1979 it was reopened under that name after being divided up during the Cultural Revolution as the Capital Middle School and the Number 135 Middle School.

POST-1949 CHINESE EDUCATION OF MUSLIMS

In 1949, there were 19 Hui elementary schools created out of former private "Muslim schools" (*Muzi xuexiao*). By 1953 there were 28 Hui elementary schools, all of which were renamed during the Cultural Revolution. Children were required to attend the schools in the neighborhoods where they lived. While this is still mainly the case for Hui elementary schools, there are now 13 Hui elementary schools and 6 Hui nursery schools in Beijing, all in Hui-concentrated neighborhoods. Elementary education, now universally required throughout Beijing, is the area of real gain. In 1949 there were only about 2,700 Hui in elementary school in Beijing. Now virtually all Beijing Hui elementary school-aged children are in school.

The curriculum in all of these state-run institutions is set by the Ministry of Education and is exactly the same as other schools, the main differences being that no pork is served at the schools and no tuition charged to Hui students. In 1984 the State Council for Nationality Affairs (CNA) published "nationality general knowledge" (*minzu changshi*) curriculum for the Hui middle schools. The state's goal to strengthen education among minorities reflects the call of the 1930s: "This research explains that whenever nationality education work is seized upon (*zhua haole*), then nationality relations and nationality unity will be greatly strengthened."[58]

Table 3.2. Ethnic Composition of Entering High School Students from Beijing, Niujie Muslim district, 1979-1981

	1979		1980		1981		Total	
	Han	Hui	Han	Hui	Han	Hui	Han	Hui
Students	54	3	37	2	35	2	123	10
Percentage of ethnic group	0.13	0.03	0.09	0.2	0.8	0.04	0.29	0.07
Percentage of class	94.7	5.3	95.0	5.0	86.0	14.0	92.0	8.0

Source: Adapted from Beijing City (1984), p. 21; see Dru C. Gladney, *Muslim Chinese: Ethnic Nationalism in the People's Republic* (Cambridge: Harvard University Press, 1996), pp. 214-219.

Despite a great deal of emphasis on minority education since the "golden period" of the 1950s, the Hui still lag behind the Han in Beijing, especially in post-elementary education. Out of 364 Han who graduated from Beijing's Number One Middle School in 1982, there were 47 (12 percent) who went on to either college or higher technical schools. Out of the seven Hui who graduated, not one went on to higher schooling.[59] Table 3.2 gives differences in Hui and Han high school entrance from 1979 to 1981 in the Oxen Street district.

From 1979 to 1981 there was a slight decline among both Han and Hui in high school entrance. Although the Hui occupy about one-fourth of the Oxen Street population, they represented only 5 to 14 percent of those entering high school. Less than 6 percent of the Oxen Street area Hui had attended middle school prior to 1955. A 1983 education survey of the Xuanwu district (where Oxen Street is located) revealed that out of every 1,000 Hui, 5.1 percent are college graduates, 22.7 percent are high school graduates, 30.7 percent are middle school graduates, and 41.8 percent are elementary school graduates. The same survey among Han in the Xuanwu District revealed that 23.34 percent are college graduates, 21.54 percent are high school graduates, 25 percent are middle school graduates, and 17.58 percent received an elementary education. There are more than four times as many Han graduates from college as Hui in this area, and there are almost two and a half times as many Hui with only an elementary school education as there are Han. In 1982, 1.2 percent the Han students who took the high school exam were admitted, whereas only .67 percent of the minority examinees were admitted.[60]

This brief examination of the educational situation of the Hui in Beijing is indicative of national trends for most Muslims in urban areas in China. It is clear, however, that there are large gaps between rural and urban Muslim education, which drives the national statistics. While it is generally true that Hui educational level is lower than that of the Han majority among whom they live, at the national level, the educational level of the Hui has apparently fared fairly well. Table 3.3 reveals that in 1982 the Hui had kept pace with the national average, and are substantially better educated than the other Muslim minorities, with the exception of the Tatars and Uzbeks.[61] The main advantage the Hui have is language: other Muslim minorities have to contend with

Table 3.3. Educational Level of Muslim Minorities in China in Percent, 1982

Educational Level	Hui	Uygur	Kazak	Dong-xiang	Kirgiz	Salar	Tajik	Uzbek	Baoan	Tatar	All Ethnic Groups	All China
University graduate	.5	.2	.4	0	.3	.2	.2	.2	.2	3.9	.2	.5
Undergraduate	2.5	.1	.1	0	.1	.2	.1	.9	.1	11	.1	.2
Senior Middle School	7	5	5	1	5	1	4	11	2	15	5	8
Junior Middle School	19	12	17	3	11	5	11	22	6	25	15	20
Primary School	30	37	49	8	40	18	38	40	12	40	37	40
Illiterate*	41	45	29	87	41	74	49	20	78	9	45	32

*Population age 6 and above who cannot read or can read very little.
Source: Adopted from Population Census Office 1987: xvi, p.29.

Table 3.4. Educational Level of Muslim Minorities in China in Percent, 1990

Educational Level	Hui	Uygur	Kazak	Dong-xiang	Kirgiz	Salar	Tajik	Uzbek	Baoan	Tatar	All China
University graduate	.6	.5	.5	.05	.3	.3	.2	2.6	.2	3.6	.5
Undergraduate	.9	.4	.7	.08	.5	.3	.3	1.9	.1	2.5	2.4
Technical School*	1.6	1.6	2.6	.3	2.4	.9	2.1	4.7	1.0	5.8	17.6
Senior Middle School	6.2	3.5	5.5	.6	3.4	1.6	2.5	10.8	2.9	11.0	6.4
Junior Middle School	19.9	11.9	16.4	2.8	10.2	6.3	9.3	20.3	7.2	22.0	23.3
Primary School	29.1	43.3	43.9	12	43.4	18.8	40.4	33.7	16.2	32.7	37.2
Semi- or illiterate	33.1	26.6	12.3	82.6	24.9	68.7	33.5	8.3	68.8	4.9	22.2

*Note that data for "Technical School" was not provided for 1982 figures.

Source: Adopted from Department of Population Statistics, 1994, pp. 70-73.

learning the Han language as a second language in order to enter middle school and a university.[62] However, the Hui speak the Han dialects wherever they live.

Since 1982, Muslims have made some gains in public education in China compared to the rest of the population, according to the 1990 census. A comparison of figures from the 1990 census (see Table 3.4) reveals that for the Hui, educational rates have remained basically the same. Significantly, college graduate rates for all Muslims except the Tatars and Uzbeks are similar to the rest of China (about .5 percent). The elementary distinction for Tatars and Uzbeks is that their numbers are small and that they are primarily concentrated in urban areas. Though their college educational rates are extraordinary compared to the rest of the population, there at least 10 other minority groups with higher educational rates in China than the Han (including Koreans, Manchus, Russians, Daur, Xibe, Hezhe, Ewenki and Oroqen). It is clear that the most rural Muslim groups (the Dongxiang, Bonan and Salar in Gansu) and the still seminomadic or pastoralist groups (Kazak and Kirgiz) suffer from the least access to state schools, though there does seem to be some gains in elementary school education among the Uygur, Kazakh and Dongxiang. The gap between rural and urban, nomadic and sedentary, shows up most dramatically in illiteracy and semi-illiteracy rates. While the Hui have made some gains between 1982 and 1990 (illiteracy reduced from 41 to 33.1 percent), the two groups with the highest illiteracy rates in 1982, the Dongxiang (87 percent) and the Baoan (78 percent), have shown only marginal gains in literacy in 1990 (reduced to 82.6 percent and 68.8 percent respectively). This compares to an overall reduction in illiteracy in China between 1982 and 1990 from 32 percent to 22 percent. This dramatic drop has apparently not reached the Muslim communities in rural Gansu.

At the other extreme, when the college educational level among Muslims is compared with the rest of China, not only have they done comparatively well, but there have been some gains between 1982 and 1990, particularly for the most educated Muslims, the Tatars and Uzbeks. Most remarkable gains have been among undergraduate education for the Uygurs, Kazaks, Kirgiz, Salars and Tajiks. Whereas the Han undergraduate college population grew from .2 to 2.4 percent, these groups experienced even greater gains (Uygur, .1 to 2.1; Kazaks, .2 to 3.3; Kirgiz, .1 to 2.9; Tajik, .1 to 2.5).[63]

For the most part, however, we have seen very little change between 1982 and 1990 in Muslim education in China, despite significant state efforts to promote education in minority and Muslim areas. Not only is elementary and secondary education provided in several primarily Muslim languages (especially Uygur, Kazak, Kirgiz and Tajik), but the state provides the normal minority nationality incentives for preferred college entrance. The state in China has made strong efforts to provide equal educational access for minorities and Han in both rural and urban areas.[64] It is noteworthy, however, that second-language education is not widely available among the least educated Muslim populations concentrated in the Hexi corridor of Gansu, the Dongxiang, Bonan and Salar. As these groups speak a mixed combination of Chinese, Turkish and Mongol, the state for the most part provides primarily Chinese language education. In all Muslim areas, however, the state has sought to adapt to Muslim needs by providing *qing zhen*, or Halal food that does not contain pork, with special Hui schools in urban areas. Yet even these efforts do not seem enough to raise Muslim minority education in China. This may have to do more with the content of education that is set by the central education bureau than its medium of adapting to local languages and Muslim customs.

For example, in my Beijing city research, many Hui parents in the Oxen Street district told me that, while they were glad for the Hui schools and the priority Hui are now receiving in education, they felt their children would be more motivated to study if there was more ethnic content in the studies. Many of them remember that Hui schools in the early 1950s often invited famous Hui scholars such as Bai Shouyi and Ma Songting to give lectures on Hui history and on historical Chinese Muslim personages. The Hui middle school in the Oxen Street district also offered Arabic as a second language, so children did not have to go to the mosque to learn it. Beijing Hui parents are not tempted to withdraw their children from school and send them to the mosque for religious education like many northwestern Hui. Instead, they argue that there is more of a need to integrate secular and religious education in order to motivate their children. They also point out that the Islamic schools, even with the course for training imams at the Chinese Islamic Association in the Oxen Street district, cannot supply enough imams for as many mosques as need them. One of the reasons for this is that upon graduation many young men use their Arabic or

Persian to become interpreters or translators overseas where they can travel and earn more money, rather than becoming imams. The distinction between ethnicity and Islam in the city is still too strong for most Hui parents, and they think it might help the country if the two were brought closer together.

Like other minorities, the Hui in Niujie receive special consideration on their exams for entrance to middle school, high school and college. In general, they receive two "levels" of 10 points each for college entrance preference. For example, if the threshold for college entrance on the state exams is 300 points, a Hui who scores 280 points will be accepted. This may make a difference. I knew a Hui who scored 281 on the exam and was admitted to Beijing Normal University (Beijing Shifan Daxue). His Han neighbor complained bitterly of this to me, as he had scored 295 and was not admitted to the college of his choice. He had thought he was assured a place, and eventually went to a "television university" (*dianshi daxue*) where most courses are taught on video cassette. Athletes who place among the top six (*qian liu ming*) in provincial competitions are also given two stage preferences. Hence, it is conceivable that a Hui athlete could score 260 on the exam and still be admitted to college with a total score of 300 since he receives four stage preferences. Preference for high school and college minority education is just beginning to show long term effects, and 1990 records should reveal a significant improvement over the 1979-1981 figures cited above.

From the government's perspective, the most important stress has been placed upon raising the educational level of rural Hui villagers. In 1958, over 90 percent of the Hui in Changying, one suburban village on the outskirts of Beijing, were found to be illiterate. By contrast, almost all of the children above the age of 10 of their Han village neighbors could read. The country had to send in outside accountants to handle the huge amount of paperwork which was too much for the few literate Hui to handle. By 1980, there were 8 Hui college students from the village, 650 high school students, 3,000 middle school students, and 3,000 elementary school students. The municipality and district government donated 300,000 yuan to build a nationality elementary school (*minzu xiaoxue*) for Hui in Changying, with the plan of making it into a cultural center for all the Beijing suburban villages to emulate. The faculty are paid higher wages than that of other elementary schools, and there is twice the budget for the children's meals and snacks. Out of 647 students, 85 percent are Hui, a proportion higher than any other nationality school in Beijing. The faculty are 30 percent Hui. Ninety-five percent of the first class entered middle school, and 50 percent of them tested into high school.

There are still problems to overcome, however. The Hui principal said that Hui parents do not value education as much as the Han. They would rather have their children help out with the family sideline enterprise. The village government has developed special training programs to help families realize the importance of a public education. One of the issues that the local officials have yet to address, however, is the nature of education for these Hui. The imam mentioned that while desire for "Han" learning was low, many of the younger Hui were quite motivated to study Islamic history and Quranic languages. The secretary of the Communist Party countered that this was not regarded as education by the state and therefore could not be encouraged by state schools. Rather, it was part of religion, he argued.

For other Muslim minorities, efforts have been made to bring state education to the minority areas, including the pastoral areas, through the novel program of setting up schools in the pastures, or more commonly, requiring Kazak and Kirgiz herders to leave their children in school until they can join them in the herding areas during vacation. Despite these efforts, Muslim illiteracy (with the exception of the Tatars and Uzbeks) remains high, and there has been little overall change in Muslim minority education in the last 8 years. The reason, again, may have more to do with what is taught, rather than how it is taught. The lack of nationality content and Muslim world history may be forcing the Muslims who are interested in their people's history to go to the mosque rather than to public schools and libraries for such "religious" knowledge. This is odd, since information on other world religions are frequently taught in the public schools, including Buddhism and Christianity, though often in a critical fashion.

The Gender Gap: Male-Female Education Discrepancies among Muslim Nationalities

It is clear that China's policy of co-education and mixing male and female students runs directly against traditional Muslim sensitivities. While it could be argued that China's Muslim women are more "liberated" than their Middle Eastern counterparts in that they are not subject to the strict rules of purdah and seclusion, the 1990 data on education suggests a significant male-female discrepancy in access to state-sponsored education at both ends of the spectrum. China, as a society dominated by male influence related to the East Asian tradition of patrilineal descent and patrilocal residence, is characterized by male preference in terms of birth, education and social mobility. For Muslims, this is even more significant in terms of public education. In terms of illiteracy and semi-illiteracy rates, the figures for Muslim females are nearly twice as high as those for Muslim males. While China's illiteracy rate in general is about 22.2 percent, the Muslim average (excluding the Tajik and Uzbeks) is about 45 percent. The rates diverge even more across gender boundaries. Hui females average 42.7 percent illiteracy and semi-illiteracy, compared to 23.7 percent among Hui males and 12.3 percent among Han males (Han females average 31.1 percent). For the three least educated Muslim groups, the Dongxiang, Baoan and Salar, the rates are even worse: Dongxiang males; 73.8 percent, females; 92 percent; Bonan males; 53.3 percent, females; 85.3 percent; Salar males; 49.2 percent, females; 88.9 percent. Earlier, Hawkins argued the importance of minority education for inter-group relations in China.[65] This data reveals that high rates of illiteracy among females and males for at least three Muslim nationalities bodes ill for inter-group relations with Han Chinese and the Chinese state.

At the other extreme, college education among Muslim males and females reveals a similar gender gap. Whereas for Han males, .4 percent have received university education, this is true for only .1 percent of females. Among the least educated Muslim groups, this gap is negligible, since so few have attended college. But it is interesting to note that three times as many Kazak males attend college than Kazak females (.35 versus .1 percent, respectively), and twice as many Uygur males as females (.16 versus .8 percent, respectively). Among the more educated Muslim minorities, the Uzbek male/female college ratio is equal (1.3 percent for both males and females) and for the Tatar, it is only slightly different (2 percent for males and 1.5 percent for females). This indicates that more educated Muslims tend to send both males and females alike to school. This is not true, however, for the more rural and less educated Muslim populations.

China's Muslim males and females never pray together, so it is no wonder that they do not want their children to study together. Although China is distinguished in the Muslim world by having many women's mosques that are often attached to or even independent from men's mosques, it is clear that they rarely mix together for ritual or religious education. On one holiday, however, that of Fatima's birthday, which is celebrated widely among Muslims in China, I have witnessed men and women praying together. In general, however, women pray at home, in the back or side of the mosque separated by a curtain, or in an adjacent or separate women's mosque (*nü si*).[66] While it is not clear how well-educated China's Muslim women are in Islam, they are active in studying the Quran and in establishing mosques. This is not true for their participation in public education. It is clear that if China wants to improve the education of its Muslim population, it not only needs to consider a more inclusive curriculum of Muslim history, but it may need to end co-education in Muslim areas. An examination of traditional Islamic education in China, though generally equally exclusive toward women, is one that is highly developed and permeates all of China's Muslim communities, male and female alike. This cannot be said for state school education.

TRADITIONAL ISLAMIC EDUCATION IN CHINA

In a recent paper, Ma Qicheng (a Hui Muslim scholar from Ningxia) and Gladney (1996) have argued that traditional Islamic education in China has been one of the primary catalysts in preserving and promulgating Hui Muslim identity.[67] This can be considered a process of indigenization assisted by the rise of a system of *jing tang jiaoyu* (literally, "education in the Classics' Hall"), that is, the *madrassah* Muslim educational system that is closely associated with the mosque.[68] It is interesting that mosque education in China was modeled on Confucian education, but instead of the lineage bearing responsibility, the entire community supported the mosque and its students. The system paralleled the Confucian literati training program, but was not supported by imperial authorities and was not recognized by the imperial government. Thus the two systems bore organizational similarities, but did not institutionally inter-mingle or overlap. So today, Chinese authorities do not recognize private, mosque-oriented Islamic education except in those larger academies set up by the China Islamic Association in Beijing and elsewhere. These institutions train imams on behalf of the state to work in official mosques and government religious affairs bureaus.

Traditionally, the *jing tang* is a *madrassah* (community school) established in and attached to the mosque. The leading ahong (teacher or imam) in the mosque is also the master of the *jing tang*. The aim of a jing tang is to train religious personnel, hence the Quran and other Islamic classics are the main textbooks. The emergence and development of jing tang education is closely related to the Hui effort of adapting Islam to the Chinese social milieu.

Mosque education can be generally broken down into three levels: that of the elementary (school), the intermediate (middle school), and the advanced (college). The elementary school (*jingwen xiaoxue*) teaches the alphabet and phonetics of Arabic; primary Quranic knowledge, often referred to in Arabic as the khatim ("seal," referring to 18 Quranic suras); and various readings on ritual practices, such as prayer, fasting, funerals, marriages, etc. Morning and evening, children would be taught the rudimentary basics of prayer, ablution and recitation. Rote memorization of the Quran was accomplished by assigning Chinese characters homophonically with Arabic syllables, leading to remarkably accurate pronunciation without any understanding whatsoever. It is not uncommon in the past for this to be compulsory for both boys and girls age 6 to 13 or 14 in many Muslim communities. Wang argues that graduation from elementary school was more important than circumcision for recognition as members of the Islamic community for young Muslims in Yunnan.[69] This clearly is not the case today in most Muslim areas of China, where mosque education is less developed.

Middle-level mosque education is more seasonal. Incorporating students from ages 12 to 18, it equips Muslim youth with the core Islamic stipulations and morals. They learned both pedagogy (Arabic grammar, syntax, logic, rhetoric and ethics) and theology (including the shariah and hadith). Students furthered their knowledge of primary Arabic, the Quran and classic religious works in Arabic or even Persian, depending on the expectations and level of the community.

The "college" level is actually the real jing tang, in which the regular students (known as *halifa* [Khalifa], or *manla*) further their knowledge of Arabic or Persian, rhetoric and commentaries on the Quran and the Hadith. While many Muslim communities had elementary and middle-level training in the mosque, only large communities could support college-level training. Ages ranged from 18 to 25 and even older, depending on the support from the community.

Often the education depended on the mastering of five Arabic and Persian textbooks, including an examination and graduation ceremony, attended by the entire community.

Finally, it also important to note that this madrassah system was characteristic of traditionalist and modernist or Yihewani Muslim communities.[70] Sufi communities followed more personalized courses of instruction after the elementary stage, in which the Shaykh personally inducted the student (*manla*) into the generally esoteric practices and traditions of the order.[71] Three stages of initiation were taught among Sufis, and while debate often centered on which stage is most important, or in what order they should be followed, they were generally given as the first stage of Jiaocheng or Changdao (in Arabic, the Sharia); the middle stage of Daocheng or Zhongdao (in Arabic, the Tariqah); and the final stage of Zhencheng or Zhidao (in Arabic, the Haqiqah). Individual Sufis would be initiated into each of these stages under the Daozu (master of the Dao), which often took place in the Dao Tang (ritual center of the Sufi shaykh).

THE RISE OF ISLAMIC EDUCATION AND ITS INFLUENCE ON CHINESE EDUCATION

It is clear from Table 3.3 and Table 3.4 that Muslim education in China varies dramatically between groups and between males and females. Not only were the Baoan and Dongxiang among the most illiterate groups in China in 1982 and 1990, but the Tatars and Uzbeks continue to be among the most educated. These trends are continuing in the 1990s, but with rising Islamic conservatism, there is some concern that gains in Chinese education may be lost. As I noted in my earlier study in Ningxia in the mid-1980s, rising Islamic conservatism led to the decline in interest in government-sponsored education. A decrease in public school enrollment, and an increase in children studying the Quran in private madrassah attached to local mosques is another phenomenon that had local Ningxia cadres concerned. This growing interest in pursuing religious education has not yet reached large proportions of the Hui in Na Homestead, as only 10 school-age children were not attending public school in 1985. Instead, they were studying the Quran at home privately. There are four officially permitted manla in the village. In more heavily populated Hui areas, however, this is becoming a more noticeable trend. In Guyuan County, Jiefangxiang

(Liberation Township), only 12 out of 104 school-age children in the village are attending school, and 27 of those not in school are studying the Quran in the mosque.

This trend has become even more pronounced in conservative Muslim areas such as Linxia Hui Autonomous Prefecture in Gansu Province, where various Muslim minorities make up 52.7 percent of the population.[72] Here, school enrollment has regularly decreased since 1978, from 77.2 percent at that time to 66.6 percent in 1979, 60 percent in 1980, 57.3 percent in 1981, and a low of 50 percent in 1982. In constrast, in Hanfeng Commune, a completely Han area, enrollment of children reaches as high as 93.9 percent overall, and among girls it is 79 percent. In the neighboring mountainous Badan Commune, an all-Muslim area, enrollment was 23.9 percent in 1982, with only 9.05 percent of girls enrolled. By the end of the school year only 2.9 percent of the girls remained in school. This reflects the common practice of children attending school for the first few weeks of registration, but returning full-time to the farm before completing the term.[73]

In a *China Daily*[74] front page article entitled "Keep rural girls in school," Liu Su,[75] the vice-governor of Gansu Province, reported that out of 157,300 school-age children not in school in Gansu, 85 percent were girls. Children leave school for a variety of reasons, including the farm's need for income-producing labor under the newly introduced responsibility system. Yet many Hui point to traditional Islamic views that have made them reluctant to send their children, especially daughters, to public schools.

When asked about their reluctance to send their children to school, Na Homestead parents expressed doubts about "the value of learning Chinese and mathematics." "It would be much more useful," I was told by one mother, "for our children to learn the Quran, Arabic and Persian." If a child excelled, he or she might become a manla, and eventually perhaps an ahong. Their status in the village would be much higher than the average middle school or even high school graduate, as would their income (estimated at 100 to 500 yuan a month for a well-known teaching ahong). Children who are in poor health are often kept at home to study the Quran. In large families with more than one son, one child is generally encouraged to study to become an ahong. Although the government officially allows each mosque to support from two to four full-time manla-who should be at least 18 years old and junior middle school graduates-many younger children study at home without official approval.

Ningxia, as the only autonomous region for China's Hui Muslims, tends to monitor ahong training and religious practice more closely than other areas where Hui are concentrated. In Yunnan's Weishan Yi and Hui Autonomous County, several mosques had over 20 resident manla studying under well-known ahong. In Gansu's Linxia Hui Autonomous Prefecture, at the South Great Mosque there were over 130 full-time students. In Linxia City's Bafang district, where most of the Hui are concentrated, there were at least 60 full-time manla in each mosque. Mirroring the spiritual importance of Mecca and the centrality of theological learning of the Iranian city of Qum for China's Hui Muslims,[76] Linxia's famous mosques and scholars attract students from all over China.[77]

Renowned mosques in Yunnan's Shadian and Weishan counties tend to attract students from throughout the southwest, including Hainan Island. At an ordination (*chuanyi*) service I attended at the Xiao Weigeng Mosque in Weishan County in February 1985, the 10 graduates included one Hainan Island student and six students from outside the county who had studied there for 5 years. The Hainan student had a brother studying the Quran in Beijing. The next class admitted 30 students, 10 from the local village, 10 from other villages and 10 from outside the county, including one from outside Yunnan. The fact that these manla travel long distances to study under celebrated ahongs demonstrates that national ties continue to link disparate Hui communities. It also reveals the growing importance of religious education in the countryside.

In the northwest, in addition to allowing from two to four students (*halifa*) to train privately in each mosque, the government has approved and funded two Islamic Schools (*yixueyuan*) in Yinchuan and Tongxin. In 1988, the state provided funding to establish a large Islamic seminary and mosque complex outside the west gate of Yinchuan near Luo Village. Similarly, in Urumqi the Islamic college was established in 1985 and other regional and provincial government's have followed suit. This indicates a "regionalization" of state-sponsored Islamic education, which until the 1980s had been officially concentrated at the China Islamic Affairs Commission in Beijing, established in 1956.

The increased promotion of exchange with foreign Muslim countries is exposing more urban Hui to international aspects of their religious heritage. Among urban Hui, Islamic knowledge tends to be higher than in rural areas, perhaps because of increased educational levels and more media exposure. The majority knew of Khomeini and the location of Mecca. Unlike the vast majority of Hui in rural areas, many urban Hui interviewed knew of and often read the magazine published by the Chinese Islamic Association, *Zhongguo Musilin* (*China's Muslims*). Few were aware of and interested in the sectarian disputes in the Iran-Iraq conflict, but most knew of Shicism.

PUBLIC AND PRIVATE DISCOURSE REGARDING ISLAMIC KNOWLEDGE IN CHINA

This chapter has examined the nature of the transmission of Islamic knowledge from two perspectives: first, from that of the public state-sponsored representation and education of China's Muslims, and second, from that of the Muslims themselves, their self-representation and methods of Islamic education. It is clear that neither of these streams of Islamic knowledge transmission is separate from the other; both have intermingled, but they have never really merged. It is surprising that though these two streams have at times ebbed over into each other, they have never fully blended, and as a result many Muslim communities continue to live in very different worlds than their Han and other nationality neighbors. These distinct educational worlds have contributed in China to producing a situation similar to that observed by John Bowen in his classic study of a Muslim Malay community.[78] Bowen found that varying forms of Islamic knowledge transmission contributed to constructing two increasingly disparate spheres, the public and private. Though the context is different in China, there is clearly a growing discrepancy between those regarded in Muslim circles as teachers (imam, ahong) with nearly 15 years of formal education and possessing wide Islamic knowledge (*erlin*), and those educated in the state system, often with only the Marxist-Leninist view of Islam and religion as promoted in the centralized curriculum.[79] This two track system has led to increasingly distinct public and private spheres among Muslims in China. Thus, while there has certainly been a great deal of integration among Muslims with Han Chinese society through state-sponsored schooling (something that was begun in the Ming dynasty with Confucian-style education), a parallel universe of Islamic education has continued, and indeed flourishes. This private, mosque-centered schooling continues to produce alternative social spheres.

Muslims in China are clearly distinguished between other Muslim groups by language, location and nationality. They are also distinguished internally within their own groups in terms of Islamic tradition and rural-urban differences.[80] However, even though responses to Chinese education will be different among the various 10 Muslim nationalities, as this chapter has found, there are important commonalities shared among all Muslims, as well as important differences. Particularly among urban and rural communities, the invidious distinction between public and private knowledge shows no indication of decreasing.

The rise of private schools in China today may see the return of private Muslim schools (*muzi xuexiao*) that arose in Beijing at the beginning of this century. Though the government has sought to prevent the proliferation of private schools that is regarded as "elitest," the market economy and Muslim interest in Islamic-oriented schooling augurs for a return of this traditional institution that proliferated in China's urban areas throughout the first part of this century. We have certainly seen a widespread revival of mosque-connected madrassahs and Islamic colleges with high levels of attendance throughout China, from Yunnan to Xinjiang. The clear revitalization of Islam in China since the early 1980s cannot be linked directly to the expansion of state schooling.[81] However, resistance takes many forms, and it is clear that Muslims can learn little if anything about their religious heritage in state schools. Certainly they learn little that is positive there, given the Marxist-atheistic critique of religion and the widespread expectation that all religion, with nationality and class, should "wither away." This very well may be driving more religious Muslims away from state schools into the private schools-exactly counter to the state's intention of integration and secularization through public schooling. While much of the data for this chapter is drawn from the Hui, shared Islamic concerns make many of the traditions and debates among Muslims in China regarding education, modernization and the state quite similar. At the same time, all Muslims in China no matter what their language or nationality have been subjected to the same government educational policy and centralized curricula.

Until state education in China begins to incorporate more Muslim information about Islam, these streams will continue to run parallel, leading to continued misunderstandings and misrepresentations. In addition, until Chinese educational policy recognizes a "cultural level" that is based on knowledge of other traditions and languages, many more conservative, and especially, rural Muslims might continue to resist sending their children-particularly their daughters-to state schools. Given the money to be made in the free market economy, at which many Muslims are quite adept, there may be even less incentive to attract and keep those Muslim children in state schools. The mosque might become an even more practical source for an alternative education, a source of knowledge that has persisted throughout China's Muslim regions since the Prophet Muhammad enjoined the new world Muslim community to seek knowledge even unto China.

NOTES

1. Eric Hobsbawm, *Nations and Nationalism since 1780,* first edition (Cambridge: Cambridge University Press, 1991).

2. A version of this chapter was first presented at a symposium, "International Conference on Islam in the 21st Century" sponsored by the Indonesian-Netherlands Cooperation in Islamic Studies and the International Institute for Asian Studies, Leiden, the Netherlands, June 3-7, 1996. I would like to thank Dick Douwes, Johannes den Heijer and Nico J.G. Kaptein for comments during the original presentation, and especially Gerard Postiglione and Mette Halskov-Hansen for later comments and suggestions.

3. John Bowen, "The Forms Culture Takes: A State-of-the-field Essay on the Anthropology of Southeast Asia," in *Journal of Asian Studies*, Vol. 54 No. 4 (1995), pp. 1,004-1,068.

4. Ann S. Anagnost, "The Politics of Displacement" in Charles Keyes, Laurel Kendal and Helen Hardacre (eds.), *State and Religion in East and Southeast Asia.* (Honolulu: University of Hawaii Press, 1994); Wurlig Borchigud, "The Impact of Urban Ethnic Education on Modern Mongolian Ethnicity, 1949-1966" in Stevan Harrell (ed.), *Cultural Encounters on China's Ethnic Frontiers* (Seattle: University of Washington Press, 1995), pp. 278-300; Pamela Kyle Crossley, "Thinking about Ethnicity in Early Modern China" in *Late Imperial China*, Vol.11, No. 1 (1990) pp. 1-35; Dru C. Gladney, "Representing Nationality in China: Refiguring Majority/Minority Identities" in *The Journal of Asian Studies,* Vol. 53, No. 1 (1994) pp. 92-123; Dru C. Gladney, "Tian Zhuangzhuang, the Fifth Generation, and Minorities Film in China" in *Public Culture*, Vol. 8, No. 1 (1996) pp. 161-175.

5. Dru C. Gladney, *Muslim Chinese: Ethnic Nationalism in the People's Republic*, first edition (Cambridge: Harvard University Press, Council on East Asia, 1991); Hadi Su Junhui, *Islamic in Beijing* (Beijing: Beijing Nationality Pictoral Academic Society, 1990).

6. Yang Kun, *Minzu xue diaocha fangfa* (*Nationality Studies Research Methodology*) (Beijing: CASS, 1992, original dedication in 1984).

7. Tong Enzheng, "Morgan's Model and the Study of Ancient Chinese Society," in *Social Sciences in China*, Summer (1989), pp. 182-205, pp. 182,184.

8. John N. Hawkins, *Education and Social Change in the People's Republic of China* (New York: Praeger Press, 1983); Gerard A. Postiglione, Teng Xing, and Ai Yiping, "Basic Education and School Discontinuation in National Minority Border Regions of China," in Gerard A. Postiglione and Lee Wing On (eds.), *Social Change and Educational Development in Mainland China, Taiwan, and Hong Kong* (Hong Kong: Centre of Asian Studies Press, 1995).

9. Gladney, *Muslim Chinese: Ethnic Nationalism in the People's Republic*.

10. Department of Population Statistics of State Statistical Bureau and Economic Department of State Nationalities Affairs Commission, People's Republic of China, *Zhongguo Minzu Renkou ziliao: 1990 nian renkou pucha shuju)* (*Population of China's Nationalities: Data of 1990 Population Census)* (Beijing: Zhongguo tongji chubanshe, 1994).

11. Dru C. Gladney, "Transnational Islam and Uighur National Identity: Salman Rushdie, Sino-Muslim Missile Deals, and the Trans-Eurasian Railway" in *Central Asian* Survey, Vol. 11, No.3 (1992), pp. 1-18; Dru C. Gladney, "Representing Nationality in China: Refiguring Majority/Minority Identities" in *The Journal of Asian Studies*, Vol. 53, No. 1 (1994), pp. 92-123.

12. Lee Chae-Jin, *China's Korean Minority: The Politics of Ethnic Education* (Boulder, CO: Westview Press, 1986); Yeo, Kwang-Kyoon, "The Koreans in China: The Most Educated Minority and Its Ethnic Education," Cultural Studies Program Seminar (unpublished seminar paper), University of Hawaii at Manoa, 1996.

13. Myron L. Cohen, "Being Chinese: The Peripheralization of Traditional Identity," in *Daedalus*, Vol. 120, No. 2 (1991), pp. 113-134.

14. Alexander Woodside and Benjamin A. Elman, "Introduction," in Alexander Woodside and Benjamin A. Elman (eds.), *Education and Society in Late Imperial China, 1600-1900* (Berkeley: University of California Press, 1994), pp. 1-15.

15. David Johnson, "Communication, Class and Consciousness in Late Imperial China," in David Johnson, Andrew Nathan and Evelyn Rawski (eds.), *Popular Culture in Late Imperial China* (Berkeley: University of California Press, 1985), p. 47.

16. Charles Stafford, "Chinese Nationalism and the Family," in *Man*, Vol. 27, No. 2 (1992), pp.362-374.

17. Richard E. Strassberg, *Inscribed Landscapes: Travel Writing From Imperial China* (Berkeley: University of California Berkeley Press, 1994).

18. Dru C. Gladney, "Salman Rushdie in China: Religion, Ethnicity, and State Definition in the People's Republic" in Charles F. Keyes, Laurel Kendall and Helen Hardacre (eds.), *Asian Visions of Authority: Religion and the Modern States of East and Southeast Asia* (Honolulu: University of Hawaii Press, 1994).

19. Gladney, *Muslim Chinese: Ethnic Nationalism in the People's Republic.*

20. Pamela Kyle Crossley, "Thinking about Ethnicity in Early Modern China," in *Late Imperial China*, Vol.11, No. 1 (1990), p. 4.

21. Thomas LaBelle and Robert E. Verhine, "Education, Social Change, and Social Stratification," in *Harvard Education Review*, No. 45 (1975), pp. 3-71.

22. Dru C. Gladney, "Representing Nationality in China: Refiguring Majority/Minority Identities," in *The Journal of Asian Studies*, Vol. 53, No.1 (1994), pp. 92-123.

23. Paul Rabinow, "Representations are Social Facts: Modernity and Post-Modernity in Anthropology" in James Clifford and George E. Marcus (eds.), *Writing Culture: The Poetics and Politics of Ethnography* (Berkeley: University of California Press, 1986), pp. 234-261.

24. Norma Diamond, "The Miao and Poison: Interactions on China's Southwest Frontier," in *Ethnology* Vol. 27, No. 1 (1988), pp. 1-25; Thierry, Franois. "Empire and Minority in China," in Gerard Chaliand (ed.), *Minority Peoples in the Age of Nation-States* (London: Pluto Press, 1989), pp. 76-99.

25. Wolfram Eberhard, *China's Minorities: Yesterday and Today* (Belmont, CA: Wadsworth, 1982).

26. Arnold Chang, *Painting in the People's Republic of China: The Politics of Style* (Boulder, CO: Westview Press, 1980); Ellen Johnston Laing, *The Winking Owl: Art in the People's Republic of China* (Berkeley: University of California Press, 1988); Felicity Lufkin, *Images of Minorities in the Art of the Peoples Republic of China*, Unpublished M.A. Thesis, University of California, Berkeley, 1990.

27. Dru C. Gladney, "Salman Rushdie in China: Religion, Ethnicity, and State Definition in the People's Republic" in Keyes, Kendall and Hardacre (eds.), *Asian Visions of Authority.*

28. Fei Xiaotong, "Ethnic Identification in China," in *Toward a People's Anthropology* (Beijing: New World Press, 1981).

29. *Minzu wenhua gong* (*The Cultural Palace of Nationalites*) (Beijing: Beijing xinguang caiyinchang, 1990), p. 12.

30. Dru C. Gladney, "Salman Rushdie in China: Religion, Ethnicity, and State Definition in the People's Republic" in Keyes, Kendall, and Hardacre (eds.), *Asian Visions of Authority.*

31. Dru C. Gladney, "Masculinity and Alterity: Other Definition of Maleness among Minorities in China" in Jeffrey Wasserstrom and Susan Brownell (eds.), *Chinese Femininities/Chinese Masculinities* (Berkeley: University of California Press, forthcoming).

32. *Minzu Huabao* (*Nationality Pictorial*) (Beijing: Minzu chubanshe, 1974); reproduced in Dru C. Gladney, "Salman Rushdie in China: Religion, Ethnicity, and State Definition in the People's Republic" in Keyes, Kendall, and Hardacre (eds.), *Asian Visions of Authority.*

33. Dru C. Gladney, "Representing Nationality in China: Refiguring Majority/Minority Identities," in *The Journal of Asian Studies*, Vol. 53, No. 1 (1994), pp. 92-123.

34. Dru C. Gladney, "Transnational Islam and Uighur National Identity: Salman Rushdie, Sino-Muslim Missile Deals, and the Trans-Eurasian Railway" in *Central Asian Survey*, Vol. 11, No. 3 (1992), pp. 1-18.

35. Dru C. Gladney, "Salman Rushdie in China: Religion, Ethnicity, and State Definition in the People's Republic" in Keyes, Kendall, and Hardacre (eds.), *Asian Visions of Authority.*

36. Joan Lebold Cohen, *The New Chinese Painting 1949-1986* (New York: Harry N. Abrams, Inc., 1987).

37. China Islamic Association, *A Collection of Painting and Calligraphy Solicited for Charity in Aid of the Disabled* (Beijing: China Islamic Association, 1985).

38. Hadi Su Junhui, *Islamic in Beijing* (Beijing: Beijing Nationality Pictoral Academic Society, 1990).

39. Dru C. Gladney and Ma Qicheng, "Local and Muslim in China: The Making of Indigenous Identities among the Uygur and Hui," Paper presented at the Annual Association of Asian Studies Meetings, Honolulu, Hawaii, April 10-14, 1996.

40. *Tulufan Fengqing Huaji* (*Picture Album of Turpan Landscape and Custom*) (Urumqi: Xinjiang renmin chubanshe, 1985).

41. See those by Huang Zhou, Zhan Jianjun, Liu Bingjiang and Zhou Cangmi.

42. *Tulufan Fengqing Huaji* (*Picture Album of Turpan Landscape and Custom*), p. 1.

43. Ibid , p. 29.

44. Ibid , p. 16.

45. Ibid , p. 35.

46. Dru C. Gladney, "Representing Nationality in China: Refiguring Majority/Minority Identities" in *The Journal of Asian Studies*, Vol. 53, No. 1 (1994), pp.92-123.

47. Joan Lebold Cohen, *The New Chinese Painting 1949-1986* (New York: Harry N. Abrams, Inc., 1987).

48. *Tulufan Fengqing Huaji* (*Picture Album of Turpan Landscape and Custom*), p. 50.

49. Ibid , p. 14.

50. Ibid , p. 15.

51. Claude L. Pickens, "The Four Men Huans," in *Friends of Moslems*, Vol.16, No.1 (1942), pp. 15-28.

52. Anonymous, "Peoples and Politics of China's Northwest," Unpublished report (Washington D.C.: Office of Strategic Services, Research and Analysis Branch, 1945).

53. Fletcher, Joseph F., "A Brief History of the Chinese Northwestern Frontier, China Proper's Northwest Frontier: Meeting Place of Four Cultures," in *China's Inner Asian Frontier,* Alonso, Mary Ellen (ed.), (Cambridge: Peabody Museum, 1979).

54. Rudolf Lowenthal, "The Mohammedan Press in China," in *The Religious Periodical Press in China* (Peking: Synodal Committee on China, 1940).

55. Anonymous, "Peoples and Politics of China's Northwest."

56. Ma Shouqian, "The Hui People's New Awakening at the End of the 19th Century and Beginning of the 20th Century," in Dru C. Gladney (ed.), *The Legacy of Islam in China: An International Symposium in Memory of Joseph F. Fletcher, Conference Volume,* Harvard University, April 14-16, 1989.

57. Wang Shoujie, "*Niu jie Huimin Shenghuo tan*" ("Discussion of the lifestyle of the Oxen Street Hui,") in *Yue Hua*, May 25, July 5, (1930), pp. 18-19.

58. Beijing City Sociology Committee et. al. (eds.), "Beijing shi canzaju xiaoshu minzu jiaoyu wenti diaocha baogao" ("Research Report on the Problem of Education among Dispersed Minorities in Beijing City,") in *Central Institute for Nationalities Journal*, No.1 (1984), pp. 18-26.

59. Ibid.

60. Ibid.

61. The Uzbek and Tatar minorities have fared very well educationally since they are almost exclusively living in urban areas in Xinjiang.

62. Note that the Dongxiang have the highest illiteracy rate in China, at 87 percent.

63. Note that the 1982 census included a category for college education, whereas the 1990 census broke that category into "undergraduate" and "technical school" figures. For 1982 and 1990 comparisons, these figures have been combined.

64. Julia Kwong and Hong Xiao, "Educational Equality among China's Minorities," in *Comparative Education*, Vol. 25, No. 2 (1989), pp. 229-243.

65. John N. Hawkins, "The Politics of Intergroup Relations: Minority Education in the People's Republic of China," in Murray Thomas (ed.), *Politics and Education* (New York: Pergamon Press, 1973).

66. For more on Muslim women in China, see the "Women in China's Islam Project" in Zhengzhou, initiated by Ms. Xie Jiejing and Maria Jaschok (of the University of Hong Kong); also see Elizabeth Alles, "L'islam chinois: femmes ahong" in *Etudes Oriental,* No. 13/14 (1994), pp. 163-168; Leila Cherif, "Ningxia, l'ecoles au femini" in *Etudes Oriental,* No. 13/14 (1994), pp. 156-162; Pang Keng-Fong, *The Dynamics of Gender, Ethnicity, and State Among Austronesian-speaking Muslims (Hui-Utsat) of Hainan Island,* unpublished Ph.D. dissertation, University of California, Los Angeles, 1992; and Barbara Pillsbury, "Being Female in a Muslim Minority in China," in Lois Beck and Nilli Keddie (eds.), *Women in the Muslim World* (Cambridge, MA: Harvard University Press, 1978).

67. Gladney and Ma, "Local and Muslim in China", paper delivered at the 1996 Annual Meetings of the Association for Asian Studies, Hilton Hawaiian Village Hotel, Honolulu.

68. For a list of educational terms and mosque personnel titles, see Dru Gladney, *Qing Zhen: A Study of Ethnoreligious Identity Among Hui Muslim Communities in China,* unpublished Ph.D. dissertation, University of Washington, Seattle 1987, pp. 387-391, 394.

69. For an interesting comparison documenting the widespread standardization of this madrassah system even in Yunnan, see the recent thesis

by Wang Jianping, "Concord and Conflict: The Hui Communities of Yunnan Society in Historical Perspective," in *Lund Studies in African and Asian Religions*, Vol. 11 (1996).

70. Dru C. Gladney, *Muslim Chinese: Ethnic Nationalism in the People's Republic.*

71. Wang, "Concord and Conflict," *Lund Studies in African and Asian Religious.*

72. Out of a population of 1.3 million in 1981, the Hui are 35.2 percent (489,571), the Dongxiang 15.9 percent (223,240), Baonan are .53 percent (7,683) and Salar are .27 percent (4,364).

73. For further information about the economic situation in Linxia, see Linxia Hui Autonomous Prefectural Basic Situation Committee (ed.), *Linxia huzu zizhizhou gaikuang (Linzia Autonomous Preferctural Basic Situation)*(Lanzhou: Gansu minzu chubanshe, 1986). Other helpful introductions to the Hui autonomous counties that I have been able to collect include: Da Chang (1985); Min He (1986); Meng Cun (1983); Men Yuan (1984); Hua Long (1984); and Chang Ji Autonomous Prefecture (1985). For the Hui in Gansu, see Ma Tong, *Zhongguo Yisilan Jiaopai yu Menhuan Zhidu Shilue (A History of Muslim Factions and the Menhuan System in China)*, first edition, 1981 (Yinchuan: Ningxia renmin chubanshe, 1983).

74. Liu Su, "Keep rural girls in school" in *China Daily*, April 17, 1987, p.1.

75. All names used in this study are true unless indicated as pseudonyms.

76. Michael M. J. Fischer, *Iran: From Religious Dispute to Revolution* (Cambridge, MA: Harvard University Press, 1980).

77. A rather new development is the sending of Hui manla to mosques in Xinjiang where Arabic language study is much more advanced due to the influence of the Arabic script in Uygur and the proximity to Pakistan with its recently opened Karakoram highway. In September 1987 while visiting a mosque in Kashgar, I met a Hui manla from Hezhou who had been studying there for 6 years for precisely those reasons. He mentioned his desire to travel to Mecca through Pakistan and how much more inexpensive and convenient the Hajj had become since the opening of the road. He served at the only Hui mosque among the 160 Uygur mosques in the city.

78. John Bowen, "The Forms Culture Takes: A State-of-the-field Essay on the Anthropology of Southeast Asia," in *Journal of Asian Studies*, Vol. 54, No. 4 (1995), pp. 1,004-1,068.

79. John Bowen, *Muslims through Discourse: Religion and Ritual in Gayo Society* (Princeton: Princeton University Press, 1993).

80. Dru C. Gladney, "Relational Alterity: Constructing Dungan (Hui), Uygur, and Kazakh Identities across China, Central Asia, and Turkey" in *History and Anthropology*, Vol. 9, No. 2 (1996), pp. 445-477.

81. Gladney, *Muslim Chinese.*

Writing Cultural Boundaries

National Minority Language Policy, Literacy Planning, and Bilingual Education

Regie Stites

The number and diversity of languages used by the non-Han peoples of China is a formidable barrier to the popularization of education in China's rural and remote frontier regions. Although Chinese law places minority languages and "the common speech" (*Putonghua*) on equal footing, the implementation of schooling in minority languages has been complicated by the fact that linguistic survey work and language and literacy planning efforts for many minority languages are still underway. In China, as elsewhere, scarcities of human resources (qualified minority language teachers) and material resources (texts and materials in minority languages) are also obstacles to the implementation and effectiveness of bilingual education policies. But the most fundamental obstacle to native language schooling and literacy for China's ethnolinguistic minorities may well be the fact that literacy in minority languages lies outside the cultural sphere defined by the Han language and writing system.

In any multilingual society, pressures to acquire the dominant language and assimilate to the majority culture are important constraints on the demand for minority language schooling and literacy. In China, these pressures are compounded by the time and intensity of effort required to acquire literacy in Chinese characters. Learning to read and write a Chinese minority language is most often seen as a detour away from literacy in Han Chinese. The gap between minority language writing systems and Chinese characters is also a physical marker of the distinctiveness as well as the marginality of national minority cultures. Although Chinese minority language and literacy planners have attempted to bridge this gap in some ways—most notably in efforts to bring the sound-symbol correspondence of alphabetic minority language writing systems into line with the Han language phonetic system (*Hanyu pinyin*)—the rationale for such efforts has always been to promote the acquisition of *Putonghua* among national minorities.

Chinese minority language policy, minority literacy planning and bilingual education policy and practices can all be interpreted as efforts to construct and maintain cultural boundaries. Languages (and especially literacies) are among the most fundamental markers of identity and difference. While linguistic diversity within the majority Han nationality is an inescapable fact, the image of Han cultural uniformity is supported by the contrast between Han and minority language literacies ("one people-one writing system"). In China, as in other multiethnic states, the representation of minority languages and cultures supports the construction and coherence of the majority identity.[1] Official policies as well as popular attitudes toward minority languages and literacies are shaped by the convergence of Chinese nationalism and Han ethnic identity. As can be seen in the cases discussed below, the politics of identity in China have lead to instability and volatility in minority language and literacy planning.

ETHNOLINGUISTIC DIVERSITY IN CHINA

At the time of the founding of the People's Republic of China (PRC) in 1949, China's central educational policymakers were only dimly aware of the ethnolinguistic diversity of the Chinese population. Mapping that diversity became one of the first tasks taken up by the new state. In the early 1950s, the organizational and methodological foundations were laid for systematic surveys of the linguistic and ethnic characteristics of the peoples inhabiting frontier regions of China. But this task remains incomplete. Even today there remains a high degree of indeterminacy in official accounts of the variety of languages and cultures existing within the borders of the PRC.

The extent and nature of language and dialectical diversity in minority areas of China has still not yet fully been explored. As

Table 4.1. Chinese National Minority Languages

Sino-Tibetan Language Family						Altaic Language Family					Austral-Asiatic Language Family
Tibetan-Burmese Group		Miao-Yao Group		Zhuang-Dong Group		Mongolian Group	Turkic Group		Manchu-Tungusic Group		
Tibetan Branch	1) Tibetan (3)	Miao Branch	21) Miao (3)			35) Mongolian (3)			Manchu Branch	49) Xibe	
	2) Jiarong (3)		22) Bunu			36) Dongxiang				50) Hezhe	
	3) Menba (2)	Yao Branch	23) Mian (3)			37) Tu (2)				51) Manchu	
Jingpo Branch	4) Jingpo	Branch uncertain	24) She (2)			38) Dagur					
						39) Bao'an (2)					
Yi Branch	5) Yi (6)					40) Eastern Yugur			Tungusic Branch	52) Ewenki	
	6) Hani (3)									53) Oroqen	
	7) Lisu			Zhuang-Dai Branch	25) Zhuang (2)						
	8) Lahu (2)				26) Buyi		Western Huns Branch	41) Uygur (3)			
	9) Naxi (2)				27) Dai (2)			42) Kazak (2)			
	10) Jinuo			Dong-Sui Branch	28) Dong (2)			43) Salar			54) Wa
Burmese Branch	11) Zaiwa				29) Shui			44) Uzbek			55) Blang
	12) Achang (3)				30) Mulao			45) Tatar			56) De'ang

Table 4.1 (continued)

Sino-Tibetan Language Family			Altaic Language Family		Indo-European Language Family	Language family uncertain
Branch uncertain	13) Bai (3)				**Indo-European Language Family**	
	14) Tujia (2)	31) Maonan				
	15) Loba	32) Lajia	Eastern Huns Branch	46) Kirgiz (2)	57) Tajik	
Li Branch		33) Li (5)		47) Western Yugur		
Gelao Branch	16) Qiang (2)	34) Gelao (4)		48) Tuva	58) Russian	
	17) Pumi (2)					
	18) Nu (3)					
	19) Deng				**Language family uncertain**	59) Korean
	20) Derung (2)					60) Gin (Vietnamese)

Information on languages and language classifications on this chart is from entries in the *Zhongguo Da Baike Quanshu* (Chinese Encyclopedia), *Yuyan Wenzi* (Languages and Scripts) Volume, Beijing: Chinese Encyclopedia Press, 1988.

illustrated in the list of officially recognized languages and ethnic identities (see Table 4.1), there is not a one-to-one correspondence between language and national identity in China.

Estimates of the number of mother tongues spoken in the PRC range from 80 to more than 100 and yet there are only 55 officially recognized minority nationalities.[2] Thus, there is considerable linguistic diversity within nationalities in China. Coming to grips with this diversity has posed a significant challenge to central educational policymakers.

In an article published in 1988, Qu Aitang characterized central knowledge of the ethnolinguistic characteristics of the Chinese population in the following manner:

> How many nationalities does China have? The answer is relatively simple—fifty-six. This is so because the definition of a nationality is intimately related to political, legal, and administrative procedures. . . . The identification and confirmation of languages is more complicated than the identification and confirmation of nationalities; it is relatively hard to answer the question of exactly how many languages are used by the fifty-six nationalities because the exact number of languages used by some nationalities has not yet been made completely clear.[3]

As Qu points out, the situation becomes even more complicated when the diversity of writing systems used to represent various Chinese languages is considered.

> Exactly how many writing systems are used by China's nationalities? This question is also a relatively difficult one to answer. . . a common view is that, of China's fifty-six nationalities, twenty-five nationalities currently use thirty-three different writing systems to record their own languages.[4]

In his article on "Writing systems of China's Minorities" in the "Languages and Scripts" volume of the *Chinese Encyclopedia*, Fu Maoji estimated that 27 Chinese minority nationalities were using 39 different writing systems.[5] In a 1991 article in the journal *Minzu Yuwen*, Zhou Qingsheng counted 47 different minority language writing systems being used by 30 of China's 55 minority nationalities.[6]

Zhou categorized minority language writing systems under five general headings. Seven languages and writing systems were described as relatively old, well-established, and currently in widespread use. Five languages and writing systems were described as being used primarily for religious matters. Another 5 were described as being used only in relatively small areas. Finally, the remaining 30 writing systems were all created, reformed or revised in the twentieth century and were either still being tried out on an experimental basis or were still in the process of being popularized (see Table 4.2). Of these 47 languages and writing systems, only 31 were being used in China's elementary school system as of 1989.[7]

At the heart of the Chinese party/state's basic position on the status of minority languages is an apparent contradiction. From 1949, when it was written into Article 53 of the Common Program of the Chinese People's Political Consultative Conference, every version of the Chinese Constitution has included a provision that guarantees the right of all nationalities to develop and use their own languages and writing systems. The current constitution, like its predecessors, also contains a provision that calls for the promotion and general use of *Putonghua* ("the common language," i.e., the standard Beijing dialect of Mandarin). What separates the 1982 version of this provision from previous ones is the explicit statement that *Putonghua* should be used by *all* Chinese nationalities. These two constitutional provisions provide the legal and ideological contexts of China's official stand on societal bilingualism. They also frame the boundaries of the arena within which Chinese bilingual educational policies are formulated and interpreted.[8]

In an essay written in 1985, a minority language specialist, Wang Jun, offered his thoughts on the correct handling of the two language policy provisions of the 1982 constitution. Wang's view was that the promotion of *Putonghua* as a common language for all of China's peoples, Han and minority alike, was necessary because China needed a standard language for the sake of communication and convenience as well as for the higher purposes of social development. Wang expressed disagreement with the idea that the promotion of *Putonghua* was aimed at the elimination of Han regionalects. While not advocating a prohibition on the use of Han regionalects at home, Wang strongly supported the general use of *Putonghua* in public.[9]

Table 4.2. Chinese National Minority Language Writing Systems

A) Writing systems in widespread use	
1) Mongolian* (Sogdian)	
2) Tibetan* (Indic)	
3) Uygur* (Arabic)	
4) Kazak* (Arabic)	
5) Korean* (other)	
6) Liangshan Yi * (other)	
7) Xishuangbanna Old Dai* (Indic)	
B) Writing systems used primarily for religious matters	
8) Old Miao* (other)	
9) Old Lisu* (Sinitic)	
10) Old Wa (Latin)	
11) Old Yi* (Sinitic)	
12) Old Lahu (Indic)	
C) Writing systems used only in limited geographic areas	
13) Dai Peng (Indic)	
14) Dai Duan (Indic)	
15) Bamboo strip syllabic Lisu (other)	
16) Russian* (Slavic)	
17) Manchu* (Sogdian)	
D) Writing systems created this century and currently in limited use	
18) Eastern Guizhou Miao* (Latin)	33) Naxi* (Latin)
19) Western Hunan Miao* (Latin)	34) Bai* (Latin)
20) Border Region Miao* (Latin)	35) Tujia* (Latin)
21) Eastern Yunnan Miao* (Latin)	36) Kirgiz* (Arabic)
22) Revised E. Yunnan Miao (Latin)	37) Xibe (Sogdian)
23) Buyi (Latin)	38) Tu (Latin)
24) Dong* (Latin)	39) Yao* (Latin)
25) Xishuangbanna Dai (Indic)	40) Yunnan Yi (Latin)
26) Delong Dai* (Indic)	41) Derung (Latin)
27) Hani* (Latin)	42) Nu (Latin)
28) Jingpo* (Latin)	43) Shui (other)
29) Zaiwa* (Latin)	44) Qiang (Latin)
30) Lisu* (Latin)	45) Dagur (Latin)
31) Wa* (Latin)	46) Blang* (Latin)
32) Lahu* (Latin)	47) Zhuang* (Latin)

Information from Zhou Qingsheng, Zhongguo shuangyu jiaoyu leixing, *Minzu Yuwen* (3): 65-69, (1991).

* Writing system used in state-sponsored schooling as of 1989.

In elaborating his arguments on the need to promote *Putonghua* and at the same time preserve the rights of minority nationalities to use their own languages, Wang Jun posited a two-level comparison. On the one hand, he noted that the position of *Putonghua* vis-a-vis the Han regionalects was clearly one of dominance. While all Han regionalects should be considered equal, *Putonghua* should be given a relatively higher status. For Wang, the higher status of *Putonghua* was based on the fact that it was the language that typified the Chinese nation as a whole. He used the analogy of the uniforms worn by athletes in a sports event to explain his point. As Wang viewed it, just as it is important that athletes on the same side all wear the same uniform so that everyone can distinguish one team from the other, in a similar fashion, the use of *Putonghua* in public affairs in China serves the important role of presenting a unified face to the world.[10] Wang went on to argue that the relationship between *Putonghua* and minority languages of China should be one of equality. In his view, state policy is very clear on this point, promoting both "ethnic equality" and "language equality" (*minzu pingdeng, yuyan pingdeng*). This does not mean that Chinese minorities should not study *Putonghua*, it simply means that they should not be compelled to do so. On the other hand, those who do choose to study *Putonghua*, do so "because they are interested in the progress and development of their people."[11]

In his foreword to a compilation of Chinese writings on bilingualism (including Wang Jun's article), Xing Gongwan expressed the apparently widespread official view that the majority of Han Chinese are already bilingual in the sense that they understand both a Han regionalect and *Putonghua*.[12] In another article reprinted in this same volume, Yan Xuejun explained that the term "bilingualism" (*shuangyu xianxiang*), though borrowed from Western scholarship, had taken on somewhat different implications in the Chinese context.[13] This point was further elaborated in yet another article reprinted in the collection, this one by the noted minority language specialist, Ma Xueliang. Ma argued that Chinese society was characterized by two types of bilingualism. The first type was characteristic of linguistic diversity within the majority Han population. Ma used the English term "diglossia" and in Chinese *shuangyan xianxiang* for the situation in which both *Putonghua* and a Han regionalect are used by an individual or group. The English term "bilingualism" was paired with the Chinese *shuangyu xianxiang* and used in reference to the use of two or more nationality languages (e.g., Han and Tibetan) by individuals or groups in China.[14]

The two different Chinese terms for bilingualism reflect official recognition of two distinct levels of linguistic differences within China. Whereas from the outsider's point of view both Han regionalects (such as Cantonese or Hakka) and national minority languages are vernaculars, only the latter are officially recognized and supported as such by the Chinese government. In his overview of bilingualism and bilingual education in the PRC, James H.Y. Tai pointed out three differences in the Chinese state's treatment of Han regionalects and minority languages. First, among the Han, *Putonghua* is the required language of instruction in all elementary and secondary schools, but *Putonghua* is only used for the instruction of minority students "in response to the wishes of the minority." Second, state-sponsored language planning work has resulted in the creation and promotion of alphabetic writing systems for many minority languages but not for Han regionalects. Third, minority languages are officially recognized for both ideological and practical reasons, whereas Han regionalects are acceptable only on practical grounds with the ultimate goal being their elimination.[15]

Tai's assessment seems to fit well with Xing Gongwan's characterization of *Putonghua* as the "dominant system" (*zhudao xitong*) and all other languages spoken in China as "offspring systems" (*zi xitong*). The constitutional provision on the general use of *Putonghua* makes this very clear and as Xing was careful to point out, this provision applies to national minorities as well as to the Han majority.[16] The central problem for Chinese bilingual education, as Xing and other Chinese officials and scholars see it, is that of fulfilling the requirement of promoting the general use of *Putonghua* and at the same time preserving the right of national minorities to develop and use their own languages.

The implications of state language policies for the educational system for China's national minorities are not clear. Both those who argue for language shift through a "direct transition" (*zhijie guodu*) to Han language instruction for minority nationality students and those who argue that all nationalities with their own language and writing system should use them in the school system can find justification for their positions in state language policies. Those with knowledge of the complexities of the linguistic variation and the language-use situation in China appreciate the fact that a uniform statewide language of instruction policy can never satisfy the diverse needs of China's linguistic minority students. As Bai Ning pointed out in an essay on the language of instruction problem in minority education, although minority languages are granted equality with the Han language in law, history has created inequities in political and economic development which make languages functionally unequal.[17] In effect, neither the constitutional guarantee of freedom to use and develop minority languages and scripts nor the stipulation to promote the general use of *Putonghua* act as guiding principles for national minority language of instruction policy. In accordance with the policy of "free choice" (*zijue ziyuan*), language of instruction policies and practices are determined for the most part by decisions made at the regional and local levels by officials who must balance central demands against peripheral exigencies. The result is tremendous variability in the goals and methods of bilingual education across China's national minority populations and regions.

The ambivalence at the core of official language policy in China is the result of a complex set of legacies which have shaped the ideology and organization of the PRC's efforts to manage ethnolinguistic diversity within the Chinese population. To a certain extent, the ambiguities entailed in the state's official position of advocating both minority language maintenance and shift to *Putonghua* are also related to inadequate central appreciation of the complexity of the vernacular language use situation in China and to the sporadic and unsuccessful history of state efforts to reduce that complexity through language and script reforms.

LANGUAGE AND LITERACY PLANNING

In an influential 1951 essay on "Marxism and Language," Stalin (or more precisely, his ghostwriter) argued that there was no such thing as a feudal language or a socialist language, since "at every stage of development, language, as a means of communication for people in society, was common and single for the society, serving the members of society, regardless of social position."[18] This formulation of an essentially non-Marxist and autonomous view of language provided both a justification of state tolerance of linguistic diversity and a rationale for state efforts to treat languages as politically neutral technologies which could be manipulated and controlled through central planning. The scope of the language planning efforts undertaken by the Soviet state was unprecedented. At the height of these efforts in the 1930s, Soviet minority languages were standardized and writing systems were revised and created in order to help create nationalities and to strengthen communication links between the minority language periphery and the Russian language center.[19] In the process, old cultural and linguistic ties were suppressed and new ties were forged. The Turkic peoples of Central Asia, for example, had historically been unified by a common heritage of Islam and a shared Arabic language literature. In standardizing the Kazak, Turkmen, Kirgiz, and Uzbek languages and replacing their Arabic writing systems with the Cyrillic script of Russian, the Soviet state effectively weakened pan-Turkic loyalties at the same time that it was building loyalty to the Soviet Union.[20]

China's minority language and script work begun in the 1950s and in some cases resumed in the 1980s has been guided not only by a Stalinist theory of the apolitical nature of linguistic variation and the example provided by language and script planning in the Soviet Union, but also by a Chinese reading of Anglo-American structural linguistics. Among the leaders of China's large-scale minority language survey and planning work in the 1950s were many scholars, such as Luo Changpei, Fu Maoji and Ma Xueliang among others, who had been trained in the theory and methods of structural linguistics. One of the central tenets of structural linguistics is the assumption of the primacy of spoken language, an assumption that implies the rejection of prescriptive grammatical description based on literary standards in favor of synchronic analyses of patterns of speech. In other words, phonological, morphological, lexical and syntactic analyses of a language were to be built from the ground up rather than from the book down. By basing linguistic description on synchronic analyses of speech, structural linguists were able to give an empirical basis to their claims for the equality of all contemporary languages. Structural and Stalinist linguistics were thus compatible in their assumption that no living language was inherently more primitive than any other. However, these two schools of linguistics were directly at odds with each other on the question of the relationship of language to culture. Anglo-American structural linguistics, in line with Anglo-American anthropology, assumed a relativistic stance on cultural differences and saw language as an integral part of culture. Stalinist linguistics, on the other hand, had to accommodate a Marxist conceptualization of social and cultural evolution and as a result posited a view of language as relatively autonomous and thus distinct from culture.

On the question of the language and culture connection, Chinese Stalinist/structuralist linguists were thus faced with a dilemma. The solution was found in the traditional Chinese equation of culture with literacy. The traditional Chinese view clearly was that Classical Chinese (*wenyan*) was superior to vernacular languages as a vehicle of education. In fact, the traditional Chinese notions of culture and learning were inseparable from the acquisition of literacy in Classical Chinese. Given this historical context, the structuralist's case for the equality of languages and cultures was a difficult one to make in China. But by disengaging language from culture, an idea that was supported by Stalinist theory, an argument for the equality of languages at the level of speech was possible. The Chinese concept of culture, on the other hand, remained linked to the acquisition of literacy, an idea that was congruent with both traditional Confucian and socialist notions of the potential for social development through education.

The Chinese vision of the value and functions of societal bilingualism must be understood within the context of this conceptual separation of language (speech) from culture and the inseparability of Chinese conceptions of culture and literacy. In effect, current Chinese language and education policies are aimed at cultivating a kind of multilevel diglossia.[21] Diversity in spoken forms of vernacular languages is accepted as a fact while one (or in some cases more than one) standard literary language is promoted for each minority nationality. At the same time, a single dominant literary language is promoted for all. This dual logic is particularly evident in discussions of the rationale for promoting *Putonghua* in minority regions.

LANGUAGE OF INSTRUCTION

Since the terms "bilingualism" and "bilingual education" first appeared in Chinese educational policy discussions in the early 1980s, there have been a series of attempts to categorize the varieties of bilingual education systems and plans that exist in China. In his 1991 article, Zhou Qingsheng summarized some of the efforts along these lines as a preface to offering his own systematic typologies of schemes for bilingual instruction and bilingual educational systems for China's national minorities. Zhou begins his summary with a typology of styles of minority language instruction devised by Yan Xuejun and published in 1985. Yan offered six categories, a Yanbian style, a Inner Mongolian style, a Tibet style, a Xinjiang style, a Southwest style and an anti-illiteracy style. Zhou points out that the last of these categories does not fit the regional scheme of the previous five and that at any rate there is a fundamental problem with a regional scheme since minority language instruction varies a great deal within regions.[22]

In devising his own categorization, Zhou set for himself two basic requirements. The first was that his classificatory scheme be logical and the second was that each of the categories in his classification corresponds to actually existing practices in China. Zhou's categorization of bilingual teaching plans consists of three main types, each of which can be further divided into subtypes. The three main types are the "maintenance type" (*baocunxing*), the "transitional type" (*guoduxing*) and the "expedient type" (*quanyixing*).[23]

Although Zhou borrowed Western terminology for his typology of Chinese bilingual education, he adopted Western terms to fit Chinese concepts and realities. The terms "maintenance" and "transitional" are most often used in English language literature to describe the two ends of the spectrum of objectives for bilingual schooling. A maintenance program is one which is basically aimed at preserving and cultivating a child's knowledge of his or her mother tongue. A transitional program is aimed at developing competence in the dominant group language. While these two aims do not appear incompatible in theory, Western scholars tend to see them as mutually exclusive in practice.[24]

Zhou Qingsheng uses the terms "maintenance type" and "transitional type" primarily to identify patterns of bilingual instruction rather than to contrast educational objectives. The defining feature of Zhou's maintenance type of bilingual teaching plan is the use of the mother tongue throughout the course of elementary and/or secondary schooling. Within the maintenance type, Zhou differentiates subtypes based on the relative weights given to Han and minority languages at various stages of schooling, the timing of the introduction of Han and minority languages into schooling and the amount of mother tongue, Han, or bilingual instruction that is provided in subject areas. Based on these criteria, Zhou identifies three bilingual teaching plans of the maintenance type currently in use in minority areas of China. In the first maintenance sub-type the mother tongue is used as the main language of instruction, with Han language introduced as a separate subject in the second or third year of elementary school and continued as such throughout elementary and secondary schooling. Zhou notes that this type of schooling is especially well-suited to areas of concentrated minority population and where the writing systems, textbooks, teachers and community support are available to make it work.

The second maintenance subtype is the converse of the first. Here Han is the main language of instruction and the mother tongue is taught as a separate subject. Zhou notes that this plan is used widely in north China in areas where minority students have lost their mother tongue or where minority language teachers are in scarce supply.

The third maintenance sub-type identified by Zhou is a plan where the mother tongue is used for some subjects and Han is used for others at all levels. This plan is used when few qualified minority teachers are available to teach technical subjects, especially at the secondary level.

Zhou lists a number of regions and nationalities in China for whom maintenance type bilingual education is available. Maintenance type plans can be found in use for Mongolian students in Inner Mongolia, Xinjiang, Heilongjiang, Jilin, Liaoning, Qinghai and Gansu; for Korean students in Jilin, Heilongjiang, Liaoning and Inner Mongolia; for Uygur, Kazak, Uzbek, Xibe and in some schools for Russian students in Xinjiang; in some schools for Tibetan students in Tibet, Qinghai, Gansu, Sichuan and Yunnan; for Zhuang students in Guangxi; and in some schools for Yi students in Sichuan. Zhou does not specify which subtype of maintenance bilingual instruction is available to the various nationalities in the regions he lists. But as Zhou points out early in his analysis, the patterns of bilingual education are not consistent within regions in China and we should therefore not assume that bilingual education of the maintenance type is available to all or even most students in the regions and of the nationalities he lists.

The second major type of bilingual instruction which Zhou Qingsheng identifies is the transitional type. Zhou asserts that the transitional types of bilingual instruction in China are designed to provide a bridge between the language of the home and that of the school, and to facilitate the transition from instruction in the minority language to instruction in Chinese. The general pattern for transitional bilingual instruction in China is for the minority language to be used as the principal medium of instruction in the first two years of elementary school, for both Chinese and the minority language to be used in grades three and four, and then for Chinese to be the principal language of instruction in the final two years of elementary school. However, there are many variations on this general plan. Zhou identifies four major "permutations" (*bianti*), and then further subdivides one of these into two varieties.

The first permutation of the transitional type of bilingual instruction is the "three-phase style" (*sanduanshi*). In this style of instruction, there are three phases in elementary language study. In the first and second grades the minority language is studied. In grades three and four bilingual texts (minority language and Han) are used for language study. Other subjects are taught in Han. Starting in the fifth grade and continuing through grade seven, the national unified (Han) language texts are used. This pattern is similar to one which Guan Xinqiu has called "link-style" (*xianjieshi*) bilingual instruction, a style of instruction which Guan observed in use in the Western Hunan Miao region. Guan felt that this style of instruction was particularly well-suited to solving the problems of meeting bilingual education's basic objectives of fluency in two languages, of linking the minority language curriculum to the national unified Han language texts and of handling dialectical variation in the mother tongue.[25]

The second permutation of transitional bilingual instruction in Zhou's classification is the "two-phase style" (*erduanshi*). There are two subtypes of this style. The first involves a bilingual and a Chinese phase. In the first through third grades both the minority language and Chinese are taught, but in grades four through six only Chinese is taught. The second two-phase style involves a first phase of teaching only the minority language and second phase of teaching only Chinese.

The third permutation is labeled the "tapered" or "pagoda" style of transitional bilingual instruction. In this style, the minority language is used for instruction in the first grade, but starting in the second grade Chinese conversational lessons are introduced and from that point on the minority language is gradually phased out.

The final permutation is called the "expedient" or "abnormal" type of transitional bilingual instruction. Zhou notes that this form of instruction violates the constitutional guarantee of the right of nationalities to use their own language. In this permutation, the minority language is taught only for a short period of time in the final year of elementary school. Zhou cites several reasons for the practice of this type of bilingual instruction, including the scarcity of minority language teachers, the (incorrect) assumption that non-Han-speaking students should receive maximum exposure to *Putonghua* during elementary school, and the strategic consideration of the need to improve student test scores on the secondary school entrance examination where the minority language accounts for only 30 percent of the total score.[26]

PROBLEMS IN MINORITY LANGUAGE AND LITERACY EDUCATION

In a 1990 article, Ding Wenlou identifies three types of obstacles to the implementation of minority language education policies in China. According to Ding, the most fundamental problem is a lack of "consensual understanding" (*tongyi renshi*) of the value of minority language and literacy education. Ding cites a variety of commonly expressed negative attitudes toward mother tongue instruction. He notes that some local leaders see schooling in minority languages as "regressive" or as a "detour" and they feel that studying a minority language will impede a student's progress in the study of Chinese. The second problem on Ding's list is that of the lack of coordination between the minority language and Chinese language curricula and texts. Finally, Ding notes the shortage of qualified teachers as a major obstacle. He estimates that at the time of his writing only about half of the approximately 140,000 Chinese language teachers in China's minority language school system were qualified to teach in the system.[27]

Beyond these three fundamental barriers to the implementation of mother tongue instruction in minority area schools, there are also other widespread subsidiary problems, including a general scarcity of appropriate texts and materials in minority languages and a shortage of funds and material resources for supporting schooling in minority language areas. Further complications and problems with implementation of minority language schooling and literacy are best perceived on a case-by-case basis. For this purpose, four brief case studies are presented below. Although each of the groups described in these case studies has been literate historically, the fate of traditional writing systems is slightly different in each case. Cases of minority languages that do not have traditional writing systems and for whom writing systems have been created since the founding of the People's Republic are not included here. Such cases present additional complexities and difficulties in implementing mother tongue language and literacy education.

Zhuang language and literacy

The Zhuang are China's largest national minority. The 1990 national census reported a Zhuang population of just under 15.5 million. This population was concentrated in the Guangxi Zhuang Autonomous Region (hereafter Guangxi) located in south China just north of the border with Vietnam. Outside of Guangxi there are also members of the Zhuang nationality living in the neighboring provinces of Yunnan, Guangdong, Hunan, Guizhou and Sichuan. The Zhuang are considered among the most advanced as well as the most acculturated of China's national minorities. They are credited with having developed bronze technology as early as the fifth century B.C.E. and have had close economic and cultural ties with the Han for more than 2,000 years.

The Zhuang language is one of 14 Chinese minority languages belonging to the Zhuang-Dong branch of the Sino-Tibetan family. Linguistic survey workers in the 1950s divided Zhuang speakers into two major dialects, a northern and a southern dialect, each of which encompassed numerous local speech variants. The Wuming County variety of northern Zhuang was chosen as the standard form, not because it had any historical claim to such status but because its phonological system was thought to be the most generalizable. Although there are no precise figures available on the number of speakers of the Zhuang language, it seems clear that the linguistic situation of the Zhuang is complex. There are apparently influential urban-dwelling members of the Zhuang nationality who do not speak Zhuang, while significant numbers of people among the 90 percent of the Zhuang population living in the countryside speak only Zhuang. In addition, there are some Zhuang in both cities and in the countryside who are bilingual to varying degrees in both Zhuang and Han. One writer estimated that in 1990 there were no more than 2 to 3 million Zhuang with any grasp of the Han language, and that as many as 7 to 8 million (or half the total Zhuang population) were illiterate in any language.[28]

When the State Council officially called for work on the creation of minority language writing systems (*"Guanyu bangzhu dang wu wenzi de minzu chuangli wenzi de baogao"*) (Report on Helping Nationalities Without a Written Script to Create One) in May 1954, the Linguistics Research Institute and the Central Nationalities Affairs Commission chose the Zhuang language as one of the first to be dealt with. This choice was a natural one, given the size of the Zhuang population and the fact that linguistic surveys of Zhuang speakers and work on specifications for a phonetic script were already underway. The traditional "square Zhuang" (*fangkuai Zhuang*) writing system which had been developed on the model of Chinese characters and was in widespread use among educated Zhuang of the Southern Song period (1127-1279) had gradually fallen out of use. By the end of the Ming period (seventeenth century), more and more potential learners of the traditional Zhuang writing system were turning to the study of the Han language and script. By the mid-twentieth century, when the PRC began its linguistic survey work in Zhuang areas, the traditional writing system was found to be lacking in uniformity and was very restricted in use.[29]

In May 1955, a meeting was convened in Nanning to discuss problems in the creation of a new Zhuang writing system. According to the recollections of Wang Jun, the issue which generated the most debate at the 1955 meeting was the question of which of the two major dialects should be used as the basis for a new standard Zhuang script. Some of the attendees felt that the Zhuang should emulate the Han experience, and therefore argued for a standardization based on the dialect and speech with the richest vocabulary and the greatest potential for widespread use. They pointed out that the use of the speech of Beijing (*Beijinghua*) rather than a "national" literary form as the standard for the Han phonetic writing system (*Hanyu pinyin*) had established the precedent of not departing from the sound pattern of a language in use. On the other hand, others argued that no version of spoken Zhuang was comparable in authority to the Beijing pronunciation of Mandarin. In the end, this latter group's arguments for a standard congruent with the sound patterns over the greatest range of spoken Zhuang won the day and a modified version of the northern Zhuang spoken in Wuming County was adopted as the basis for a new phonetic script.[30]

Once the basic dialect (northern Zhuang) and speech (*Wuminghua*) had been determined, specifications for the new script were finished in August 1955. Because this occurred before the central decision to have all minority scripts conform to the sound-symbol correspondence of *Hanyu pinyin*, the first version of the new Zhuang script, though based on the Latin alphabet, also incorporated several letters from the Cyrillic alphabet as well as symbols from the International Phonetic Alphabet. Efforts to promote the new script began immediately but were short-lived.[31] The emphasis on rooting out vestiges of "local nationalism" that accompanied the Great Leap Forward slowed down efforts to promote the new Zhuang script and by 1964 this work had come to a complete stop.[32]

After a 16-year hiatus, the Guangxi Regional Party Committee decided to resume promotion of the new Zhuang script in May 1980. At the same time, a decision was made to remove all non-Latin letters from the writing system in order to take better advantage of modern communications technology and to facilitate the study of other Latin-based scripts (including *Hanyu pinyin*).[33]

In the fall of 1981, the use of the new standard Zhuang language and writing system in the schooling of Zhuang children was begun on an experimental basis in four schools serving rural areas of Wuming County located about 60 kilometers north of Nanning, Guangxi. The following year, experimental classes were also begun in three schools in Debao County, 200 kilometers west of Nanning. In 1986, local officials reported that 92 students had graduated from the Zhuang-Han classes in Wuming County. These students had studied only Zhuang in grades one and two and then began the transition to Han study in the third grade. Another 70 students were expected to graduate from the Debao classes in 1987.[34] By 1988, there were a total of 22,994 primary school students enrolled in Zhuang-Han bilingual classes in 306 schools spread over 45 counties in Guangxi. There were also 1,260 junior middle school students enrolled in Zhuang-Han classes in 17 counties.[35]

There are a number of obstacles standing in the way of the implementation of a complete Zhuang language-based school system. One of the chief obstacles seems to be a lack of support for mother tongue literacy among the urban Zhuang intelligentsia. The high degree of acculturation of this group and their shift to Han language and literacy makes it unlikely that they will choose to render themselves "illiterate" by promoting the general use of the Zhuang language and script. According to one observer, because Zhuang cadres and intellectuals are accomplished in Han language and literacy—as are their children—they have no use for Zhuang literacy and think that the masses have no use for it either.[36] According to another source, Zhuang cadres in north central Guangxi are so concerned about their children's chances for educational advancement that they will not only not allow them to study the Zhuang language but also discourage them from using *Guilinhua,* the Han dialect in common local use.[37] Without a base of support among this important segment of the Zhuang population and as long as the Zhuang language and script are confined to use as a means of introducing basic literacy skills to rural peasants and elementary school students, it seems unlikely that a Zhuang language-based school system can be fully developed.

The other major obstacle to the development of a Zhuang language-based educational system is a shortage of teachers and texts. Given the fact that the new Zhuang writing system is just a little more than a decade old, the range and scope of literature published in the new script is bound to remain extremely limited for quite some time to come. Without adequate texts, it will be difficult to expand the Zhuang language school system, particularly at the middle school level and above. Without a rapid and large-scale expansion of secondary level and higher teacher training, it is difficult to imagine where the teachers needed to raise the quality of Zhuang language schooling at the elementary level will come from.

Tibetan language and literacy

As a group, China's Tibetan population is among the least assimilated of the national minorities. The remoteness and underdevelopment of the vast area of the Chinese periphery where the majority of the speakers of Tibetan dialects reside has stymied the government's efforts to integrate these people into the cultural, political and economic mainstream of Chinese society. Within the borders of the PRC, the Tibetan language is divided into three principal regional dialects. Central, Kham and Amdo. The phonological differences among these dialects are great enough to make them mutually unintelligible, and each has numerous local speech variants. The traditional Tibetan writing system, developed in the seventh century, is a phonetic alphabet that is capable of representing each of the major dialects.[38] However, the spelling conventions for the standard literary form of Tibetan diverge greatly from the current pronunciation of the central dialects. In spite of this divergence, the Tibetan script is one of only three historically important minority language writing systems in China (the others are Korean Hangul and the Cyrillic Russian script) that central language planners have made no effort to revise or reform.[39] Part of the reason for this, beyond the remoteness of the Tibetan plateau, may be the vast body of Tibetan literature. This literature is of two types: indigenous and non-indigenous. The non-indigenous literature consist of the large canon of Buddhist texts, most of which were translated from the original Sanskrit. The indigenous literature is both voluminous and varied, ranging from works of philosophy, religion and ethics to historical, philological and scientific-technical works to belle lettres and travel literature.[40]

Tibetan-speaking children in China live and attend schools in the Tibetan Autonomous Region (TAR), and in Qinghai, Sichuan, Gansu and Yunnan provinces. The majority of these children belong to families of seminomadic pastoralists who inhabit the vast territory of the Tibetan plateau, one of the poorest and most inaccessible regions of China. The 1982 national census reported that more than 70 percent of Tibetan adults were non-literate, the highest rate for any of China's nationalities.

There are no reliable figures on the extent of Tibetan-Han bilingualism in the Chinese Tibetan population. But given the relatively low level of contact between the Tibetan and Han populations, it seems reasonable to assume that Tibetans with anything beyond a rudimentary grasp of *Putonghua* comprise a very small portion of the total population. No one argues, as some have done in the Zhuang case, that Tibetan-Han bilingualism is already so widespread that schooling in Han only is both feasible and appropriate. On the other hand, it was not until the 1980s that the Chinese government officially sanctioned the promotion of a minority language-based educational system in Tibetan areas.

As late as September 1983, the TAR government was able to discuss problems in improving education in the region without giving priority to the question of mother tongue instruction.[41] In June 1984, however, a regional conference on the problem of low enrollment in elementary schools decided that it was necessary to establish an educational system with Tibetan as the main medium of instruction. It was therefore decided that beginning that fall, elementary schools that had a majority of Tibetan students must use the Tibetan language as the principle medium of instruction. Moreover, in schools that already offered Tibetan instruction, Han language classes would no longer be required for first graders. The conferees noted that due to the lack of qualified teachers available to implement their plan immediately, a transitional period would be needed in which to recruit and train teachers. They suggested that cadres who spoke Tibetan could be recruited to teach, that Tibetan-speaking intellectuals from Sichuan, Qinghai, Gansu and Yunnan might be enticed to come to Tibet to teach, and that more Tibetans should be enrolled in teacher training schools and colleges. The goal for normal school enrollments would be to increase the percentage of minority students to 60 percent in tertiary teacher training institutions and to 70 percent in secondary teacher training schools.[42]

The cause of Tibetan language instruction was given a further boost in 1988 with the founding of a regional language commission. The commission was established by joint decree of the TAR party and government, and was assigned the task of protecting and promoting the use of Tibetan as the "dominant" language in Tibet. In a press report on the first meeting of the Tibetan language commission in March 1988, one member was quoted as saying poor work by the commission would result in "mistakes for which we will have to apologize to the Tibetan people."[43]

The 1990 census reported a degree of progress in popularizing basic education in the Tibet. It was estimated that 54 percent of school-age children living in pastoral and farming areas of Tibet were enrolled in school, compared to just 35 percent in 1985.[44] This degree of progress in increasing enrollments appears to have been one by-product of efforts to implement a Tibetan language-based educational system. The traditional locus of Tibetan language and literacy instruction was the lamasery. In looking for persons qualified to provide instruction in Tibetan literacy, local educational officials could not ignore the human resources represented by lamas and Tibetan Buddhist nuns. As Chen Hongshou reports in a 1989 article arguing for an accommodation between religious and state-sponsored educational system in China, religious personnel are a ready source of minority language instructors. Chen suggests that religious figures can help serve the goal of modernization in several ways. First, the status of religious figures can make them good vehicles for promoting higher levels of enrollment in public schools. Chen cites the example of a bodhisattva (*huo fo*) from the Xiaxin Temple in southern Gansu who traveled over 20,000 kilometers in order to visit 800 nomadic families and encourage them to enroll their children in boarding schools. As a result, one primary school in the region was able to increase its enrollment from 25 to 253 students. Chen also suggests that the "temple economy" may be a source of financial support for education. The same bodhisattva mentioned above reportedly donated 1,000 yuan, 50 head of cattle and the use of pasturage to one local primary school. Finally, Chen suggests that religious personnel can be recruited to teach or to be leaders of public schools. He notes that the Gannan Tibetan prefecture in southern Gansu contains 94 temples housing more than 5,000 monks and nuns. Chen suggests that recruiting only 5 percent of these people to teach could have a great impact on minority language education. Four pastoral counties in this region have already invited bodhisattvas to become honorary principals of primary schools.[45]

There can be little doubt that many Chinese leaders would be hesitant to endorse Chen's open invitation to lamas to become teachers in the state-sponsored educational system. In one interesting case, the argument against the inclusion of Tibetan religion, culture and to some extent even the Tibetan language in state-sponsored education has been supported by empirical research. Three researchers from Northwest Normal University recently employed a variety of instruments and statistical analyses to investigate math achievement of Tibetan and Han children in a variety of monolingual and bilingual elementary school classroom settings in schools in the Gannan Tibetan Prefecture. They found that cultural background variables, including parental educational attainment and home language, were highly correlated with math achievement. In discussing their results, they single out language and cultural attitudes as possible causes of relatively low levels of math achievement by Tibetan students as compared with their Han counterparts. Tibetan students in bilingual programs that stressed Tibetan language study were seen to be disadvantaged relative to Tibetan students in Han language immersion classes. The chief explanation for this was the fact that Tibetan children in bilingual classes did not learn enough Han vocabulary to be able to understand the early volumes of the national unified text series in mathematics.

The researches also felt that Tibetan parents and religious figures encouraged the development of negative attitudes toward mathematics among the children.[46]

The achievement levels of Tibetan children in technical subjects becomes even more of a problem at the secondary and tertiary levels. Above the primary level, a Tibetan language-based school system remains a distant goal. According to a report published by the Tibetan Nationality Educational Science Research Institute in 1989, graduates of Tibetan language elementary programs in Tibet really had nowhere to go to continue their studies at the secondary level. Although they found 2,250 primary schools in the region offering Tibetan language instruction, they counted only one Tibetan language lower middle school class. In contrast, many of the students who graduated from the 370 Han language primary school classes in the region were able to continue their studies in a Han language system that included 40 lower middle schools, 13 secondary technical schools, 16 ordinary upper middle schools and 23 programs of study at the tertiary level.[47]

Given the length of time that will be needed to develop a secondary educational system to serve Tibetan students and the difficulty of recruiting qualified secondary school teachers to come to the remote areas where Tibetan students live, the short-term solution has been to send Tibetan students to special boarding schools in China proper. Beginning in 1985, 20 middle school classes for Tibetan students were organized in 17 provinces and municipalities, including Liaoning, Hunan, Tianjin, Beijing and Chengdu. Entire middle schools for Tibetan students were founded in Beijing and Chengdu in that year. By 1991, the number of inland programs for Tibetans had expanded to 49 and more than 9,000 Tibetan students were receiving secondary vocational schooling in 21 provinces and municipalities. The program is supported by the State Education Commission, which furnishes each student with free food, housing and clothing. Local governments also chip in 300 to 500 yuan per student.[48] Meanwhile, TAR regional educational authorities are trying to develop training programs to produce the large number of Tibetan language teachers needed to implement the planned expansion of Tibetan language instruction to all middle schools in the region. As of 1988, there were only 129 Tibetan language instructors teaching in Tibet's middle schools.[49] In 1989, 300 students were enrolled in a tertiary course of study which would lead to their appointment to jobs as middle school Tibetan language instructors.[50]

While some progress has been made in Tibet toward the provision of Tibetan language instruction at the elementary levels and, to a much smaller degree, at the secondary levels, there seems to be a very long way to go toward the provision of Tibetan language-based schooling. Outside of language lessons, subject matter instruction in schools for Tibetan students still relies primarily on Han language instruction and texts. This situation is not likely to change for quite some time, and as long as it persists Tibetan students will be unlikely to match the subject matter achievement levels of their Han counterparts. In addition, the divide between the cultural spheres of Tibetan and Chinese literacies is unlikely to be bridged by state-sponsored Tibetan language schooling.

Liangshan Yi language and literacy

The 1990 national census counted roughly 6.6 million members of the Yi nationality living for the most part in concentrated settlements in mountainous areas of the four southwestern provinces of Yunnan, Sichuan, Guizhou and Guangxi. The Yi are thought to have developed a "slavery system" social organization as long ago as the second century B.C.E.[51] Remnants of this system in the form of a caste-like hereditary social system with nobles at the top of the hierarchy and domestic servants at the bottom survived until the "victory of democratic reform" in 1958. The largest compact community of Yi is the Liangshan Yi Autonomous Prefecture in Sichuan with an Yi population exceeding 1.5 million.[52] The Yi language belongs to the Yi branch of the Sino-Tibetan family. In 1956, the "number four group" from the Linguistic Research Institute identified six separate Yi dialect areas.

The Yi (Lolo) writing system is known to have been in existence since at least as early as the Tang Dynasty (618-907 A.D.). Like the square Zhuang script, it was developed on the model of Chinese characters, but unlike Zhuang, the Yi script developed out of use of Chinese characters to represent syllables rather than words. As a result, different Yi dialect areas developed very different scripts. The scripts used in the Sichuan and Guizhou dialect areas contained roughly eight to nine thousand characters. The script used in the Yunnan dialect areas employed a smaller number. Literacy among the Yi was traditionally confined to a small number of nobles and shamans (*bimo*).

The Yi were the first nationality for whom a new script was proposed after the founding of the People's Republic in 1949. In February 1951, a plan for a new version of written Yi based on the Latin alphabet was devised at a regional meeting in Xikang Province (part of contemporary Sichuan). By July of the same year, courses in the "new Yi script" (*xin Yiwen*) were being offered at the newly formed Southwest Nationalities Institute in Chengdu. The Linguistic Research Institute first sent a linguistic survey team to the Liangshan Yi in November 1951. In April 1954 they were followed by the "number four work group," which was assigned responsibility for the Yi and Tujia languages. The results of these investigations were reviewed at meetings in Beijing, Chengdu, Xichang and Zhaojue between July and October 1958 and resulted in the promulgation of a revised version of the new Yi script specifications which brought the new Yi script into line with *Hanyu Pinyin*.

In commenting on the course of the "new Yi script" work, Chen Shilin noted several basic problems. First, the survey work conducted between 1951 and 1955 failed to reveal the full social significance of the traditional Yi script and thus did not give due weight to the implications of replacing it with a new script. The "number four work group" was also faulted for the superficiality of its findings. Chen felt that the most critical error occurred during the period of the "democrat reform" when the focus on overturning the Yi slavery system caused neglect in following the mass line in the resolution of the script problem.[53]

The Yi linguist, Maheimuxia, reported that early in 1958, the "tide of left thinking" within the Chinese Communist Party (CCP) caused a general move toward assimilationist (*gongtongxing*) policy, which was reflected in the idea that nationality language and script work could also take a "great leap forward" by promoting the spread of the Han language and writing in the minority areas.[54] By 1960, the effect of promoting the "direct transition" (*zhijie guodu*) method of using *Putonghua* and Chinese characters in rural literacy work had been to undermine completely the implementation of the revised Yi script. According to Maheimuxia, by 1964, when the failure of the direct transition process had become clearly evident, the Liangshan party committee put together a list of eight thousand commonly used Yi characters. In 1965, they began to use this list of characters (*changyong yiwen*) to produce literacy materials. The advancement of literacy in using these materials was interrupted by the start of the Cultural Revolution, but throughout this period the Liangshan Yi cadres are reported to have continually sent letters to the central government urging the official endorsement of the traditional Yi script. Finally, in 1974, the Sichuan party committee's Yi language and script work group sent a survey team to the Liangshan area to begin work on "standardizing" and "organizing" the Yi script. The result was official provincial approval of "standardized Yi" in December 1975. The State Council recognized "standardized Yi" in 1980 after the usual five-year waiting period.[55]

At a time when the promotion of the Latin-based scripts created for other southwestern minority languages in the 1950s was being vigorously renewed, the decision to abandon the alphabetic new Yi in favor of the traditional, restricted and complex script seems somewhat odd. In his article on the evolution of scripts based on Chinese characters, Zhou Youguang notes that the Yi are the only Chinese nationality currently making use of a Chinese character-style syllabic script. His opinion on this is reflected in his further comment that standardized Yi is not used beyond the secondary level of schooling and is further restricted to "certain levels and parts" of areas of concentrated minority population.[56]

In understanding the complete failure of attempts at Latinization of the Yi script, it may be useful to compare the Yi situation with that of the Zhuang, where attempts to promote a new script met with little resistance. As noted above, the relative ease with which script reforms proceeded among the Zhuang may be attributed to the limited sphere in which the new Zhuang script has operated and the high levels of assimilation and bilingualism among the existing literate Zhuang population. The Yi as a whole and the Yi literati in particular are much less integrated into Han society. The failure of the attempt to impose a more "democratic" script on the Yi may also be related to the extreme disruption entailed in the reordering of the Yi social hierarchy. The small number of Yi literate in the traditional script did not prevent the script from serving as a powerful symbol of group loyalty at a time of strong acculturating pressures.

Uygur language and literacy

The Uygurs are thought to be the descendants of several different Turkic peoples whose names appear in Chinese historical records as early as the third century B.C.E. The 1990 national census counted 7.2 million Uygurs in the PRC, mostly concentrated in Xinjiang, where they are the majority of the population. The Turkic language spoken by the Uygurs is closely related to Kazak, and the writing systems for the two languages have similar paths of development and reform. If these two groups are considered together, it could be said that their combined population is evenly split on either side of the former Sino-Soviet border, though Uygurs greatly outnumber Kazaks in China and the situation is reversed in Kazakhstan. As a result of this situation, the reform of the Uygur (and Kazak) writing system in China has been profoundly shaped by shifts in Sino-Soviet relations.

The ancestors of China's present day Uygurs have used various writing systems in different times and places. At the time of the Zhou dynasty (1100-771 B.C.) the use of a runic script called *Tujiwen* was widespread. In the eighth century, the Turkic peoples inhabiting the area of the Silk Road city of Gaochang made use of the phonetic Sogdian script, which had its origins in Aramaic. This script, which survived among Buddhist Uygurs into the fifteenth century and became the basis of the Manchu script as well as the Mongolian writing system currently in use in both Inner Mongolia and Mongolia. Beginning in the tenth century and accompanying the spread of Islam, the Uygurs adopted the Arabic writing system. A revised version of this Arabic-based script is currently the official writing system for Uygur.[57]

From 1950-1957, the Cyrillic alphabet was adopted as the official writing system for Uygur and the other Turkic languages of Xinjiang in emulation of Soviet policy and practice and in order to make use of texts and materials produced in the Soviet Union. However, after the Sino-Soviet split in 1957, efforts to popularize Cyrillic-based writing systems in China were abandoned. In 1959, a Latin-based script was introduced for both Uygur and Kazak. It was argued at the time, just as it had been in the Soviet Union in the 1920s, that the Arabic script was not well-suited to Turkic languages. According to one source, by 1962, all official communications had been converted to the new Latinized writing system, and from 1964-1965 use of the new script is reported to have spread to all public schools and to have served as the basis for rural literacy work. By 1972, the old Arabic script had been nearly completely supplanted by the new script.[58]

Actually, the decline of central authority during the Cultural Revolution probably allowed for the repopularization of the Arabic script through the medium of private Islamic schooling. As a result, after the fall of Gang of Four in 1976, the Xinjiang provincial government felt it necessary to pass a regulation banning the use of the old Arabic-based script for Uygur. By 1979, the Xinjiang government had decided that it would be necessary to sanction the use of the old writing system while at the same time continuing to promote the new one. However, by 1982, the use of the Latin-based script was abandoned and public schools took up the Arabic writing system. This move may be seen as the state accepting the inevitable, but it also came at a time of general decentralization and of increasing interest by the state in fostering better ties with the Islamic world. At the same time, provincial authorities were acting to combat the influence of religious schools by outlawing the dissemination of "Islamic propaganda" to anyone under the age of 18.[59]

It is no small irony that, while the Latin-based writing system for Uygur was developed and promoted as a way of improving communications and relations between Han and Uygur, its net effect was to further strain already tense inter-ethnic relations.

CONCLUSION

The existence of wide disparities in levels of social, political and economic development and the extreme linguistic and cultural diversity of China's minority nationalities presents a complex array of problems in the provision of education for ethnolinguistic minority children. As Chinese writers on the topic often put it, the problems of bilingual educational policy and practice in China cannot be "sliced with one stroke" (*bu neng yidao qie*). China's highly centralized educational system must cope with tremendous regional diversity, which manifests itself in different levels of development, in profoundly different cultures, and not least of all, in a wide variety of spoken and written languages. While China's central educational policymakers often express their belief in the inevitability of the long-term persistence of cultural and linguistic diversity within the Chinese population, the ultimate goal of resolving the "nationalities question" through the development of a "socialist spiritual and material civilization" which would embrace all of China's peoples remains as a backdrop for any discussions of the status and functions of bilingualism and bilingual education in Chinese society.

At this point in history, China has no choice but to make every effort to construct a viable bilingual educational system for its national minority students. Without mother tongue instruction, China cannot possibly enroll and keep monolingual linguistic minority children in school. Without providing minority children with instruction in *Putonghua*, the Chinese party/state cannot socialize these children into the political, cultural and economic mainstream of Chinese society, nor can it provide them with the skills and knowledge needed to support the development goals of the Four Modernizations. What the Chinese party/state wants and needs is a bilingual educational system capable of producing people who are both "ethnic and expert." But there are tensions inherent in this dual objective just are there were in the old pairing of "red and expert." To paraphrase Marshall McLuhan, the medium of instruction is the message.[60] Minority languages are not entirely autonomous systems that can be easily engineered to promote the central government's goals for social, political and economic development. Even in the case of the new scripts, such as that being promoted for the Zhuang language, the available literature may remain so marginal as to be useless or it may serve ends in direct conflict with those envisioned by central planners. For a language and script with a long history and institutional bases beyond the reach of the state, such as Tibetan, the potential for that language and its literature to become weapons in the struggle against central control and objectives becomes even greater. With the resurgence of ethnic nationalism in the newly independent states carved out of the former Soviet Union, China's central authorities will undoubtedly be looking hard for signs of what went wrong in the nationalities policies of their former role model. Policies on mother tongue schooling in minority areas will certainly be scrutinized closely, particularly those policies affecting education in border regions where issues of state security are likely to be given high priority. But significant changes in the current orientation of bilingual educational policy are unlikely. If anything, the heightening of inter-ethnic conflict within and across the borders of the PRC will reinforce the central government's desire to extend its reach into peripheral minority regions by expanding state-sponsored minority language schooling. ᴉₙₑ degree to which central efforts to popularize mother tongue schooling and literacies will succeed in China's national minority regions will be shaped by the politics of ethnic identity. Central control of minority language literacies will most likely be contested on many fronts.

NOTES

1. See Dru C. Gladney, "Representing Nationality in China: Refiguring Majority/Minority Identities," in *The Journal of Asian Studies,* Vol. 53, No. 1 (1994), pp. 92-123.

2. See Sun Hongkai, "Yuyan shibie yu minzu" ("Distinguishing Minorities and Languages"), in *Minzu yuwen (Nationalities Languages and Scripts),* No. 3 (1988), pp.1-5; and S. Robert Ramsey, *The Languages of China* (Princeton: Princeton University Press, 1990).

3. Qu Aitang, "Zhongguo de minzu yu yuyan"("Nationalities and Languages of China"), in *Minzu Yanjiu (Nationalities Research),* No. 1 (1988), pp. 26-27.

4. Ibid., p. 27.

5. Fu Maoji, "Zhongguo zhuminzu wenzi" ("Writing Systems of China's Minorities"), in *Zhongguo da baike quanshu: yuyan* wenzi *(Chinese Encyclopedia: Languages and Scripts)* (Beijing: Zhongguo dabaike quanshu, 1988), pp. 521.

6. Zhou Qingsheng, "Zhongguo shuangyu jiaoyu leixing" ("Varieties of bilingual education in China"), in *Minzu Yuwen,* No. 3 (1991), pp. 65-66.

7. Ibid., p. 68.

8. C. B. Paulston, "Bilingualism and bilingual education: an introduction," in C.B. Paulston (ed.), *International Handbook of Bilingualism and Bilingual Education* (New York: Greenwood Press, 1988), pp. 2-3.

9. Wang Jun, "Tuiguang putonghua he guanche luoshi minzu yuwen zhengce" ("Promote the Common Language and Support The Implementation of National Minority Language and Script Regulations,") in China National Minority Bilingual Education Research Committee (ed.), *Zhongguo minzu shuangyu yanjiu lunji (Collected Works on China National Minority Bilingual Research)* (Beijing: Minzu chubanshe, 1990), pp. 31-38.

10. Ibid., p. 31.

11. Ibid., p. 33. Wang supported this point by quoting Lenin's expression of his opposition to the forced study of Russian by Soviet minorities: "We are

only the slightest bit opposed (to the use of Russian by minority nationalities). It is not possible to force someone into heaven with a club."

12. Xing Gongwan, "Xu" ("Foreword"), in China National Minority Bilingual Education Research Committee (ed.), *Zhongguo minzu shuangyu yanjiu lunji* (*Collected Works on China National Minority Bilingual Research*) (Beijing: Minzu chubanshe, 1990), p. 1.

13. Yan Xuejun, "Lun shuangyuzhi de helixing" ("Rationale for a Bilingual System") in ibid., p. 4.

14. Ma Xueliang, "Lun shuangyu yu shuangyu jiaoxue" ("On Biligualism and Bilingual Instruction,") in ibid., pp. 21-22.

15. J.H.Y. Tai, "Bilingualism and bilingual education in the People's Republic of China," in C. B. Paulston (ed.), *International Handbook of Bilingualism and Bilingual Education* (New York: Greenwood Press, 1988), p. 199.

16. Xing Gongwan, "Xu" ("Foreword"), p. 5.

17. Bai Ning, "Minzu jiaoyu zhong de jiaoxue yuyan wenti" ("The Language of Instruction Question in National Minority Education"), in *Minzu Tuanjie (Nationalities Unity)*, No. 7, (1989), pp. 28-29.

18. Quoted in M. Adler, *Marxist Linguistic Theory and Communist Practice: A Sociolinguistic Study* (Hamburg: Helmut Buske Verlag, 1980), p. 61.

19. M. I. Isayev, *National Languages in the USSR: Problems and Solutions* (Moscow: Progress Publishers, 1977).

20. P. Henze, "Politics and Alphabets in Inner Asia," in J. Fishman (ed.), *Advances in the Creation and Revision of Writing Systems* (The Hague: Mouton, 1977).

21. The classic definition of the term "diglossia" comes from the work of Charles Ferguson. Ferguson used the term to describe a situation in which a literary language was superposed on a variety of dialects of a language. The situation in imperial China, with Classical Chinese (*wenyan*) and spoken forms of Chinese co-existing is a good example of a diglossia. Some authors have argued that bilingual situations are always characterized by imbalance, with one language occupying a "strong" position relative to social, political and economic interaction and the other occupying a "weak" position; thus, societal bilingualism is always diglossic. See M. Siguan and W. Mackey, *Education and Bilingualism* (London: Kogan Page, 1987), pp. 32-34. See also J. Norman, *Chinese* (New York: Cambridge University Press), p. 251. According to Jerry Norman, the current situation in China is less one of diglossia than what Ferguson would call "standard-with-dialects," since Putonghua is not just a

literary standard and is actually used for daily communication by some segments of the Chinese population.

22. Zhou Qinsheng, "Zhongguo shuangyu jiaoyu leixing" ("Varieties of bilingual education in China") in p. 65.

23. Ibid., p. 66.

24. J. D. Williams and G. Snipper, *Literacy and Bilingualism* (New York: Longman, 1990), pp. 51-53. See also C. Baker, *Key Issues in Bilingualism and Bilingual Education* (Philadelphia: Multilingual Matters, Ltd., 1988).

25. Guan Xinqiu, "Xianjieshi shuangyuzhi" ("Link-style Bilingualism,") in *Minzu Jiaoyu Yanjiu (Nationalities Education Research)*, No. 2 (1990), pp. 46-52.

26. Zhou Qingsheng, "Zhongguo shuangyu jiaoyu leixing" ("Varieties of bilingual education in China") in pp. 65-66.

27. Ding Wenlou, "Renzhen luoshi dang de minzu yuwen zhengce, dali kaizhan 'shuangyu' jiaoxue" ("Earnestly Carry Out the Party's Nationality Language Regulations, Energetically Develop 'Bilingual' Instruction,") in *Minzu Jiaoyu Yanjiu (Nationalities Education Research)*, No. 3 (1990), p. 63.

28. Liang Tingwang, "Zhuangwen jiaoyu de xingqi jiqi zhanwang" ("The Current Situation and Prospects for Zhuang Language Education"), in *Minzu Jiaoyu Yanjiu (Nationalities Education Research)*, No. 3 (1990), pp. 66-70.

29. Qin Yaoting, "Zhuangyuwen zai shehui zhuyi xin shiqi zhong de zhongyao zuoyong" ("The Important Utility of Zhuang Language and Script in the New Era of Socialism"), in *Minzu Yuwen*, No. 2 (1987), pp. 1-7.

30. Wang Jun, "Zhangwen gongzuo mantan" ("Chat on Zhuang language work"), in Fu Maoji (ed.), *Zhongguo Shaoshu Minzu Yuwen Yanjiu Lunji (Collected Research on China's National Minority Languages)* (Chengdu: Sichuan minzu chubanshe, 1986), pp. 1-18.

31. Ibid., p. 19. Wang Jun reported that by the end of 1958, 2.9 million Zhuang speakers had received literacy training using the new script and that 700,000 had thus acquired basic literacy.

32. Chen Zhulin, "Zhuangwen gongzuo de huigu" (A Review of Zhuang Language Work"), in Fu Maoji (ed.), *Zhongguo Shaoshu Minzu Yuwen Yanjiu Lunji (Collected Research on China's National Minority Languages)*, pp. 19-30.

33. Wang Jun, "Zhangwen gongzuo mantan" ("Chat on Zhuang language work"), p. 11.

34. "Guangxi experiments with bilingual education," in *Foreign Broadcast Information Service, China, Daily Reports*, (July 2, 1986), p. P1.

35. Lu Ruichang, "Lun Zhuangwen yu minzu zhili de kaifa" ("On Zhuang Language and Nationality Intellectual Development"), in *Minzu Jiaoyu Yanjiu (Nationalities Education Research)*, Vol. 4 (1990), pp. 37-41.

36. Liang Tingwang, "Zhuangwen jiaoyu de xingqi jiqi zhanwang" ("The Current Situation and Prospects for Zhuang Language Education"), p. 69.

37. Zhang Wei, "Lun shuangyuren de yuyan taidu jiqi yingxiang" ("On the language attitudes and influence of bilinguals"), in *Minzu Yuwen (Ethnic Nationality Languages)*, No. 1 (1988), p. 58.

38. *"Zangyu"* ("Tibetan language"), see *Zhongguo da baike quanshu: yuyan wenzi (China Encyclopedia: Languages and Scripts)*, p. 512.

39. Scripts that have been revised or reformed include Mongol, Uygur, Bai, Thai, Yi, Miao and Zhuang, among others. See R. D. Stites, "Literacy and Loyalty: the Politics of Minority Languages and Literacy in the People's Republic of China, 1950-1958," paper presented at the meeting of the Comparative and International Education Society, Anaheim, CA, March 1990.

40. R. A. Stein, *Tibetan Civilization* (Stanford: Stanford University Press, 1972), pp. 250-265.

41. "Xizang holds conference on improving education," in *Foreign Broadcast Information Service, China, Daily Reports*, September 30, 1983, pp. Q2-3.

42. See "Xizang Meeting Views Education in Tibetan language" in *Foreign Broadcast Information Service, China, Daily Reports* June 1, 1984, pp. Q3-4, and "Xizang to Enroll More Minority Nationalities," *Foreign Broadcast Information Service, China, Daily Reports*, June 1, 1984, p. Q4.

43. See "Xizang Commission to Guide Language Use," in *Foreign Broadcast Information Service, China, Daily Reports*, February 12, 1988, pp. 35-36, and "Tibet Commission Stresses Tibetan Language," in *Foreign Broadcast Information Service, China, Daily Reports* (March 14, 1988), p. 45.

44. "Tibet Census Reveals Improvements in Education," *Foreign Broadcast Information Service, China, Daily Reports* (January 22, 1991), p. 36.

45. Chen Hongshou, "Lun minzu jiaoyu yu zongjiao" ("On Nationality Education and Religion,") in Geng Jinsheng and Wang Xihong (eds.), *Minzu jiaoyu gaige yu tansuo (Nationality Education Reform and Investigation)* (Beijing: Zhongyang minzu zueyuan chubanshe, 1989).

46. Sun Mingfu, Lo Shihu and Wang Zhongchun, "Zang, Han ertong shuxue siwei nengli fazhan chayixing de yanjiu" ("Research on Differentiation Between Tibetan and Han Children's Development of Conceptual Abilities in Math"), in *Jiaoyu Yanjiu (Educational Research)*, No. 8 (1991), pp. 57-63.

47. Tibetan Autonomous Region (TAR) Nationality Educational Science Research Institute, "Guanyu Xizang jianli yi Zangzu shouke weizhu de jiaoxue tixi chutan" ("Preliminary Report Regarding Tibet's Formulation of a Curricular Framework Handbook for Tibetan Education"), in Geng and Wang (eds.), *Minzu jiaoyu gaige yu tansuo (Nationality Education Reform and Investigation)*.

48. "Tibetan Students Enrolling in Inland Areas," in *Foreign Broadcast Information Service, China, Daily Reports*, October 29, 1991, pp. 27-28.

49. Tibetan Autonomous Region (TAR) Nationality Educational Science Research Institute, "Guanyu Xizang jianli yi Zangzu shouke weizhu de jiaoxue tixi chutan" (Preliminary Report Regarding Tibet's Formulation of a Curricular Framework Handbook for Tibetan Education") p. 295.

50. "Tibet Develops Tibetan Language Education," in *Foreign Broadcast Information Service, China, Daily Reports*, April 29, 1991, pp. 59-60.

51. Hu Qingyao, "Yizu" ("Yi nationality"), in *Zhongguo da baike quanshu: minzu (Chinese Encyclopedia: Nationality)*, p. 500.

52. Maheimuxia, "Yiwen guifan fang'an de dansheng ji qi shixian xiaoguo" ("The Emergence and Some Practical Results of the Yi Script Standardization Specifications"), in *Zhongguo shaoshu minzu yuyan wenzi lunji (Studies of China's Ethnic Minorities Written Language)* (Chengdu: Sichuan minzu chubanshe, 1986), p. 42.

53. Chen Shilin, "Guifan yiwen de shiyan xiaoguo he you guan de jige wenti" ("The Results of Putting the Standardized Yi Script into Practice and Several Related Issues"), in *Minzu Yuwen*, No. 4 (1979), p. 247.

54. Maheimuxia, "Yiwen guifan fang'an de dansheng ji qi shixian xiaoguo" ("The Emergence and Some Practical Results of the Yi Script Standardization Specifications"), p. 44.

55. Ibid., pp. 45-46.

56. Zhou Youguang, "Hanzi wenhua chuan de wenzi yanbian" ("The Evolution of Writing Systems in the Chinese Characters Cultural Sphere"), in *Minzu Yuwen*, No. 1 (1989), p. 53.

57. Hu Zhenhua, "Weiwu'erzu de wenzi" ("The Uygur Nationality Script"), in *Minzu Yuwen*, No. 2 (1979), pp. 152-157.

58. Chen Shengyuan, "Wei, Ha wenzi gaige" ("Uygur and Kazak script reform"), in *Zhongguo jiaoyu nianjian, 1949-1984: Difang jiaoyu (China Education Yearbook, 1949-1984: Local Education)* (Changsha: Hunan jiaoyu chubanshe, 1986), pp. 1,312-1,315.

59. Ibid., p. 1,315.

60. Marshall McLuhan, Quentin Fiore, and Jerome Agel. *The Medium Is the Message,* New York, NY: Touchstone, 1989.

PART II

Educational Disparities: Literacy Levels and Access to Higher Education

CHAPTER 5

National Minority Education in China
A Nationwide Survey Across Counties
Jacques Lamontagne

The rapid economic development in China over the past 15 years has entailed increasing socioeconomic, cultural and educational disparities among China's regions. The reduction of the gap between the coastal areas and those of central and western China has become a priority objective of the ninth five-year plan (1996-2000) adopted by the National People's Congress (NPC). Some recent intranational comparative studies have shown manifestations, determinants and consequences of the unequal development of education in China.[1] Other recent studies, employing quantitative, macrosociological and longitudinal data, have revealed a varying magnitude of regional and/or ethnic and/or gender disparities in Chinese educational development.[2]

This chapter addresses three questions: (1) what are the educational disparities among the regions and among the nationalities in China? (2) are there patterns of increase/decrease of these disparities over time? and (3) what are the factors that facilitate most or that hinder most the development of education in the regions and within the nationalities?

The study of regional, ethnic and gender disparities in Chinese educational development is still in need of analytical model-building as well as of corresponding systematic and detailed data analyses. This chapter attempts to contribute to filling this void: (1) by introducing a model applicable to the comparative analysis of educational development in social entities (such as regions, ethnic groups and men versus women), focusing on the notions of degree of educational development, speed of educational development and educational gap; (2) by analyzing, in terms of the model introduced, quantitative, macrosociological and longitudinal data on Chinese educational development; and (3) by interfacing our quantitative analyses with our ongoing and forthcoming fieldwork qualitative analyses. The quantitative data analyzed in this chapter are mainly from the last two Chinese censuses (1982 and 1990).

AN ANALYTICAL MODEL OF EDUCATIONAL DEVELOPMENT

Both absolute and relative numbers, can be used to measure the extent of diffusion of a phenomenon, as well as the magnitude of a change, in a society. When used to compare the situation of various social entities in certain respects, numbers may uncover social disparities. The measurement of social disparities is important because the latter, especially when they are highly visible, may become a source of envy, dissatisfaction, disruption and conflict. Thus, the study of social disparities may help understand the origin, orientation and implementation of social change.

In the field of education, numbers are commonly used to measure achievement. Judgments are made on past achievements and plans are made for future achievements, often involving the intervention of special facilitating measures. The magnitude of educational achievement of a given social entity can vary over time, and the magnitude of educational disparities between social entities is also subject to variation over time.

Rogers conceived a model to analyze the way innovations are diffused in society, in particular to observe the various moments when the various members of a society adopt a given innovation.[3] Rogers' model is based on a normal (i.e., bell-shaped and symmetric) distribution of events (i.e., the adoption of a given innovation) applied over time. Each event consists of the adoption of a given innovation by a particular member of a given society. According to Rogers' model, very few people adopt the innovation at the onset. But as time goes on, the number of new adopters grows exponentially. The bulk of the population will be adopting the innovation within a period of time well within the two extreme time limits defined by the normal curve. Beyond the mid-point of the normal curve, the number of new adopters begins to dwindle gradually. As we approach the far right-hand side of the curve, we find fewer and fewer laggards adopting the innovation.

Our purpose is to develop an analytical model of educational development that could measure a social entity's educational progress per se; that is, in comparison with this social entity's own past level of educational development; and with reference to what is considered as its potential maximum degree of educational development; and which could also measure this social entity's educational progress in comparison with that of other social entities, at a given point in time as well as in a longitudinal perspective.

One may look at literacy as a phenomenon that can be diffused in a given population over time according to a normal distribution. In the beginning, literacy would spread very slowly. Then, after an educational takeoff, literacy would spread exponentially, that is, faster and faster. After reaching a peak, the increase in the number of literates would begin to slow down gradually. As the potential total number of literate persons is approached, fewer and fewer newcomers would join the ranks of the literate society. This total potential number of literate persons could be the entire 15-year-old-plus population, or the 15-50 age group, or some other age group.

Our analytical model of educational development is built on two dimensions: degree of educational development and time (see Figure 5.1). The degree of educational development in a social entity is measured in terms of the percentage of the population in that social entity having attained a given educational level (i.e., elementary, secondary or higher). For instance, the degree of development of higher education in a given region is measured in terms of the percentage of the population of that region having attained the higher education level. The speed of development of a given educational level in a social entity is measured in terms of the difference between the degrees of educational development in the social entity at two successive time units. We assume that, initially, and until an educational takeoff, the degree of educational development is low and increases slowly. After the educational takeoff, the degree of educational development increases at an accelerating speed, until it reaches a threshold; then the speed decelerates as the educational development approaches a ceiling or saturation point (i.e., 100 percent, or a certain other percentage). The latter is the maximum potential degree of development of a given educational level (i.e., elementary, secondary or higher) in a social entity. The entire development process is illustrated in Figure 5.1 by the sigmoidal curve. At different points along this curve, we distinguish four successive phases of educational development: Low-slow, Low-fast, High-fast and High-slow. Figure 5.2 expresses the model in terms of illiteracy, instead of education; consequently, the sigmoidal curve is simply reversed.

We consider a value situated at any point along the sigmoidal curve to be an expected value. Reality would conform to these expected values unless some exogenous factor intervenes. Let us see how a real curve fits with the theoretical curve. Figure 5.3 shows the evolution of illiteracy among the Yugur nationality (the data is from the 1990 census). The time units are represented by 5-year age groups: from 65+ to 15-19. The curve in Figure 5.3 fits with the theoretical curve with one exception, caused by an exogenous factor. This exception is seen in age groups 30-34 and 35-39. Indeed, according to the expected curve, the level of illiteracy of these two age groups should be lower. We see this departure from the expected values as having been caused by the Cultural Revolution. Indeed, people who, in 1990, were between the ages of 30 and 40 had been school-age children during the Cultural Revolution, and a higher than expected percentage of them did not become literate. The "Cultural Revolution bump illustrated in Figure 5.3 is especially obvious in the case of the Yugur nationality; but it can also be seen in most of China's 56 nationalities.

Looking again at Figure 5.3, one might think that there was also an exogenous factor affecting the 65+ age group, because the slope between the 65+ and the 60-64 age groups is steeper than expected by the model. However, this phenomenon is not caused by an exogenous factor, but simply by the fact that all 5-year age groups above 64 (65-69, 70-74, 75-79, etc.) have been lumped together. If they had been separated, the slope would have appeared more gradual, as expected by our model. So we do not take this to be a departure from the model, nor do we see there any sign of intervening factors.

To appreciate the relative importance of educational progress in a given social entity, one must look at the expected value as well as the real value. For instance, a hypothetical decrease of illiteracy by 10 percent among the Dongxiang nationality would be more significant than a decrease by 10 percent among the Jingpo nationality, because the Dongxiang are in the Low-slow phase and are expected to progress slowly, whereas the Jingpo are in the Low-fast phase and are expected to progress rapidly. In this example, to achieve respectively a decrease of illiteracy by 10 percent, the Dongxiang need stronger intervening factors than the Jingpo.

A comparative analysis of the educational development of two social entities (for instance, two territories, two nationalities and men versus women) may show an educational gap, that is, the educational lagging of a social entity in comparison with the educational advancement of another social entity. According to the model, the magnitude of the educational gap, which is initially non-existent or small, increases more and more after the educational takeoff of one of the two social entities. Eventually, the backward social entity begins its own educational takeoff: the educational gap then widens less and less and, later, narrows more and more. The end point is attained when both social entities have finally reached the maximum possible degree of educational development (100 percent or a certain other percentage). An example of this pattern is given in Figure 5.4 here we see the comparative evolution of the illiteracy of men and women and the evolving magnitude of the illiteracy gender gap.

Figure 5.5 shows a hypothetical comparative development of elementary, secondary and higher education. The evolution of the curve is basically the same for each of the three levels of education. In Figure 5.5, we see the complete process for elementary education, that is, the complete universalization of elementary education. Thus, the percentages for elementary education run from 0-100 percent. However, only part of the potential curve appears for secondary education: at the end of the time period covered by Figure 5.5, the generalization of secondary education has reached 68 percent of the people. For higher education, the percentage at the end of the time period covered is still much lower (only 11 percent). If the time period of the figure were to be extended, we would eventually see the universalization of secondary education. The overall curve for secondary education would resemble that of elementary education, except that it would materialize with a time lag. Eventually, if higher education were to reach a very large percentage of the population, its evolution would gradually follow the same kind of curve as elementary education and secondary education. It follows from the above that even when the equality of two social entities concerning elementary education has been achieved, there remain disparities between the two social units concerning secondary education and higher education.

Figure 5.1. Analytical model of educational development

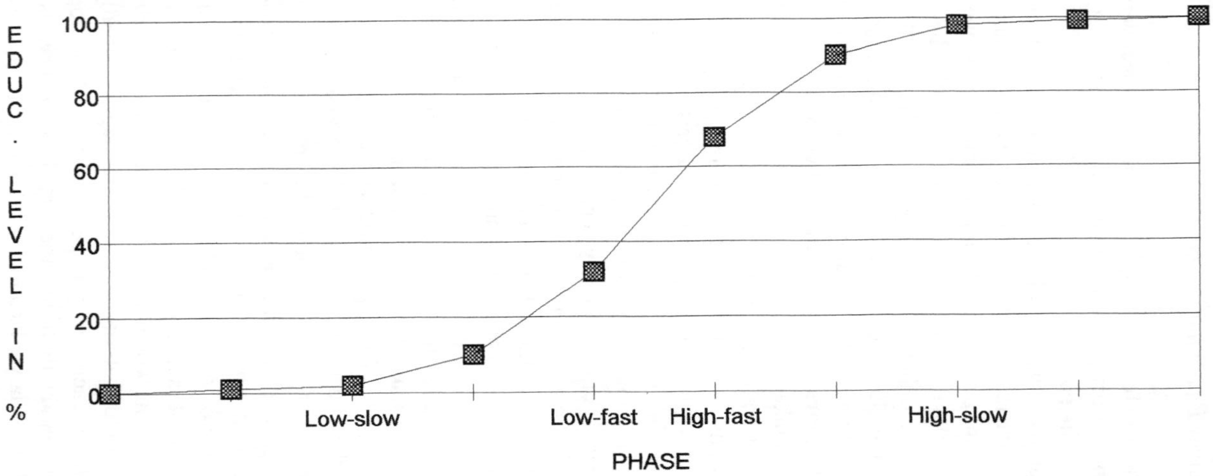

Figure 5.2. Expected evolution of illiteracy level

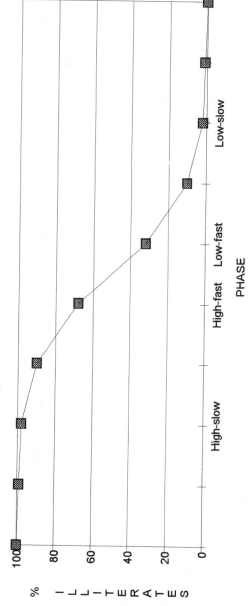

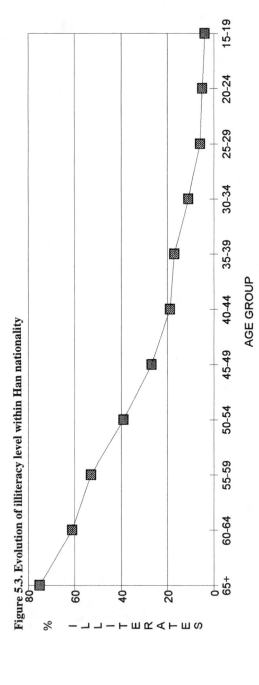

Figure 5.3. Evolution of illiteracy level within Han nationality

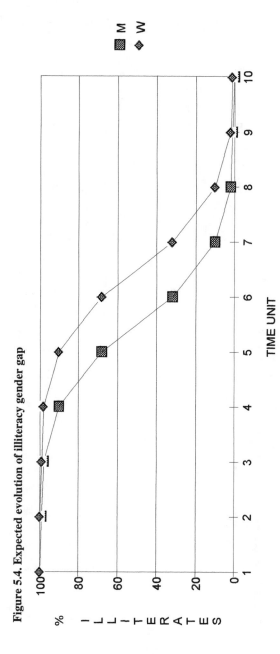

Figure 5.4. Expected evolution of illiteracy gender gap

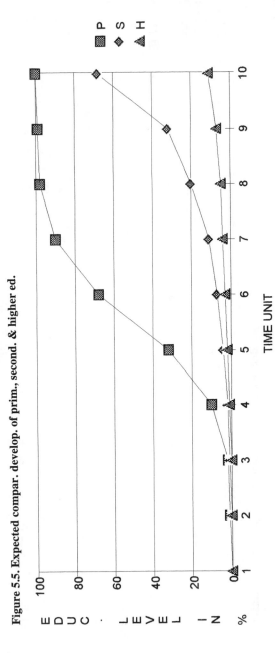

Figure 5.5. Expected compar. develop. of prim., second. & higher ed.

Indeed, we have already noted[4] that just as equality between two social entities concerning literacy is reached, there appear increasing disparities between these two social entities concerning secondary and, especially, higher education.

Exogenous factors may cause reality to deviate from the comparative expected values of elementary education, secondary education and higher education. For instance, let us say that we break down the literate population in a territory into a portion that has elementary-level schooling only and another that has post-elementary schooling. As the territory reduces its rate of illiteracy, one would expect first to note an increase in the relative volume of the elementary-level population and later an increase in the relative volume of the post-elementary-level population. Thus, among the educated population, the proportion of the elementary-level-only population would be smaller in the territories with the largest overall percentage of educated population. This situation indeed prevails in most province-level territories of China. However, there are exceptions pointing to the presence of intervening factors. In Qinghai, Gansu and Ningxia, the proportion of elementary-level-only population (about half) is relatively low, considering the overall educational lack of advancement of these territories. This suggests that, in these three northwestern territories, there is a relatively sizable population with post-elementary-level education alongside a relatively large illiterate population. A contrary situation is found in Guangxi and Sichuan, which have an above-average overall percentage of educated people: 6 out of 10 educated persons in these two territories are educated at the elementary level only. In other words, education in Guangxi and Sichuan is relatively widespread, but it tends to be concentrated at the elementary level.

APPLICATIONS OF THE MODEL

Following are applications of our model to the analysis of quantitative, macrosociological and longitudinal data on illiteracy. The illiteracy data pertains to the province-level territories, the counties and cities, the nationalities and gender.

Province-level Territories

In 1990, illiteracy (and semiliteracy) among the Chinese 15-year-old-plus population varies from 11 percent in Beijing to 69 percent in Tibet.

The 10 most literate province-level territories are Beijing, Tianjin, Shanghai, Liaoning, Jilin, Heilongjiang, Shanxi, Guangdong, Guangxi and Hunan. The 7 least literate province-level territories are Tibet, Qinghai, Gansu, Ningxia, Yunnan, Guizhou and Anhui. From 1982 to 1990, on average, the various province-level territories reduced their level of illiteracy by 10 percent. The progress made by the province-level territories, in terms of reduction of illiteracy, was such that, except for the seven least literate territories, the inter-territory gap has been narrowed. This means that the most literate territories have now reached the High-slow phase, while less literate territories are now in the Low-fast phase or the High-fast phase. The seven least literate territories are still in the Low-slow phase; they made significant progress during the 1980s (especially Anhui, Yunnan and Guizhou), but this progress was not commensurate with their level of illiteracy, and the seven territories remain far behind the 23 others.

Counties and Cities

Data on illiteracy (15-year-old-plus percentage of illiterates and semi-literates in total population) in China's counties and cities displays a curvilinear relationship between the degree of illiteracy in 1982 and the progress made during the following 8 years (i.e., the difference between the 1982 degree and the 1990 degree). When the counties and cities are lumped together ($n = 2,188$), the correlation coefficient is negligible ($r = .099$). But when they are separated into two subgroups, according to their level of illiteracy in 1982 (at least 27 percent in one subgroup, $n = 830$; and less than 27 percent in the other subgroup, $n = 1,358$), two opposite-sign and larger correlation coefficients are obtained ($r = -.395$ and $r = .657$). The counties and cities where the greatest progress was made, in terms of illiteracy reduction, are those where the degree of illiteracy in 1982 was neither very low nor very high. What this means is that, in terms of illiteracy reduction, the most advanced counties and cities have reached the High-slow phase, while the least advanced counties and cities are still in the Low-slow phase. The other counties and cities are either in the Low-fast phase or the High-fast phase. This also means that, in terms of illiteracy reduction, some moderately advanced counties and cities (in the Low-fast phase or the High-fast phase) have made progress toward catching up with the most advanced counties and cities (in the High-fast phase or in the High-slow phase), while the gap separating the least advanced counties (in the Low-slow phase) from the moderately advanced counties/cities (in the Low-fast phase or the High-fast phase) has widened.

Nationalities

National minorities/Han

The national minorities in China constitute 8.1 percent of the total population (1990 census), but they are very unequally distributed among the 30 province-level territories. In 9 territories, their share of the total population is less than 1 percent. In 11 other territories, their share is at least 10 percent: their presence is overwhelming in Tibet (96 percent) and Xinjiang (62 percent); they are in proportionately quite large numbers in Qinghai (42 percent), Guangxi (39 percent), Guizhou (35 percent), Yunnan (33 percent) and Ningxia (33 percent); and they are proportionately numerous in Inner Mongolia (19 percent), Hainan (17 percent), Liaoning (16 percent) and Jilin (10 percent). A significant proportion of national minorities is also found in Gansu (8 percent), Hunan (8 percent), Heilongjiang (6 percent) and Sichuan (5 percent).

In 1990, the level of illiteracy (in terms of percentage of illiterates and semiliterates in the 15-year-old-plus population) of the national minorities as a whole (30.8 percent) is markedly higher than that of all Han combined (21.5 percent). However, this average 9.3 percent illiteracy gap between the national minorities and the Han is far from being the same in each province-level territory. There is a very strong correlation ($r = .908$) between the level of national minority illiteracy and the minorities/Han illiteracy gap: the highest levels of minority illiteracy are those where the minorities/Han illiteracy gap is the largest. The largest illiteracy gaps are in Hainan (7 percent), Guangxi (8 percent), Hunan (9 percent), Guizhou (10 percent), Yunnan (12 percent), Xinjiang (12 percent), Ningxia (23 percent), Sichuan (31 percent), Gansu (31 percent), Qinghai (37 percent) and Tibet (70 percent). Thus, in most province-level territories with a large national minority presence, illiteracy is a discriminating characteristic between the national minorities and the Han. However, there are territories where the illiteracy ethnic gap, albeit not very large, is negative, that is, the level of illiteracy of the Han is somewhat higher than that of the national minorities. This situation prevails in Jilin (-6 percent), Inner Mongolia (-5 percent), Heilongjiang (-5 percent) and Liaoning (-2 percent). Among the province-level territories, and except for Tibet, there is much less variation in Han illiteracy than in illiteracy of the national minorities. In other words, the inter-provincial illiteracy disparities are much smaller among the Han than among the national minorities. Nevertheless, with the exception of Tibet (where the minorities and the Han are poles apart, illiteracy being at 73 percent for the minorities and only 3 percent for the Han), the levels of illiteracy of the national minorities parallel those of the Han within the various province-level territories (r = .677, when Tibet is excluded from the analysis).

The 56 nationalities

The level of illiteracy (in terms of percentage of illiterates and semi-literates in the 15-year-old-plus population) varies greatly among the 56 nationalities of China. In 1990, at the extremes are the Tatars (5 percent) and the Dongxiang (83 percent). The 10 most literate nationalities (illiteracy level of 10 percent or less) are the Tatars, Xibe, Koreans, Russians, Oroqen, Uzbeks, Hezhe, Gaoshan, Ewenki and Daur; and the 10 least literate nationalities (illiteracy level of more than 60 percent) are the Hani, De'ang, Lisu, Salar, Bonan, Tibetans, Lahu, Loba, Monba and Dongxiang.

As observed above concerning the counties and cities, there is a curvilinear relationship among the nationalities between the level of illiteracy in 1982 (measured in terms of the percentage of illiterates and semiliterates in the 12-year-old-plus population) and the progress made between 1982 and 1990 (measured by the difference between the 1982 level of illiteracy and the 1990 level of illiteracy). By separating the 56 nationalities into two subgroups of equal size according to their 1982 level of illiteracy (one subgroup with more than 46.5 percent, n=28; the other sub-group with less than 46.5 percent, n = 28), the resulting two subgroups display strong correlation coefficients, one negative (r = −.711) and one positive (r = .783). Consequently, each of the four phases of the model is represented by nationalities, on the basis of the 1982 level illiteracy and the degree of progress made between 1982 and 1990. The following nationalities are typically in one of the four phases with regard to illiteracy: (1) the Low-slow phase Salar, Tibetan, Bonan, Dongxiang; (2) the Low-fast phase Achang, Jingpo; (3) the High-fast phase Jing, Mulao; (4) the High-slow phase Tatar, Korean, Xibe. These trends mean that, in terms of eradicating illiteracy, the moderately advanced nationalities have made significant progress during the 1980s toward catching up with the most advanced nationalities. Meanwhile, although the least advanced nationalities have made some progress, the gap separating them from the moderately advanced nationalities has widened.

Intra-provincial analyses

There are several patterns of territorial distribution of the various nationalities in China. In many nationalities, although the members tend to concentrate in a particular territory, several smaller clusters of the nationality members are scattered in several territories. Given this territorial dispersion, one may ask: is the degree of educational development of a given nationality more or less the same for all of its subgroups living in various parts of the country, or is the degree of educational development more closely related to the characteristics of a territory and less related to ethnicity? In other words, what is the respective relationship of the variables of *ethnic group* and *territory* with regard to educational development?

This question can be approached by a comparative analysis of the educational development of each nationality in each territory. Table 5.1 gives an idea of this kind of analysis. The territory chosen here is Qinghai Province, and the question addressed is: Is the degree of educational development of a given nationality living in Qinghai typical or atypical of the degree of educational development of that nationality viewed as a whole at the national level? Eventually, a more specific analysis could compare the educational development of a given nationality in a certain territory with the educational development of the same nationality in another territory.

The degree of educational development (measured by the percentage of literate population, at all levels combined, in the total population) of the population of Qinghai Province is somewhat lower (54 percent) than that of the national population (70 percent). In addition, there are large disparities among the nationalities living in Qinghai, in terms of degree of educational development.

The least educated nationalities in Qinghai are the Hui, Dongxiang, Mongol, Tu and, especially, the Salar and Tibetans. In contrast,

Table 5.1. The Nationalities in Qinghai Province: Their Percentage of Educated Population (At all Levels Combined) in the Total Population, and Their Comparative Percentage for the Whole Country

NATNAM*	QALLP0	ALLEP0	QPONA0	POPNA0
All nat.	54.07	69.81	4,456,952	1,130,510,638
Salar	26.41	28.46	76,818	87,546
Tibetan	27.30	26.47	912,160	4,593,072
Hui	38.39	58.49	639,766	8,612,001
Dongxiang	40.27	16.17	1,475	373,669
Mongol	40.80	69.17	71,510	4,802,407
Tu	44.86	46.03	163,463	192,568
Kazak	52.58	69.77	523	1,110,758
Bonan	55.15	28.07	602	11,683
Uygur	65.57	61.32	122	7,207,024
Han	69.09	70.67	2,578,912	1,039,187,548
Yi	77.36	44.99	106	6,578,524
Korean	82.79	82.25	308	1,923,361
Man	84.07	76.32	8,527	9,846,776
Tujia	84.93	67.13	823	5,725,049
Zhuang	85.10	69.15	671	15,555,820
Miao	85.30	51.45	381	7,383,622
Xibe	86.36	78.54	132	172,932
Bai	86.44	63.02	118	1,598,052

Note: Only nationalities with a population of more than 100 in Qinghai Province are reported in this table.

*NATNAM = Nationality name; QALLP0 = Qinghai Province, 1990, % of educated population (all levels combined) in total population; ALLEP0 = China, 1990, % of educated population (all levels combined) in total population; QPONA0 = Qinghai Province, 1990, total population; POPNA0 = China, 1990, total population

Sources: Department of Population Statistics, State Statistical Bureau, People's Republic of China. *China Population Statistics Yearbook, 1992.* Beijing: China Statistical Publishing House, 1993, pp. 74-93. Population Census Office of Qinghai Province. *Tabulation on the 1990 Population Census of Qinghai Province (Computer Tabulation).* Three Volumes. Xining, Qinghai: China Statistical Publishing House, 1992, Volume 1, pp. 252-255. Population Census Office under the State Council, and Department of Population Statistics of the State Statistical Bureau, People's Republic of China. *Tabulation on the 1990 Population Census of the People's Republic of China.* Four Volumes. Beijing: China Statistical Publishing House, 1993, Volume 1, pp. 300-319 and 722-727.

several other nationalities in Qinghai have a very high degree of educational development: the Yi, Koreans, Man, Tujia, Zhuang, Miao, Xibe and Bai.

Of the 18 nationalities in Qinghai Province (i.e., those with a total population of more than 100), six have a percentage of educated population typical of the corresponding percentage found at the national level. The six nationalities are the Salar, Tibetans, Tu, Uygur, Han and Koreans. For the Hui, Mongols and Kazaks, the percentage of educated population in Qinghai is much smaller than the corresponding percentage at the national level. For the following seven nationalities, the percentage in Qinghai is very much higher than the corresponding national percentage: the Dongxiang, Bonan, Yi, Tujia, Zhuang, Miao and Bai. All of these seven nationalities are in small numbers (less than 1,500) in Qinghai Province, and their members in Qinghai represent a very small fraction of the total respective nationality in the country as a whole. The bulk of their members not being in Qinghai, but elsewhere in China, one could surmise that they are minority nationality cadres sent to Qinghai on assignment. Thus, they might be referred to as immigrant national minorities in Qinghai. The fact that they are cadres would explain why their degree of educational development is relatively high. For the Man and the Xibe, the national percentage of educated population is very high, but the corresponding percentage in Qinghai is even higher.

The question of the relative importance of the variables of *ethnic group* and *territory* concerning the degree of educational development could be examined even more precisely by pursuing the analysis at the prefectural level, and even at the county level. The question would be: Do all nationalities living in the same prefecture or the same county have more or less the same degree of educational development? We have just noted very large educational disparities among the nationalities within Qinghai Province. An examination of the ethnic composition of the various autonomous prefectures and autonomous counties of Qinghai reveals that some poorly educated minority groups live alongside relatively advanced minority groups. The Salar and the Tibetans, who are at the bottom of the educational ladder, often co-exist in the same autonomous prefecture or autonomous county. But they are also found alongside relatively more advanced nationalities, such as Mongols, Tu, Hui and Kazak. Salar and Tibetans co-exist with Mongols, Tu and Hui in Huangnan Tibetan Autonomous Prefecture, in in Hainan Tibetan Autonomous Prefecture, in Haixi Mongol-Tibetan-Kazak Autonomous Prefecture (where Kazaks are also present), and in Menyuan Hui Autonomous County. There are also Salar and Tibetans alongside Hui in Hualong Hui Autonomous County and in Xunhua Salar Autonomous County. To proceed with this analysis, quantitative and qualitative data gathering through sociological surveys and fieldwork would have to be made at the prefectural level and the county level. In order to shed more light on the inter-relationships of educational development, ethnicity and territory, several local phenomena could then be investigated, among which the following would be especially relevant: economic structure, occupations, social stratification, residential patterns, traditions, language use and cultural change. Ma Rong's observations on Han and Tibetan residential patterns in Lhasa are a step in this direction.[5]

GENDER

Province-level territories

At the national level, as of 1990, the percentage of illiterates and semi-literates in the 15-year-old-plus population was markedly different for men (13 percent) and women (32 percent). This average 19 percent gender gap varies a great deal among the 30 province-level territories, from 8 percent in Xinjiang to 32 percent in Guizhou. There is a strong correlation ($r = .842$) between the 1990 level of female illiteracy and the magnitude of the illiteracy gender gap: in general, the gender gap is at its maximum where female illiteracy is also at its maximum, and vice versa. This relationship is a reflection of the four phases of educational development. In educationally less advanced territories, such as Qinghai, Gansu, Yunnan, Guizhou and Anhui, women are still in the Low-slow phase, whereas men have begun their educational takeoff some time ago and are now in the Low-fast phase. This explains the very wide illiteracy gender gap in these territories. In Tibet, the educational lagging for both men and women is even more striking. The men of Tibet started their educational takeoff later than the men in the aforementioned educationally less advanced territories. Consequently, the illiteracy gender gap in Tibet has not yet reached its peak. At the other end of the continuum, the women in the three municipalities and in the three northeastern provinces have made tremendous progress, and the illiteracy gap separating them from the men in these territories is now rather small. These women have reached a point where not much more progress can be made, because the upper limit is near: they have entered the High-slow phase. Xinjiang women are in the High-slow phase, but the situation in Xinjiang is somewhat out of line, in comparison with the other provinces: given the overall (men and women combined) level of illiteracy in Xinjiang (20 percent), one would expect the illiteracy gender gap in that territory to be wider than it actually is (8 percent). For instance, in Sichuan, the overall level of illiteracy is 21 percent and the gender gap is 17 percent. Eventually, an analysis of economic, geographical, political, cultural, ethnic, historical and linguistic characteristics specific to Xinjiang might be helpful in explaining this phenomenon. The other province-level territories are distributed along the continuum between the two extreme situations and represent either the Low-fast phase or the High-fast phase.

In all province-level territories except Tibet, the illiteracy gender gap decreased between 1982 and 1990. The reduction of the illiteracy gender gap at the national level is 7 percent, dropping from 26 percent to 19 percent. In Tibet, the gap increased by 5 percent (from 23 to 28 percent). As noted above, the women of Tibet have not yet begun their educational takeoff, and the men of Tibet have only recently begun their own educational takeoff. This means that, in Tibet, the illiteracy gender gap is currently widening, as women remain in the Low-slow phase and men have just entered the Low-fast phase.

In the 22 most advanced territories (1982 female illiteracy level of no more than 57 percent), there is a strong correlation (r = .757) between the 1982 female illiteracy level and the magnitude of the gender gap reduction between 1982 and 1990: the territories with the highest 1982 female illiteracy level are those where the gap has been reduced the most. In other words, in these territories, women have been making significant progress toward catching up with men, in terms of literacy, and the territorial disparities between women are smaller in 1990 than they were in 1982. These 22 territories are either in the Low-fast, High-fast or High-slow phase. The least advanced territories (excluding Tibet) have made relatively little progress in terms of reduction of the illiteracy gender gap: the women of Qinghai, Gansu, Ningxia, Yunnan, Guizhou and Anhui are still in the Low-slow phase.

Nationalities

Among the 56 nationalities, there are several extreme situations, as well as several intermediate situations, in terms of female illiteracy. In 1990, the lowest proportion of illiterates and semi-literates among 15-year-old-plus women is found in the Tatar nationality (6.6 percent) where the complete eradication of female illiteracy has almost been achieved. The level of illiteracy among Xibe and Oroqen women is also very low (9 percent and 10 percent). The proportion of women illiterates and semi-literates varies between 10 percent and 16 percent among nine other nationalities: Russians, Uzbeks, Koreans, Hezhe, Ewenki, Daur, Gaoshan, Kazaks and Man. In eight more nationalities, women are moderately advanced, in terms of illiteracy (20-33 percent): Mongols, Mulao, Maonan, Uygur, Jing, Kirgiz, Han and Zhuang. The highest level of female illiteracy (92 percent) is among the Dongxiang nationality. Female illiteracy is between 80 percent and 90 percent in the Tibetan, Monba, Bonan and Salar nationalities. In nine other nationalities, the percentage of women illiterates and semi-literates ranges between 70 percent and 80 percent: Tu, Pumi, De'ang, Shui, Blang, Loba, Hani, Lisu and Lahu. The women of six other nationalities can also be considered educationally slow (60-70 percent): Achang, Buyi, Drung, Yi, Nu and Wa.

Obviously, when the total literacy of women is close at hand, as in the case of the Tatars, the illiteracy gender gap dwindles to naught and the equality of the sexes concerning literacy is achieved. In 1990, the illiteracy gender gap of the Tatars is the smallest (3.4 percent) of all the nationalities in China. The illiteracy gender gap is also small (less than 9 percent) for 11 nationalities with a low level of female illiteracy (less than 16 percent): Oroqen, Ewenki, Daur, Xibe, Uzbeks, Russians, Hezhe, Kazaks, Koreans, Man and Gaoshan. Normally, when the gender gap is small, the level of female illiteracy is low. Such is the case in the foregoing examples. Exceptionally, the Uygurs have a very small gender gap (4.3 percent) along with a level of female illiteracy that is somewhat high (29 percent). We noted earlier that in Xinjiang there is an unusually small illiteracy gender gap. The Uygur nationality being concentrated in Xinjiang, there could be a connection between the two phenomena. Further research into this question could eventually contribute to determine the respective effect of the variables of *ethnic group* and *territory* on the illiteracy gender gap in the Uygur nationality and in Xinjiang Uygur Autonomous Region.

Nationalities with a very high level of female illiteracy and a very wide illiteracy gender gap are nationalities where women are still in the Low-slow phase and men are well into the Low-fast phase. Examples of this type of nationality (female illiteracy level more than 70 percent and illiteracy gender gap more than 25 percent) are Tibetan, Blang, Lisu, Hani, Bonan, Tu, Salar, Pumi and Shui.

Nationalities with a very high level of female illiteracy and a relatively narrow illiteracy gender gap are nationalities where the educational takeoff has not yet started for neither men or for women: both men and women are still in the Low-slow phase, although there is a visible comparative slowness for women. Examples of this type of nationality (female illiteracy level more than 75 percent and illiteracy gender gap less than 13 percent) are the Loba, Lahu and Monba. The Dongxiang may be included in this type (female illiteracy, 92 percent; male illiteracy, 74 percent; illiteracy gender gap, 18 percent).

Another type of nationality is one where the male illiteracy level is relatively low (less than 20 percent) alongside a somewhat wide illiteracy gender gap (more than 20 percent). Examples of this type are the Jing, Zhuang, Bai, Tujia, Dong, Naxi, She, Yao, Li and Gelao. In these nationalities, the male illiteracy rate is relatively low because the men have already made much progress toward literacy: they have gone through the Low-fast phase and are now in the High-fast phase. The illiteracy gender gap is relatively wide because the women of these nationalities have only recently entered the Low-fast phase.

As noted earlier, at the national level, from 1982-1990, there was a 7 percent reduction of the illiteracy gender gap (from 26 percent to 19 percent). Among the nationalities, the relationship between the 1982 female level of illiteracy and the magnitude of the reduction of the illiteracy gender gap is curvilinear: the reduction of the gap was smallest both for the highest and lowest percentages of the 1982 female level of illiteracy. The breaking point is 50 percent. Above that, the correlation is negative ($r = -.604$): women in the least literate nationalities made the least progress; in some cases the gender gap even increased. Below 50 percent, the correlation is positive ($r = .600$): the smallest progress was made by women in the most advanced nationalities. This pattern of relationships makes sense in terms of the four phases of educational development. Women in the least literate nationalities are still in the Low-slow phase, and women in the most advanced nationalities have reached the High-slow phase. Generally speaking, among the nationalities, the fastest female literacy advances between 1982 and 1990 were made by the nationalities where the female level of illiteracy in 1982 stood somewhere between 45 and 70 percent: the women of these nationalities had then reached the Low-fast phase or the High-fast phase.

With regard to the following nationalities, women are in the Low-slow phase and men are in the Low-fast phase: Yi, Wa, Tu, Pumi, De'ang, Blang, Hani, Lisu, Shui, Tibetans, Lahu, Bonan, Salar and Dongxiang. Women, as well as men, of the following nationalities are in the High-slow phase: Tatar, Xibe, Koreans, Oroqen, Ewenki, Uzbek and Daur. Among some other nationalities, the illiteracy gender gap has been reduced tremendously because of the huge progress that women have made, both in absolute terms and in comparison with the progress of the men of the same nationalities. Among these nationalities, women are in the Low-fast phase and men are in the High-fast phase. These nationalities still have a long way to go to achieve complete literacy of both sexes, but both their men and women are progressing rapidly. The progress of men in these nationalities has begun to slow down as the men approach the High-slow phase; consequently, the greater much larger progress of the women of these nationalities results in a swift narrowing of the illiteracy gender gap. This situation is characteristic of the following nationalities: Zhuang, Jing, Mulao, Yugur, Bai, Yao, Dong and Qiang.

FUTURE TRENDS

On the basis of our analytical model of educational development and of the foregoing research findings concerning recent trends in the evolution of illiteracy in China, we predict the following trends in regional, ethnic and gender disparities during the next few years.

Province-level Territories

The illiteracy disparities will continue to decrease between the most advanced province-level territories (the three municipalities, the three northeastern provinces, Guangdong, Shanxi, Guangxi, Hunan and Xinjiang) and the moderately advanced province-level territories (Hainan, Sichuan, Hebei, Inner Mongolia, Hubei, Jiangsu, Zhejiang,

Shandong, Henan, Fujian, Jiangxi and Shaanxi). Some territories will move up to the High-slow phase from the High-fast phase, while others move up to the High-fast phase from the Low-fast phase. For some time to come, Tibet, Qinghai, Gansu and Ningxia will remain in the Low-slow phase of development. Yunnan, Guizhou and Anhui, which have been progressing toward literacy somewhat faster than the other four highly illiterate territories, will reach the Low-fast phase in the near future, at which point they will begin to narrow the gap separating them from the moderately advanced territories.

Counties and Cities

The illiteracy disparities will continue to decrease between counties and cities in the High-slow phase and counties and cities in the High-fast phase or the Low-fast phase. But the counties and cities in the Low-slow phase will lag further behind the moderately advanced counties and cities, despite some progress toward literacy.

Nationalities

There will be a decrease of the illiteracy disparities between nationalities in the High-slow phase (such as the Tatar, Korean and Xibe), those in the High-fast phase (such as the Jing and Mulao) and those in the Low-fast phase (such as the Achang and Jingpo), as an increasing number of these nationalities achieve near-complete literacy. However, nationalities still in the Low-slow phase (such as the Salar, Tibetan, Bonan and Dongxiang) will not make so much progress, and the gap separating them from the moderately advanced nationalities will continue to widen.

Gender

At the national level, the illiteracy gender gap will continue to narrow, but will not totally vanish. In the three municipalities and the three northeastern provinces, as well as in Xinjiang, where women have already attained the High-slow phase, the illiteracy gender gap will continue to dwindle slowly to a very small percentage, as those province-level territories come close to achieving the complete literacy of women as well as of men. At the other extreme, in Tibet, Qinghai, Gansu, Ningxia, Yunnan, Guizhou and Anhui, women will move from the Low-slow phase to the Low-fast phase, that is, their progress toward literacy will accelerate, and the illiteracy gender gap will continue to narrow, except in Tibet, where female illiteracy is at its highest, and where the illiteracy gender gap will continue to widen before it begins to narrow. In these seven highly illiterate territories, the illiteracy gender gap will remain relatively wide, and female illiteracy will still exist in sizable proportions. The moderately advanced province-level territories, in the Low-fast phase and the High-fast phase, will continue to advance quickly toward literacy for both men and women, and toward the reduction of the magnitude of the illiteracy gender gap. Some of these territories, such as Shanxi, Inner Mongolia and Hunan, will eventually attain the High-slow phase for women, that is, near-complete literacy for both sexes and a very small illiteracy gender gap. For several nationalities, female literacy will be complete or quasi-complete. These nationalities are the Tatar, Xibe, Oroqen, Russian, Uzbek, Korean, Hezhe, Ewenki, Daur, Gaoshan, Kazak and Man. By the same token, these nationalities will have achieved an equality of the sexes concerning literacy. The High-slow phase will also be reached by women of the following nationalities: Mongol, Mulao, Maonan, Uygur, Jing, Kirgiz, Han and Zhuang. Some women in the Low-slow phase will reach the Low-fast phase: for example, women of the Achang, Buyi, Drung, Yi, Nu and Wa nationalities. However, there will still be women in the Low-slow phase, in particular, women of the Dongxiang, Tibetan, Monba, Bonan, Salar, Tu, Pumi, De'ang, Shui, Blang, Loba, Hani, Lisu and Lahu nationalities.

INTERFACING QUANTITATIVE ANALYSES AND QUALITATIVE ANALYSES

A Research Strategy and an Integrated Approach

In our strategy of analysis of the factors of educational development in China (see Figure 5.6), we distinguish two levels of explanation. At the first level, we analyze the effect of the variables of *territory, ethnic group* and *gender* on educational development. At the second level, we analyze the effect of various socioeconomic, geographical, political, ethnic, cultural and historical variables on educational development. We measure educational development in two ways: (1) the degree of educational development; and (2) the speed (slow or fast) of educational progress.

Figure 5.6. A research strategy for the study of educational development in China

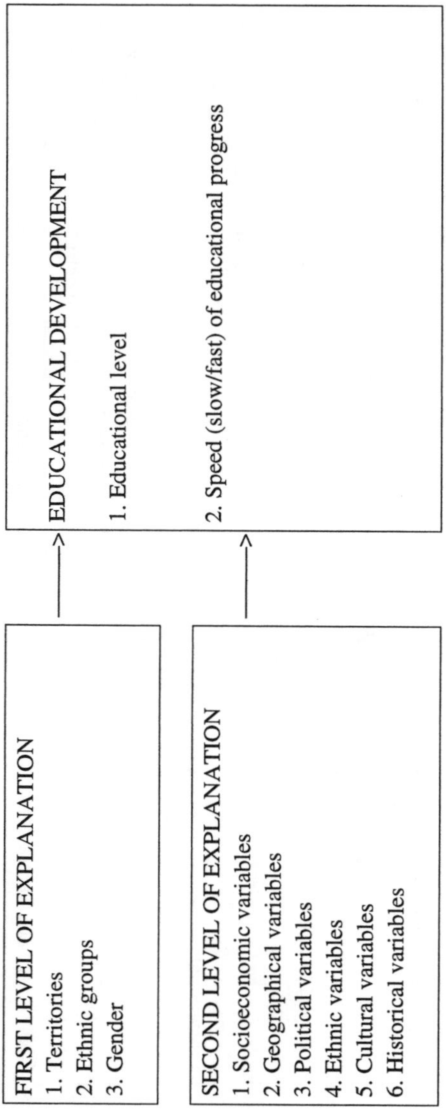

FIRST LEVEL OF EXPLANATION
1. Territories
2. Ethnic groups
3. Gender

⟶ EDUCATIONAL DEVELOPMENT

1. Educational level

2. Speed (slow/fast) of educational progress

SECOND LEVEL OF EXPLANATION
1. Socioeconomic variables
2. Geographical variables
3. Political variables
4. Ethnic variables
5. Cultural variables
6. Historical variables

Table 5.2. An Integrated Approach for Analyzing Educational Development in China: Methods, Phenomena and Types of Analyses

| | Territorial Level of the Analyses | | |
	Inter-provincial Analyses	Inter-county Analyses	Intra-county Analyses
Methods	Comparisons between the provinces	Comparisons between counties of a same province, and between counties all over the country	Direct observation in each selected county: analysis of documents concerning each selected county
Phenomena	Educational development and its relationship with socioeconomic development	Educational development and its relationship with socioeconomic development, and with variables territory, ethnicity and gender	Educational development and its relationship with the socioeconomic, geographical, political, ethnic, cultural and historical characteristics specific to each selected county
Types of analyses	Quantitative and longitudinal analyses	Quantitative and longitudinal analyses	Qualitative analyses

Our research program in comparative education consists of intra-national comparisons; that is, comparisons between territories, between ethnic groups and between men and women in China. It is also characterized by the longitudinal approach that we have adopted; this perspective leads to the analysis of the comparative evolution of educational development in China, especially over the last 15 years.

Our methodological approach is founded on the research methods in comparative education elaborated by L Theh Kho.[6] These methods are comparative and interdisciplinary and consist of the analysis of educational phenomena through their relations with society, culture and the economy. Our research method is also an example of the multilevel analysis recently advocated by Bray and Thomas.[7] Indeed, our research in comparative education focuses on two administrative levels of Chinese society: the provincial level and the county level. These two levels give rise to three types of analyses (see Table 5.2): (1) inter-provincial comparative analyses; (2) inter-county comparative analyses; and (3) analyses of intra-county dynamics in selected counties.

An especially interesting problem is that of the overlap in the effect of the variables of territory and ethnic group. Since certain ethnic groups are scattered over several territories, the comparative analysis of the educational development of members of a given ethnic group may facilitate the measurement of the respective effect of territory inhabited and ethnic belonging on educational development.

The analysis of variable gender, at the intra-provincial level, could lead to important precision on the level of education of both sexes, on the evolution of this level, on the magnitude of the educational gender gap, and on the evolution (increase/decrease) of this magnitude. The magnitude of the educational gender gap may vary according to territories and ethnic groups, and may evolve in a predictive way. Intra-county analyses could lead to the identification of socioeconomic, geographical, political, ethnic, cultural and historical factors at the root of the observed differences and tendencies.

SELECTION OF COUNTIES FOR THE FIRST FIELDWORK

The following sampling technique has been applied to an ongoing research project on the regional development of education in China. Before selecting the counties, a selection was made of the province-level territories where the fieldwork was to take place. Of the 30 provinces, autonomous regions and municipalities, six were selected for the fieldwork, on the basis of two criteria: (1) diversity in the provincial overall level of education (i.e. high or low), measured with a composite index of educational development; and (2) a fair representation of the various parts of the country, that is, North, South, East and West.

The composite index of educational development was constructed by grouping three educational variables: percentage of illiterates and semi-literates, percentage of senior high school graduates, and percentage of college and university graduates. It was constructed for 1990 data (variable EDIND0) and for 1982 data (variable EDIND2). The difference between the two indexes was viewed as a measure of the magnitude of the educational progress during the intervening years (variable EDID20). The data for these variables was excerpted from the China Population Statistics Yearbook, 1992.[8]

We used the following components for the indexes:

ILLIT0	1990, 15-year-old-plus percent of Illiterates and Semiliterates in Total Population
ILLIT2	1982, 15-year-old-plus percent of Illiterates and Semiliterates in Total Population
HSLEV0	1990, Senior High School Graduates per 10,000 Persons in Total Population
HSLEV2	1982, Senior High School Graduates per 10,000 Persons in Total Population
COLEV0	1990, College and University Graduates per 10,000 Persons in Total Population
COLEV2	1982, College and University Graduates per 10,000 Persons in Total Population

The formulas for computing the three indexes were:

EDIND0	1990, Educational Index
EDIND0	$= ((COLEV0 \times .2) + (HSLEV0 \times .15)) \, ILLIT0$
EDIND2	1982, Educational Index
EDIND2	$= ((COLEV2 \times .2) + (HSLEV2 \times .15)) \, ILLIT2$
EDID20	1990-1982, Difference in Educational Index
EDID20	$= EDIND0-EDIND2$

On the basis of the two above-mentioned criteria, the following six province-level territories were selected: Gansu, Inner Mongolia, Jilin, Shandong, Guangdong and Yunnan.

We decided to do fieldwork in four counties in each of the six selected province-level territories: two educationally advanced and fast-developing, and two educationally less advanced and slow-developing. The aim of the fieldwork was to identify, through observation and comparison, the various factors that either facilitate most or hinder most the development of education in the counties.

To select these counties, a composite index of educational development for each county, analogous to the one described above for the province-level territories, was constructed. Within each of the six selected province-level territories, the counties were first categorized according to two criteria: (1) their educational index in 1990 (EDIND0); and (2) the magnitude of their educational progress between 1982 and 1990 (EDID20). Then, the cutting point of the 20th and the 80th percentiles for variables EDIND0 and EDID20 were obtained, respectively. The conjunction of these two variables produced a short list of the two kinds of counties: the educationally most advanced and fastest developing, and the educationally least advanced and slowest developing.

In each of the six selected province-level territories, we found that the great majority of the most advanced counties were also the fastest developing counties, and that the great majority of the least developed counties were also the slowest developing counties. Incidentally, this means that, in most cases, the gap between the educationally advanced counties and the educationally slowest counties widened between 1982 and 1990.

For each of the six province-level territories, the short list was longer than necessary. To reduce the short list to our final selection of four counties per province-level territory, we applied the following criteria: (1) preference was given to the counties with either the highest scores or the lowest scores concerning the level of educational development in 1990; (2) although the counties would preferably be scattered in various parts of the province, preference was given to counties where transportation is not too great a hurdle; and (3) the county selected should still be a county at the time of the selection, that is, it had not been elevated to the rank of city, or been integrated into a city. Table 5.3 shows the 24 counties thus selected for the fieldwork.

Table 5.3. The 24 Counties Selected for the First Fieldwork (1994 and 1995)

Gansu	Guangdong	Shangdong
Dongxiang Aut. County*	Dianbai County*	Juye County*
Zhangjiachuan Hui Aut. County*	Yangshan County*	Shanghe County*
Jingchuan County**	Lianshan Zhuang-Yao Aut. County**	Yiyuan County**
Jingyuan County**	Gaoming County**	Changdao County**
Jilin	Inner Mongolia	Yunnan
Lishu County*	Xinghe County*	Jinping Miao-Yao-Dai Aut. County*
Changling County*	Shangdu County*	Yiliang County*
Antu County**	Sonid Right Banner**	Simao County**
Wangqing County**	Xianghuang Banner**	Anning County**

* Educationally less advanced and slow-developing county

** Educationally advanced and fast-developing county

Note: We define the expressions "educationally less advanced and "educationally advanced within the respective context of each province-level territory. There are large inter-provincial educational-level disparities, and the meaning of these two expressions varies according to the overall educational level of each province. For instance, Jingchuan County of Gansu Province is considered as an "educationally advanced county when compared with the other counties of Gansu Province, an "educationally less advanced province. Jingchuan County would appear "educationally backward if it were compared with the counties of an "educationally advanced province, such as Jilin. For instance, the educational level of Jingchuan County is lower than the educational level of Changling County of Jilin Province, although Changling is considered as an "educationally less advanced county when compared with the other counties of Jilin Province.

The first fieldwork took place in 1994 (Inner Mongolia, Shandong, Yunnan) and 1995 (Gansu, Jilin, Guangdong). Our fieldwork research method consisted of the identification of socioeconomic, geographical, political, ethnic, cultural and historical factors which are conducive to or which inhibit educational development in each investigated county, and then in the comparison of the characteristics of the two types of counties selected: advanced/fast developing and less advanced/slow-developing.

SELECTION OF NATIONALITIES FOR THE SECOND FIELDWORK

For our second fieldwork, forthcoming in 1997 and 1998, we decided to select nationalities on the basis of three criteria: the degree of educational development, the magnitude of educational progress and the magnitude of the educational gender gap. To apply each of these three criteria, we use a measure of the level of illiteracy, that is, the percentage of illiterates and semiliterates.

We decided to select nationalities that contrast according to one of the three criteria, in order to compare these nationalities and discover factors which facilitate or inhibit their educational development. Tables 5.4 to 5.7 illustrate contrasting situations between nationalities in terms of degree of educational development, educational progress and educational gender gap. All of the nationalities listed in tables 5.3 to 5.6 could be compared. For fieldwork, we shall select a few of them.

Selecting the specific territories (provinces, prefectures, counties, towns, townships, villages) where the fieldwork will actually take place, taking into account each nationality's specific population distribution over the Chinese territory (compact group versus dispersion over vast areas, isolation versus co-residence with other nationalities, etc.) and ascertaining that the educational pattern specific to the nationality living in the particular territory under consideration is the overall educational pattern shown in the nationality in question. The purpose of the fieldwork will be to uncover the various factors that facilitate or inhibit educational development within the respective nationalities under study, and to analyze these factors in a comparative perspective.

Table 5.4. Most Literate and Least Literate Nationalities, 1990

Percentage of Illiterates and Semiliterates	Nationalities
-13%	Tatar, Xibe, Koreans, Russians, Oroqen, Uzbek, Hezhe, Gaoshan, Ewenki, Daur, Man, Kazak
+58%	Wa, Blang, Hani, De'ang, Lisu, Salar, Bonan, Tibetans, Lahu, Loba, Monba, Dongxiang

Source: Population Census Office under the State Council, and Department of Population Statistics of the State Statistical Bureau, People's Republic of China. *Tabulation on the 1990 Population Census of the People's Republic of China.* Four Volumes. Beijing: China Statistical Publishing House, 1993, Volume 1, pp. 300-319 and 734-739.

Table 5.5. Magnitude of Illiteracy Difference between 65+ and 15-19 Age Groups in Selected Nationalities, 1990

Difference	Nationalities
-40%	Tibetans, Dongxiang, Salar, Bonan, Monba, Loba
+70%	Li, Jingpo, Qiang, Achang, Tajik, Jinuo

Source: Department of Population Statistics of the State Statistical Bureau, and Economic Department of the State Nationalities Affairs Commission, People's Republic of China. *Tabulation on China's Nationalities: Data of 1990 Population Census.* Beijing: China Statistical Publishing House, 1994, pp. 76-115.

Table 5.6. Magnitude of Illiteracy Reduction between 1982 and 1990 in Selected Nationalities

Reduction	Nationalities
Small	Tujia, Hui, Tu, Pumi, Drung, Nu, Salar, Tibetans, Loba, Dongxiang
Large	Russians, Mulao, Kirgiz, She, Gelao, Miao, Jingpo, De'ang, Blang, Lahu

Sources: Population Census Office under the State Council, and Department of Population Statistics of the State Statistical Bureau, People's Republic of China. *The 1982 Population Census of China: Results of Computer Tabulation.* Beijing: China Statistical Publishing House, 1985, pp. 32-33 and 244-247. Population Census Office under the State Council, and Department of Population Statistics of the State Statistical Bureau, People's Republic of China. *Tabulation on the 1990 Population Census of the People's Republic of China.* Four Volumes. Beijing: China Statistical Publishing House, 1993, Volume 1, pp. 300-319 and 734-739.

Table 5.7. Magnitude of Illiteracy Gender Gap in Selected Nationalities, 1990

Gap	Nationalities
Small	Uzbek, Ewenki, Daur, Kirgiz, Uygur, Tajik, Jinuo, Jingpo, Drung, Nu, Wa, De'ang, Loba
Large	Koreans, Jing, Mulao, Maonan, Zhuang, Bai, Dong, She, Gelao, Buyi, Shui, Pumi, Salar

Source: Population Census Office under the State Council, and Department of Population Statistics of the State Statistical Bureau, People's Republic of China. *Tabulation on the 1990 Population Census of the People's Republic of China.* Four Volumes. Beijing: China Statistical Publishing House, 1993, Volume 1, pp. 300-319 and 734-739.

SUMMARY AND CONCLUSION

An analytical model of educational development was introduced at the beginning of this chapter. The model was built on two dimensions: degree of educational development, and time. A measure of the speed of educational development was obtained by combining these two dimensions. According to the model, a social entity (for instance, a region, an ethnic group, or women as a group) goes through four successive phases of educational development: Low-slow, Low-fast, High-fast and High-slow. The model allows the comparative analysis of the educational development of two social entities by focusing on the notion of an educational gap. On the basis of the model, a quantitative, macrosociological and longitudinal analysis was made of regional, ethnic and gender disparities in illiteracy in China. The data used to apply the model are mainly from the last two censuses in China (1982 and 1990).

Province-level Territories

There are province-level territories in each of the four phases. The following 10 territories are the most literate, and they have reached the High-slow phase: Beijing, Tianjin, Shanghai, Liaoning, Jilin, Heilongjiang, Shanxi, Guangdong, Guangxi and Hunan. The following 7 territories are the least literate, and they are still in the Low-slow phase: Tibet, Qinghai, Gansu, Ningxia, Yunnan, Guizhou and Anhui. During the 1980s, all province-level territories progressed toward literacy, at varying speeds. This entailed a narrowing of the gap separating the territories in the High-slow phase and those in the High-fast phase or in the Low-fast phase. However, the territories in the Low-slow phase continue to lag far behind all others.

Counties and cities

The most advanced counties and cities have reached the High-slow phase, while the most backward counties and cities are still in the Low-slow phase. The other counties and cities are either in the Low-fast phase or in the High-fast phase. During the 1980s, the gap narrowed between the most advanced counties and cities and the moderately advanced counties and cities, but it widened between the least advanced counties and cities and the moderately advanced counties and cities.

Nationalities

The level of illiteracy varies greatly among the 56 nationalities of China. The 10 most literate nationalities are the Tatars, Xibe, Koreans, Russians, Oroqen Uzbeks, Hezhe, Gaoshan, Ewenki and Daur. The 10 least literate nationalities are the Hani, De'ang, Lisu, Salar, Bonan, Tibetans, Lahu, Loba, Monba and Dongxiang. The following nationalities are typically in one of the four phases: (1) the Low-slow phase—Salar, Tibetans, Bonan, Dongxiang; (2) the Low-fast phase—Achang, Jingpo; (3) the High-fast phase—Jing, Mulao; (4) the High-slow phase—Tatars, Koreans, Xibe. The moderately advanced nationalities have made significant progress toward catching up with the most advanced nationalities. Meanwhile, although the least advanced nationalities have made some progress, the gap separating them from the moderately advanced nationalities has widened.

Gender

In educationally less advanced territories, such as Qinghai, Gansu, Yunnan, Guizhou and Anhui, women are still in the Low-slow phase in terms of illiteracy, whereas men began their educational takeoff some time ago and are now in the Low-fast phase: this explains the very wide illiteracy gender gap in these territories. In Tibet, where the educational lack of advancement for both men and women is even more profound, and the illiteracy gender gap in Tibet has not yet reached its peak. At the other end of the continuum, the women in the three municipalities and in the three northeastern provinces have made tremendous progress, and the illiteracy gap separating them from the men in these territories is now rather small; these women have reached the High-slow phase. The other province-level territories are distributed along the continuum between the two extreme situations, and the women in these territories are either in the Low-fast phase or the High-fast phase. Except in Tibet, the illiteracy gender gap has narrowed in all province-level territories during the 1980s, which is especially the case in the territories where women are in the Low-fast phase or in the High-fast phase.

Women of 12 nationalities have reached the High-slow phase; they are close to achieving total literacy and, consequently, their illiteracy gender gap has narrowed to a very small percentage. These women belong to the Tatar, Oroqen, Ewenki, Daur, Xibo, Uzbek, Russian,

Hezhe, Kazak, Korean, Man and Gaoshan nationalities. There are other combinations of male and female illiteracy phases in the nationalities. Combination men-Low-fast/women-Low-slow is found among the Tibetan, Bulang, Lisu, Hani, Bonan, Tu, Salar, Pumi and Shui nationalities. Combination men-Low-slow/women-Low-slow is characteristic of the Loba, Lahu, Monba and Dongxiang nationalities. And combination Men-high-fast/Women-low-fast is now typical of the Jing, Zhuang, Bai, Tujia, Dong, Naxi, She, Yao, Li and Gelao nationalities.

Future Trends

On the whole, elementary education for all is now within the horizon in China and, with some exceptions, educational disparities at the elementary level are being reduced at an accelerating pace. During the next few years, social entities (i.e., province-level territories, counties versus cities, nationalities, and women versus men) in the Low-fast phase and in the High-fast phase will continue to progress rapidly and, thus, reduce the gap that separates them from social entities in the High-slow phase. Social entities in the Low-slow phase will also progress, but will nevertheless lag further behind social entities in the Low-fast phase.

Future Research Agendas

Aside from our ongoing and forthcoming research, which we described in this chapter, other avenues of research could eventually be explored on the basis of some of the findings in the foregoing analysis. They are discussed below.

An illiteracy gender gap that is smaller than expected was found, separately, in the Uygur nationality and in Xinjiang Uygur Autonomous Region. An explanation for the apparent connection between the two phenomena could lie in economic, geographical, political, ethnic, cultural, historical, demographic and linguistic conditions specific to the Uygur and/or to Xinjiang. The purpose of this future research would be to determine the respective relationship of the variables of *ethnic group* and *territory* with regard to educational development.

The educational development of the various nationalities in Qinghai Province is characterized by very large disparities among the nationalities. In addition, analogous disparities among nationalities possibly exist within prefectures and counties of Qinghai. This phenomenon could be investigated in selected prefectures or counties in Qinghai, by addressing the question: Is the degree of educational development of a given nationality more or less the same for all of its subgroups living in various territories, or is the degree of educational development more closely related to the characteristics of a territory and less related to ethnicity? In other words, this is the same question as posed above: What is the respective relationship of the variables of *ethnic group* and *territory* for educational development? The same kind of study could also be made in several other parts of China, where various nationalities co-exist.

Other comparative studies could be undertaken with selected minority ethnic groups in selected areas of China. The studies would focus on territorial, ethnic and gender disparities in educational development. The selection of the minority ethnic groups and areas to be studied could be based on a number of criteria, such as the following: (1) type of territorial distribution (concentration in one or in a few areas, or dispersion in several areas) of the minority ethnic group; (2) presence or absence of other ethnic groups (including the Han) in the same territory (e.g., prefecture, county); (3) social distance (i.e., conviviality or separateness) between the minority ethnic group and the other ethnic groups; (4) size of the population of the minority ethnic group (in absolute numbers, and in proportion with the size of the population of neighboring ethnic groups); (5) existence or non-existence of a written language for the minority ethnic group; (6) proportion of illiterates in the minority ethnic group; and (7) occupational characteristics of the minority ethnic group.

Practical Use of the Model

The evaluation of past educational development should be made with reference to expected educational development, which, as we have seen, varies according to the four phases. When analyzing past educational development of a magnitude that deviates significantly in a positive or negative way from the expected magnitude, one should look for specific intervening factors that have influenced the outcome positively or negatively. The model can be used to measure the effect of planned interventions in a given social entity to accelerate its educational development. Given no such interventions, the educational development would likely follow its course at the speed expected by the model. The effect of interventions is measured by the difference between the expected degree of development, as predicted by the model, and the real degree of development, as observed. Of course, there can also be negative intervening factors, that is, factors that reduce the speed of educational development. The magnitude of the impact of the negative intervening factors can similarly be measured by the difference between the expected and the observed level of educational development.

Looking ahead, setting educational goals realistically requires that the expected educational development be taken into account. For example, within a certain time period, a given educational goal might be attainable for a social entity in the Low-fast phase, but might be out of reach for a social entity in the Low-slow phase. Knowing the specific phase and the expected educational development of a given social entity helps setting educational goals for that social entity that are commensurate with its current specific capacity for educational development.

NOTES

1.   Gerard A. Postiglione and Wing On Lee (eds.), *Social Change and Educational Development: Mainland China, Taiwan and Hong Kong* (Hong Kong: Center of Asian Studies, The University of Hong Kong, 1995); Keith M. Lewin and Wang Yingjie, *Implementing Basic Education in China: Progress and Prospects in Rich, Poor and National Minority Areas* (Paris: International Institute for Educational Planning, UNESCO, 1994); Jacques Lamontagne and Ma Rong, "The Development of Education in China's Cities and Counties, in Gerard A. Postiglione and Wing On Lee (eds.), *Social Change and Educational Development*, pp. 153-173; Jan-Ingvar, Lofstedt, *Education in Multi-Ethnic and Disadvantaged Areas: The Case of Gansu in China* (Stockholm: Institute of International Education, 1994).

2.   John Bauer, Wang Feng, Nancy E. Riley and Zhao Xiaohua, "Gender Inequality in Urban China: Education and Employment, in *Modern China*, Vol. 18, No. 3 (July 1992), pp. 333-370; Jacques Lamontagne, "Educational Disparities in Mainland China: Characteristics and Trends, in Bih-jaw Lin and Li-min Fan (eds.), *Education in Mainland China: Review and Evaluation* (Taipei: Institute of International Relations, National Chengchi University, 1990), pp. 130-151; Jacques Lamontagne, "Improving the Education of China's

National Minorities, in Douglas Ray and Deo Poonwassie (eds.), *Education and Cultural Differences: New Perspectives* (New York: Garland Publishing, 1992) pp. 183-209; William Lavely, Xiao Zhenyu, Li Bohua and Ronald Freedman, "The Rise in Female Education in China: National and Regional Patterns, in *The China Quarterly*, No. 121 (1990), pp. 61-93.

3.   Everett M. Rogers, *Diffusion of Innovations*, third edition (New York: Free Press, 1989).

4.   Jacques Lamontagne and Ma Rong, *Trends in Chinese Educational Development: An Analytical Model and Its Applications to Regional, Ethnic and Gender Disparities* (Montreal and Beijing: Faculte des sciences se l'education, Universite de Montreal, and Institute of Sociology and Anthropology, Peking University, 1995).

5.   Ma Rong, "Han and Tibetan Residential Patterns in Lhasa, in *The China Quarterly*, No. 128 (1992), pp. 814-835.

6.   L Theh Kho, *L'education Compare* (Paris: Armand Colin, 1981).

7.   Mark Bray and R. Murray Thomas, "Levels of Comparison in Educational Studies: Different Insights from Different Literatures and the Value of Multilevel Analyses, in *Harvard Educational Review*, Vol. 65, No. 3 (Fall 1995), pp. 472-490.

8.   Department of Population Statistics, State Statistical Bureau, People's Republic of China (ed.), *China Population Statistics Yearbook, 1992* (Beijing: Zhongguo tongji chubanshe, 1993).

Expanding Access to Higher Education for China's National Minorities

Policies of Preferential Admissions

Barry Sautman

The People's Republic of China (PRC) has one of the oldest and largest programs of state-sponsored preferential policies (*youhui zhengce*) for ethnic minorities. While preferential policies have been explicitly touted by national leaders only since the mid-1980s,[1] the program dates from the inception of the state[2] and is a variant of a concept pioneered in the ex-Soviet Union.[3] As of 1995, preferential policies for minorities encompassed 9 percent of China's population, about one hundred ten million people.[4]

Preferential policies are applied to minority areas[5] and minority individuals. Lower-level minority areas receive infrastructural subsidies from higher jurisdictions. Budgetary subventions, disproportionate investment in public works and the provision and training of personnel are common features.[6] For minority areas, these measures are a trade-off; in exchange, they are expected to make "extensive efforts to support the country's construction by providing more natural resources.[7]

It is recognized, however, that ethnic relations will be stabilized only when living standards in minority regions are greatly improved.[8] Aid measures arise in part from the overlap of minority and impoverished areas.[9] Preferential treatment is also accorded minority areas in terms of liberal investment laws, exemption from tariffs for certain imported goods, etc. This policy has become so important to development that the leaders of Qinghai, a province whose territory is 98 percent Tibetan autonomous prefectures, would like the whole province to be converted into an autonomous region or be given the same preferences accorded the Tibet Autonomous Region (TAR). Because it has autonomous powers, Xinjiang is said to have better economic prospects than mainly Han Shanxi and Gansu provinces.[10]

Major aspects of the lives of minority individuals are also impacted by preferential policies. There are preferential policies for family planning (exemption from minimum marriage age and one-child strictures), education (preferential admissions, lowered school fees, boarding schools, remedial programs), employment (extra consideration in hiring and promotion of cadres), business development (special loans and grants, exemptions from some taxes) and political representation.[11] In Yunnan province, where the population is 34 percent minorities, there are in all about 150 different preferential policies.[12]

Preferential policies are intended to narrow the economic and social gap between Han and minority people.[13] The posited goal is "equality in fact" (*shishishangde pingdeng*).[14] It is argued that if equal treatment were the basis for determining entry into universities, equality of opportunity would sharply diminish. Unequal treatment is thought to be needed to propitiate equal opportunity, with equality of results as the eventual goal.[15] Because most minorities live in the relatively remote interior where development lags increasingly behind the growth of coastal regions, however, the gap between minorities and Han living standards has widened despite preferential policies. Equality in the economic and educational spheres remains illusive.[16]

In Hainan, where minorities are 17 percent of the population, a 1995 study carried out by provincial officials revealed that whereas in 1987 Hainan's minority autonomous counties and two cities with autonomous powers produced 25.9 percent of provincial gross domestic product, in 1992, these areas produced only 21.5 percent; in 1993, 20.1 percent; and in 1994, 17.7 percent.[17] In Yunnan in 1996, it was estimated that the richest Han area of the province has an income level 20 times that of the poorest minority area. The income level of Han peasants near the capital, Kunming, was 4 to 5 times the income level of minority peasants in impoverished Guangnan county.[18] Officials in minority areas acknowledge the growing Han-minority economic gap and some accuse the government of aggravating it through anti-redistributive tax reforms carried out in China from 1994.[19]

Preferential policies do nevertheless provide benefits to broad sections of the minority population, particularly with regard to family planning and education. In higher education, preferences are aimed at creating a reliable minority elite and are deemed essential to the drive for prosperity and increased state legitimacy in the nearly two-thirds of China's territory that is officially designated as autonomous areas (*zizhi difang*). The scope and effect of these admissions preferences is addressed in the discussion that follows.

THE BASIS FOR PREFERENTIAL ADMISSIONS

Preferential policies in family planning provide a valued benefit for which the vast majority of minority people become eligible at some point in their lives. Preferential admissions to higher education encompass a much smaller number of minority people. They are, however, a key facet of minority elite formation, as university education has become a requisite of hiring and promotion to higher cadre positions.[20] In contrast to most preferences, which are available only to minorities who remain in autonomous areas, preferential admissions are extended without regard to residence in the minority areas, and therefore can be used by the one-quarter of the minority population that live in the mainly Han areas.[21] Preferential admissions, moreover, are the only policy provided to every minority ethnie, including groups such as the Koreans, Mongols and Tatars, who on average surpass the Han in their level of tertiary schooling.

For example, in relatively prosperous Jiangsu province, the proportion of minorities, at .25 percent, is the smallest in the country, although they still number over 100,000. The bulk of this minority population is Huizu (Chinese Muslims) whose educational level is higher than that of the Han. Moreover, the Huizu, who have a background in commerce, are more prosperous than the Han. Jiangsu Hui applicants nevertheless receive preferences in admissions: 20 points are automatically added to their scores on the national entrance examination (*gaodeng xuexiao ruxue kaoshi* or *gao kao*) if they apply to nationalities institutes (*minzu xueyuan*), or 5 points if to other schools.[22] The national policy that universities are supposed to "relax their admission standards to an appropriate extent[23] has a legal basis in

Section 65 of the 1984 Law on Regional Autonomy for Minority Nationalities (*minzu quyu zizhi fa*):

> The state shall set up institutes of nationalities and, in other institutions of higher education, nationality-oriented classes and preparatory classes that enroll only students from minority nationalities. Preferred enrollment and preferred assignment of jobs may also be introduced. In enrollment, institutions of higher education and secondary technical schools shall appropriately set lower standards and requirements for the admission of students from minority nationalities.[24]

Other national laws also endorse preferential admissions for minorities in higher education. For example, Article 14 of the "Regulations on Ethnic Township Administration of 1993[25] states that quotas for preferential admission to higher education institutions of students from ethnic townships may be used, if higher-level government bodies agree to set up special ethnic "classes or cohorts" (*minzu ban*) at such institutions.[26] These classes generally, although not always, consist of students from the same ethane or minority area who live and study together. Their existence depends partly on the influence of the minority areas, since the autonomous areas negotiate with universities to run the classes. For example, before it was abolished in 1988, the Hainan Li-Miao Autonomous Prefecture ensured that there were Hainan *minzu ban* at some *neidi* (interior) universities, for example, East China Normal University (*Huadong shifan daxue*) in Shanghai.[27]

Some of these classes are accorded a year of remedial education before beginning the regular four-year curriculum. Other classes are provided with special tutoring. Many prominent universities now have one or more *minzu ban*. There were, for example, *minzu ban* at 16 Beijing universities in 1994-1995, including 6 national and 10 locally controlled institutions.[28] At most universities, participation in a minority class means, in effect, an additional year of undergraduate study in a preparatory class (*yuke ban*), but in some universities *minzu ban* students have been expected to finish in 4 years.[29]

In 1994, there were "Tibetan classes (*Xizang ban*) at 28 inland universities, and in 1987 "Xinjiang classes (*Xinjiang ban*) totaled 450 students at 14 inland universities.[30] By 1991, some 3,600 Xinjiang minority students were studying at inland universities, and in 1993 there were 110 Xinjiang classes at 46 universities. Similar classes exist for some other ethnies.[31] *Minzu ban* also exist in upper secondary schools, where their main task is to prepare students to go to universities. In Hainan, for example, there have been upper secondary school *minzu ban* since the early 1980s and every year 20 to 25 minority students from the cohorts of 45 to 55 go on to a university. Hainan's universities also have *minzu ban*, with 40 students at each institution and one year preparatory classes required of each cohort.[32]

Since the early 1980s, there have also been one-year preparatory courses (*yuke ban*) for minorities at key universities and nationality institutes. These classes, which may be arranged by agreement between minority areas and universities,[33] can serve students who failed to enter a university through the national enrollment system. They may also be part of a long-term program involving promising minority pre-college students who will study at nationality institutes for 3 to 6 years.[34]

By the end of the 1980s, 40,000 minority students had gone through preparatory courses at over 140 institutions of higher education.[35] In 1995-1996, more than 11,000 minority students were said to be enrolled in *yuke ban* at 128 institutions in 20 provinces.[36] In Ningxia, for example, such classes exist at Ningxia University, Guyuan Normal University (*Guyuan shifan daxue*) and Guyuan Ethnic Minority Normal University (*Guyuan minzu shifan daxue*).[37] At Beijing University, there are *yuke ban* for Mongol students, each enrolling 30 students, and at Jilin University, such classes exist for Tibetan students.[38] Liangshan Yi Autonomous Prefecture, Sichuan has Yi preparatory classes at its teacher training schools. Students study an advanced secondary school curriculum for one year and then take the national entrance examination. If their scores are high enough, they go to universities, if not, they remain at the normal school. Liangshan University, which is actually a college-level technical school (*dazhuan*) with an engineering emphasis, also has a preparatory class.[39]

PREFERENTIAL ADMISSIONS AND THE EDUCATIONAL GAP

When the Communist Party achieved national power in 1949, ethnic minority university students amounted to less than 1 percent of students in higher education. The proportion increased fairly rapidly in the

1950s, peaking at 3.7 percent in 1956-1957 and declining somewhat thereafter, so that it stood at 3.2 percent on the eve of the Cultural Revolution in 1964-1965. Universities were closed during the first few years of the turbulent decade that followed. When they reopened-with a hyper-politicized curriculum and without examinations-preferences for minority admittees were doubled. By the end of the Cultural Revolution in 1976, 6.5 percent of university students were minorities. With the reinstitution of the national entrance examination in 1977,[40] the proportion of minority students fell sharply, bottoming out at 3.7 percent in 1978-1979. In 1980, it was announced that minimum score requirements would be lowered for minority applicants to universities.[41]

The percentage of minority students then began a steady climb again, peaking in 1991-1992 at 7 percent and thereafter declining to 6.4 percent in 1992-1994 and, circa 5.7 percent in 1994-1995 (See Table 6.1).[42] The most recent decline is likely related to the very rapid expansion of Chinese higher education in the 1990s. There were nearly three million students at mid-decade, and as many as seven million are expected to be enrolled at PRC universities in the year 2000.[43]

The imposition of university tuition may also discourage some minority students, who are generally from poorer backgrounds than Han students. The central government has announced a policy of discounts or exemptions from tuition in order to reduce financial obstacles to minority enrollment,[44] but tuition is now significant for most majors, even at some universities that recruit a large number of minority students. At the Central Nationalities University (*Zhongyang minzu daxue*) in Beijing, at least 90 percent of the students must be minority group members and about 95 percent of students are. Tuition for the 1996-1997 school year stood at 1,400 yuan for journalism majors; 1,200 yuan for such majors as banking, trade and economics, taxation and law; and 1,000 yuan for the education management, foreign trade, secretarial and history majors. Only ethnic language & literature, linguistics and anthropology were tuition-exempt. Although the university provides 80 yuan per month subsidies to students, the tuition is still judged by minority area officials to be too high to be affordable to many minority students.[45]

At Southwest Nationalities University (*Xinan Minzu Daxue*) in Chengdu, where the quota for minority students is 80 percent and about 88 percent of students are minorities, tuition for 1996-1997 was 1,700 yuan for all majors except bilingual Han/Tibetan administration, which is 500 yuan. Teachers colleges (*shifan daxue*), however, remain tuition-exempt and a disproportionate percentage of minority students attend such institutions. Minority cohorts and preparatory classes at many universities outside the autonomous areas may also waive tuition.[46]

The effect of the introduction of tuition in Xinjiang is not atypical: a greater percentage of prospective students will be Han. As of 1995, about half of the students in the Xinjiang higher education system were self-supporting (*zifei* or *zikaoban*). Han applicants are mostly urban and therefore more likely to be able to pay the fees, which in 1995 amounted to about 2,000 yuan per year. Some 77 percent of Xinjiang's minority higher education students are from peasant families and, while many are government-supported and need only pay 900 yuan per year, this fee may be beyond the reach of some students.[47] In any case, the proportion of minority students in the region's institutions of higher education decreased from 56-60 percent in the early 1990s to 51.7 percent in 1994.[48] Officials in other areas where minorities tend to be poor also note that many minority families cannot bear the cost of their children going to universities. In Xishuangbanna Daizu Autonomous Prefecture, Yunnan, officials maintain that the cost of attending university discourages minority students from even enrolling in upper secondary schools, which are viewed as useless without the prospect of going on to university.[49]

At the same time that the proportion of undergraduate minority enrollment has stagnated or declined in the mid-1990s, there has been relatively little progress in heightening the number of minority students admitted to graduate study. In 1993, only 3 percent of graduate students were minorities.[50] This remains the case despite the fact that minority preferences for admission to China's relative small contingent of graduate students are also accorded. For example, at Inner Mongolia University, the minimum examination score for Han applicants to graduate studies in 1995 was 315, while for minorities the minimum could be dropped to as low as 280.[51]

One reason for the low percentage of minority graduate students is that many minority undergraduates intend to become cadres, rather than

Table 6.1. Minority Students at PRC Universities

Year	Number of Students	Percentage	Year	Number of Students	Percentage
1949-1950	1,285	0.93	1978-1979	37,378	3.66
1950-1951	2,117	1.36	1979-1980	42,944	3.75
1951-1952	2,948	1.52	1980-1981	51,220	4.00
1952-1953	5,536	2.56	1981-1982	53,739	4.66
1953-1954	7,999	3.10	1982-1983	59,630	4.94
1954-1955	8,883	3.04	1983-1984	69,633	5.0
1955-1956	14,159	3.47	1984-1985	94,095	5.3
1956-1957	16,101	3.62	1985-1986	99,468	5.3
1957-1958	22,421	3.39	1986-1987	118,735	6.1
1958-1959	28,163	3.47	1987-1988	125,422	6.1
1960-1961	29,921	3.16	1988-1989	131,599	6.3
1961-1962	28,729	3.45	1989-1990	137,948	6.6
1962-1963	24,825	3.31	1990-1991	141,767	6.9
1964-1965	21,870	3.24	1991-1992	152,858	7.0
1974-1975	30,607	6.11	1992-1993	163,224	6.4
1975-1976	36,578	6.48	1993-1994	178,000	6.4
1976-1977	34,460	5.51	1994-1995	160,000	5.7
1977-1978	36,030	4.21			

Table 6.1 (continued)

Sources: *Zhongguo minzu tongji nianjian* (1949-1994) (Chinese Minority Statistical Yearbook), pp. 244-245; Guo Sheng et al. *Xin zhongguo jiaoyu sishi nian* (Forty Years of Education in New China) (Fuzhou: Fujian jiaoyu chubanshe, 1989), p. 298; data from State Education Commission, Minority Education Department (personal communication, 1996); Liu Yingjie, ed., *Zhongguo jiaoyu dashidian, 1949-1990 (Book of Main Educational Events in China 1949-1990)*, Zhejiang Educational Press, 1993, p. 2,048; *Zhongguo shehui tongji ziliao*, pp. 170, 182. Zhang Yenming, op. cit., pp. 1,600, 233; He Jiangcheng, "China's Policy on Nationalities, in Dae-sook Suh and Edward Schultz, eds., *Koreans in China* (Honolulu: University of Hawaii, Center for Korean Studies, 1990), pp. 1-30; Chen Hongtao, *Zhongguo minzu jiaoyu fazhan tujing tantao (An Inquiry into the Way for China's Minority Education to Develop)* (Beijing: Zhongyang Minzu Xueyuan Chubanshe, 1990), pp. 363, 383; Guojia Jiaowei, *Zhongguo jiaoyu chengjiu (Achievements of Education in China, 1949-1983* (Beijing: Renmin Jiaoyu Chubanshe, 1984); p. 107; Ismail Amat, "Guanyu fazhan minzu jiaoyu de ruogan wenti" (Certain issues in developing minority education), Minzu yanjiu no. 3 (1991), pp. 1-5; Amat, "Growing Role of Minority Cadres, *China Today*, 41, no. 7, 1992; *Xinhua*, "China to Improve Ethnic Education, November 21, 1995, Item no. 1121097; *Xinhua*, "Ethnic Regions Experience Rapid Economic and Social Development, September 29, 1991, Item no. 00929117; *Zhongguo Xinwenshe*, "Number of minority nationality students increases," September 23, 1993, in *BBC/SWB*, September 25, 1993, FE/1803/G; Daniel Kwan, "Mao's Philosophy Set to Stay on Curriculum," *South China Morning Post*, December 22, 1995, p. 9; *Reuters*, "Sixty Percent of China HIV Carriers Under 30," October 25, 1995.

Table 6.2. Minority Faculty at PRC Universities

Year	Number of Students	Percentage	Year	Number of Students	Percentage
1953	623	1.85	1985	12,775	3.7
1957	1,941	2.8	1986	14,236	3.8
1965	3,311	2.4	1987	15,400	4.0
1976	3,020	1.8	1988	16,900	4.3
1978	5,876	2.8	1989	18,000	4.4
1979	7,150	3.0	1990	17,533	4.4
1980	7,808	3.2	1991	18,900	4.8
1981	8,364	3.4	1992	19,400	4.9
1982	9,150	3.2	1993	19,000	4.9
1983	10,791	3.6	1994	21,000	5.3
1984	10,841	3.4			

Sources: State Education Commission, Department of Ethnic Minority Education, personal communication; Guo Sheng, et al., *Xin zhongguo jiaoyu sishinian* (*Forty Years of Education in New China*) (Fuzhou: Fujian jiaoyu chubanshe 1989), p. 300; Liu Yingjie, *Zhongguo jiaoyu da shi dian, 1949-1990* (*Book of Great Events in Chinese Education, 1949-1990*) (Hangzhou: Zhejiang Education Press, 1993), Vol. 2, p. 2055; *Zhongguo shehui tongji ziliao* (*China's Social Statistics*) (Beijing: Zhongguo tongji chubanshe, 1993), pp. 146, 170, 179, 182; Liu Yingjie, p. 1,546.

academics, although the percentage of minority academics does surpass the proportion of minorities receiving graduate training (see Table 6.2). Indeed, preferential admissions have mainly been directed toward overcoming the problem of the dearth of educationally qualified minority cadres by turning out more bachelor's level graduates. Within this context, the affirmative action drive has had some effect.

In 1982, minorities had less than 70 percent of the overall educational level of the Han, and 60 percent fewer university graduates per 1,000 people.[52] There were 15.5 university students nationally per 10,000 people, but only 10.1 minority students. There were also large differences among minority groups. At the high end of the scale, the ethnic Korean average was 65.2, the Mongol 36.9, Man 21 and Hui 18.1. At the low end, the Tujia and Buyi had 2.4, the Miao 2.1, the Tibetans 1.5 and the Yi 1.3. By 1990, 1.42 percent of Han had attained a higher education and the highest rate of educational attainment among minority groups in China was 4.3 percent (of Koreans), while only .52 percent of Tibetans had reached that level. These figures represented a dramatic rise from those of 8 years earlier, when only 1.57 percent of Koreans and .117 percent of Tibetans had achieved higher educational levels. Altogether, the proportion of the minority population with a higher education increased by .74 percentage points in 1982-1990.[53]

PREFERENCES IN TAKING THE ENTRANCE EXAMINATION

Preferential admissions are facilitated by several factors. One element is to make the process of taking the national entrance examination easier for minority students by allowing them, in many cases, to use indigenous languages. Minority students who seek admission to the 12 nationalities institutes (*minzu daxue; minzu xueyuan*) and to some of the approximately 110 minority region universities and polytechnic schools can become *min kao min,* "minorities taking the examination in a minority language." Minority students who take the examination in Chinese are known as *min kao han* "minority students taking the examination in *Hanyu* (i.e., Chinese)," and these students will study in *Hanyu* as well. Many *min kao min* students do take some of their classes in their autonomous region's main minority language, but it is fully possible to take the entrance exam in an indigenous language and then enroll in classes taught solely in *Hanyu.*

Some 16-18 percent of minority students of higher education are enrolled in nationalities universities.[54] An indeterminate percentage, but surely the majority, of the remaining minority students attend minority region universities, rather than schools in the predominantly Han coastal areas, where some three-quarters of the prestigious "keypoint" (*zhongdian*) universities are located.[55] Many minority students thus may not be particularly disadvantaged by becoming *min kao min*. Students in the autonomous regions with a large number of non-*Hanyu* speakers, that is, Xinjiang, Inner Mongolia and Tibet, can easily become *min kao min*; students from minorities without written languages (Li, Bai, etc.) or who live in areas where the minority population is linguistically diverse (Yunnan, Guizhou, etc.) or consists overwhelmingly of *Hanyu*-speakers (Guangxi, Ningxia, etc.) generally cannot.

In addition to being able, in many cases, to take the national examination in their indigenous languages, minority students can apply to some minority area institutions that have their own entrance exams. These are arranged by the local government and given in the local language. Even a student who seeks to enter a university that uses *Hanyu* as the sole medium of instruction may have the opportunity to take the national exam in a minority language, if he or she takes it in a region such as Tibet, Xinjiang or Inner Mongolia. Alternatively, a student who graduates from a secondary school in which a minority language is used can take a "B Text" (*B juan*) entrance exam. Although the exam is in *Hanyu*, it is easier than the standard one.[56]

The amount of preferential advantage given to minority students to some extent depends on whether a student has chosen the *min kao min* or *min kao han* path. For example, in Kashgar prefecture, Xinjiang, the number of "bonus points" (*jia fen*) awarded to the few non-native *Hanyu*-speaker minority students who take the national examination as *min kao han* varies annually, but generally is in the 80-140 point range, considerably higher than the points awarded to *min kao min* students. Huizu applicants, who are native *Hanyu* speakers, are given bonus points as minorities, but usually only 10-20. In Liangshan, *min kao min* applicants to normal universities take both the national examination and a test of their Yi language skills. They receive 40 bonus points for being minorities and have the score on the Yi language exam (50 points possible) added to their score.[57]

PREFERENCES THROUGH QUOTAS

Minority students benefit from quotas that set aside a certain percentage of the spaces in classes for them. In Yunnan, every year about 24 percent of applicants to the province's universities are minority students, and 24 percent of admittees are minorities.[58] In Xinjiang, the minimum points needed by minority students on the national entrance examination to qualify to apply to universities is also a function of an ethnic quota system. At Xinjiang University, the region's comprehensive (*zonghe*) and keypoint institution, the exact percentage of minority admittees varies annually. However, roughly 55 percent of spaces in new classes are to be filled by minorities.[59]

The cutoff point (*fenshuxian*) for passing the national exam also varies annually in different parts of Xinjiang, in instances where the local government intervenes to fulfill its own needs for minority admitees. For example, in Kashgar prefecture, a list is submitted annually to mesh the needs of the prefecture's counties with admission quotas for universities where the prefecture's students can be *min kao min*. The quota will be specific to each county in the prefecture. For example, the Northwest Nationalities University (*Xibei minzu daxue*) accepts about one-third of applicants. Taking into account the needs of each of Kashgar's counties to staff work units with institute graduates and the number of minority students from each county who apply for admission, a determination is made of the cutoff point for minority applicants from Kashgar. It is understood that the "quotas" submitted by the work units are for reference only and not determinative, since many work units are over staffed. Local education authorities do nevertheless fix the actual number of admittees higher than the number desired by the work units.[60]

In Hainan, the provincial government announces quotas for minority students, and the cutoff point for qualifying to apply for universities may depend on whether the award of bonus points is sufficient to fill the quotas. For example, in Tongzha municipality, where the population is 60 percent minorities, 60 percent of students at Tongzha University must be minorities.[61] The mechanism to ensure minority enrollment is the award of 100 bonus points or more to minorities from Tongzha who apply to nationalities institutes and, generally, 20 points to those who apply to other institutions, with the precise number of points depending upon how many minority applicants there are in a given year.[62] In Liangshan, all students who apply to universities receive 20 bonus points as an area preference (*dichu youhui*). Minority students receive an additional 20 points. Minimum score requirements can be lowered further, however, in order to fulfill minority quotas if these bonus points prove to inadequate.[63]

It was decided in the early 1980s that 20 to 25 percent of higher education students in Inner Mongolia should be from minority groups, and the actual proportion initially rose to almost 25 percent. This was accomplished in part by giving local minority students 10 bonus points on the entrance examination if they were liberal arts majors or 15 points if they intended to major in the natural sciences. It was estimated that without these bonus points, not more than 2 percent of admittees would have been from minority backgrounds. By 1994-1995, Inner Mongolia's 19 institutions of higher education generally provided only a 5-10 point advantage to minority applicants, depending upon local circumstances. Minority students in higher education amounted to 20.5 percent of all university students, and the 16-17 university students per 10,000 people was higher than the national average. At the region's leading institution, the keypoint Inner Mongolia University, the minority student population was 33 percent in 1995, a stable ratio required by regulation.[64]

Inner Mongolia Normal University, the main training ground for teachers at schools in grasslands areas, had a 1995 student body that was 49 percent ethnic Mongol, with many in the *minzu ban* that were in place in 11 of the university's 16 departments. About 45 percent of the faculty were Mongol. These figures approach the 50 percent goals maintained by the university for both students and faculty. Minority applicants to the university's Mongolian or bilingual streams generally have their entrance examination minimums lowered by 10 points, while minorities who seek entry to the *Hanyu* stream have typically received an extra five points. In 1995, however, it was determined by the university authorities that no preferential policy was needed, as the minority quota could be filled with applicants who met the standard admission requirements.[65]

In most minority areas, however, the proportion of minority higher education students has been below (and sometimes well below) the proportion of minorities in the general population. In Ningxia, for example, minorities made up about 33 percent of the population in the late 1980s, but they constituted only 18 percent of students at the seven regional institutions of higher learning. This figure nevertheless represents a substantial rise from the 14.5 percent figure of 1983. A quota is now in place for Ningxia University, Ningxia Agricultural Institute and Ningxia Medical School, to recruit 20 percent of each school's incoming classes from the region's southern mountain areas and other districts where Hui minority people are concentrated.[66]

In Tibet, where it is claimed that as of 1995, 96.7 percent of the population were ethnic minorities,[67] it was decided in 1980 that at least 60 percent of new entrants to institutions of higher education be from minority groups.[68] By 1989, four such institutions were under the Tibet Autonomous Republic (TAR) government and, in 1995-1996, these were attended by more than 4,000 students. The student body of Tibet University (*Xizang daxue*; founded 1985), according to a 1995 official source, is over 90 percent minority students.[69] Western reporters have given figures of 72 percent in 1989 and two-thirds in 1995 for ethnic Tibetan enrollment at the university.[70] A 1995 study by leading Tibetologists in Beijing reported that, in 1992, 1,004 of 1,092 students enrolled at Tibet University, or 92 percent, were minorities.[71]

There are two other institutions of higher learning in the TAR, the Tibet Institute of Agriculture and Animal Husbandry (*Xizang nongmu xueyuan*, founded 1978) and the Tibetan Traditional Medical Institute (*Yao wang shan zang yi xueyuan*, founded 1989). Some 60 percent of students at the former and 100 percent of the students at the latter were ethnic Tibetans in the early 1990s.[72] The TAR government also supports a Tibet Institute of Nationalities (*Xizang minzu xueyuan*, founded 1957). It is located in Xianyang, Shaanxi, however, and had a 40 percent minority enrollment in 1993.[73]

In Guangxi, where 39 percent of the population was of minority ethnicity as of 1995, 39.6 percent of the region's higher education students were from minorities, up from 17.7 percent in 1978 and 34.9 percent in 1989. Three of 24 institutions of higher learning in Guangxi are devoted especially to training minorities.[74] In Yunnan, minority enrollment accounted for 24 percent of students in higher education in 1995. The stability of that percentage over recent years indicates that it represents a goal if not a quota. The figure, however, is an overall one: Yunnan University, the province's keypoint school, had a minority student body of only 8 percent in 1993.[75] This percentage may be the result of a quota. This is the case, for example, with Hainan University, the province's top institution, where only 5 percent of students need be from minority groups.[76]

In some minority areas, there is a further ethnically related desegregation of university applicants. This may or may not involve quotas. In Xinjiang, quotas *are* set in terms of numbers of minority students from given regions and ethnicities, so that there is some relationship between the size of at least the major ethnicities and number of admittees from those groups. The cutoff is fixed at the points attained by the lowest-scoring student within the ethnic cohort needed to fill a particular quota. At Xinjiang University, there is an effort to achieve a distribution among the region's 13 substantial ethnic groups that approximates their representation in the population.[77]

In Yunnan, in contrast, there is no strict relationship between the representation of particular minority groups in the province's population and the admission of students from these groups. Some minorities are very much over represented or underrepresented in this regard (see Table 6.3). For the 10 minority groups that are least represented in the university student population,[78] however, the province sponsors upper secondary school cohorts in each of its eight autonomous prefectures. These are set up in the best county-level high schools and the best teachers in the county are assigned to teach these *minzu ban*. It is hoped that 85 percent of the graduates of these cohorts will go to a university. To ensure that students can attend, an 80 yuan monthly subsidy is provided to each, with 60 yuan coming from the provincial minority affairs commission (*sheng minwei*) and 20 yuan from the local government.[79]

Some university applicants from minorities officially deemed "advanced" receive lesser preferences or even no preferences. Applicants from some small or assuredly primitive minority groups benefit from especially preferential admission policies. For example, in Yunnan, the authorities consider that certain minorities (Man, Bai, Hui, Naxi) are on a plane of development similar to the Han and accord them a lesser degree of preference than other ethnies among the province's 25 minority groups. On the other hand, Drung, Nu and Jinuo applicants, who are very few in number, are given sizable preferences, generally 30 points or more (see Appendix A).[80] In Inner Mongolia, greater latitude is given to Daurs than Mongols in terms of

Table 6.3. Minority University Admittees for Various Ethnic Groups (total = 5,200 per annum) in Relation to Population of Minority Groups in Yunnan Province

Ethnic Group	Population (in millions)	Admittees
Bai	1.39	1,400
Yi	1.05	1,200
Hani	1.20	120-130
Zhuang	1.04	200
Dai	1.06	200
Miao	1.00	50-60
Lahu, Jinbo	.3-.4	20-30
Hui, Meng, Man, Naxi	less than .3	more than 200 each

entrance exam scores, and even more eased requirements are allowed for Ewenkis. Oroqen applicants are admitted without taking the entrance examination if they are senior secondary school graduates.[81]

In some cases, the use of quotas benefits students from ethnic minorities that have an educational attainment higher than that of the Han. Although the Korean minority is much better educated on the whole than the Han and supplies a disproportionately high number of cadres in Yanbian Korean autonomous prefecture,[82] all higher educational institutions in China's three northeastern provinces and in Inner Mongolia have to enroll fixed quotas of Korean students.[83] At Yanbian University, the ratio of minority students, including Koreans, is fixed at 70 percent.[84]

PREFERENCES THROUGH "BONUS POINTS"

Almost all minority students who apply to universities benefit from the award of bonus points on the entrance exam. These may add up to an advantage already provided by admission with lowered scores for minority applicants. There is considerable variation, however, in the number of points awarded to minority students. Statements often appear in the literature published outside of China to the effect that minorities receive a bonus of anywhere from 10 to 30 points, depending on the field and university.[85] Specialists in China, however, acknowledge that the range of bonus points is much wider. One has stated that the extra points accorded minority status vary according to region and may be between 10 and 80 out of the 630-640 points typically needed to gain admission.[86] Another expert notes that the bonus points given to minorities can range from 20 to 100.[87]

The situation of bonus points for minority students, however, is even more complicated. The State Education Commission varies by province the minimum scores needed to qualify to apply to three categories of higher education: keypoint universities, ordinary (*putongde*) universities and higher technical schools, with a higher minimum always needed to apply to the first of these categories. The variation in the minimums by province is based on the relationship between the total quota for students taken from each province by the universities in each of these categories to the scores actually achieved by students from each province who apply to schools in each category. Thus, the cutoffs are reconfigured annually, although minimums for each province have a more or less predictable relationship to each other. For example, the minimum score for students from Jiangsu, where average scores tend to be relatively high, always greatly exceeds the minimum score for students from Guizhou, where average scores tend to be relatively low.

Alongside the small variation from year to year in how each province's students perform relative to students from other provinces, there is also a variation in the quotas for each province's sons and daughters who seek admission. These quotas are negotiated between the universities and central authorities. If the center decides to increase the number of students coming from a certain province, it can be expected to prevail upon universities to dip down further into the pool of applicants from that province, thereby effectively lowering the minimum score needed for students from that province.

For example, in 1989, the central authorities decided that they wanted to boost the enrollment of Xinjiang minorities studying at *neidi* universities (those not in the far western border areas) by effectively lowering the minimum score for all applicants from the region.[88] Such moves benefit not only minority students, but also some Han students who live-or successfully claim residence (*hukou*)-in minority areas. At the same time, they do also allow for an increase in minority admittees. To further fine-tune the mix, the authorities may also vary the number of bonus points given to *min kao han* and *min kao min* students, and even vary the points according to whether students are from a particular part of a minority area, for example, southern Xinjiang or northern Xinjiang.[89]

The minimum score needed to apply also varies according to whether the student's prospective major is in the sciences (*li ke*) or liberal arts (*wen ke*), there being a different examination for applicants to these two fields. Moreover, incoming university classes have to be balanced by sex, with institutions attempting to select 50 percent males and 50 percent females in the social sciences and 80 percent males and 20 percent females in science and technology. The sexual quota system in social sciences, incidentally, is effectively a preference for males, who are accepted with much lower scores than females.[90]

Besides lowering minimum scores for areas with significant minority populations, the number of bonus points for Han and minority students may be varied within a province. In Hainan, the number of bonus points accorded minority students may change radically from year to year, depending on how large the gap is between the actual scores of minority and Han students. If the gap is small, then only 40-50 bonus points may be awarded, but if the gap is large, 100 points are possible.[91]

Variations in bonus points can also be found within individual universities, although these generally reflect the cumulative variation among and within provinces. There are exceptions in response to central policy decisions, however. For example, at Central Nationalities University, bonus points usually vary from 5 to 80 points, "depending on the students backgrounds."[92] In *min kao han* students (students who take the exam through Chinese) who came to that university from Xinjiang in 1990, however, were accepted after receiving a 100 point advantage and were aware that earlier cohorts had received an even larger number of bonus points. At the same time, in response to another policy stance, the bonus points awarded to the university's applicants have steadily decreased over the years.[93] Minority students have been encouraged to "engage in self-strengthening" (*ziqiang*), so that the award of bonus points based on minority status will eventually not be needed.[94]

The top national universities present another variant with regard to preferential admissions. The minority student bodies at these schools generally hover around the national average. For example, in 1993, 6 percent of Beijing University and 5 percent of Lanzhou University students were minority students.[95] The number of bonus points awarded varies with the ethnicity of the applicant. Those from relatively highly educated minorities may receive only a 5 to 10 point advantage; those from generally less educated ethnicities will receive more points. Whether all the points that minority students are accorded by their native places are honored in the admissions process of top universities is another matter. Top schools, after all, are the places of choice for many minority students, as they are for Han students, and these universities can afford to be highly selective. Given the fierce competition for places in top PRC universities, however, even an advantage of one or two points often makes a difference.

The top schools take a considerable number of students from particularly sensitive minority regions, but whether there are any special quotas in this regard is unclear. During the 1994-1995 academic year, about 800 Tibetans were studying at universities outside the TAR, many of them at keypoint schools.[96] A large share of these students are products of the *neidi* Tibetan boarding secondary school system, whose graduates on average have scored over 100 points higher on the national entrance examination than examinees who did their studies in Tibet.[97] In 1991, 745 of 1,600 students who took the entrance exams in the TAR were minorities. Some 350 were admitted to study at *neidi* universities, in part because of lowered minimum scores.[98] Without lowering admission standards, the enrollment levels of Tibetan undergraduates would only amount to 50-70 percent of what is actually attained.[99]

Further preferences may be given to students from frontier, mountainous and pastoral regions. At Lanzhou University, for example, the minimum score needed by minorities from these areas is lowered by 25 percent. Minority applicants from these remote areas who apply to nationalities institutes, such as the Yunnan Institute for Nationalities and the Southwest University for Nationalities, also have their minimums lowered by an additional 10-40 points. Han students who apply from remote areas may also benefit. At Northwest University for Nationalities in 1993, the minimum score for Han applicants from remote areas was lowered by 50 points, while the minimum for minority students was lowered by 105 points.[100] In Yunnan, Han border area students (*bianjiang hanzu*), who are often from very poor backgrounds, receive 15-20 bonus points.[101] In Hainan, Han students from minority areas are, in effect, deemed to be from remote regions and accorded 10 bonus points in applying to universities within the province. Minority students from the same areas automatically receive at least 10 additional bonus points.[102]

As a result of lowered minimums and bonus points, minority students are, in many circumstances, admitted with much lower scores on average than Han admittees. For example, in 1986, Han students admitted to Xinjiang universities averaged 435 points in science and 440 points in liberal arts; minorities averaged 300 points in science and 245 points in liberal arts. In 1987, Han students from Xinjiang admitted to keypoint universities averaged 470 points in science and 445 points in liberal arts; minority students averaged 313 and 269 points, respectively.[103] In the late 1980s, when a score of about 400 was the average minimum needed for admission in Han areas, Han students in Tibet needed 250 points for admission in Tibet; Tibetans could be admitted in Tibet with about 190 (210 for liberal arts; 170 for sciences).[104] In Qinghai province, "the required grades for college enrollment have been lowered for minority middle school students, while a certain number of them will be directly sent to college without taking the annual national examination."[105]

Despite the gap in the actual scores of Han and minority students, there is no evidence that retention rates or graduation rates for minority students are any lower than for Han students. The apparent reasons for the absence of a gap include the very high retention and graduation rates of Chinese undergraduates in general, the high concentration of minority students in minority area universities and nationalities institutes and the provision of supports, particularly preparatory classes and minority cohorts, for many minority students.

CONCLUSION: THE FUTURE OF PREFERENTIAL ADMISSIONS

Preferential admissions for ethnic minorities are among the most valued of "positive discrimination" measures accorded minorities in China. From 1982 to 1990, some 14 million minority people who previously had elected to be classified as Han had themselves reclassified as minority group members. While the Han population rose about 10 percent in the period 1982-1990, the minority population increased by more than 35 percent. About half that increase was attributable to the large-scale changes of ethnic status (*minzu chengfen*). Five million people had applications to change ethnic status pending in 1990 when the process of reindentification was basically brought to a close by government fiat.[106] Many Han-some claiming a minority progenitor who lived hundreds of years earlier-have applied for minority status in order to make themselves eligible, *inter alia*, to enter a university with lower scores.[107] Other Han with no minority background have purchased forged papers identifying themselves as minorities, in many cases to give their offspring an advantage in applying to universities.[108] It has been observed, for example, by minority scholars in Yunnan, that the main reason for people to seek ethnic reclassification in their province has been the availability of preferences in university admissions.

There is anecdotal evidence that preferential admissions for minorities are not only envied, but also resented by many Han. Calls emanating from elite circles to scrap preferential admissions on grounds of quality control and equity date back at least to the mid-1980s.[109] In some places, such as rural Yunnan, these are echoed because the Han there are only slightly better off than their impoverished minority neighbors.[110] While special admissions to higher education institutes for minorities are more resented than any other preferential policy in China save family planning preferences,[111] the resentment is not strong enough to have been publicly manifested by any social group. This is the case despite the fact that grievances of all kinds have, from time to time (e.g., during the Cultural Revolution and in 1989) been very publicly aired in China. It has been claimed that the lack of tensions over preferential admissions in China can be traced to the relatively small difference in social rewards, particularly in income, made by a university degree.[112]

While this explanation is likely valid, there are additional reasons why preferential admissions have not produced obvious tensions. First, preferential admissions are, in the main, practiced by minority institutions. While many predominantly Han institutions of higher learning engage in "affirmative action" as well, the bulk of preferential admissions are out of sight and out of mind, scarcely, if at all, diminishing the opportunities of Han students. In fact, it can be argued that preferential admissions for minorities have actually benefited some Han. These include not only Han with residence in certain minority areas who may get bonus points on this account, but also the Han who have benefited from the rapid expansion of higher education in China that was, in some measure, impelled by the need to accommodate an increasingly larger number of minority students. The majority of the population of the minority areas, after all, is Han.

Second, the PRC state has long maintained that minority people were sharply oppressed in the "old society and by elites that were, in the main, Han. Moreover, the state has seen to the establishment, in most of the minority regions of the country, of the autonomous areas. Just as in the former Soviet Union the Slavic majority of the country regarded the Central Asian "republics" of the USSR as under the rightful control of their eponymous minorities,[113] many Chinese have probably come to accept that having an autonomous government must and, indeed, should result in some special rights for at least the predominant minority of that area governed.

As social differentiation accelerates and economic reform matures in China, so that fewer opportunities will be available to those with a relatively low level of education, university training will likely become more closely correlated with economic success. Already the blossoming of the "socialist market economy" since the early 1990s has impacted preferential policies in a number of negative ways. For example, hiring quotas for minority workers, which exist on paper in some minority areas, have been rendered unenforceable by the National Industrial Law (*qiye fa*),[114] and minority officials complain that:

> [W]ith the transition from planned economy to market economy, some preferential policies designed for minority areas have been weakened or made defunct. On the other hand, some new policies, do not take enough consideration of the special situations of minority areas [and] our development has been restrained by these policies.[115]

Preferential admissions may then become a subject for debate, at least in elite circles, despite the fact that the absolute number of places in universities will probably continue to expand very rapidly in China. That debate, should it occur, will be a major diversion from the more critical questions caused by the reforms, for example, the growth of illiteracy occurring both among minority and Han populations due to the demand by rural parents for the labor-power of their children.[116]

It may also be queried whether support for the continuation of preferential policies will be sustained in the face of the ever-rising crescendo of Chinese nationalism. Despite the disclaimers of the PRC state, the latter is firmly Han-centered, with the Han seen as the epitome of the *Zhonghua minzu* (Chinese ethnie) that is being forged from an amalgamation of the Han and minorities. As misplaced efforts to "Sinicize" (*Hanhua*) the origins and identity of minority people go forward,[117] it is not inconceivable that elite voices against emphasizing the "special characteristics" of minorities, including the continued need for autonomy and preferences, will be raised in the early twenty-first century, as they were during the Cultural Revolution.

The other side of the coin of resentment toward preferential policies is that some minority people regard such policies with reservations. In the main, minority intellectuals criticize preferential policies as too weak; for example, they help get one into the university, but do not provide sufficient support for promotion once one has graduated and entered a work unit.[118] It has also been reported, however, that some minority students who were admitted under a quota system and had a hard time with their studies felt inferior to their Han classmates. This was the case, for example, at Xinjiang Teacher's University (*Xinjiang shifan daxue*) in the mid-to-late 1980s, and the reaction has been even more pronounced at national universities.[119] Some minority students may therefore view preferential admissions as a double-edged sword, which improves their lot, but at a psychological cost. At this point, most minority students seem quite willing to pay that price, but if attacks on preferences of the kind found elsewhere emerge in China, the burden on minority students can expect to increase exponentially.

At this point, economic reforms and other factors have not reversed the policy of preferential admissions. In absolute terms, the number of minority graduates has even slowly increased from year to year. The type of training provided to minorities, moreover, has changed, so that an increasingly larger percentage qualify as technical and professional cadres upon graduation.

While preferential admissions have proven to be a success in creating minority educated elites, a number of problem areas can also be observed. The percentage of minority students still lags significantly behind that of minorities in the general population of China. There is a recent trend for minority graduates to seek economic opportunities outside their relatively poor native regions. If the effort to produce trained elites for the minority regions is dissipated because of the mobility that attends the reform, then support for preferential admissions may wane among national and minority leaders, both of whom want to see highly trained minority people mainly working in the minority areas.

Preferential admissions, by their very nature, emphasize the ethnicity of the benefited students. Moreover, the grouping of minority students in preparatory classes and separate cohorts at the national universities promotes, rather than diminishes, ethnic consciousness.[120] This process contributes to occasional manifestations of ethnic consciousness among Uygur, Tibetan and some other minority students in cities like Beijing and Shanghai.[121] While these events may sometimes be worrisome to the PRC leadership, it does seem that most beneficiaries of preferential admissions will become the professionally competent and politically loyal graduates that the policy is designed to produce. This alone may guarantee the future of preferential admissions in China.

Appendix A: "Minority Students Special Consideration Policies"

(*Minzu sheng zhaogu zhengce*), handwritten document, Yunnan Education Commission, September 9, 1994.

1. In border counties and counties that practice border policies, minority applicants will receive 30 bonus points. Han applicants born and raised in those areas and Han who have gone there with their parents for at least ten years will have 20 bonus points, but if the latter have gone to high schools in (*neidi*), they will have 10 points subtracted from their bonus points.

2. The 20+ minorities in Yunnan, except the Bai, Hui, Naxi, Yi and Zhuang, will receive 10 bonus points, even if they live in *neidi* [but apply to universities in Yunnan].

3. Yi and Zhuang applicants who live in *neidi* will receive 10 bonus points if they have a rural *hukou* (household registration).

4. Minority applicants from high, cold, and poor mountainous areas, so designated by provincial or prefectural governments, and children of teachers who have worked for more than 10 years in these areas and continue to work there, will receive 10 [additional] bonus points.

5. Bai, Hui and Naxi applicants from *neidi* and Yi and Zhuang urban applicants from *neidi* and minorities who enter Yunnan

198 _Barry Sautman_

from outside, will have priority for admission if they have the same qualifications [as Han students].

NOTES

1. See, for example, _Xinhua,_ "Li Peng Joins Xinjiang Deputies in Discussion, March 3, 1988, Item No. 03300224.

2. June Dreyer, _China's Political System: Modernization and Tradition_ (New York: Paragon House, 1993), pp. 364-365; Fang Youyan, "Shinian laide shaoshu minzu jiaoyu" ("Education of the National Minorities in the Past Ten Years,) in _Guangming Ribao,_ September 21, 1959, in _Current Background,_ No. 609 (1959), pp. 10-12.

3. On Soviet preferential policies, see Nancy Lubin, _Labour and Nationality in Soviet Central Asia: an Uneasy Compromise_ (London: Macmillan 1984); Rasma Karklins, "Ethnic Politics and Access to Higher Education: the Soviet Case," in _Comparative Politics_ Vol. 16, No.3 (April 1984), pp. 277-294; William Mandel, _Soviet But Not Russian: the Other Peoples of the Soviet Union_ (Edmonton: Alberta, 1985), pp. 312-215; Zvi Gittelman, "The Politics of Ethnicity and Affirmative Action in the Soviet Union," in Michael Wyzan (ed.), _The Political Economy of Ethnic Discrimination and Affirmative Action_ (New York: Praeger, 1990), pp. 167-196.

4. _Reuters,_ "China population growth slows survey," February 14, 1996.

5. There are 159 minority autonomous areas (5 regions [_qu_], 30 prefectures [_zhou_] and 124 counties [_xian_]), plus more than 1,500 ethnic townships and villages (_minzu xiang, minzu cun_). In 1990, minorities were 46 percent of the population of the autonomous areas. One-third of the areas had a population in which the titular minority exceeded half the population. _Zhongguo minzu jingji (China's Ethnic Nationality Economy)_ (Beijing: Zhongguo tongji chubanshe, 1994), pp. 222-224; Xinhua, "Li Peng Addresses National Conference on Nationalities Affairs," February 20, 1990, in _BBC/SWB,_ February 22, 1990, FE/00695/B2.

6. _Zhongguo Xinwenshe,_ "China's Policy to Boost Ethnic Minority Regions," January 25, 1996, in _BBC/SWB,_ January 26, 1996, EE/D2520/G; _Xinhua,_ "Economic Development of Areas Inhabited by Minority Nationalities," April 5, 1991, Item No. 0405034; interview with Ordos district ethnic affairs officials, Dongsheng, Inner Mongolia, April 11, 1995; Ma Rong, "Economic Patterns, Migration and Ethnic Relationships in the Tibet

Autonomous Region, China," in Calvin Goldscheider, ed., *Population, Ethnicity and Nation Building* (Boulder Co: Westview, 1995), pp. 37-75.

7. Hua Juxian, "Stability Reigns Supreme," in *Beijing Review* (November 7-13, 1994), pp. 18-21.

8. Wu Zongjin, "Lun wo guo minzu guanxi fazhi tedian" ("On the Special Characteristics of the Legal System with Regard to Our Country's Ethnic Relations") in *Minzu Yanjiu*, No. 1, (1992), pp. 8-14.

9. Of 311 poor counties listed by China's State Council, 143 are mainly inhabited by minorities. See *Xinhua*, "Educational Help Offered to Poor Areas," January 14, 1996, Item No. 011498. In 1992, when the population of autonomous areas was 13.6 percent of China's total, the Gross Value of Industrial and Agricultural Output (GOV) of the autonomies was only 6.7 percent of national GOV. Huang Gongxue, *Dangdai Zhongguo minzu renwu* (*Contemporary China's Ethnic Tasks*) (Beijing: Dangdai Zhongguo, 1993), pp. 221-223.

10. Cheung Lai-kuen, "Income Chasm Still Yawns Wide," in *South China Morning Post*, February 8, 1996, p. 6.

11. For a case study, see Barry Sautman, "The Impact of 'Affirmative Action' on Han-Minority Relations: the Case of Xinjiang," paper presented at the Association of Asian Studies annual meeting, April 1995, Honolulu, Hawaii.

12. Interview with head of Yunnan Minority Affairs Committee Policy Institute (*Minwei zhengce yanjiusuo*), Kunming, July 9, 1996.

13. See Chen Kuiyuan, "Study the Marxist Nationality Theory and Correctly Understand the Nationality Issues in the New Period," in *Shijian* (*Hohhot*), No. 10 (October 1, 1991), pp. 4-17, in *Joint Publications Research Service* (*JPRS*)-CAR-92-0021 (April 16, 1992), pp. 1-11.

14. Interview with Zhao Shu, Deputy Director of the Beijing Ethnic Affairs Commission (*minwei*), interview, June 23, 1995.

15. Interview with Li Zi, Director of the Institute of Ethnic Studies of the Xinjiang Academy of Social Sciences (*Xinjiang shehui kexue yuan, minzu yanjiusuo*), June 27, 1995.

16. Deng Bihai, "Cursory Discussion of Specific Characteristics of Family Planning in Minority Nationality Areas," in *Zhongguo renkou bao* (China Population Report), December 22, 1989, p. 3, in *JPSR*-CAR-90-13 (February 21, 1990), pp. 58-60.

17. Interview with Hainan provincial People's Congress Standing Committee Minority Work Committee (*Renda changwei hui minzu gongzuo weiyuan hui*), Haikou, July 8, 1996.

18. Interview, with an official of the Yunnan Minority Affairs Commission Economic Office (*Minwei jingjichu*), Kunming, July 10, 1996.

19. Interview with officials of the Systems Reform Commission (*tigaiwei*), Zhaojue County, Liangshan Yi Autonomous Prefecture, Sichuan, Zhaojue, July 24, 1996.

20. For a history of minority enrollment policies through the end of the 1980s, see Zhang Yenming, *Effects of Policy Changes on College Enrolment of Minority Students in China, 1949-1989* (Unpublished Ed.D. dissertation, Harvard University, 1991).

21. *Xinhua*, "China Makes Progress in Work on Minority Nationalities," October 3, 1991, Item No. 1003079.

22. Interview with officials of the provincial Ethnic Affairs Commission (*Sheng minwei*) and Islamic Association (*Yisilanjiao xiehui*), Jiangsu Province, Nanjing, June 9, 1995.

23. *Xinhua*, "State Council Issues Circular on Minority Autonomy Law," January 12, 1992, Item No. 00112091. See also Ismail Amat, "Guanyu fazhan minzu jiao yu de ruogan wenti" ("Certain Issues in Developing Minority Education") in *Minzu Yanjiu (Nationality Research)*, No. 3 (May 10, 1991), pp. 1-5.

24. "Law of the People's Republic of China on Regional National Autonomy," in Legislative Affairs Commission, National People's Congress, *The Laws of the People's Republic of China, 1983-1986*, Vol. 2 (Beijing: Foreign Language Press, 1987), pp. 87-101.

25. Reproduced by *Xinhua*, October 22, 1993, in *BBC/SWB*, November 9, 1993, FE/1841/S1.

26. Article 9 of the "Regulation on Work with Urban National Minorities" (*Xinhua*, October 22, 1993, in *BBC/SWB*, November 9, 1993, Fe/1841/S1) states that "City people's governments should take appropriate measures to run ethnic classes efficiently at all levels and to give preferential treatment to ethnic classes in the allocation of funds and teachers."

27. Interview with Institute of Nationalities, Office of Research on the National Economy *(Hainan sheng minzu yanjiusuo, guojia jingji yanjiuchu)*, Tongzha, Hainan, July 5, 1996.

28. Anonymous, "Qieshi gaohao shaoshu minzu diqu dang de jianshe-qingzhu zhongguo gongchandang chengli qishi zhounian" ("Conscientiously Build the Ethnic Minority Areas—Celebrate the 70th Anniversary of the Founding of the Communist Party of China") in *Minzu Tuanjie (Ethnic Unity)*, No. 7 (November 10, 1991), p. 3. For statistics on the numbers of students in *minzu ban*, by school and by province of origin, for each year 1980-1990, see

Liu Yingjie, *Zhongguo jiaoyu da shi dian, 1949-1990 (Book of Great Events in Chinese Education, 1949-1990)*, Vol. 2 (Hangzhou: Zhejiang jiaoyu chubanshe, 1993), p. 2094.

29. Gerard Postiglione, "China's National Minorities and Educational Changes," in *Journal of Contemporary Asia*, Vol. 22, No. 1 (1992), p. 39; Zhang, *Effects of Policy Changes on College Enrolment of Minority Students in China*, pp. 183-186.

30. *Xinhua*, "Friendly Tie Between Han and Tibetans Cemented by Education Funding for Tibetans in China," 31 July 1994, in *BBC/SWB*, 2 August 1994, FE/2063/G; Ba Jiankun, "Xinjiang minzu jiaoyu de zongjie" ("Overview of Minority Education in Xinjiang"), in *Zhongguo jiaoyu nianjian 1988 (Chinese Education Yearbook, 1988)* (Beijing: Renmin jiaoyu chubanshe, 1989), pp. 302-310.

31. *Xinhua*, "Xinjiang Develops Higher Education for Ethnic Minorities," November 11, 1991, Item No. 1111072; *Xinhua*, "Strives to Raise Educational Level," January 27, 1993, Item No. 0127407.

32. Interview with Dong Xieming, head of Minority Education Office of the Provincial Education Commission of Hainan (*Hainan sheng jiaowei minzu jiaoyu chu*), Haikou, July 1, 1996.

33. *Xinhua*, "Education for Ethnic Minorities in Xinjiang Blossoming," September 12, 1995; in *BBC/SWB*, September 18, 1995, EE/DD2411/G.

34. *Zhongguo jiaoyu nianjian, 1949-1981 (Yearbook of Chinese Education, 1949-1981)* (Beijing: Renmin jiaoyu chubanshe, 1984), pp. 413.

35. *Xinhua*, "China Develops Minority Nationality Preparatory Courses," November 23, 1989, Item No. 1123065.

36. *Xinhua*, "National Conference on Pre-college Education for Minorities," June 17, 1996; in *BBC/SWB*, June 18, 1996.

37. Ningxia huizu zizhiqu jiaoyu ting (Ningxia Hui Autonomous Region Education Department), "Zai tansuo he gaige zhong fazhan minzu jiaoyu" ("Develop Minority Education in the Process of Exploration and Reform") in *Minzu jiaoyu yanjiu*, No. 1 (1990), pp. 7-11.

38. Edward Kormondy, "Observations on Minority Education, Cultural Preservation and Economic Development in China," in *Compare*, 25, No. 2 (1995), pp. 161-178.

39. Interview with Liangshan Ethnic Affairs Commission (*minwei*), Xichang, Sichuan, July 25, 1996.

40. On the restoration of entrance examinations in 1977, see Xiaodong Niu, *Policy Education and Inequalities in Communist China Since 1949* (Lanham: University Press of America, 1992), Chap. 5; Suzanne Pepper,

China's Universities (Ann Arbor: University of Michigan, Center for Chinese Studies, 1984).

41. Robert Klitgaard, *Elitism and Meritocracy in Developing Countries* (Baltimore: Johns Hopkins University Press, 1986), p. 26.

42. The number and percentage of minority university students during many of the years from 1950 to 1994 are set out in Table 7.1. The 1994-1995 figure is based on the most conservative estimate of the number of PRC university students (2.8 million) and the announced figure of 160,000 minority students in China in 1995.

43. Chan Wai-Fong, "Confucius Revival May Hinder Higher Learning," in *South China Morning Post*, June 2, 1994, p. 10.

44. *Reuters*, "China to Aid Poor Students Through University," April 19, 1995.

45. Interview with officials of the Ethnic Minority Secondary School (*Minzu zhongxue*) of Liangshan Yi Autonomous Prefecture, Xichang, Sichuan, July 25, 1996.

46. *Yunnan Jiaosheng Bao*, May 26, 1996.

47. Interviews with officials of the Xinjiang Education Commission (*jiaowei*) (June 28, 1995) and Xinjiang Ethnic Affairs Commission (minwei) (June 30, 1995).

48. *Xinhua*, "Xinjiang Boosts Education for Ethnic Minorities," 10 July 1994, in *FBIS*-CHI-94-133 (12, July 1994), p. 86; *Xinhua*, "Ethnic Education, 28, May 1994, Item No. 0528130; *Xinhua*, "More Ethnic Minority Students Receive Education in Xinjiang," Item No. 0120097; *Xinhua*, "Xinjiang Develops Education for Ethnic Minorities," November 11, 1991, Item No. 1111072; *Xinhua*, "Xinjiang Stresses Education for Ethnic Minorities," August 15, 1991, Item No. 0815044; *Xinhua*, "Minority Education Thrives in Xinjiang," November 9, 1989, Item No. 1109138; *Xinhua*, "Ethnic Discrimination Claim Rejected," September 3, 1988, in *BBC/SWB*, September 9, 1988, FE/0252/B2/1.

49. Interviews with officers of the People's Political Consultative Conference (*zhengxie*) of Xishuangbanna, Jinghong, April 21 and 24, 1996.

50. Kormondy, "Observations on Minority Education, Cultural Preservation and Economic Development in China," p. 162.

51. Interview with Inner Mongolia University officials, Hohhot, April 9, 1995.

52. Minority university graduates per 10,000 persons equalled 62 percent of the nationwide figure. *Zhongguo shehui tongji ziliao* (*China Social Statistical Data*) (Beijing: Zhongguo tongji chubanshe, 1987), pp. 170, 182.

53. Postiglione, "China's National Minorities and Educational Changes, p. 39; Deng Bihai, "Cursory discussion of specific characteristics of family planning in minority nationality areas," *Zhongguo Renkou Bao,* December 22, 1989, p. 3 in JPRS-CAR-90-13 (February 21, 1990), pp. 58-60; Zhang Tianlu, "Population Development and Changes of China's Minority Nationalities," in Li Chengrui (ed.), *A Census of One Billion* (Beijing: Population Census Office, State Statistical Bureau, 1987), p. 449; Zhang Tianlu, *Zhongguo minzu renkoude yanjiang (Lectures on China's Minority Population)* (Beijing: Haiyang chubanshe, 1993), pp. 131, 199; Yan Ruxian, "Marriage, Family and Social Progress of China's Minority Nationalities," in Chien Chiao and Nicholas Tapp (eds.), *Ethnicity and Ethnic Groups in China* (Hong Kong: Chinese University of Hong Kong, New Asia College 1989), pp. 79-88; Yang Chunpu, "Wo guo shaoshu minzu wenhua shuiping da fudu tigao" ("Our country's minorities cultural level is being raised to a great extent.") *Minzu,* No. 6 (1994), pp. 40-41; Amat, "Guanyu fazhan minzu jiaoyu de ruogan wenti" ("Certain issues in developing minority education"), *Minzu yanjiu,* No. 3 (1991), pp. 1-5.

54. *Xinhua,* "Guangxi Boosts Education in Minority Areas," July 14, 1994, Item No. 0714089; *Zhongguo jiaoyu shiye tongji nianjian (China Educational Statistics Yearbook, 1994)* (Beijing: Guojia jiaoyu weiyuanhui jihua jianshe ce, 1994), pp. 140-141. For an overview of the nationalities institutes at the end of the 1980s, see Liu Yingjie, *Zhongguo jiaoyu da shidian,* pp. 2,079-2,081; Gregory Guldin, "The Organization of Minority Studies in China," in *China Exchange News* Vol. 19, No. 2 (Summer 1991), pp. 7-12.

55. Kormondy, "Observations on Minority Education, Cultural Preservation and Economic Development in China," p. 166. For example, the vast majority of the 952 tertiary students of higher education from Xinjiang's Turpan prefecture who matriculated in 1994 did so at Turpan institutions; almost all the rest attended other Xinjiang institutions. Interview with a Turpan bureau chief, Turpan, July 2, 1995. Lijiang Naxi district produces about 40 minority university students each year, but only a few go to keypoint universities and most go to nationalities institutes. Interview with official, Lijiang District Education Commission (*Lijiang dichu jiaowei*), Lijiang, July 17, 1996. Every year, seven to eight Zhaojue County students go on to higher education, but most go to Southwest Nationalities University (*Xinan minzu daxue*) or the Central Nationalities University. Interview with head of Zhaojue County Personnel Office (*Zhaojue xian renshichu*), Zhaojue, July 24, 1996).

56. Postiglione, "China's National Minorities and Educational Changes," p. 38; Bernard Olivier, *The Implementation of China's Nationality Policy in the*

Northeastern Provinces (San Francisco: Mellen Research University Press 1993), p. 242; Jan-Ingvar Lofstedt, "Education for National Minorities in China: an Overview," in *Journal of Negro Education* Vol. 36, No. 3 (1987), pp. 326-337; Zhang, *Effects of Policy Changes on College Enrolment of Minority Students in China*, p. 208.

57.   Interview, Liangshan Ethnic Affairs Commission. Minorities are 45.4 percent of the Liangshan population.

58.   Interview, official of the Yunnan Minority Education Commission (*sheng minzu jiaowei*), Kunming, July 10, 1996.

59.   Interviews with Prof. Wang Jiamin and Uyghur students, Central Nationalities University, June 12, 1995; interview with a Turpan prefecture bureau chief, July 8, 1995. Because the cohort of college-level technical students *(dazhuan xuesheng)* at the university is disproportionally Han, overall Han and minority students each make up a half-share of the student body.

60.   Interview with an official of the Kashgar Prefecture Ethnic Affairs Commission, Ethnic and Religions Office (*Minwei de minzu zongjiaochu*), July 7, 1995.

61.   Interview with Dong Xueming.

62.   Interview with officials of the Tongzha Li Autonomous Prefecture Education and Science Office (*Tongzha Lizu zizhi jiaoyu yu kexue ju*), Tongzha, July 3, 1996.

63.   Interview with Liangshan Ethnic Affairs Commission.

64.   Interview Mongolian intellectuals, *Hohhot*, April 9, 1995; interview with Rong Shen, vice director of the Inner Mongolian Ethnic Affairs Commission (minwei), *Hohhot*, April 13, 1995.

65.   Interview with officials of Inner Mongolia Normal University (*Neimenggu shifan daxue*), *Hohhot*, April 13, 1995.

66.   Ningxia huizu zizhiqu jiaoyu ting (Ningxia Hui Autonomous Region Education Bureau), "Zai tansu he gaige zhong fazhan minzu jiaoyu" ("Develop Minority Education in the Process of Exploration and Reform"), in *Minzu jiaoyu yanjiu (Nationality Education Research)*, No. 1 (1990), pp. 7-11.

67.   *Xinhua*, "China Denies Population Transfer into Tibet," in *World Tibet Network*, August 13, 1996.

68.   Zhang, *Effects of Policy Changes on College Enrolment of Minority Students in China*, p. 209.

69.   *Xinhua*, "Tibetan Language Used Widely in Tibetan Classrooms," July 11, 1995, Item No. 071182. Supporters of the exiled Dalai Lama dispute this figure. See Anders Andersen, "Development and Cultural Destruction in Tibet," paper presented at the conference on "Social Development: a Tibetan

Experience, 9 March 1995, Copenhagen, in *WTN*, 19 March 1995, which asserts that 55 percent of the students enrolled at Tibet University are Chinese. Pema Thinley, "Educating Chinese at Tibetan Expense," in *Tibetan Bulletin* (July-August, 1996), pp. 11-14, states that "[I]n all the faculties of modern subjects in the Tibet University, Lhasa, the overwhelming majority of the students are Chinese

70. Teresa Poole, "Paying the Price of Progress," in *Independent*, August 20, 1995, p. 10; Guy Dinmore, "Tibetans and Chinese Divided by Gulf of Misunderstanding," in *Reuters*, October 31, 1989.

71. Gele and Jin Xisheng (eds.), *Zhongguo guo qingkuang shu—bai xian shi jing shehui diaocha: Lasa juan* (*Book on China's National Condition: Economic and Social Investigation of One Hundred Counties and Cities: Lhasa Volume*) (Beijing: Zhongguo da baikequanshu chuban she, 1995), p. 544.

72. Yang Chaoji, "Lizu xizang shiji; cujin goajiao gaige" ("Gain a Foothold in Tibet's Reality; Promote the Reform and Development of Higher Education"), in *Zhongguo gaodeng jiaoyu* (October 1993), pp. 18-19; *Xinhua*, "Tibet Trains More Agricultural Managers, Technicians," May 8, 1990, Item No. 0508168; *Xinhua*, "College of Tibetan Medicine Set Up in Lhasa," September 3, 1989, in *BBC/SWB*, September 6,. 1989, FE/0554/B2/1. The Agricultural and Animal Husbandry Institute for 1990 was 80 percent minority, if higher technical students (*dazhuan xuesheng*), middle technical students (*zhongzhuan xuesheng*) training students (*peixun xuesheng*), and preparatory students (*jichu yuke xuesheng*) were added to the figure for regular university students (*benke xuesheng*). See Yin Zhang, ed., *Zhongguo gaodeng yuanxiao* (*China's Higher Institutes and Schools*) (Beijing: Kexue puji chubanshe, 1991), p. 384.

73. Kormondy, "Observations on Minority Education, Cultural Preservation and Economic Development in China," p. 162. Applying the ethnic proportions stated above to total enrollment figures for 1993 derived from *Zhongguo jiaoyu shiye tongji nianjian, 1994*, pp. 114-141, the overall percentage of minorities at Tibetan higher learning institutions depends on whether the Nationalities Institute is within that category. If so, minority enrollment in the four schools is 64 percent. See also *Zhongguo jiaoyu nianjian, 1993* (China Education Year Book 1993), (Beijing: Renmin jiaoyu chubanshe, 1993), p. 691 (in 1992, the overall percentage for the four institutions was 63.4). If the Nationalities Institute is excluded from the calculations, the overall enrollment in the three institutions in Tibet is actually about 78 percent.

74. *Xinhua*, "Minorities Benefit from Autonomous Administration," June 8, 1995, Item No. 068097; *Xinhua*, "Higher Education for Minorities Thrives in Guangxi," November 30, 1989, Item No. 1109138.

75. *Xinhua*, "Success in Ethnic Minority Education in Yunnan," August 24, 1995; in *BBC/SWB*, August 30, 1995, EE/D2395/G; Kormondy, "Observations, p. 162.

76. Interview with officials of the Tongzha Municipal Ethnic and Religious Affairs Office (*Tongzhashi minzu zongjiao shiwu ju*), Tongzha, July 3, 1996.

77. Interview with Wang Jiamin,; Dong Xueming,; Lu Yumin and Zhang Tianlu.

78. Miao, Yao, Lahu, Jingpo, Wa, Lisu, Hani, Dai, De'ang and Bulang.

79. Interview with Yunnan Education Commission officials.

80. Interview with faculty of Yunnan Ethnic Studies Institute (*minzu yanjiusuo*), Kunming, April 19, 1996.

81. Interview with Inner Mongolia Normal University officials.

82. In the late 1980s, Koreans had a university attendance rate twice that of the national average. They were 41 percent of the Yanbian population, but 52 percent of its cadres. See Jin Shangzhen, "The Rights of Minority Nationalities in China: the Case of the Yanbian Korean Autonomous Prefecture," in Dae-Sook Suh and Edward J. Schultz, (eds.) *Koreans in China* (University of Hawaii, Center for Korean Studies, October 1990), pp. 44-78; Chae-Jin Lee, *China's Korean Minority: the Politics of Ethnic Education* (Boulder Co: Westview, 1986).

83. Olivier, *The Implementation of China's Nationality Policy in the Northwestern Provinces*, p. 245; Postiglione, "China's National Minorities and Educational Changes," p. 32.

84. Yoshiharu Hara, "University Hones Skills of Chinese-Koreans," in *Daily Yomiuri*, February 24, 1995.

85. Klitgaard, *Elitism and Meritocracy in Developing Countries*, p. 164, fn. 64; Arthur Rosett, "Legal Structures for Special Treatment of Minorities in the People's Republic of China," in *Notre Dame Law Review*, Vol. 66, No. 5 (1991), pp. 1,503-1,529 (10 points); Kormondy, "Observations," p. 167 (20 points); Julia Kwong and Hong Xiao, "Educational Equality Among China's Minorities," in *Comparative Education*, Vol. 25, No. 2 (1989), pp. 229-243 (30 points); Guldin, "The Organization of Minority Studies in China" (10 points, at nationalities institutes); Zhang, *Effects of Policy Changes on College Enrolment of Minority Students in China*, p. 186 (up to 30 points).

86. Interview with Lu Yumin, State Minority Affairs Commission, Education Department Deputy Office Chief, June 30, 1994. The figure of 630-640 points needed to gain admission doubtless refers to keypoint universities. The maximum number of points on the 1996 entrance examination was 750.

87. Interview with Zhang Tianlu, specialist in minority population studies, Beijing Economics University, June 22, 1995.

88. *Xinhua*, "Minority Education Thrives in Xinjiang," November 9, 1989, Item No. 1109138.

89. Interview with a Kirgiz student, Central Nationalities University, June 12, 1995.

90. Hu Xiaolu, *The Role of the Entrance Examination in the Admissions System to Higher Education in the People's Republic of China*, Unpublished Masters thesis, Kent State University, 1986.

91. Interview with Dong Xueming, director of Hainan Provincial Ethnic Minority Education Department (Hainansheng minzu jiaoyu chu); Interview with officials of the Hainan Province Institute of Nationalities, Office of Research in the National Economy (*Hainan sheng minzu yanjiusuo, guojia jingji yanjiu chu*), Tongzha, July 5, 1996. It is estimated that only two or three minority students per year from Sanya, the second largest Hainan city, would be admitted to keypoint universities without "special consideration" (*zaogu*). Interview with officials of Sanya, Hainan People's Congress Standing Committee (*renda changwei*), CCP party committee (dangwei), Ethnic Affairs and Religion Office (*min zong chu*), July 5, 1996.

92. Pat Harper, "GSU, China School Share Similar Goal," in *Chicago Tribune*, July 26, 1995, p. 3.

93. Interview with Kirgiz student; Interview with Wang Jiamin, professor at Zhongyang minzu daxue (Central University of Nationalities).

94. Interview with Lu Yumin.

95. Kormondy, "Observations on Minority Education, Cultural Preservation and Economic Development in China," pp. 162, 166, 168.

96. *Xinhua*, "More Tibetan Students Studying in China," July 30, 1995 in *BBC/SWB*, August 1, 1995, FE/2370G.

97. *Xinhua*, "Tibetan Schools in the Interior Region Successful," April 22, 1995, Item No. 04023.

98. Xinhua, "Tibetan Students Depart for Universities in China," September 11, 1995; in *BBC/SWB*, September 14, 1991, FE/1177/B2/1. The Department of Information and International Relations of the Tibetan exile administration in "The State of Education in Tibet Today," in *World Tibet Network*, November 18, 1994, argues that the majority of seats at universities

inside and outside the TAR that are reserved for Tibetan students actually "go to Chinese students due only to the fact that they have finished school from the TAR or due to their Tibet residency registration."

99.   Postiglione, "China's National Minorities and Educational Changes," citing Wang Tiezhi, "Shaoshu minzu jiaoyu de xin fazhan" ("New Developments in Ethnic Minority Education") in *Jiaoyu jianxun*, No. 4 (1987), p. 40.

100.   Zhang, *Effects of Policy Changes on College Enrolment of Minority Students in China*, p. 211; Kormondy, "Observations on Minority Education, Cultural Preservation and Economic Development in China," pp. 167-168.

101.   Interview with faculty of Yunnan Ethnic Studies Institute.

102.   Interview with Sanya Education Office (*Jiaoyuju*) officials, July 6, 1996; interview with Hainan People's Congress officials.

103.   Cheng Shengykuan, "Xinjiang jiaoyude fangxiang zhanxian shi tigao zhiliang" ("Raising Quality is the Orientation of the Front in Xinjiang's Education") in *Xinjiang shehui kexue (Xinjiang Social Sciences)*, No. 3 (June 15, 1989), pp. 38-62; Ba Jiankun, "Xinjiang minzu jiaoyu de zongjie" ("A summary of Ethnic Minority Education in Xinjiang"), *Zhongguo jiaoyu nianjian 1988* , (Beijing: renmin jiaoyu chubanshe, 1989), p. 304.

104.   Zhou Runnian, "Chuyi xizang minzu jiaoyu fazhang" ("My Humble Opinion on Developing Minority Education in Tibet") in *Minzu yanjiu*, No. 5 (1988), pp. 46-55; Panchen Lama, "Address to the TAR Standing Committee Meeting of the National People's Congress held in Peking" on 28 March 1987, in Pierre Donnet, *Tibet: Survival in Question* (London: Zed, 1993), p. 231.

105.   *Xinhua*, "Adopts Favorable Policy for Education of Minorities," February 16, 1993, Item No. 0216145.

106.   I. Johnson, "Manchu Culture Makes a Tentative Comeback in a More Tolerant China," in *Baltimore Sun*, June 4, 1995, p. 4A; Sheila Tefft, "Ethnicity Stirs in a China Set on Wealth," in *Christian Science Monitor*, June 27, 1995, p. 1; June Dreyer, "Ethnic Minorities in Mainland China Under Teng Hsiao-p'ing," in Bih-Jaw Lin and James Myers, eds., *Forces for Change in Contemporary China* (Columbia SC: University of South Carolina Press, 1993), p. 255.

107.   *Xinhua*, "Minorities Regaining Preferential Status," March 10, 1988 in *FBIS*-CHI-088-047, March 11, 1988, pp. 19-20; "Five Million Seek New Ethnic Identity," in *Beijing Review*, Vol. 33, No. 35 (August 27, 1990), pp. 10-11; *Reuters*, "Ten Million Chinese Opt to Be Minorities," May 17, 1993; G. Crothall, "Millions Claim Ethnic Roots," in *South China Morning Post*, May 18, 1993, p. 10; Dreyer, *China's Political System*, p. 255. In Tongzha, many

hundreds of people have changed from Han to minorities. Family histories are checked for three generations in such cases. Interview with Religious Affairs Office official, Tongzha, July 4, 1996.

108. *Reuters*, "China Officials Nabbed in False Papers Scam," November 16, 1995.

109. Ye Zhaoyang, "Colleges Enrolling Students Throughout the Country Should Set a Unified Test Score Requirement and Practice Unified Admissions," in *Gaodeng Jiaoyu Zhanxian*, No. 10 (1984), pp. 13-14.

110. Interview with Yunnan Ethnic Studies Institute official.

111. See Dru Gladney, *Muslim Chinese: Ethnic Nationalism in People's Republic of China* (Cambridge: Harvard, 1991), p. 164; Arthur Rosett, "Legal Structures for Special Treatment of minorities in the People's Republic of China," in *Notre Dame Law Review*, Vol. 66 No. 5 (1991), p. 1,522; C. Wren, "China's Policies on the Size of Families is Extended to Include Minorities," in *New York Times*, February 10, 1983, p. A16; Bill Brugger and Stephen Reglar, *Politics, Economy and Society in Contemporary China* (Stanford: Stanford University Press, 1994), p. 337.

112. Pyong Gap Min, "A Comparison of the Korean Minorities in China and Japan," in *International Migration Review*, Vol.26, No. 1 (1990), pp. 4-21.

113. See Gittelman Z., "The Politics of Ethnicity and Affirmative Actions in the Soviet Union," in M. Wyzan, ed., *The Political Economy of Ethnic Discrimination and Affirmative Action*, (New York: Praeger, 1990), pp. 167-196.

114. Interview with a Turpan bureau chief.

115. Commission of Minority Affairs of Dali Prefecture (*Dali zhou minwei*), "Guanyu qingqiu gei wo zhou minzu youhui zhaogu zhengce de wenti" ("On the Question of Requesting Preferential Special Consideration for Our Minority Area") mimeographed document, dated July 4, 1996.

116. Interview with Zhang Tianlu, demographer at Beijing Economics University.

117. See Barry Sautman, "Myths of Descent, Racial Nationalism and Ethnic Minorities in the People's Republic of China," in Frank Dikotter (ed.), *The Construction of Racial Identities in China and Japan* (Hong Kong: Hong Kong University Press, 1997).

118. Interviews with Mongolian intellectuals, Hohhot, April 9, 1995.

119. Zhang, *Effects of Policy Changes on College Enrolment of Minority Students in China*, p. 238.

120. Interview with Tibetan students of Central Nationalities University, June 13, 1995.

121.   For example, it was reported that in January 1992, 200 Tibetans at the Central Nationalities Institute boycotted classes because Jiang Ping, the vice chair of the United Front Work Department, termed the idea of rich cultural traditions in Tibet "useless nonsense. *Tibet Press Watch*, "Tibetans Stage Boycott," Vol. 4, No. 1 (1992), p. 2.

PART III

Case Studies of Ethnic Minority Schooling
The Yi, Tai, Tibetan and Monguor

CHAPTER 7

Folk Theories of Success
Where Han Aren't Always the Best[1]
Stevan Harrell and *Ma Erzi (Mgebbu Lunze)*

MINORITY PEOPLES AND EDUCATIONAL SUCCESS

For a long time, scholarship in the anthropology of education has concentrated on the problem of the failure of minority students in various countries, especially the United States, to match the educational achievements of students from dominant majority peoples.[2] Quite early on, anthropologists evolved what Ogbu calls the "cultural discontinuity hypothesis," the idea that linguistic and cultural barriers or differences between the home environment of a minority group and the school environment in which they were expected to learn the values of the dominant majority were the primary cause of poor performance by minorities. Minority children either spoke different languages or non-standard varieties, or they came from cultural backgrounds with different approaches to, and perhaps less emphasis on, educational attainments than were prevalent in the cultures of the majority.[3]

This simple explanation, however, founders on the fact that different minorities have differential rates of success and some, in fact, such as recent Asian immigrants to the United States, tend to overcome linguistic and/or cultural barriers to perform in school as well as or sometimes even better than members of the dominant majority.[4] In addition, several studies have shown that among Native American populations in the American Southwest, individuals whose linguistic and cultural backgrounds are more different from the majority language and culture often do better than their partly acculturated peers.[5] The question then becomes one of why certain minorities, or certain members of particular minority, perform well in spite of what seem like great handicaps, while others fail to overcome these handicaps.

One way to approach the differential school success of different minorities is by considering the ways in which members of minority groups perceive the cultural differences and linguistic differences between their family and community environments and those of the school. Ogbu maintains that immigrant minorities, who are in some sense voluntarily in their minority status, see cultural and linguistic differences as surmountable barriers to success in the host society, and thus strive to do well in school. By contrast, involuntary minorities (such as former slaves or displaced native peoples), see cultural and linguistic differences, as well as resistance to dominant ideologies[6] as necessary components of an oppositional identity that needs to be maintained in the face of pressure to assimilate on unequal terms, and thus resist the demands of the school system. Ogbu sums up this approach in his idea of "folk theory of success." If members of a minority hold the view that they can use education to achieve success, they devise ways to surmount the obstacles posed by cultural divergences. If they hold, on the other hand, that the education system will merely strip them of their own culture or identity without giving them equal opportunity in the wider society, they will respond with resistance. Most involuntary minorities hold the oppositional folk theory of success, while most voluntary minorities hold the positive theory.[7]

Minorities in the People's Republic of China clearly suffer educationally in comparison with the majority Han. As a general rule, members of minority groups are less likely to enter school , are likely to do less well while there, and tend to drop out of school sooner than members of the Han Chinese majority. For example, in Liangshan prefecture, where this research was carried out, only 49.6 percent of minority (mostly Yi) children entered school in the mid-1980s;[8] the approximate same percentage held for all three minority prefectures of Sichuan Province, of which Liangshan is one: about 70 percent of all school-age children entered school, but this was true for only 50 percent of the minority (mostly Yi and Tibetan) children.[9]

Given these clear indications of inferior educational performance, it is not surprising that the national minorities of China superficially resemble the "involuntary minorities" described by Ogbu. They are certainly not immigrants, having inhabited their current territories or nearby regions for hundreds or thousands of years. Their traditional territories, ruled either loosely or not at all by previous Imperial Chinese governments, have recently come under direct rule of the Chinese Communist Party and its subordinate organization, the People's Government, and many minority intellectuals consider maintaining an identity separate from the majority Han to be an important goal for their own ethnic groups.

Chinese educational policy and scholarship explain poor minority school performance in terms of a rather different version of the cultural divergence hypothesis. Chinese ethnology classifies all peoples according to their position on a universal social-evolutionary scale from primitive, through slave, to feudal, capitalist and socialist. At the time of the establishment of the People's Republic in 1949, most of the minorities were considered to be lagging behind the majority Han on this scale. And despite over 40 years of equal opportunity and even affirmative action, universal consensus says that the Han are still ahead. This universal scale of social progress applies to education as to every other aspect of life, so it is no surprise that minorities lag behind in academic achievement, as they also lag behind in income, public health and other areas. Compounding this lagging in social progress are linguistic differences, adding up to the statistics on lower school enrollment and completion rates.

At the same time, there are documented exceptions to the poor school performance of minorities in general. The Korean minority, located mostly in Yanbian Korean Autonomous Prefecture in Jilin Province in the northeast, is well-known in this regard: in 1985, it was claimed that over 95 percent of children in Yanbian started junior middle school, and about 50 percent went on to upper middle school; these percentages applied both to Koreans, who formed 40 percent of the prefecture's population, and to Han, who composed much of the remaining 60 percent.[10] The Manchu, descendants of the rulers of the last imperial dynasty, and now scattered around northern and northeastern China, also do well in school. At least 18 of China's ethnic minorities have a higher literacy rate than the majority Han groups. These are also ethnic minorities studying at universities overseas; for example, at least eight members of China's minority ethnic groups who are graduate students in literature and social sciences at the University of Washington.

It appears, in fact, that the situation in China is more complex than can be explained simply by comparing one minority as a whole with another minority or with the Han majority. As with the Chinese in the Netherlands studied by Pieke, there are differential strategies, differential theories of success, and different rates of educational achievement within particular minority groups in any society.[11] In order to understand the aggregate statistics, then, we need to be anthropological, and investigate minorities in the schools in particular local social contexts.

When we do undertake such a local, ethnographically based examination of educational success and failure, we find that the notion of folk theories of success is very useful in understanding some of the observed variations. At the same time, neither the American explanation in terms of voluntary versus involuntary minorities, nor the Chinese explanation in terms of differential progress through the stages of history really accounts for the differences among folk theories of success. What is left out of both of these explanations is the nature of the educational project undertaken by modern governments, and the effect this project has on the folk theories. In secular schools everywhere, the manifest purpose of education is to instill certain skills, such as literacy, numeracy and logical reasoning, as well as certain kinds of scientific and cultural knowledge. But as Keyes writes of Thai schools, the acquisition of such skills "pales beside . . . [the role] which [the school] has played in preparing villagers to accept a subordinate position in the centralized bureaucratic world of the . . . nation state."[12] In other words, the most important mission of the school in any modern nation is to prepare children for the obligations of citizenship. But the obligations of citizenship can be perceived either as an opportunity to be seized or as a burden to be resisted. In cases where pupils and their parents perceive participation in the state as a platform for personal advancement, they will be motivated to work hard in school, and will fairly easily overcome linguistic and cultural barriers and do well. In other cases, where they perceive that the state is merely trying to subordinate them without affording them opportunities for participation, they may well develop a culture of resistance that includes, among other things, perfunctory school performance, dropping out or disruptive behavior.[13] In other words, it is not so much whether people perceive their own group's lower educational level as a barrier to be surmounted or a component of a valued ethnic identity,[14] but rather the degree to which they accept the proffered citizenship and its advantages as a worthwhile goal. They can want to preserve an ethnic identity and still opt into the school project, because they think this will allow their own group to flourish, even as citizens of a multiethnic state. Foley, in his study of Mexican-Americans in south Texas, for example, found "many middle-class Mexicanos expressing their ethnicity oppositionally *and* succeeding in school and life."[15]

Whether or not people perceive citizenship as a worthwhile goal, we submit, depends on a variety of factors. In our case, set out below, the evidence of whether people from the same background-relatives, affines, fellow-villagers-have turned schooling into upward mobility as citizens seems an extremely important factor. If objective barriers to advancement exist for members of a particular minority, and if there are segregation, quotas, job ceilings, other forms of discrimination, upward mobility will be seen as blocked. If there are no objective and discrete barriers, then individual and local experience become much more salient, and pockets of people within a minority group may cultivate education as a mobility strategy,[16] a particular tactic they as a group use to promote the position of their individual members and by doing so perhaps raise the group's position in society as a whole.

It is important to realize that when members of a minority group adopt education as a mobility strategy, they are not necessarily validating the educational project of making them into compliant and subordinate citizens. The number of revolutionaries and anti-colonial activists produced by colonial mission and secular schools testifies to the possibility of schooling for citizenship being turned into schooling for resistance.[17] Members of dominated groups may pursue schooling as a means to localistic ends rather than, or in addition to, pursuing the proffered benefits of citizenship. Nevertheless, even the perceived opportunity to use schooling for localistic ends is still a perceived opportunity, and can lead to the use of schooling as a kind of heterodox or oppositional mobility strategy.

Perceived chances of occupational mobility, orthodox or heterodox, can account for differential folk theories of success, but our study has led us to be wary of total rejection of the cultural distance or discontinuity explanation. We find, in particular, that in order to explain gender differences in school attendance and success, we need to rely on some version of the theory of cultural distance: in the schools studied in our project, girls' participation in state schools depends on cultural distance in a way that boys' does not.

We have examined the perception of citizenship as an avenue to social mobility, as well as the effect of evidence of the existence of role models on folk theories of success, in an attempt to explain differential educational success among different ethnic groups in Baiwu *zhen* (township), Yanyuan County, Sichuan, a community where both statistics and popular perception agree that certain groups of minority students are better students and have greater success than others, and that many of these groups of minority students consistently do better in school than their Han neighbors.

THE CHINESE EDUCATIONAL SYSTEM

In China, since the establishment of the People's Republic in 1949, and especially since the inception of the Reform program in the late 1970s, education has been characterized by attempts to universalize at least elementary education, a uniform national curriculum heavily laden with a nationalist message, achievement measured almost entirely by examinations, and a teaching style that emphasizes the authority of the teacher and demands great amounts of memorization and recitation. It is in the context of this kind of schooling that parents and students form their perceptions of the utility of education.

Universal education has been a dream of Chinese reformers all through the twentieth century, but only during the communist period has education become near-universal at even the elementary level. This is partly due to the enormous strain on resources caused by trying to build nearly a million schools, but it is also due to the perception among many peasants, Han and minority alike, that schooling is minimally useful for a life of agriculture. After decollectivization in the late 1970s and early 1980s, education became even more of a drain on family resources, and in many areas rural elementary enrollments declined.[18] Nevertheless, education is available in all but the remotest sections of the country, and probably 80 to 90 percent of children at least begin elementary school.[19]

Quality of schools of course varies widely in China, but in striking contrast to U.S. schools, where curricula are locally determined, there are standard textbooks and curricula for all subjects at all levels. Textbooks are referred to as *tongbian jiaocai* (uniformly written teaching materials) and are written and even printed centrally; meaning, for example, that any school offering eighth-grade mathematics offers the same version of eighth-grade mathematics. Despite wide variation in geography, agriculture, climate, language and local customs, the same subjects are taught with the same materials almost all over the country.[20]

These materials and the message they seek to convey are, like textbooks everywhere, very nationalistic in content. Everything from history texts to story problems in mathematics books carries the message that China is a unified, glorious country with a great past, an uncertain but improving present and a bright future. As in almost all modern countries, students in China are being introduced through school to what Keyes has called a "national world," in contrast to the local world of the village and the kinship network.[21]

This message is conveyed in a system driven almost entirely by the idea that completion of a certain number of years of schooling, and passing of the requisite examinations, is not only the primary goal of education but the standard by which it is to be measured. Students are typically evaluated at all levels, primarily by examinations coming at the end of each year of study; the content of the examinations is almost entirely contained in the Unified Teaching Materials. Thus, students who have completed a certain number of years of study are considered to have reached what is called a certain "cultural level" (*wenhua chengdu*), and are reported as such in official statistics, social scientific surveys and ordinary conversation.

It is no surprise, then, that the teaching style in Chinese schools involves recitation, a considerable amount of shaming, but more than anything else the assumption that the teacher tells the single and absolute truth and the job of the students is to impart the knowledge conveyed by the teacher. We have visited a number of rural and urban schools in many provinces of China and found this kind of assumption to be nearly universal, and wholly universal in rural schools.[22]

Such a uniform, universalistic system of educational policy and practice runs into problems in areas inhabited by national minorities, who are linguistically and culturally different from the majority Han, and universally known to be "backward" (*luohou*) in many ways, not only economically but in terms of their "cultural level," or number of years of schooling. From the beginning of the People's Republic, the nationally unified system of education has been modified somewhat in light of the very different reality in minority areas.[23]

Modifications made in minority areas have been significant, but they have not altered the basic nature and goals of the system. Modifications include some instruction in local languages, some special classes and sometimes separate secondary schools for members of minorities and a system of separate institutions of higher education-the Nationalities Institutes (*minzu xueyuan*)-which exist primarily to train members of minority groups as teachers and bureaucrats to serve in their native areas. In addition, since the inception of the reforms members of minority groups have been given affirmative action consideration in admission to colleges and universities (see Chapter 6).

Despite these modifications in the system of minority education (*minzu jiaoyu*), most schools in minority areas or schools expressly for minorities do not deviate from the unified national model in their basic philosophy, methods, or, except for classes in minority languages and literature, their content. The degree to which minority students have classes in their own language varies greatly, from none at all to almost the whole curriculum, but probably the most typical pattern in the southwest is to have the majority of the curriculum in Chinese, with their own language as a second language; in remote areas, this distribution is sometimes reversed. In addition, minorities may get special consideration in examinations for entrance to higher schools with somewhat lower test scores. But the basic methods are the same everywhere: they are educated by rote learning, evaluated by testing and inculcated with the same nationalist ideology as their Han counterparts.

Minority students who have to learn the same material as Han children in what to them is a second language are of course at something of a disadvantage, but as Ogbu and others have commented, in certain circumstances it is a disadvantage that they can overcome if they perceive the rewards as great enough. [24] Another, perhaps greater disadvantage is the perception on the part of almost all Han and many minority educators that minorities really are "backward," that they need more help and have farther to go to succeed than do Han students. When, however, minority educators take charge of local education in a minority area, as has happened in some of the primarily Yi schools in areas such as Yanyuan County, described later in this chapter, education becomes a way in which minority teachers help minority students to succeed in the national system, and in the process sometimes help to moderate or even destroy for these students any idea that minorities might be inherently inferior, and in some cases even subvert the nationalist message of universal participation in a countrywide project of development through education. In such cases, minority students and parents may perceive schooling not only as a means for individual social mobility, but also as a way of subverting what they perceive as unfair or repressive Han rule over their own minority areas. This kind of strategy should bolster the folk theory that education is a possible avenue toward social mobility.

EDUCATION IN BAIWU TOWNSHIP

Baiwu *zhen* (township) is located in the northeast of Yanyuan County Town, in the southwestern part of Liangshan Yi Autonomous Prefecture, in the southernmost portion of Sichuan Province. The township seat stands at an elevation of 2,600 meters (8,500 feet) on the windswept high plateau where most of Yanyuan's people live. It is too high to grow much rice, but just the right elevation for the commercial production of apples, which in a few years may begin to displace traditional cereal crops such as corn, potatoes, beans and buckwheat. Rainfall, about 900 millimeters per year, comes mostly during the summer; in wintertime it is cold and dry, with frost almost every night, ice on the streams in the morning, and biting winds in the afternoon and evening. Fruit trees stand bare-limbered in neat rows within pounded-earth walls; farmhouses, pounded of the same earth and in recent years almost all bearing tile roofs, blend almost imperceptibly into the landscape. The fields, plowed in the fall, sit bare and lifeless; only the spindly pines which have regrown on the hillsides since deforestation of the 1950s through 1970s, along with the dormant rhododendrons and hollies growing underneath them, lend any green to the stark landscape. More distant slopes, not recently logged over, grow tall conifers and denser undergrowth, reminiscent of the time before progress and socialism were defined in terms of cutting down trees. Occasionally it clouds up and snows; usually nighttime snow is gone from the lowlands by early afternoon, but it lingers on the mountain slopes above 9,000 feet.

The town of Baiwu, which is the administrative center for Baiwu *zhen* and for Yuanbao *qu* (district) of which Baiwu is a part, is basically a one-street affair. Reached by a good dirt road in a little under an hour from Yanyuan County Town, the main street, paved for a few hundred meters, is lined with little shops selling liquor, batteries and other household sundries; one-table pool halls; a couple of small hotels; government offices of various sorts; and two video parlors showing mostly Hong Kong martial-arts movies. At market time every morning, stallkeepers set up shop, selling bright-colored yarn for Yi girls to wrap their headdresses, yardage goods, cigarettes and other sundries. A few offer fresh fruit, but no vegetables are available in the wintertime. Occasionally someone will have slaughtered a yak or a hog, and shoppers crowd around haggling over meat. More people stroll than shop-Yi girls in their horizontally striped pleated skirts, appliqué blouses and finely embroidered headdresses, and at this time of year probably wrapped in heavy felt capes; Yi boys in similar capes worn over store-bought pants, shirts and heavy sweaters; Zang (Tibetan) and Naxi women in black turbans, frog-closing vests over long-sleeved blouses, and long, black pleated skirts with colorful aprons; Han people of both sexes in practical Chinese clothes, some of them nicely tailored, but devoid of ornamentation.

Government cadres and teachers live in apartments attached to their offices; electricity was connected to the houses and offices on the street in January 1993, and by 1996 had reached the traditional mud-walled houses where everyone else lived. The population of Baiwu *zhen* was 10,532 in the 1990 national census; the people are distributed in the town itself and in the seven administrative villages (*cun*) that made up the township. *Per capita* income for 1992 was reported as 240 yuan per person, well below the government's official poverty line of 300, but informal estimates raised this to somewhere between 300 and 400 yuan, still only about half of the national rural average, and well under even the Liangshan prefectural average of 385 yuan in 1990.

Of the total population of Baiwu *zhen* in 1990, 9734, or 92.4 percent, were of the Yi, or Nuosu ethnic group. The Yi are relative newcomers to Yanyuan, having migrated west from their homeland in the heart of the Liangshan range to the east of the Anning River beginning in the late eighteenth century. By the early twentieth century they had displaced the Naze and Prmi people who were the previous inhabitants of the area, and their aristocratic clans controlled much of the land on the plains around Baiwu.

The Yi[25] are a farming and herding people who speak a Tibeto-Burman language that is fairly closely related to Burmese. At least since the Ming dynasty (1368-1644), their priests and a few others have been literate in their indigenous syllabic script, used primarily for writing ritual texts. They were organized into several exogamous social strata—*nzymo* or "royalty," the families of local rulers; aristocrats or *nuohxe* (called Black Yi in Chinese) commoners or *qunuo* (White Yi), lower-caste retainers or *ngajie* and slaves (*gaxy* in Nuosu; *wazi* in Chinese). Both the ruling aristocrats and their commoner retainers were organized into exogamous patricians; localized segments of these clans are still important social and political groups today, and one Nuosu meeting another will inevitably ask the other's clan. (Asking the stratum directly would be impolite, but everyone knows which clans are aristocrats and which are commoners.) Either aristocrats or commoners could hold slaves, who were usually descendants of captured Han or other ethnic groups, or commoner Nuosu enslaved for bad debts. Yi think of themselves as honest, hot-tempered and warlike, and lovers of song, dance and poetry.

The population of Baiwu in the 1990 census also included members of three nominally Buddhist peoples: 359 Zang,[26] 58 Meng and 46 Naxi, making a total of 463, or 4.3 percent of the total population. They were concentrated in the town of Baiwu and in a few rather distant villages. These are peoples who were largely displaced by the Nuosu between the eighteenth and the early twentieth centuries. These peoples, all speakers of Tibeto-Burman languages, were converted from their aboriginal religions to Tibetan Buddhism between the thirteenth and the eighteenth centuries, and in the 1990s were culturally identical and intermarried regularly, though they still preserved some of their original languages. Finally, the Baiwu area in 1990 was home to 307 Han people, about half of them teachers and cadres living in their work units, and the rest local peasants. The latter were a motley lot, most of them descended from people who came to the area from the 1920s through the 1940s, either from the Han areas near the county seat or as refugees of some sort from other counties. Several are the descendants of freed slaves; at least one set of related families descends from a school teacher that was brought in as a household servant by a Yi aristocrat leader in the 1940s.

There are eight elementary schools and one middle school in Baiwu. Each administrative village (*cun*) has a village school (*cunxiao*), with from three to five grades. In Baiwu Town there is a complete elementary school (*wanxiao*) that goes from first to sixth grade, and where students from outlying villages must come if they are to go beyond the third, fourth or fifth grade where their own local school stops. For some children, it can be a two-hour walk each way. Even to get to their local school, students may have to walk as much as 45 minutes or an hour-children from the hamlet of Yangjuan, for example, attend school in town, and it takes about 40 minutes for an adult to walk at a moderate pace. All told, in 1993 there were about 800 students in the eight elementary schools, probably about half of the elementary-age population.

Instruction in all the schools in 1993 took place primarily in the Han Chinese language. Since over 90 percent of the incoming students are Yi, most of whom speak no Han at home, especially if they come from villages, teachers have to "practice bilingual education" (*shixing shuangyu jiaoyu*), which consists of using spoken Nuosu to explain the Han-language lessons, for at least the first few years. Eventually, Yi students learn enough Han to facilitate its use as the primary classroom language, except for the classes in Yi written language and literature, which begin in the third grade and are optional for Han and Buddhist students. Still, the junior author of this chapter remembers not really feeling comfortable speaking Han until the upper elementary grades.

The first elementary school, in Baiwu town, was founded in 1956, at the time when the Communist Party began the programs known as the Democratic Reforms, in which local power holders and local economic arrangements were replaced through a basically peaceful but nevertheless coercive process. Yang Zipuo, who until 1996 was Yanyuan County party secretary, and Dong Yunfa, first magistrate and then party secretary of neighboring Muli County, were in the first class. But this was not the first school in Baiwu. In about 1942, one of the important men of the local aristocratic Luohxo clan went to Xichang, the large Han city in the Anning River valley, because the local Yi leaders realized that they would not be able to maintain a semi-independent existence forever, so they wanted their sons and perhaps their daughters to get a Chinese-language education. In Xichang, he met a 20-year-old Han man with the last name Wu, who did well in school but was not allowed by his stepmother to go beyond the fourth grade because the family could not pay his tuition. So he accepted the Luohxo clan's offer to come and be a teacher for Yi children in a private school financed by the clan. This school was open not only to the aristocrats of the Luohxo clan, but to the commoners of the Mgebbu and other clans (including the junior author's father), and also to some children (including at least one daughter) of the Zang and Naxi landowner families. It was in this school that many Yi men now in their sixties got a year or a few years of formal education, the only formal education available until the first school opened in 1956. The teacher is now reverently referred to as Wu *Xiansheng* ("Master"), and his widow and descendants still live in Baiwu.

There is also a secondary school in Baiwu, which was founded in 1970; the junior author of this article was a member of its second graduating class. It now has 150 students in the seventh, eighth, and ninth grades, one *ban* (a class that changes teachers but has all its classes together) for each grade. Students study Chinese language, mathematics, politics, history, geography, chemistry, physics, biology and personal hygiene, physical education, music and Yi language and literature. About 50 percent go on to senior high school in the county seat. Many graduates of the full elementary school in Baiwu do not go to Baiwu Middle School, which has fairly low prestige; if they can test in they go to middle school in one of the Han townships or in the county town itself, where the two most prestigious six-year middle schools are Yanyuan Middle School and the Nationalities Middle School.

All in all, Baiwu does not seem like the kind of place likely to produce very many scholars, and in fact, it has not. Fifty-seven percent of adult males and 93 percent of adult females were reported as illiterate in the 1990 census, and only 128 out of 6,570 people over 15 years of age, or 2 percent of the adult population, had as much as a high school education.[27] About 60 percent of elementary-age children are in school here, but many drop out after a few years. Of those who do graduate, almost all (80 to 90 percent) go on to junior middle school, but again many drop out of middle-school before finishing. Within Baiwu *zhen*, if any place might be an exception to this rather discouraging pattern of educational attachment, one would not expect it to be Yangjuan. Yangjuan is a village of 83 households located about a 40-minute walk, mostly on level roads, from Baiwu Town. Its original aristocratic lords of the Luohxo clan all moved away before or during the Democratic Reforms of the mid-1950s, leaving the principal clan of commoner retainers, the Mgebbu, as a majority in the village. Of the current households, 69 have a male or female head of the Mgebbu; the other 14 are former slaves of the Mgebbu or their descendants.

Yangjuan is an ordinary-seeming Yi settlement. Its mud-walled houses are arranged in no particular order, each family inhabiting two to five buildings within a walled compound. Inside the houses, there is little furniture; people sleep on wooden beds but do all their other indoor activity seated on straw mats or felt capes arranged around the hearth in the middle of the dirt floor. As of 1996, there was still no electricity, piped water or plumbing. The living standard of the Yangjuan people is probably average for Baiwu-most families keep some livestock, and slaughter a pig or a sheep for important occasions, as well as eat chickens fairly frequently. With little rice available, potatoes and bitter buckwheat cakes are the staple grain foods.

One of the authors of this chapter grew up in Yangjuan and still visits frequently; the other has only been there three times, in order to observe rituals and conduct interviews. Yet native and outsider alike must take note of the fact that in our 1993 survey, 60 percent of the male adults of the Mgebbu clan in Yangjuan were junior high school graduates, 35 percent were high school graduates, and 7 people had graduated from or were attending college, constituting half of the 14 people from the entire *zhen* who had gone beyond high school or normal school since the current educational system was established.[28] In many ways, Yangjuan is like its surrounding towns and villages-very few girls have gone beyond elementary school, adult illiteracy is still very high and only slightly over half of the school-age children are in school. But the ability of so many Yangjuan residents to attend college is illustrative of a pattern of education in Baiwu *zhen* that is at odds with the stereotypes of minority education in China and indeed elsewhere in the world. It is this pattern that piqued our interest and prompted us to compile and try to explain comparative statistics on educational success among different ethnic populations in Baiwu.

A SURVEY OF EDUCATIONAL LEVELS

We spent three intensive weeks in Baiwu in January 1993, as part of our own intersecting projects on Yi history (Ma) and of ethnic relations (Harrell) in the Liangshan area. As part of this project, we collected survey information on 191 households in the Baiwu area, containing 625 people of school age and above (young children not yet of school age are irrelevant to this study). We collected, as far as possible, data on age, marital status, clan affiliation (if married in), place of origin (if married in), job history (if any) and educational history (if any) for all members of these households (See Table 7.1).[29] The households came from six different populations in the Baiwu area:

1. *The Mgebbu clan households resident in their native village of Yangjuan, or recently moved to the county seat or other places; 66 households.* Before the Democratic Reforms, the Mgebbu were retainers of the local aristocratic Luohxo clan, but many of the Mgebbu were as wealthy in land and slaves as their nominal aristocratic overlords. Several members were classified as slave lords or descendants of slave lords, and suffered greatly because of this classification; in particular, former slave holders or people of other class backgrounds were beaten and tortured during the Great Proletarian Cultural Revolution, and others were prevented from attending school during that time. At present, the Mgebbu as a whole are neither particularly rich nor particularly poor as local households go. Of the 66 households interviewed, 26 reported having some apple orchards in cultivation, though most of these were new trees that had not yet borne significant amounts of fruit.

2. *Former slaves of the Mgebbu clan, resident in Yangjuan, 17 households.* Despite the formal abolition of slave status that came with the Democratic Reforms, and the total abolition of actual slave labor, these people still show the effects of their customary low status. There has still been only one marriage between a former slave and a household of their previous commoner owners. Some of them appeared malnourished, while others were becoming quite prosperous in 1993, with 6 of the 17 households owning apple orchards.

3. *Nuosu households, all of them from commoner clans, resident in Hongxing cooperative, contiguous with Baiwu Town.* At the time of democratic reforms and collectivization in the 1950s, Yi who had been scattered around the countryside near the town were gathered together in an area adjacent to the administrative center on the uphill side, and named Hongxing (Red Star). They represent six different commoner clans: the Lama, Ajie, Synze, Molie, Ashy and Jjike. Economically, they show little difference from the Mgebbu in Yangjuan; culturally, they are perhaps slightly less "traditional," with more access to films in the town video parlors and more tendency among the women to wear

"modern" dress, but the differences are not great. They all speak Nuosu as a first language, but most are fluent in the local Han dialect also.

4. *Buddhist households in Lianhe cooperative, contiguous with Baiwu Town.* When the local Nuosu were collected into Hongxing, all members of other nationalities, including the generally agnostic Han, were collected into Lianhe (Unity) cooperative, gathered in an area adjoining the administrative center to the downhill side. The Buddhists tend to live in the area immediately adjacent to the main street. There were 20 households in 1993; 11 Naxi, 8 Zang and 1 Meng. Some of these households are descendants of the former *bazong*, or local agent of the Muli *tusi* (tribal chief), while others are descendants of plain farmers. The Naxi all now speak *Hanyu* (Chinese) as a first language, with the older generation still remembering a few words only of their ancestral language. Zang and Meng tend to grow up more bilingual, learning both Han and the ancestral Prmi or Naze tongue. Some young and most older women wear distinctive "ethnic" dress; many younger women wear this clothing only for festivals, weddings and other special occasions.

5. *Han people in Lianhe Cooperative.* A little farther down the hill and in some places across the stream that runs below Baiwu Town live 25 households of Han people, the only Han peasants in all of Baiwu *zhen*. They come from a variety of backgrounds, and if anything are somewhat poorer than their Zang and Naxi neighbors, though there is as much variation among the Han households as among the other groups. They speak almost exclusively the local Han dialect, but most of them can understand and perhaps speak Yi as well.

6. *Prmi (Zang) and Nuosu people in Changma Village, a sample of 15 households.* Changma is about an hour and a half's walk from Baiwu Town, and among its inhabitants, slightly over half are Nuosu and the rest Prmi; the Nuosu include both aristocrats and commoners, though there is now no difference in their economic status. The Prmi were the original inhabitants. Everyone in the village is reported to be bilingual by the middle of childhood; they also develop a functional knowledge of the local Han dialect even if they do not attend school. The cooperative head, with whom we spoke, told us that the area has great economic prospects, because it has perfect soil and plenty of water for fruit cultivation, and villagers are also well-situated to raise livestock for profit. It lacked only transportation in 1993, and there

TABLE 7.1. Differential Educational Attainment of Ethnic Groups in Baiwu *Zhen*

Area	Mgebbu (Yi) Yangjuan				Former Slaves (Yi) Yangjuan				Yi Clans Hongxing				Buddhists Lianhe				Han Lianhe				Yi and Zang Changma			
Marital Status	Single		Married		Single		Married		Single		Married		Single		Married		Single		Married		Single		Married	
Sex	M	F	M	F	M	F	M	F	M	F	M	F	M	F	M	F	M	F	M	F	M	F	M	F
Illiterate	2	16	23	50	2	11	6	12	10	13	22	33	2	0	6	12	4	2	9	12	7	9	5	12
Self-ed Old-style Few years	7	9	15	4	1	0	7	3	6	3	9	0	2	1	11	4	7	3	14	3	10	0	5	0
Elem. Grad	0	0	12	1	0	0	1	1	1	0	4	0	1	0	5	3	1	0	0	0	0	0	5	0
Jr. High	6	0	12	1	0	0	1	0	4	0	10	1	2	0	6	4	7	2	5	1	1	0	1	0
Sr. High	3	0	4	3	0	0	0	0	0	0	1	0	0	1	1	0	0	0	0	0	0	0	0	0
College	5	0	2	1	0	0	0	0	0	0	0	0	0	0	0	0	0	0	0	0	0	0	0	0
In school	34	13	—	—	8	2	—	—	23	5	—	—	12	8	—	—	13	7	—	—	5	0	—	—
TOTAL	57	38	68	60	11	13	15	16	44	21	46	34	19	10	31	23	32	14	28	16	23	9	16	12
In school Pct.(%)	70	34	—	—	73	15	—	—	52	24	—	—	63	80	—	—	41	50	—	—	22	0	—	—
Jr. HS + Pct.(%)	60	0	26	8	0	0	7	0	19	0	24	3	28	50	23	17	37	28	18	6	6	0	6	0
Sr. HS +Pct.(%)	36	0	9	7	0	0	0	0	0	0	2	0	0	50	3	0	0	0	0	0	0	0	0	0

were plans to build a road within the next couple of years. There is a village school in Changma, but it only has three grades; children who wish to go on to upper elementary or junior high school must board with relatives in town or make the long trek both ways each day.

RESULTS

What does our research tell us about factors contributing to differential educational success among different groups in Baiwu?

First, ideology or perceptions of success are insufficient to explain the differences in educational attainment that are transparently due to practical difficulties in attending school. The worst record by far in all categories belongs to the Yi and Zang people in Changma village, where the village school has only three grades. Children who wish to go on to the fourth grade must walk all the way to Baiwu Town, at least an hour and a half, some of it across treacherously icy trails on winter mornings. This accords with several studies of Navajo dropout rates, in which distance from school was a major factor.[30]

Second, social status is still extremely important. The descendants of former slaves held by the Mgebbu clan rank toward the bottom in every category, and in every category are either equal to or lower than the descendants of their former slave lords. This differential exists in spite of the fact that it is just as easy or difficult for former slaves or for commoners to get to school, and the fact that, while there are economic differences between families belonging to the two strata, these are not as great as are the educational differences. The issue of slave status is still an extremely sensitive one in Baiwu; when we interviewed members of former slave families, their status was never mentioned, and the senior author of this article was warned repeatedly not to ask about the social status of families who were formerly slaves. As mentioned above, there has been only one marriage between commoners and former slaves in the villages around Baiwu. It appears that the stigma of low social status still confers a perceptual disadvantage on many students and their parents, and while a few members of former slave families have done well educationally, they are in a small minority.

Third, and central to our argument about the determinants of folk theories of success, we find that, other things being equal, that the educational attainments of the Mgebbu clan far exceed expectations.

Fully 60 percent of the unmarried males have finished middle school, and 35 percent have finished high school; the corresponding figures of 23 percent and 9 percent for married men are not as impressive, reflecting as they do the almost total lack of education for men born before 1940, but they still exceed the comparable figures for the three Buddhist nationalities and non-Buddhist Han. And rather startlingly, 10 members of the Mgebbu from Yangjuan village have gone to college—four to the Southwest Nationalities College in Chengdu, one to the Central Nationalities Institute in Beijing, three to Liangshan University in Xichang, one to Southwest Finance University in Chengdu and one to the Central Music Conservatory in Beijing, where he studied Italian opera.

It is also the perception of the teachers we interviewed in Baiwu that minority students are better students than local Han children-they try harder in school and quickly overcome their linguistic and cultural disadvantages. The junior author of this chapter remembers that he was behind his Han schoolmates in the first two grades, but had passed them by the fourth and fifth, and in fact allowed some Han friends to copy his homework in return for the loan of some comic books, which the Yi at that time were too poor to afford. One first-grade teacher said that whereas Yi students have to be shown such basic things as how to hold a pencil when they first came to school, and whereas they cannot always answer questions in spoken Han even at the end of the first year, they have already become better at reading texts than are their Han schoolmates. The perception of these teachers, then, is that Nuosu not only go father in school, but do better than Han.

What we do not find here is any indication that cultural and linguistic divergence from the national Han norm is a factor in school failure. With the exception of the Changma people, who simply live too far from schools, the educationally successful Mgebbu clan rank with their former slaves as those least exposed to Han culture-they have no television, no Han people in their local community and few if any newspapers or books. They are also ordinarily monolingual in Nuosu until they begin school. In addition, like their counterparts in town they are mostly farmers, and can often use their children's labor on the land. And while problems of access are not so great for them as for the people in Changma (they only have to walk 45 minutes, and the way is level), still the school is less convenient for them than it is for people who live five minutes' walk away in town. And, of course, the elementary and middle schools they attend are the same ones the town people attend, so they are not receiving better or different instruction.

Given that the Mgebbu are minority people living in a remote location with mediocre schools at an inconvenient distance, what accounts for their educational success? We would suggest two factors, both of them leading to the perception of formal education as a mobility strategy. First, there is a tradition of formal education. Several men now in their sixties, including the father of one of the authors of this chapter, were pupils of the private classical school established by schoolmaster Wu in 1942. This enabled them to learn to speak the local Han dialect well, as well as to write simple letters and read documents in the Han Chinese language, all skills that served them well in dealing with the increasing incursions of outsiders, culminating in the intense involvement of the Communist Party in the social transformation of the area, which began with the Democratic Reforms in 1956. One member of the Mgebbu, now in his early fifties, first graduated from the private school and then went on to finish regular elementary school in a Han area, and then became principal of the elementary school in neighboring Dalin township. Others began in the private school and then went on to regular schools after the Democratic Reforms. Men who had gained only the rudiments of literacy in the private school still sent their sons to the first government school when it opened in 1956, and their success there has in turn led to more and higher education. Many of them have used education to move into such posts as head of the Yanyuan County Livestock Bureau, Secretary of the *Qu* (district) government, researcher at the Liangshan Nationalities Research Institute and several are now elementary and secondary schoolteachers. There is thus a proven tradition of education as a successful mobility strategy.

The other major factor leading to the perception of education as a way to mobility is the general dominance of political and educational institutions in much of Yanyuan by Nuosu people. Yanyuan is part of the Liangshan Yi Autonomous Prefecture, and as such is organized to favor members of the Yi and other minorities in several ways. Rural Yi can bear three children, for example, while Han can only bear two. But most importantly, most of the government and educational positions, from county party secretary and vice secretary down through the heads of various bureaus and offices, along with a large number of school administrators and teachers, are Yi people. There is a perception among most Yi in Baiwu that many of the policies of the Han-dominated central government have retarded development in the area; many people are bitter over the foolish economic policies of extreme collectivism during the Cultural Revolution, wanton destruction of forests for fuel during the Great Leap Forward and what they perceive as the uncompensated extraction of resources. This is particularly true of the most educated and politically aware members of the community. But especially since the economic reforms of the early 1980s, the party and government have encouraged local economic initiative, and have given most posts to local people, primarily members of Yi and other minorities. So people with a strong ethnic consciousness such as the Nuosu have, people who sometimes go so far as to blame the "Han" government for their own lack of development, still see the possibility of participating in local development and construction through channeling government initiatives to local advantage. To do this, however, they must be able to operate in the wider modern Chinese society, and this means formal education, primarily in the Han language. Perceived successes in the initial stages of this development process in the last decade also point to education as a viable mobility strategy.

Fourth, gender differences are very apparent in most Nuosu groups, but not among the Han or the three major Buddhist nationalities in Baiwu. The Buddhist groups have the best record of female education by all measures, with an impressive 8 out of 10 school-age girls in school in 1993; and the Han also have a good record of school attendance, as well as a fairly high number of middle school graduates. The Mgebbu clan, whose male scholastic achievements far outstrip those of any other group in the study, are somewhat behind the Buddhists and Han in their record of female education. This finding is difficult to explain conclusively, but we might cite several factors, including the strength of patrilineal tradition. All the groups in the survey are patrilineal, in the sense that they trace descent through male genealogical lines, the Han people through the transmission of last names, and both the Yi and the Buddhists though oral genealogy recitation. But the patrilineal clan as an organized unit and point of social reference exists only among the Nuosu. All Nuosu consider their clan as the most basic unit to which they belong, and in fact one means of explaining the difference between slaves and commoners is that slaves have no clan and are therefore not fully established members of society. Han people, on the other hand, have no strong patrilineage organization in this area, having originated in the scattered and random migration of a few families from various places. And whereas Buddhist peoples do have clan names, they rarely use them.

It is also possible that the rather more retiring role played by women in Nuosu life may be a factor in educational decisions. In Nuosu households, men socialize primarily with other men, while women stay in the background, contributing opinions from time to time but not taking an active role. It is the impression of the American author of this chapter that Zang, Naxi and Meng women are much more forward and assertive with visitors, more often taking leading roles in interviews and casual conversations. This may also translate into decisions that place equal value on male and female schooling.

More interesting, however, we think that because of the Nuosu patrilineal ideology and the retiring role of women in Nuosu life, the cultural distance explanation of differential success may be relevant for girls, even though it is clearly not so for boys. We base this belief on two pieces of evidence: the fact that for Nuosu, there is a much greater linguistic and cultural distance between home and school than exists for Han or for Hanophone Buddhists; and our observation of a rather extraordinary phenomenon that began in the Spring of 1994, when the principal of the Baiwu elementary school decided to organize a *Yiwen ban*, a class to be taught primarily in the Nuosu language. The regular classes teach written Nuosu only as a single subject, and starting only in the third grade. But the *Yiwen ban*, the first to be recruited since 1984, would teach all subjects except Han language and literature in the Nuosu language. Word went out to the villages, and the place was mobbed with registrants; 117 children signed up for the Yi language class and, reluctant to turn anyone away, the principal recruited another teacher (with no state salary available, the second teacher had to be *minban*, or paid for out of local tuition and fees). The most notable thing about the registrants, however, is that they were mostly girls-66, as opposed to 51 boys, in contrast with 22 girls and 40 boys in the same year's entering first grade Han-language *ban* class-and that many of them, the girls especially, were in their middle or even late teens.

The Baiwu elementary school classroom thus presented the odd but inspiring spectacle of first-grade-age children in the front rows, in front of fully grown young adult women and a few adult men, as well. The teenage students had exchanged their skirts and head cloths for ordinary trousers and bright-colored scarves, but they stood out in a situation where no Han girl would wear a scarf, and they appeared very intent and serious about the first-grade lessons. We tried to interview the students about their experience, but they were embarrassed and we were mobbed by younger students coming to look at the foreigner, so we could only ask a few basic questions of the students, and we talked to several of the teachers (all local Nousu) about what had happened.

When the call went out for students to register for the *Yiwen ban*, teenage girls in several surrounding villages apparently got together and talked about the possibility of starting school, even at their relatively advanced ages. They did not want to go through life illiterate, but had previously felt daunted by having to study in a language with which they felt insufficiently familiar. So they came in groups; in almost every case, there was more than one teenage student from a particular village. Many parents supported the girls' decision initially, but others opposed it, and some girls surreptitiously took *huajiao* (Sichuan brown peppercorns) from their families' harvest and sold them in the market to be able to pay for tuition and books. One 24-year-old woman, already married but not yet living with her husband, initially came but was taken back home by her father, who did not want her to jeopardize the marriage. Everyone whom we spoke with about this phenomenon stressed that it was the teenage girls themselves who made the decision to attend schools, and that this caught the authorities by surprise. The decision to establish the *Yiwen ban* was not made specifically with girls in mind, nor was the curriculum designed for their needs. They simply felt more comfortable with education in their own language.[31]

It is difficult to predict how long this trend of Nuosu-language education for female students might last. Certainly the obstacles are formidable, not least of them the fact that someone who starts school at age 17 will not finish elementary school until age 23, by which age almost all women are married. And there is no possibility of skipping grades, since there are no higher-level *Yiwen ban* as yet, though this of course may change for subsequent classes. For this reason, one young teacher persuaded his 19-year-old first-grade sister to transfer to the *Hanwen ban* classes in Han, where she could move faster, and of course offered her help, something that would not be available to most of the teenage girls. By 1996 she was in the sixth grade. But the eagerness of these teenagers to get a Nuosu-language education, even an elementary one, when they had not pressed their parents earlier to allow them to attend school in the Han language, seems to lend partial credence to the idea that for females, at least, cultural and linguistic difference were indeed a barrier to school attendance and success, even when they appear to have presented no barrier for males of the same ethnic group.

CONCLUSIONS

This case study, we believe, challenges certain assumptions about the educational success of minority peoples in multiethnic states. First, it shows that ethnic education is not impossible, even for "involuntary minorities," among whom we must certainly classify the Yi. One way to protest one's status as an involuntary minority is to draw from within oneself, preserving cultural traditions and ethnic identity and refusing to participate in the state educational project. Another way is to participate in the educational project in order to turn it to what one perceives as localistic ends, in this case promoting Yi control of local politics and economics in what is, after all, part of the Liangshan Yi Autonomous Prefecture. In this sense, Ogbu is certainly correct when he attributes differential educational achievement to different folk theories of success, but somewhat overly simplistic when he assumes that folk theories of success will divide neatly along lines of voluntary versus involuntary minorities.

A second conclusion is a reaffirmation of the view that an ethnic group as a nationwide or region wide aggregate is a poor unit for measurement of educational success or the factors leading to it. Even in such a small area as Baiwu, we find distinct differences *among* different Yi populations, based at least partly on differential perception of the possibility of success. There are other Yi areas, such as Tianba in Ganluo County and Yuehua in Xichang Municipality, that are known much more widely than Yangjuan for producing college graduates and successful politicians and officials. Yet the Yi as a whole remain less educated than the Han. It is only when we observe differential educational success at a very local level that we gain insight into the factors that lead members of minority groups to do well or poorly in school. Third, we cannot entirely discard the explanation of differential success in terms of cultural and linguistic distance. Gender differences in Baiwu school attendance disappeared or were even reversed when Yi-language education was offered as a choice alongside Han-language schooling. This might be true because the teenage girls who decided to start first grade were not seeking success in terms of occupational or social mobility; they just wanted to be literate, so that they wouldn't have to go through life feeling ignorant. For these girls, few if any of whom were interested in mobility, Han language education seemed too daunting. Nuosu language education, on the other hand, seemed like a good idea.

NOTES

1. This research was organized under the auspices of the Sichuan Provincial Minorities Research Institute and the Liangshan Prefectural Minority Research Institute. We are grateful to Zhou Xiyin and Qubi Shimei, the respective directors, for their help, support and constructive criticism, and to Gaga Erri of the Liangshan Institute for short-term collaboration on this research. Harrell's research was sponsored by a grant from the Committee on Scholarly Communication with China, whose help is gratefully acknowledged, and by professional leave from the University of Washington. For comments on earlier drafts of this paper, we are indebted to Tsianina Lomawaima, Janet Upton and Martin Schoenhals.

2. See John Ogbu, "Cultural Discontinuities and Schooling: A Problem in Search of an Explanation," in *Anthropology and Education Quarterly*, No. 13 (1982), pp.290-307; "Variability in Minority School Performance," in *Anthropology and Education Quarterly*, No.18 (1987), pp. 312-334; Frederick Erickson, "Transformation and School Success: The Politics and Culture of Educational Achievement," in *Anthropology and Education Quarterly*, No. 18 (1987), pp.335-356.

3. See Ogbu, "Cultural Discontinuities," *Anthropology and Education Quarterly* pp. 291-292 for a review of the early history of anthropological thinking about this problem.

4. Ogbu, "Cultural Discontinuities and Schooling;" Ogbu, "Variability in Minority School Performance," both in *Anthropology and Educational Quarterly*.

5. K. S. Chan and B. Ostheimer, *Navajo Youth and Early School Withdrawal: A Case Study* (Los Alamitos, CA: National Center for Bilingual Research, 1993); D. Deyhle, "Pushouts and Pullouts: Navajo and Ute School Leavers," in *Journal of American Indian Education*, Vol. 6, No. 2 (1989), pp. 36-51; P. R. Platero, E. A. Brandt, G. Witherspoon and P. Wong, *Navajo Students at Risk: Final Report for the Navajo Area Dropout Study* (Window

Rock: Navajo Division of Education, 1986). For summaries of work both promoting and questioning the cultural discountinuity hypothesis, see Douglas E. Foley, "Reconsidering Anthropological Explanations of Ethnic School Failure," in *Anthropology and Education Quarterly*, Vol. 22 (1991), pp. 60-86; and Susan Ledlow, "Is Cultural Discontinuity an Adequate Explanation for Dropping Out?" in *Journal of American Indian Education*, Vol. 31, No. 3 (1992), pp. 21-36.

6. Erickson, "Transformation and School Success," in *Anthropology and Education Quarterly*.

7. Ogbu, "Variability in Minority School Performance," in *Anthropology and Education Quarterly*.

8. Shang Jinfa, "Liangshan minzu jiaoyu zhanlue chutan" ("Preliminary Discussion of Strategy for Ethnic Education in Liangshan"), in Chen Hongtao (ed.), *Sichuan minzu jiaoyu yanjiu (Research on Ethnic Education in Sichuan)* (Beijing: Zhongyang minzu xueyuan chubanshe, 1989), pp. 209, 211.

9. Zhou Chenghou, "Shehui zhuyi chuji jieduan sichuan minzu jiaoyu de sikao" ("A Consideration of Ethnic Education in Sichuan During the Early Stages of Socialism"), in Chen Hongtao (ed.), *Sichuan minzu jiaoyu yanjiu* (Research in Ethnic Education in Schuan), p. 61.

10. Qian Hongfan and Piao Taichu, "Jilin sheng bianjing qu minzu jiaoyu xianzhuang yu fazhan duice" ("The Current Situation and Policy for Development of Minority Education in Border Areas of Jilin Province"), in Wang Xihong (ed.), *Zhongguo bianjing minzu jiaoyu (Minority Education in Border Areas of China)* (Beijing: Zhongyang minzu xueyan chubanshe, 1990), pp. 633-646.

11. Frank N. Pieke, "Chinese Educational Achievement and Folk Theories of Success." in *Anthropology and Education Quarterly*, No. 22 (1992), pp.162-180.

12. Charles F. Keyes, "The Proposed World of the School: Thai Villagers' Entry into a Bureaucratic State System," in Charles F. Keyes (ed.), *Reshaping Local Worlds: Formal Education and Cultural Change in Rural Southeast Asia* (Monograph 36/Yale Southeast Asia Studies. New Haven: Yale Center for International and Area Studies, 1991), p. 89.

13. This distinction appears to be at the root of the differences Hansen describes between the educational strategies of the Naxi in Lijiang (who buy into the state system and use it to validate their own position as an ethnic group), and the Tai in Sipsong Panna (who reject the state educational system as an agent of unwanted assimilation). See Mette Halskov Hansen, "Lessons in

Patriotism: Ethnic Education in Southwest China," Ph.D. dissertation, Asian Studies, University of Aarhus, Denmark, 1996.

14. Ogbu, "Variability in Minority School Performance," in *Anthropology and Education Quarterly*.

15. Foley, "Reconsidering," pp. 82-83.

16. G. William Skinner, "Mobility Strategies in Late Imperial China: A Regional Systems Analysis," in Carol Smith (ed.), *Regional Systems, vol. 1: Economic Systems* (New York: Academic Press, 1976), pp. 327-64.

17. See Wurlig Borchigud, "The Impact of Ethnic Education on Modern Mongolian Ethnicity," in Stevan Harrell (ed.), *Cultural Encounters on China's Ethnic Frontiers* (Seattle and London: University of Washington Press, 1994), pp. 278-300.

18. See Suzanne Pepper, *Radicalism and Educational Reform in 20th Century China* (Cambridge: Cambridge University Press, 1996).

19. Suzanne Pepper, *China's Education Reform in the 1980s* (Institute of East Asian Studies, University of California, Berkeley, China Research Monograph Series, No. 36, 1990), pp. 75-92.

20. Partial exceptions to this pattern exist in areas where there are schools that teach complete elementary education in minority languages. These include many Tibetan-speaking areas in Tibet and elsewhere, as well as some pastoral regions of Inner Mongolia. Our thanks to Janet Upton for pointing this out. Also, in the Liangshan area where we have conducted research, Nuosu-language teaching materials are locally produced and contain a considerable amount of local content. In addition, there are a small number of locally produced *xiangtu jiaocai* in many local areas, but they play only a small subsidiary role in the curriculum. Our thanks to Gerard Postiglione for drawing our attention to this point.

21. Charles F. Keyes, "State Schools in Rural Communities: Reflections on Rural Education and Cultural Change in Southeast Asia," in Charles F. Keyes (ed.), *Reshaping Local Worlds: Formal Education and Cultural Change in Rural Southeast Asia* (Monograph 36/Yale Southeast Asia Studies. New Haven: Yale Center for International and Area Studies, 1991), pp. 10-11.

22. The one school one of us has visited where students were encouraged to question, even to explore knowledge on their own, was an elite experimental school in Beijing, whose students were almost all children of intellectual or political elites, and all of whose students went on to higher education, many of them to the country's best universities.

23. Borchigud, W., "The Impact of Urban Ethnic Education on Modern Mongolian Ethnicity, 1949-1966," in Stevan Harrell, ed., *Cultural Encounters*

on China's Ethnic Frontiers (Seattle: University of Washington Press, 1995), pp. 278-300.

24. See for example: Gibson, Margaret A. and Ogbu, John U. (eds.), *Minority Status and Schooling: A Comparative Study of Immigrant and Involuntary Minorities,* (New York: Garland Publishing, 1991), p. 407.

25. *Yi* is a Chinese term for a *minzu* (nationality) composed of a rather broad variety of peoples in Yunnan, Sichuan, and Guizhou who speak a group of related Tibeto-Burmanese languages. In Yanyuan, there is only one variety of Yi, people who call themselves *Nuosu* in their own language. In this article, we thus use the terms *Yi* and *Nuosu* interchangeably. For more detailed information in English on how various Yi do or do not relate to each other, see Stevan Harrell, "Ethnicity, Local Interests, and the State: Yi Communities in Southwest China," in *Comparative Studies in Society and History*, Vol. 32, No. 3 (1990), pp. 515-548; and "The History of the History of the Yi," in Stevan Harrell (ed.), *Cultural Encounters on China's Ethnic Frontiers* (Seattle and London: University of Washington Press, 1995), pp. 63-91.

26. The people classified as Zang in this area are not what Westerners would call Tibetans, but rather members of an ethnic group that calls itself Prmi in its own language, and who are classified as a separate Pumi *minzu* across the nearby border in Yunnan. Similarly, those classified here as Meng are not Mongols in the conventional sense, but members of a group that calls itself Naze, who are classified in Yunnan as the Mosuo branch of the Naxi *minzu*. See Stevan Harrell, "The Nationalities Question and the Prmi Problem," in Melissa J. Brown (ed.), *Negotiating Ethnicities in China and Taiwan* (Berkeley: University of California Institute for East Asian Studies, 1996); and Charles F. McKhann, "The Naxi and the Nationalities Question," in Stevan Harrell (ed.), *Cultural Encounters on China's Ethnic Frontiers* (Seattle and London: University of California Press, 1995).

27. Local sources provide a series of different tables, none of which appear to have been cross-checked with each other. These figures are taken from unpublished local statistics. A semi-published compendium of statistics from the 1990 census in Yanyuan (Yanyuan xian renko pucha bangongshi, *Sichuan sheng yanyuan xian disici renkou pucha shougong huizong ziliao [Hand-tabulated General Materials from the Fourth Census in Yanyuan County, Sichuan Province*, 1991]) gives the figure of 67 percent of adults being illiterate or semiliterate (*wenmang, ban wenmang*) (p. 31), and a figure of 47 percent being unable to recognize characters, or able to recognize only a very few characters (*bu shi zi huo shi zi hen shao*) on (p. 61). The figures for people with a high school education, however, are consistent in all sources. The point is that

little or no school education was still very much the norm among all ethnic groups in Baiwu in the early 1990s.

28. By 1996, there were at least three more Yangjuan residents who had been admitted to colleges in various parts of Sichuan.

29. Our information on females appears to be somewhat incomplete; if anything, this should strengthen our findings about gender differences in education, as people would be more likely to forget to mention the educational status of illiterate women than of those who had gone to school.

30. Platero et. al., "*Navajo Students at Risk,*" Chan and Ostheimer, "*Navajo Youth.*"

31. These findings resonate with the findings of the senior author in another Nuosu village in another county, an area where there is much less Han cultural influence than in Baiwu. There, in a lowland village, 90 percent of adult males but only 54 percent of adult females in a household survey were reported to be able to speak *Hanyu* (Chinese); in a semi-remote mountain community (an hour and a half walk from the road), 73 percent of adult males but only 20 percent of adult females could speak Han.

Teaching Backwardness or Equality

Chinese State Education Among the Tai in Sipsong Panna[1]

Mette Halskov Hansen

Chinese education of non-Han peoples living in the geographic periphery of the Chinese state is one of the most important components of what Stevan Harrell has called "China's civilizing projects," in which a center, claiming to be on a superior level of civilization, interacts with its peripheral peoples and attempts to raise their levels of civilization.[2] The ideology of inequality is legitimized by the conviction that the dominance of the center is truly helping and thus is to the benefit of the culturally inferior peoples. Many aspects of the communist "civilizing project" come into play within the education of minorities, which is the main arena for transmitting Chinese language, Chinese history, atheism and patriotism to the non-Han peoples. However, the civilizing and nationalist aspects of Chinese minority education have rarely been debated, and our knowledge about local ethnic minorities' reactions to these aspects of Chinese state education is particularly limited.[3]

Due to the immense discrepancies in the various minority regions in terms of educational practice and local people's responses, both with regard to academic attainment and ethnic identity, the generalizing descriptions of minority education in China tend to suffer from the lack of detailed knowledge about local situations. This essay analyses and discusses, on the basis of fieldwork, how the form and content of Chinese state education has a direct influence on local expressions of

ethnic identity among the Tai (also called Tai Lue/Lü/Le[4]) people in
Sipsong Panna (*Xishuangbanna*[5]) on the borders of Burma and Laos.[6] I
shall argue that the patriotic message of national unity and equality of
the nationalities transmitted through education is largely undermined by
other aspects inherent in the Chinese state education, which on one
hand preaches constitutional equality of the nationalities (*minzu*), and
on the other hand impresses on the Tai students immense feelings of
cultural inferiority.

THE BEGINNING OF CHINESE EDUCATION IN SIPSONG PANNA

When the first Chinese schools were established in Sipsong Panna in
1911, the area was still ruled by a Tai government, a Tai king (*chao
phaendin*) and the local princes (*chao meeng*), who ruled together with
local governments in the subdistricts (*panna* and *meeng*). The main
populace of Sipsong Panna were the Tai, who inhabited the prosperous
plains and rarely interacted socially with the other ethnic groups (such
as the Akha, Jinuo, Blang, Lahu, etc.) who lived higher up in the
mountains. Sipsong Panna had been under nominal rule of the Chinese
empire since the Yuan dynasty, but it was only in 1911 that the Chinese
government seriously attempted to install direct Chinese rule in the area
by establishing a system whereby two official governments, the
indigenous officials (*tusi*) and the Chinese appointed magistrate existed
simultaneously.[7] During this period of increasing Chinese dominance in
Sipsong Panna, the establishment of Chinese schools became for the
first time part of a strategy to integrate Sipsong Panna and its
population into the Chinese state under Chinese rule.

For the local representatives of the government of the republic, it
was not an easy task to establish Chinese education in an area that
already had a developed form of Buddhist education reaching most of
the male population. For hundreds of years, the Tai had been Theravada
Buddhists, and each village had its own temple (*wat*), monks (*tu*) and
novices (*pha*). The Tai language and script were taught in the
monasteries, and knowledge of and interest in Chinese language and
culture was extremely limited. The first Chinese schools were meant for
children of the locals as well as for offspring of Han immigrants in
Sipsong Panna. Through the teaching of Chinese, the government
hoped to break the authority of the *chao* class and the influential

Buddhist monks who conducted all education of Tai boys in the monasteries. The lack of knowledge of Chinese among the ethnic groups in the border areas was regarded as a major obstacle for the imposition of Chinese rule, and in 1921 the provincial government in Yunnan issued regulations for expanding border education with the purpose of consolidating Chinese control in the areas that were generally regarded as being culturally backward.

New schools had to be financed through the tax system, and the existence of the double government (Tai and Chinese) created heavy economic burdens on the population in Sipsong Panna. Among the heaviest tax burdens were the two kinds of taxes that financed education.[8] Since few Tai voluntarily sent their children to the Chinese schools, a quota system was introduced, forcing each middle-sized village to send at least one boy to the nearest school. This created new financial hardships for Tai villagers, who started to pay Chinese, Akha, poor Tai or boys from other local ethnic groups to fill their quota and attend the unpopular schools. There were other reasons why the attempted spread of Chinese school education during the republican period largely failed: most schools were in fact not started in the Tai plains, but higher up in the mountains where most Han lived in fear of malaria; although Tai students were entitled to economic support during their education, they usually never received it; and although the royal family supported Chinese education in public, it was against it in reality. Therefore, most students in the new schools were Han, many schools only operated on paper in order to get financial support and, finally, in 1942 all schools stopped in Sipsong Panna due to the Japanese bombing of the area.[9]

Real expansion of Chinese school education in Sipsong Panna took place after the Communist Party established control in the area in 1950. As part of the new nation-building project, a large number of mostly Han Chinese cadres, teachers and members of work teams were sent to disseminate knowledge of the Communist Party and its policies, set up new governments, prepare land reforms, recruit adult students for cadre training and start new schools. Special research teams conducted the economic and cultural investigations that later served as the basis for accomplishing land reforms and provided the communist government with its first thorough knowledge of the social and political system among the Tai in Sipsong Panna. Researchers, heavily influenced by the theories of social evolution developed by Friedrich Engels and

Lewis Henry Morgan.[10] concluded that generally speaking, the ethnic groups in Sipsong Panna, like most of the minority nationalities, were at a lower feudal stage of social evolution than the Han.

Especially in a border area such as Sipsong Panna where the knowledge of the Chinese language was so limited, where the ruling class was the absolute authority in the minds of the people, and where Buddhist temples were the centers not only of religion but also of education, it was essential for the communists quickly to foster loyal cadres who could act as a connecting link between the commoners and the party. For the same reasons, the party provided special treatment for those members of the upper class who did not flee the country (quite a few did flee). Many of them received positions in the autonomous government established in 1953 when the Communist Party put an end to all previous royal titles and positions. Many of them also received short-term cadre education together with local headman or villagers who were selected by the communist work teams. The majority of the incoming Han Chinese cadres, teachers and farmers were convinced that their presence greatly benefited the Tai and the other ethnic groups in the area. They believed that their mission was to develop, civilize and integrate this outpost of the People's Republic. One of the Han who arrived in the late 1950s recalled:

> Already by the 1960s the Tai were quite civilized (*kaihua*). They welcomed us and wanted to learn Chinese. A large amount of Han were sent from all over China to help develop Sipsong Panna. If we *Hanzu* had not come, this place would not have developed. The Tai welcomed us because they realized that we, as a more advanced (*xianjin*) nationality, could help them develop this place. I believe that Sipsong Panna is the place in China where education has developed fastest because the sudden influence of Han culture (*Hanzu wenhua*) was so strong. [11]

In 1953, there were 23 elementary schools and one teacher training school in the whole of Sipsong Panna. The first secondary schools were established in 1958. Eighty percent of the students were non-Han and teachers were encouraged to learn the Tai script, which was taught in a number of elementary schools. However, the script was not standardized, and in line with the communists' wish to simplify the Chinese characters and create new scripts for those minorities without one, it was decided to make a simplified version of the Tai script. Thus, from the mid-1950s, three writing systems were taught to the Tai in Sipsong Panna: Chinese in all schools, the simplified "new Tai" in some schools and the traditional "old Tai" in all the temples. The locals' attitudes toward the "new Tai" were divided then, as they are today.

Although Chinese education spread steadily throughout Sipsong Panna in the 1950s, it did not manage to pull the Tai boys out of the monasteries. For the first time, Tai girls were able to get a school education, but for the Tai at that time the prospect of having a child educated in a Chinese school was not economically or culturally attractive and was considered irrelevant to daily life. Nevertheless, the government, the work teams and an increasing number of enthusiastic teachers (mainly from outside Sipsong Panna) managed to multiply the number of Chinese schools by 10 within the first 7 years of communist rule, and for the first time in Sipsong Panna an increasing number of Tai pupils in villages attended Chinese schools, at least for short periods of time. The Communists had adopted a strategy of cooperation with the Tai nobility, which paid off by achieving the Tai commoners' equal cooperation, for instance in the matter of sending children to the Chinese schools.

However, the real increase of Tai students in schools took place in periods where state policy became very restrictive and anti-religious. As a result, large numbers of monks were forced to return to secular life, and it became difficult or even impossible for boys to study as novices. At the same time more children attended schools, because they had no alternative and because local cadres stressed the demands for sending children to the Chinese schools rather than to the monasteries. In 1950, statistics indicated that there were 574 temples, 930 monks and 5,550 novices in Sipsong Panna. As early as 1957, the numbers were down to at least a half of these figures, according to interviews, and after the launching of the Cultural Revolution in 1966 all novices and monks were compelled to discard their yellow robes and resume a secular life: many of them fled the country. Buddha images and temples were smashed, and books written in Tai script burned. For almost fourteen years no Tai novices were trained and teaching of the old Tai script was only conducted in families where the father or grandfather secretly taught their children to read. Thus, in spite of the later official condemnation of the repressive policy of the Cultural Revolution, it achieved, at least for a period of time, what less oppressive policies had not been able to, namely, a large number of Tai students in Chinese schools, an increased influence of Chinese language and culture and a decline of Buddhist and Tai traditions.

THE REVIVAL OF BUDDHIST EDUCATION

According to interviews, the so-called "religious fever" (*zongjiao re*) started in 1982 when people finally dared to believe that they were free to restart religious practices. However, at this time a whole generation had not studied in temples and all monks had either fled the country or resumed lay life. Therefore, the Tai faced the practical problem of finding monks who could teach the new novices in the local temples that they had started to rebuild, mostly with their own money. Most Tai families have family members in Thailand or Burma, and mainly through contacts with them many villages were able to invite foreign monks to Sipsong Panna. It was the gradual improvement of the Tai peasants' economy which made possible the increasing number of temples, monks and novices. In 1982 there were 145 temples, 36 monks (*tu*), and 655 novices (*pha*) in the whole of Sipsong Panna. Twelve years later, in 1994, there were 435 temples, 509 *tu* and 5,336 *pha* (see Table 8.1).[12]

Between 1980 and 1983 the government in Sipsong Panna faced a situation where school attendance was less than 60 percent and the dropout rate was very high, especially south of the Mekong River. This was partly a result of the renewed possibilities of sending boys to the temples, and partly a result of the new system of contracting fields that caused parents to keep their children home in order to work. Some schools were almost empty; some had only female pupils; and most boys stopped after a few years. A number of measures (special regulations for novices in schools, Tai classes, "novices classes," etc.) were introduced to convince parents to send their children to school, and still today the education departments, teachers and educators discuss how to increase the number of graduates at all levels. Although almost 90 percent of children start school in Sipsong Panna today, only 55.5 percent complete 5 years of study.[14] About 67 percent of novices enroll in school today, but the problem for the government is that it is

Table 8.1. Temples, Monks and Novices in Sipsong Panna[a13]

year	temples	monks	novices
1950	574	930	5,550
1982	145	36	655
1994	435	509	5,336

difficult to make them stay there for more than a few years. Very few novices manage to continue into secondary education. Whereas the number of novices enrolling in school is registered, there are no local statistics on how many of them drop out and when they drop out. However, my fieldwork clearly indicated that especially in villages with many novices, the dropout rate for boys is high. One Tai village, for instance, had an elementary school with one teacher who taught for 2 years. After that, the children had to continue in the schools of the nearest administrative village. After 2 years of school (in 1994) 8 out of 19 children dropped out rather than continue in the other school. All 8 pupils were boys, 7 of them turned novices.

In the first years of the religious upsurge when many villages still did not have a monk, novices were often alone in the monasteries with nobody to teach them and without any idea of how to lead a Buddhist life. Often one of the elderly villagers who had been a monk or novice earlier in his life would try to guide the boys. Today there are still some poorer villages that do not have a learned monk to teach their novices, and in some villages peasants complain that their monk is not well enough educated. In the numerous villages where foreign monks have been invited, or where local monks have been properly trained before taking over the Buddhist education, villagers today express satisfaction with the situation. They are happy to send their boys to the monastery and hold the monk in high esteem. However, during interviews some parents explained that even if they would like their children to go to a Chinese school, they had no way of forcing those boys who themselves preferred the monasteries. I did not find this explanation very convincing, since most of the boys referred to were only between 7 and 10 years old when they became novices. Teachers, however, confirmed that this was an explanation commonly heard among parents in villages. It was probably a strategic way for some parents to excuse themselves for not insisting on keeping the boys in school when facing representatives of the Chinese educational system.[15] However, it also indicated that even though most Tai have accepted the Chinese schools as part of village life and are mostly happy to have a school in their neighborhood, many of them do not consider it essential for their own children to attend it. Indeed, they very seldom try to force their children to stay there if they themselves do not want to. Most villagers feel that children should try the school for a few years and if they do not like it, or if they are not good enough, they might as well stop. If they have a good monk in the village, parents consider the Buddhist education at least as good as the school education in terms of learning how to read and write. Equally or more important, they regard it as essential for moral training and for earning merit for their sons and themselves. The practice of sending boys to receive a Buddhist education is a tradition built on religious belief, and it is a habitual practice for most Tai. It is a significant component of Tai ethnic identity, and at the same time a practical way of transmitting the Tai script, history and cultural values. In comparison to this, the Chinese school in Sipsong Panna is a poor competitor.

In several monasteries, monks have now started to extend education to include mathematics, the Thai language (standard Thai of Thailand) and, more rarely, Chinese. The most important temple in Sipsong Panna, Wat Pa Jie Maharajatan in Manting Park, has recently set up an institution for a sort of higher education for novices and monks who are then sent back to village temples after completed studies. In this way, the temple has established an education that attempts to solve the antagonism between school and monastery education, as expressed in this statement by a Tai monk: "In the temple children do not learn modern knowledge. In school they do not learn how to be a good human being."[16] All monks and novices I talked to were very excited about the prospects for the new school that attempts to bridge the division between Buddhist teaching and the demand for knowledge in modern subjects as well as the Chinese language. Only a very few boys who have been novices for more than a few months manage to get a Chinese education beyond elementary school level, for several reasons: their level of Chinese is insufficient, it is difficult for them to participate in school education while spending time studying in the monastery, they get very little credits for having learned to read and write their own language, some parents consider it a waste of money to pay for a school education that does not lead to a job or further education, and finally many are not motivated to get a Chinese education at all. Therefore, the higher Buddhist education in the temple in Manting is a welcome alternative at least for the small percentage of novices who get a chance to study there.

In the early 1980s, religious activities in Sipsong Panna were centered on rebuilding temples and restarting the tradition of temple education from scratch. In the last few years, encouraged by the increasing contacts across the borders, with Tai and Thai in Thailand especially, attitudes toward temple education are slowly changing. Even though most Tai in the mid-1980s wanted to educate at least one son in the temple for religious purposes, many had been influenced by the extensive government propaganda that insisted that only Chinese schools could promote modernization of the economy. Buddhist teaching and modern education—equivalent to Chinese state school education—were presented as mutually exclusive. Through their contacts across the borders, more and more Tai people in Sipsong Panna have learned that in Thailand there is a closer connection between schools and temples, monks sometimes participate in common teacher training courses, teachers in elementary schools may take a special course in teaching Buddhism, larger temples offer courses for girls and boys who are not novices, and nevertheless Thailand has a developed economy. Thus, it slowly seems that an increasing number of Tai are starting to question the theory of the mutual exclusiveness of modern and Buddhist education.

Most Han Chinese cadres, teachers and researchers in and outside Sipsong Panna continue to express negative views on the influence of Buddhist education among the Tai. Also, many local Tai schoolteachers and government members, trained in Chinese schools, share this view, but government members and teachers who have themselves been monks, especially elderly ones, tend to be more positive. The most concrete criticisms of temple education are that it employs backward teaching methods, that too many novices are illiterate after they leave the temples because of the monks' poor educational level and that it does not include girls in its education. These are problems that some of the most highly educated Tai monks attempt to solve at the moment, but other objections are far more extensive and directed toward the very institution of temple education. It is, for instance, said that temple education obstructs modernization by preventing the spread of Chinese culture. Such negative points of view are summarized in a comprehensive Chinese study from 1990 of education among national minorities that has, for instance, the following characterization of temple education in Sipsong Panna:

> The Buddhist temple education is a religious, theological education the purpose of which is to teach people to stand aloof from worldly affairs, detest life, escape the present to jump out of the sea of bitterness and into Nirvana. It wants people to seek a passive life, not an active life. It gives people the knowledge of how to follow the way of Buddha, but not the strength to understand and change the world. . . . This kind of education fosters, to a large extent, people who follow religion, the feudal ruling clique and the traditional culture. Their function is to defend the feudal and religious rule. This is a force that restrains and blocks development for the Tai society and culture that is facing a conflict with the historical tide of modernization, and the basically negative effect of this malpractice is evident. [17]

The text goes on to argue that the only way to promote a modern style education in Sipsong Panna is to penetrate the traditional outlook of the Tai, who tend to prefer the well-known, old-fashioned style of education. According to the text, forbidding temple education is no solution, but ways have to be found to convince people that only in Chinese schools are their children brought up to adapt to the modernizing world. Buddhism, on the contrary, is held responsible for bringing up a population of self-centered and xenophobic people.[18]

The people within Sipsong Panna who are most negative toward the temple education and see no potential in it are generally the Han Chinese who possess high positions in school administration, headmasters, older teachers in administrative posts and Han cadres in the government education departments. They tend to see Buddhist education as the main force that prevents boys from having a Chinese education, and they rarely seek out problems within the Chinese educational system itself. Many of them are worried that the Tai might even become more "backward" than the minorities living in the mountains who have always been considered to be most backward by the incoming Chinese and the Tai themselves.[19]

Many Tai teachers and cadres share this critical view on the institution of temple education. The Tai who have a Chinese education themselves would never let their sons participate in Buddhist education because it would prevent them from moving upward in Chinese society. However, they often tend to be more open toward the idea of cooperation between schools and temples. In the early 1950s, some monks were invited to teach in the new schools, but during the resurgence of religious activities since 1980, cooperation between monasteries and schools has been extremely limited. Monks and teachers are mostly only in contact with each other when teachers go to the monasteries to inform the monks that novices must go to school, or when monks go to the schools to obtain permission for novices in school to participate in temple activities.

A few highly educated Han and Tai in Sipsong Panna have a more positive view of temple education, mainly because they regard it as an opportunity for boys who do not manage to pass the examinations within the school system. However, with the recent attempts from scholarly monks in Sipsong Panna to set up higher education for novices, a more respectful attitude toward temple education seems to be slowly developing among some of the Tai with a Chinese higher education. Some of them are (mostly privately) putting forward the view that Buddhist education has not prevented Thailand from modernizing, and that it is therefore wrong to hold that educating novices is responsible for slow economic development among the Tai in Sipsong Panna. By claiming that Buddhist education is undergoing change, they indirectly reject the common Chinese interpretation of temple education as a static form of education. However, it is beyond dispute that temple education today is an obstacle to the spread of Chinese education and thus Chinese culture, language, nationalism, knowledge of Chinese history, etc. This is basically the reason why the Chinese authorities, including most Han Chinese teachers, are firmly against it.

Local statistics on school enrollment rates, retention rates, etc., are unreliable and should not be used as bases for any conclusions about the educational situation of the Tai and other ethnic groups in Sipsong Panna.[20] In general, schools had many students in periods when religion was severely suppressed and the demands for school attendance strict. However, the statistical data does not indicate what numerous interviewees told me: that students who were enrolled went to school only once or twice a week, that many dropped out after a

Table 8.2. Number of Schools, Students, School Employees and Enrollment Rates from 1953 to 1990 in Mengla County

Year	Number of Schools	Number of Students	Employees in Schools	Enrollment Rate %
1953	15	950	42	13.8
1958	40	3,310	87	50
1962	60	2,462	127	28.3
1966	62	5,714	267	62
1970	160	8,312	297	68
1975	283	19,255	697	92
1983	239	13,138	1,131	85
1988	245	18,904	1,184	89.4
1990	260	19,729	1,260	88.1

Table 8.3. Some Statistical Data Concerning the Whole of Sipsong Panna Prefecture

Year	Number of Schools	Number of Students	Number of Teachers
1950	11	390	22
1957	More than 100	More than 9,000	—
1964	About 400	More than 35,000	About 1,000

few months, that students were not registered according to nationality, and that teachers and cadres over-reported the number of students. Tables 8.2 and 8.3 show local statistics concerning number of schools, students and employees in schools in Mengla County in Sipsong Panna from 1953 to 1990 and in the whole of Sipsong Panna. These tables lack the figures from 1980 to 1982, when the number of students fell considerably, according to the Education Department.

There is different local statistical data for the whole of Sipsong Panna which suffers from the same shortcomings as the above-mentioned data. Table 8.3 is made on basis of the different sources of information from local education departments and other reports concerning education.[21]

Statistical data concerning the whole of Sipsong Panna in 1990 suggests that the enrollment rate of school-age children was 88.1

percent, but only 55 percent finished 5 years of elementary school. Minority students (that is, all students not classified as *Hanzu*) made up 76 percent of pupils in elementary school, 58 percent of students in lower secondary schools (*chuzhong*) and 37 percent of students in higher secondary schools (*gaozhong*). Thirty-five percent of all Sipsong Panna's teachers and school administrators, and 60 percent of teachers in elementary school were national minorities. In the two key point schools in Sipsong Panna (the elementary and regular secondary schools with the best facilities outside of the local state farms, which have their own schools as well) the majority of teachers and students belong to the Han nationality. In secondary school, 78 out of 84 teachers are Han, and out of 1,370 students in 1992, 227 were Tai whereas 830 were Han. Most of the minority students in this school are children of cadres working in the prefectural capital of Jinghong, and many of the students classified as *Daizu* (Dai nationality) have one Han Chinese parent. In 1993 and 1994, not a single Tai graduate form the key point higher secondary school managed to pass the university entrance examination.

THE POSITION OF THE TAI LANGUAGE IN SCHOOLS

Facing the obstacles against the development of Chinese education in Sipsong Panna in the early 1980s, the government decided to reintroduce the Tai script as a subject in some elementary schools and in one bilingual class a year in the teachers training school. This, it was hoped, would make the schools more attractive for the Tai and facilitate their learning of the Chinese language. Elementary schools in Sipsong Panna may decide to start classes in Tai language, and school teachers in Tai villages are encouraged by the Education Department to use Tai to explain Chinese terms and sentences that students do not understand. In reality this is seldom practiced, due to the shortage of Tai teachers. The same problem exists in villages of other ethnic groups in Sipsong Panna, where most teachers do not speak the local language. In principal, the Education Department wants to appoint local elementary school teachers who speak the language of the local pupils. However, until now such people were in short supply, and so is the necessary outside funding to train more Tai teachers.

Most elementary schools that offer Tai lessons have one class of students, who in addition to following the regular curriculum participate in 1 or 2 hours of Tai per week for the last 1 to 3 years of elementary school.[22] Often pupils may decide themselves if they want to participate, and although Han and other nationalities are allowed to attend these classes, they never do. Only very few schools conduct experiments with teaching all lessons in Tai from the first year of elementary school and teaching Chinese as a second language.[23] In 1986 the prefecture government decided to abandon the use and teaching of "new Tai" and return to a standardized version of "old Tai." This created new problems, because a whole generation of Tai had only learned "new Tai" in schools: girls and women who had attended schools or literacy courses since the mid-1950s, and boys and young men who had grown up in periods where few were able to become novices and learn "old Tai" in the temples, so had only learned "new Tai" and/or Chinese. The local newspaper, which had always been published in "new Tai", started printing in "old Tai" in 1993, but according to one of its editors many people were against this, because they were not able to read "old Tai," and the journalists themselves had problems adapting to it. On the other hand, many of the Tai who were against the reintroduction of "old Tai" seem to be gradually changing their opinions now because of the increasing contacts with Thailand, Burma and Laos.

Whereas most people in Sipsong Panna agree on the necessity for the bilingual class at the teacher training school, there is a standing disagreement on the issue of bilingual education and the teaching of Tai in regular elementary and secondary schools. Teachers, school administrators and members of the Education Department in the three counties and the prefecture are roughly divided between a majority, who see the teaching of Tai as a temporary necessity, and a minority who want an expansion and improvement of Tai language instruction in elementary schools, in examinations and in secondary education.

The main argument for maintaining Tai lessons in elementary schools, while not expanding them, is that they are looked upon as a necessity in a transition period until more (eventually all) Tai understand and read Chinese, and as a means of persuading Tai parents to have their children, especially their boys, participate in Chinese education. Therefore, some administrators emphasize that the goal of the bilingual Tai class in the teacher training school is not to spread the knowledge of Tai language and culture, but on the contrary, to facilitate its gradual, natural and voluntary disappearance:

> The final goal is to make all people of China speak Chinese
> (*Putonghua*). So the final goal of the bilingual class is to make
> everybody in Sipsong Panna speak our mother tongue. They can use
> Tai to explain in schools when necessary, but the idea is certainly not
> that everybody should learn Tai script or that Tai language should be
> spread further. There are too many languages in China, it would be
> impossible to teach them all. Teachers in elementary schools may
> themselves decide when it is necessary to speak Tai. They have to
> teach Tai script, but not to all the pupils.[24]

Some cadres fear that because the Tai are concerned about learning their own script, they run the risk of becoming "more backward" than the minorities from the mountains who have always been considered to be most backward. They consider the rapid development of Chinese education among the small Jinuo minority, in particular, to be proof of the educational advantages and civilizing effects of teaching more Chinese and less Tai. Another common argument in this connection is that the Tai language is simply not developed for use in a modernizing society.

A small but seemingly increasing number of Tai teachers, cadres and students have started to raise the question of introducing the Tai language into secondary schools, expanding the use of it in elementary schools and making the study of Tai history and culture part of the common school curriculum and examination. They criticize the fact that parents are forced to send their boys to the temples if they want them to learn Tai, and some believe that schools would be much more attractive to the common people if they were based on the Tai language and included Tai history and literature as part of the curriculum. Others have a more practical point of view, and argue that schools will only become relevant among the Tai peasants when they teach useful knowledge of agriculture in the Tai language. Some of the more pragmatic Han cadres feel that teaching the Tai language in schools should be extended mainly to convince people that they do not need to send their boys to the temples.

CREATING BACKWARDNESS: TAI CULTURE IN SCHOOL EDUCATION

Through their participation in the Chinese standardized state education, the Tai (and the other) students are presented with certain images of themselves as members of a national minority, of their own religion, language and customs, and of their relation with the Han majority. While the formal curriculum intends to stress national unity, equality between the nationalities and patriotism, the students are as much influenced by what is left out of the curriculum, by the structure of the educational system and by their daily experience of the actual position of their own inherited cultural values in the context of the education system.

Except for the Tai in the bilingual class in the teacher training school, minority students in Sipsong Panna use the same textbooks as students in the rest of China. Together with most other students in Yunnan they also study Yunnan history, and some classes in secondary education in Sipsong Panna study the recently locally edited "Sipsong Panna Geography" (*Xishuangbanna dili*). When asked directly what they have learned about their own ethnic group's history, literature and religion during their time in school, most students answered "nothing" without hesitation. However, when talking more generally about what they knew about the different *minzu* in China, when reading their school books, and listening to some of their classes, it was clear that they do learn about their own *minzu*. However, what they learn is mostly presented indirectly and tends to instill in students a negative image of their own cultural heritage. For instance, merely the fact that Tai language and literature does not have any place in secondary education gives the students the impression that it is not important and not relevant for modern education, or even that it stands in opposition to it.

Like other students in China the Tai are imbued, through their school education, with the official construction of the 56 nationalities (*minzu*) in China and, not least, their respective levels of development.[25] The Tai students often realize for the first time that their classification as *Daizu* also implicates a number of Tai people in other places of China with whom they have no contact and know nothing about. All the Tai students I have talked to are (sometimes painfully) aware that they belong to what is considered a "backward" minority group. Some of them find a certain comfort in the fact that the other minorities in Sipsong Panna are considered to be even more backward: they have no script, no "real" religion like Buddhism, and they are poor. Before entering school, the Tai students have not been used to interacting with the minorities from the mountains while living in their villages, and even before they encounter the official descriptions of the social evolution of the *minzu*, they already regard these groups as inferior. The following quotation is from a class in politics for the second year of lower secondary school in a nationalities boarding school in Sipsong Panna. The subject of the class was "when mankind entered the era of civilization (*wenming shidai*)." Approximately half of the students in the class were Tai, the other half belonged to various other ethnic groups in Sipsong Panna, such as Akha, Blang, Jinuo, Lahu, etc., who have generally been described in Chinese publications as belonging to the low evolutionary stage of "primitive society" (*yuanshi shehui*) at the time of the communist takeover in 1949. These non-Tai students belong to minorities without a script:

Teacher: "What is the characteristic of a 'primitive society'?"
Class: "IT HAS NO SCRIPT."
Teacher: "Right. Therefore mankind in the primitive society had not yet entered in the era of civilization (*wenming shidai*). From the time of slave society mankind entered the era of civilization. Before the time of slave society man had no culture (*wenhua*), no science (*kexue*). The most important characteristic of the era of civilization is the existence of script. In the primitive society people used knots, carvings in wood, etc., to remember things. Genuine script developed from pictographic script. Therefore we have the following stages: from no script, to knots and carvings, to pictographic script, and finally to genuine script. Then, why was there no division between physical and mental work in the primitive society?"
Class: "BECAUSE THERE WAS NO SCRIPT." [26]

The Tai students learn that the other *minzu* in Sipsong Panna were more backward than themselves at the time of the 1949 liberation, but on the other hand, they also learn through their education that they themselves belong to a group more backward than the majority.

According to books, the different stages of development among the nationalities in the early 1950s constituted "a living history of social evolution."[27] Students learn that the Tai (together with the Tibetans and Uygurs) had preserved their own typical "feudal serf society" (*fengjian nongnu zhidu*), and that today the area they inhabit is still considered to be backward in terms of both economy and culture.[28] This last point was put very directly by another teacher who was giving a lecture about the unequal economic development in China to a third-year class in lower secondary school in a nationalities boarding school. Although mainly talking about the economy, it was implicitly understood that cultural development was always directly related to the level of economic development. The teacher was talking about "backwardness" as a relative term:

Teacher: Is there a gap between our Panna [Sipsong Panna] and Kunming?
Class: "YES."
Teacher: "Right. Our Panna is very backward. Is there a gap between Jinghong City and Menghai County?"
Class: "YES."
Teacher: "Right. Menghai is more backward. Is there a gap between Menghai County and the small villages?"
Class: "YES."
Teacher: "Right. We all know which is most backward." [29]

The methods of teaching leave no room for discussions or questioning of the interpretations of *minzu* and cultural development presented in the schoolbooks. The most common way of teaching is to follow the book strictly with students answering questions by repeating sentences from the books, mostly all together. The classification of *minzu* in China, based upon Stalin's criteria of common language, territory, economy and culture, is presented as a scientific truth, and the students learn the criteria by heart. Their previous conceptions of the various local ethnic groups were not as strict and definite as those they now come to perceive as scientifically proven and final.

At the same time, the students learn about the Communist Party's minority policy that advocates equality of the *minzu*, equal rights to economic development and education, etc. They learn how the party established autonomous minority regions to ensure the minorities' rights to self-determination, and how the party even helped certain minorities "to jump over some stages of history in their development."[30] The language in the books is generally positive and presents a picture of all the *minzu* as part of "one family," making up one common *minzu*, the *Zhonghua minzu* (Chinese nation) to which all the *minzu* have contributed: the Han mainly with science; the minorities mainly with songs, dances and medical herbs.[31] Indirectly, the positive language and the interpretation of the relation between the *minzu* makes it clear and unquestionable that not only the party, but also the advanced Han as a whole, have helped the more backward minorities to develop. Before liberation, the Mongols with all their leather were not able to produce leather shoes, the Tibetans with all their timber could not make matches, some minorities still practiced slash-and-burn agriculture, minority areas had no institutions for higher education, and Tibet, for instance, did not have one public road. However, the text continues, "Today the differences between the levels of cultural and economic development in the minority areas and the Han areas are decreasing."[32]

The Tai students, like students in the rest of China, do not have any specific courses in religion, but teaching about religion is part of the political lessons. Since all the Tai are Buddhists and most Tai students (with the exception of some from Jinghong Town) have been brought up with this belief, the anti-religious attitudes in the schools have a direct impact on their self-esteem and perception of their own culture. Many Tai students seem to find a certain relief in the fact that they have a "real" religion (*zongjiao*) which is acceptable in China, and not just "superstition" (*mixin*), which is more "backward" and even forbidden. Unfortunately for the other minorities in Sipsong Panna their religious practices are not considered to be related to one of the world religions and may easily fall under the category of "superstition." In lower secondary school, students learn that superstitious people believe in gods (*shen*) and spirits (*gui*) that "do not really exist."[33] Superstition (unlike China's "five major religions" of Islam, Buddhism, Catholicism, Protestantism and Daoism) is "a result of human benignity" from the earlier times of human society when peoples' ability to reflect upon things was developing, but still not to the degree that they were able to produce scientific knowledge.[34] According to the political teaching material, superstition prevents the development of modern science and keeps people in ignorance and poverty. In senior secondary school, students read about the characteristics of "primitive religion" (*yuanshi zongjiao*), but it remains unclear what the actual difference is between so-called "primitive religion" and "superstition." The characteristics of religion are religious scripts, doctrine, church or temple and priests or monks. These characteristics do not apply to "primitive religion" which ends up having more in common with the description of "superstition."

The students are presented with a very simple, basically Marxist analysis of religion that describes it as a social phenomenon that evolved in the class society and basically functioned as a means of suppressing the working people who used religion to escape poverty and misery. Therefore, religion in the long run is doomed to disappear in the socialist society where the exploiting class has been eradicated, and science, political consciousness and human cognition continue to develop.[35] On a general level, the political teaching material explains that religion in the socialist Chinese society is no longer directly connected to a small, exploiting class except in the few cases where members of minorities advocate secession from China and use religion for this purpose.[36] It refers to the constitution, which guarantees the freedom to believe or not to believe in religion and, of greatest relevance for the Tai, which maintains that religion is not allowed to interfere with or obstruct the national education system. Thus, the students study the party's interpretation of why religions still exist in the socialist society, how it will eventually disappear, why the government allows freedom of religion, and what this freedom implies. Students learn nothing about the contents of the various religions, so when asked what they have learned about their own religion, most Tai students answer "nothing" or "that religion is free in China."

Some secondary schools in Sipsong Panna, use the recently locally edited booklet *Sipsong Panna Geography* (*Xishuangbanna dili*) as teaching material. The purpose of this book is to increase students' knowledge of the geography of Sipsong Panna and to promote patriotic education by teaching about local conditions. Therefore, the book also has a short chapter about the history of Sipsong Panna where it is repeatedly emphasized that Sipsong Panna has always been part of the Chinese state. It informs about the climate, the natural resources and the development since 1949, and it has a special section about the tourist spots of Sipsong Panna. This book (taught for a total of 10 lessons during the 6 years of lower and upper secondary school) is the only material about their own area which students in the regular secondary schools study.

THE NATIONAL MESSAGE: "MOTHERLAND, I LOVE YOU FOREVER!"

Ever since the early 1980s, patriotic education (*aiguozhuyi jiaoyu*) has been given high priority in the minority areas on the borders of the People's Republic. Like in the rest of China, it was further enforced after the crushing of the demonstrations in Tiananmen in 1989 and the government's subsequent campaign against "counterrevolutionary rebellion." Nationalism has become a dominant theme in official Chinese rhetoric, media and education. It has become a means to strengthen China vis-à-vis the international community, and to erode actual or potential internal ethnic conflicts. In Yunnan Province, where one-third of the population belongs to national minority groups, the government has put great efforts into spreading and extending patriotic education, especially in higher education and in the areas closest to the borders. Since Sipsong Panna borders Burma and Laos and the ethnic groups here have strong and historically close ethnic and cultural relationships across the borders, patriotic education is vigorously promoted in this area.

After the crushing of the democracy movement in June 1989, the local government held several meetings for all the students in secondary schools in Sipsong Panna to inform them about what had happened in Beijing and to make clear that political and ideological work would now be strengthened among them. Most students had only heard rumors about the demonstrations in addition to the official versions, and few of them knew much about what had taken place. Apart from the campaign to study Lei Feng and other revolutionary heroes, all schools and teachers were informed of the need for strengthening patriotic education as the main element in political and ideological work. The introduction of a course in Sipsong Panna geography in secondary schools was a direct result of the central guidelines as to how patriotic education should be conducted in minority areas, making "love of the local area" the fundament for "love of the country." Thus, the most important reason why teaching about local conditions is gaining ground within the educational system today is its role in "patriotic" education.

Patriotic education is incorporated into teaching on politics, and history in particular. In addition, the government has arranged special "speech competitions" in the last years, with patriotism as the topic. In 1994, secondary school students took part in a provincial competition for the best patriotic speech in standard Chinese *Putonghua* (as opposed to the local Yunnan Chinese dialect). A number of local competitions were set up in secondary schools, and the winners of each school within the prefecture competed against each other. The other students also wrote essays about patriotism and many blackboard messages in schools had patriotism as their theme.[37] Since it was just after the Asian Games, many of the patriotic speeches concerned China's greatness, as reflected in its number of gold and silver medals. Otherwise, the non-Han students' speeches and short essays were very much alike in their emotional way of repeating the official, nationalist rhetoric from the books:

> I love my own China. Some people from outside have asked me if I am a Korean or Japanese just because being an Aini*zu* my skin is dark. I answered, "I AM A PURE CHINESE!" (*dididaodao de Zhongguoren*).[38]

> Motherland, my mother, I love you!

> Even though our country is poor and backward, I still love it just as much as my own mother!

> We young people need patriotic education and to love the fatherland is to love the party.

> China has changed, so today she is a rich country. A country with Chinese socialist characteristics. SO LET US ALL RISE UP AND STRUGGLE FOR THE *ZHONGHUA MINZU*!

> The whole of Sipsong Panna is singing the same song about our motherland, our mother.[39]

One of the most central elements in the patriotic education in schools is that all *minzu* should be convinced that they belong to the *Zhonghua minzu*, a national identity covering all ethnic identities in

China. Furthermore, it is propagated that all *minzu* have contributed to the history and development of China, and that therefore "the Han can never depart from the minorities, the minorities never from the Han, and the minorities never from each other." Thus, the nationalistic content in education focuses on common history and the common political/economic/cultural interests of all people within China. Common symbols are the mythical Yellow Emperor, the *Zhonghua minzu*, the Olympic sports heroes, the national flag, emblem and anthem:

Teacher: "What is the subject of today?"
Class: "THE NATIONAL FLAG, THE NATIONAL EMBLEM, THE NATIONAL ANTHEM."
Teacher: "What should all citizens do?"
Class: "LOVE THE NATIONAL FLAG, LOVE THE NATIONAL EMBLEM, LOVE THE NATIONAL ANTHEM."
Teacher: "The national emblem symbolizes the unison of all people under the leadership of the great Communist Party. How should we treat our national emblem?"
Class: "WE SHALL ALL LOVE AND RESPECT OUR NATIONAL EMBLEM."
Teacher: "We have to love our fatherland and love socialism. Can love of the fatherland and love of socialism be separated?"
Class: "NO."[40]

The people engaged in promoting patriotic education among minorities emphasize that one of the most important factors is to avoid Han chauvinism and to prevent the minorities from getting the impression that they are backward.[41] In order to prevent minorities from turning against China and becoming "local nationalists," they should be convinced of their contribution and role in the socialist Chinese state as minorities. The edition of local teaching material is an attempt to solve the dilemma between the official propaganda and policy, which praise the equality of the *minzu*, and the minorities' practical experiences, which demonstrate the low evaluation of their own languages, histories and religions within China. Within the educational system, there is a clear conflict between the government's wish to show how the *minzu* contributed equally to the history of China, and the presentations of the alleged scientifically proven

backwardness of minorities. These presentations undermine the
government's nationalistic propaganda among minorities, and the Tai
students seem more influenced by the construction of themselves as
members of a backward group than by the superficial statements about
their contribution to Chinese history and society.

TAI STUDENTS' ETHNIC IDENTITY: THE CONFLICT
BETWEEN FAMILY AND SCHOOL EDUCATION

Most Tai students in Sipsong Panna have learned at least some Tai
script in elementary school; they can recognize the consonants and
vowels. With the exception of the 40-odd Tai students per year in the
bilingual class in the teachers training school, only few have learned
enough to be able to actually read and write Tai. Due to the
standardized curriculum and the small proportion of Tai teachers, the
Tai students have heard very little from individual teachers about their
own history, stories, traditions, religion, language, etc. Many Tai
students beyond the level of junior secondary school are profoundly
influenced by the images of the Tai as a slowly developing, even
backward, ethnic group. They tend to be ashamed of "the backward
habits of their family," "the tradition of sending boys to temples" and
"the low level of education among Tai in general."[42]

There is, however, one aspect of ethnicity which Tai students
repeatedly mentioned as a source of pride; namely, their script. One
reason for this might be that the content of their school education
allows them to view their script as a proof of "relative development"
and "literary tradition." Their religious practices, on the other hand, are
presented as "obstructing modernization," their belief in spirits is
labeled as "superstition" and the history of the Tai king and the state of
Sipsong Panna is not likely to be part of the curriculum. Thus, while
attempting to disassociate themselves from the cultural practices of
their Tai families in the villages, they retain the Tai script as an
accepted ethnic marker. In his study of Tai history and ethnicity Shih-
Chung Hsieh found that the institution of the Tai king, the *chao
phaendin*, was the most crucial factor in Tai ethnic identity and
solidarity.[43] My fieldwork convinced me that the *chao phaendin*'s role
in the ethnicity of the Tai has been profoundly challenged during the
last 40 years, when the Tai to an increasing degree have been forced to
identify themselves in relation to the Chinese rather than to the other

Tai people south of Sipsong Panna. The *chao phaendin* has been physically absent from Sipsong Panna for the last 50-odd years, and refrains from attempting actively to maintain his influence in the Tai community. Furthermore, school education presents the Tai students with an interpretation of history that minimizes the role of the *chao phaendin* and makes it clear that a Tai identity focusing on the previous king would run counter to the interests of the Chinese state. All the students I have talked to know that in history, Sipsong Panna was ruled by the *chao phaendin*. Many of them know that the *chao phaendin* is now in Kunming; some think he is long dead; and most students have no idea of why he is in Kunming rather than in Sipsong Panna. To the younger generations of Tai today, the *chao phaendin* does not seem to play a significant role in their identification as Tai. Whereas the *chao phaendin* (and other living *chao* as well) still enjoys very high status among the Tai, I found that it was especially among the monks and among the rural Tai above 50 years that the *chao phaendin* was one of the main symbols of Tai identity. For most Tai it is language, script and religion that more than anything else identify them as Tai in China and contrast them with the Han and the other local ethnic groups.

The Tai students are all interested in learning their script, and they often emphasize that if they had the chance they would participate in training in their own language even if it was not part of the examination. The majority argue that learning proper Chinese is indispensable, first of all to increase their chances of further education, but that learning Tai also ought to be part of school education. Students from the other ethnic groups without a script feel that learning Chinese is the most important task, and that studying a local language would be a waste of time. Partly for this reason, local teachers generally praise other groups, specifically the Akha and Jinuo, for being more open than the Tai toward the Han, and for putting more effort into learning Chinese and succeeding in school. Unlike the Tai, they regard the school as the only way to escape poverty and backwardness. Many of the other minorities in Sipsong Panna know some colloquial Tai, but they find that learning the Tai script would merely be an extra burden on them. It would not help them within the educational system or to get a job later on. In this respect there is a conflict of interest between the Tai (one-third of the population) and the other minorities (together totally one-third of the population as well), and on these grounds many

cadres argue that the Tai language has no place in secondary education
or in any of the non-Tai villages.

The Tai who have attended Chinese schools at a higher level are
generally not very explicit and demanding in their wishes to strengthen
the position of Tai culture within education. The Tai intellectuals have
no organization to promote "Tai culture" (such as, for instance, the Yi
and the Naxi nationalities have), they have very few researchers, and
there are few of them at decisive administrative and political levels.
Except for the few students who are also novices or monks, the
Chinese-educated Tai tend to disassociate themselves from their
cultural heritage and upbringing in their villages to the point of being
embarrassed about their religious practices and the poor knowledge of
Chinese in their villages. It is mainly in the course of their education
beyond elementary school that they experience a contradiction between
the things they learn during their childhood in the Tai villages and the
content of school education. In their families, religion constitutes a
significant part of village life, the only language employed is Tai,
novices and monks enjoy high status and most of them have heard
stories of the Tai king and his kingdom from parents and grandparents.
In school, all these aspects of life in the Tai villages are repudiated as
being worthless or even an impediment to modernization and the
students' own careers, and therefore, in practice, most students seem to
have no choice but to disassociate themselves from it.

While students in the bilingual classes in the teachers training
school and in the Tai classes in Yunnan Institute of Nationalities in
Kunming (approximately 15 students per year) are well-trained in their
own script, the only Tai students in secondary and higher education
who have a profound knowledge of their own religion, language and
history, are those few male students who are also novices or monks. All
monks today are aware of the law of compulsory education in China,
and many of the better educated among them want their novices to
learn mathematics, history, other languages than Tai, etc. Some of the
monks now support novices attending higher Chinese education in
order to return to the temple afterwards as qualified teachers. Many
other monks accept that their novices go to school, mainly because they
have no other options, but they would rarely force them to stay in
school if they did not want to.

The few novices who have made it into secondary education have
all attended a central elementary school (*zhongxin xiaoxue*) during the

last 2 years of their studies, and they did not get extra points at the examination. Although they agree that it was very difficult for them to pass the examination, none of them regret having been novices and all speak with affection about the education they received in the temple. They emphasize that all their knowledge of Tai language, history, religion and literature has been acquired in the temple or from their grandparents, not in school. They consider it to be a great advantage to have learned Tai script so well and they use it for taking notes in school, transcribing Chinese and English words, writing letters home, etc.

The few novices and monks who continue into secondary education encounter contradictions between their religious belief and the content of education in the Chinese schools. They are also faced with a basic indifference toward their religion in the daily life of the boarding school. They come from an environment where their lives are centered around the activities in the temple. School ignores the Buddhist festivals held in all Tai villages and regards their religious activities as a waste of time and a hindrance to further development. During secondary education, the monks and novices learn that all *minzu* have the right to have their own religious beliefs in China. At the same time, they are taught that religion teaches people to escape life and prevents them from modernizing their economy. Still, the novices and monks in secondary and higher education whom I have talked to deny that school education has in any way influenced their opinions about their religion. Their previous temple education and continued ties with other novices and monks make them less inclined than the other students to deviate from previous beliefs and opinions about their own cultural background:

> During my education all teachers taught according to Marxism and dialectic materialism. I always disagreed with their viewpoints on religion and history. I have learned a lot of new things, but I do not agree with everything and I have not changed my mind about my own religion.[44]

And in the words of another student and novice: "Before starting in school we already knew what it meant to be a Tai and believe in Buddhism. No school can ever change this." However, since the Chinese schools have a negative attitude toward religion, and Tai language has no place in the Chinese educational system beyond elementary school, many monks who want an education prefer to obtain it in Thailand, where "they really appreciate us monks." Every year 10 monks may get an official scholarship to go and study in Thailand, but in fact a much larger number leaves every year (some also to visit family members or even to do business). Monks may go freely to Thailand, and every year several monks and older novices from Sipsong Panna, manage to raise private financial support for being educated in the temples in Thailand. Therefore, Chinese education is no longer the only alternative for boys to the education in the temples in Sipsong Panna and with the improvement of the economy and the increasing contacts with Thailand, more novices and monks will probably look for educational opportunities there. Many parents regard the temple education in Thailand as a higher (sort of secondary) education after the training in the local monastery.

Obviously, the novice and monk students are very positive toward the institution of temple education, but among the other students this topic often sparks heated discussions. During my interviews with students, it became increasingly clear that the young students in lower secondary school tend to be much more sympathetic toward the customs of their own family and other people in the villages than are the students in upper secondary school. This is especially so with regard to religion. One of my questions, which never failed to arouse laughter, giggling and lively discussions, was whether or not a female student would prefer her boyfriend to have been a novice and whether she would let any future son become a novice:

Discussion between three Tai girls, all 13 years old and all attending first year of lower secondary school:

A: "I would prefer my husband to have been a novice because then he could teach our children Tai script."
B: "I would also rather marry a novice."
C: "Sure, I would prefer to marry somebody who had been a novice. We Tai believe in superstition [sic!] and if a boyfriend has not been a novice he might say nasty things and behave badly."
All in agreement: "Certainly! It is best to marry a man who has learned something in the temple".

Interviewer:	"What if you have a son?"
B:	"My son has to be novice!"
Interviewer:	"Why?"
A:	"Boys should be novices. They can study at the same time, it is no problem."
B:	"Or he can become a novice after he finishes elementary school. Many boys do that."[45]

The majority of female students in junior secondary school have a positive view toward the temple education, whereas most female students beyond the level of junior secondary school firmly state that they do not want a boyfriend who has been a novice and that they will certainly never let their sons become one. Male students generally tend to be more positive toward temple education. They all have friends and close relatives who are or have been novices, and many of them have had to make what they thought was a difficult choice between school and monastery. Again, the youngest male students were most positive toward temple education.

Generally, students are very realistic in their attitudes toward temple education and their own school education. They are all very much aware of the fact that Tai language, culture and history play no role whatsoever if you want to be successful within the educational system. While saying that they would welcome more Tai training in schools, they emphasized that schools would never expand Tai education as long as it was useless for obtaining higher education, for the Chinese state as a whole and therefore also for their own ambitions. Of course, the difference in age between students in lower and upper secondary school explains some of the major difference in, for instance, level of reflection and the ability to express one's own thoughts. However, at the same time I found that the students' increasing repudiation of their own cultural background can be partly explained by their long-term stay in boarding schools, which prevents them from participating in village life. The majority of Tai students who graduate from senior/specialized secondary or higher education have lived in boarding schools in the cities since they were 13 years old, sometimes even since they were eleven (since higher elementary school). For 6 or 7 years (in secondary school), and an additional 3 or 4 years (in college or university), most of them visit their families only once every 6 months, they only speak Tai with fellow Tai students and they stop participating in religious activities. In order to succeed within the school system students are simply forced to disassociate themselves from their religious background, their language, the things they have learned from elderly people about Tai history and their own assumptions that they belong to a dominant group with valuable traditions. Only when putting aside what they have learned from home and realizing the overwhelming importance of learning Chinese, studying Chinese history, criticizing backwardness, propagating the *Zhonghua minzu*, repeating the nationalist/patriotic messages, etc., will they have a chance to continue in the educational system. Therefore, most Tai intellectuals and students who have ambitions to continue into higher education are more preoccupied with adapting to the cultural values supported by schools and propagated in the broader context of Chinese society than with struggling to win a place for Tai culture within this system. This also helps to explain why the number of Tai students who manage to study beyond lower secondary school is still so small.

To a certain extent, the hopes of many officials and school administrators of changing the cultural habits of the Tai by placing them in the "new surroundings" of Chinese boarding schools have been fulfilled. Students do start to have doubts about their religious background and play down the role and significance of their own experiences in their Tai villages, their history and their language. Therefore, the Chinese-educated intellectual Tai have no contacts or feelings of shared interest with the other strata of educated Tai, the monks. Many of the Tai students and intellectuals become stigmatized in the sense that they express embarrassment about their cultural heritage to the point of rejecting it. However, some students and graduates, particularly those who have passed their mid-twenties, have recently started to express regret and discontentment for not having had the opportunity to study their own language properly, for not having had the chance of developing and adapting Tai language to the modern vocabulary and for having been taught that Buddhism is incompatible with modernization. They have started to question the theory that the Tai are a xenophobic, slowly developing group of people. However, these Tai constitute a small group of individuals with no scholarly or official positions to enable them to raise and push these questions within the Chinese political system.

CONCLUDING REMARKS

Chinese authorities have encountered huge problems in their efforts to establish Chinese education in Sipsong Panna. As in other minority areas of China, the basic purpose of education is to train a population to become literate in Chinese, and in this way become capable of participating in political administration and in modernizing the economy. Ideologically, the further development of the education of minorities is seen as needed in order to unite the population of China in an atmosphere of ethnic brotherhood, to play down and ultimately eradicate ethnic differences while promoting Chinese language, culture and history. In this sense, minority education constitutes an essential part of the Communist Party's nation-building and civilizing project. Education in the post-Cultural Revolution era has to demonstrate, especially to the national minorities in the border areas, that it is only participation in modern school education based upon Chinese language and history, socialism, patriotism and atheism that will bring about the desired economic development. Minority languages are granted a place in the educational system only when facilitating the learning of Chinese, or when it is considered to be an inevitable necessity to persuade people to attend the schools. Local history and culture are normally only incorporated to the degree that they prove to be instrumental for promoting the common national identity of the *Zhonghua minzu.*

Due to scarce resources and limited national financial support at the local level, the lack of teachers with a knowledge of the Tai language and disagreement among cadres on the issue of bilingual education, most Tai children receive all their elementary education in Chinese, which they mostly do not speak when they start in school. The language problem is one important reason for the low proportion of Tai with a secondary or higher education. Some researchers, local teachers and cadres argue that the introduction of Tai courses in more schools will not only make it easier for Tai children to learn Chinese, but will also result in more Tai boys attending school instead of participating in temple education. However, sporadic Tai training in school will not eliminate the fundamental contradiction between the content and form of the Chinese school system and the Tai people's cultural practices and ethnicity, which is one of the major reasons for the low number of Tai with a Chinese higher education.

The intellectual Tai with a Chinese higher education constitute a very small part of the Tai population, and are currently rather passive and aloof in their expressions of ethnic identity. On the whole, they tend to distance themselves from the cultural aspects that characterize Tai identity and are in direct conflict with their Chinese education. The Tai who have received a longer Chinese education are those who focus most on language, less on religion, and not at all on the king and the kingdom when expressing their Tai ethnicity. First of all, a Tai ethnicity centered around the king and the history of the kingdom would oppose and offend the party's propaganda of the *Zhonghua minzu* and its historically legitimized power in Sipsong Panna. This particular aspect of Tai ethnicity is probably the most sensitive and politically unacceptable. Second, the religious beliefs of the Tai collide directly with Chinese education due to the practice of temple education; therefore, this aspect of ethnicity is also problematic for the Tai intellectuals to defend. Finally, the Tai script plays an important symbolic role as the proof of a "high culture" and as a transmitter of religion, history and traditional Tai literature. However, it also has a practical value in the villages where many parents want their children to know the script of which they themselves have at least a modest knowledge of. This means that a focus on Tai script and language in fact also tends to run counter to the promotion of Chinese education, which emphasizes the advantages of abandoning one's language in favor of Chinese. Thus, it seems that Chinese education for the minority of Tai who participate beyond secondary level to a certain extent causes them to abandon their religion, accept the construction of themselves as members of a backward group, disregard their history as a kingdom and support the theory of the uselessness of the Tai language. However, a number of factors have begun to pull the Tai intellectuals and students in the opposite direction. With the increasing contacts with neighboring countries especially Thailand, many of them find for the first time that their language is in fact of use outside the Tai villages because of the speech communities in Thailand and Burma, and because it is relatively easy for them to learn Thai. Many express the wish to continue their studies in Thailand. Furthermore, they seem to find in Thailand the proof that Buddhism does not necessarily impede economic development. As a consequence, a minority of younger Tai students and intellectuals have started to see new potential in their own language and in their religion. In this particular respect, they are developing a new, growing solidarity with Tai peasants and monks.

Very few Tai go through the educational system at all, and most drop out after elementary school. For the vast majority of Tai living in the villages, Chinese school education has little impact on their ethnic identity and their cultural practices. If the government sincerely wants to change this and increase the influence of school education, it will probably have to change the form and content of school education to make it directly relevant to the Tai, their language, religious beliefs and economic conditions. In this event, many cadres and teachers fear that school education would not live up to its ideological purposes because it would directly support the already strong Tai ethnicity rather than attempting to break it. Running counter to the government's intentions, the Chinese education system in Sipsong Panna excludes the majority of Tai from participation. The low level of Chinese education among the majority of Tai that results from this makes them largely incapable of strongly and efficiently formulating and promoting their own cultural, political and economic interests within the context of the Chinese state. At the same time, by insisting upon an educational system that excludes all aspects of Tai culture and diminishes its values, the Communist Party involuntarily creates a strengthening ethnicity among the vast majority of Tai who do not participate in this education. Realizing that their language and religion are the main reasons for being excluded from Chinese education, they seek alternatives that support, rather than reject, their way of life and they turn toward the monks, the improvement of education in temples and their connections with other Tai and Buddhists outside China. The few who do participate in long-term Chinese education and become affected by its assimilative intentions tend to become stigmatized, and therefore they also welcome alternative explanations of their culture as valuable and useful. Thus, since many Tai seem to find alternatives especially in the increasing economic and cultural contacts with Thailand, the government might be paying a high price for not establishing a school system that takes Tai culture seriously.

NOTES

1. This paper is largely based upon chapter 10 of my Ph.D. thesis, "Lessons in Patriotism: State Education and Ethnic Identity among Naxi and

Tai in Southwest China," Aarhus University, Denmark, February 1996. I am
especially grateful for comments and suggestions from Marianne Bastid, Stevan
Harrell, Stig Thøgersen, Koen Wellens and Gerard A. Postiglione.

2. Stevan Harrell, "Introduction: Civilizing Projects and the Reaction to
Them", in Stevan Harrell (ed.), *Cultural Encounters on China's Ethnic
Frontiers* (Seattle and London: University of Washington Press, 1995).

3. So far, most Chinese and Western publications on the so-called
minority education (*minzu jiaoyu*) have focused on general aspects of policy;
for instance, Julia Kwong (ed.), *Chinese Education*, No. 22 (1989), p. 1; Gerard
A. Postiglione, "The Implications of Modernization for the Education of
China's National Minorities," in Ruth Hayhoe (ed.), *Education and
Modernization* (Oxford: Pergamon Press, 1992); Zhou Yaowen, "Bilingualism
and Bilingual Education in China," in *International Journal of the Sociology of
Language*, No. 97 (1992); Xie Qihuang et al. (eds.), *Zhongguo minzu jiaoyu
fazhan zhanlüe jueze* (*Choosing a Strategy for Developing China's Minority
Education*) (Beijing: Zhongyang minzuxueyuan chubanshe, 1991); Feng
Chunlin, "Qiantan Yunnan minzu jiaoyu de tedian ji qi fazhan yuanze" ("A
Brief Discussion of the Characteristics of Yunnan's Minority Education and the
Principles for its Development,") in Chen Hongtao et al. (eds.), *Yunnan minzu
jiaoyu yanjiu* (*Yunnan Ethnic Minority Educational Research*) (Beijing:
Zhongyang minzu xueyuan chubanshe, 1989); Wang Xihong et al. (eds.),
Zhongguo bianjing minzu jiaoyu (*Education of Minority Nationalities Living in
China's Border Areas*) (Beijing: Zhongyang minzu xueyuan chubanshe, 1990);
Sun Ruoqiong et al. (eds.), *Zhongguo shaoshu minzu jiaoyuxue gailun* (*An
Introduction to the Education of China's National Minorities*) (Beijing:
Zhongyang minzu xueyuan chubanshe, 1990); Jacques Lamontagne,
"Improving the Education of China's National Minorities," in Douglas Ray and
Deo H. Poonwassie (eds.), *Education and Cultural Differences: New
Perspectives* (New York: Garland Publishing, 1992). Among the few
exceptions are Wurlig Borchigud's article about Mongolian education in the
1960s: Wurlig Borchigud, "The Impact of Urban Ethnic Education on Modern
Mongolian Ethnicity, 1949-1966," in Stevan Harrell (ed.), *Cultural Encounters
on China's Ethnic Frontiers* (Seattle: University of Washington Press, 1995).
Also Lee Chae-Jin's study of education among the Korean minority (Lee Chae-
Jin, *China's Korean Minority: The Politics of Ethnic education* (Boulder, Co:
Westview Press, 1986).

4. The term "Thai" is used only to refer to citizens of Thailand whereas
"Tai" only refers to the ethnic group "Tai Lüe." Concerning the category of
"Tai" see for instance Charles F. Keyes, "Who are the Tai? Reflections on the

Invention of Identities," in Lola Romanucci-Ross and George A. De Vos (eds.), *Ethnic Identity* (Walnut Creek/London/New Delhi: Alta Mira Press, 1996).

5. Sipsong Panna Tai Nationality Autonomous Prefecture was established in 1953 and comprises the two counties of Menghai, Mengla and the city of Jinghong, where the prefectural government is seated. Of the 798,086 inhabitants in 1994, 36 percent were Dai (278,955 people), 26 percent Han, 19 percent Hani, 6 percent Lahu, 4 percent Bulang, 4 percent Yi and 2 percent Jinuo.

6. The main part of the fieldwork was carried out during 10 months in 1994-1995 in Kunming and Sipsong Panna, Yunnan Province. I conducted a large number of interviews with students, parents, teachers, cadres, monks, etc. in Sipsong Panna especially, listened to classes in secondary schools, read schoolbooks and participated in various local and school events (see Mette Halskov Hansen, "Lessons in Patriotism: State Education and Ethnic Identity among the Naxi and Tai in Southwest China," Ph.D. dissertation, Aarhus University, 1996, pp. 7-25 for more details on fieldwork methods.)

7. See especially Hsieh Shih-Chung, "On the Dynamics of Tai/Dai-Lue Ethnicity," in Stevan Harrell (ed.), *Cultural Encounters on China's Ethnic Frontiers*; Jiang Yingliang, *Baiyi de shenghuo wenhua (The Cultural Life of the Baiyi)* (Beijing: Zhonghua shuju yinxing, 1950); Jiang Yingliang, *Daizu shi* (The History of the *Tai Nationality*) (Chengdu: Sichuan minzu chubanshe, 1983); Gao Lishi, *Xishuangbanna Daizu de lishi yu wenhua (The History and Culture of the Tai Nationality in Sipsong Panna)* (Kunming: Yunnan minzu chubanshe, 1992); and Chen Han-seng, *Frontier Land Systems in Southernmost China* (New York: Institute of Pacific Relations, 1949) concerning the history of Sipsong Panna.

8. Chen Han-Seng, *Frontier Land Systems in Southernmost China* (New York: Institute of Pacific Relations, 1949), pp.47-49.

9. Jiang Yingliang, *Baiyi de shenghuo wenhua (The Cultural Life of the Baiyi)* (Beijing: Zhonghua shuju yinxing, 1950), pp.288-289.

10. Friedrich Engels, *The Origin of the Family, Private Property, and the State* (New York: International Publishers 1972 [1883]); and Lewis Henry Morgan, *Ancient Society* (Tucson: University of Arizona Press, 1985 [1877]).

11. From an interview with Han Chinese teacher and administrator.

12. Temples have to report the number of novices to the religious department that keeps statistics on the numbers of monks, novices and temples.

13. These figures are based on information from religious departments in Sipsong and are certainly not exact: while it is possible to count temples, all monks and novices do not necessarily register. Furthermore, there have been

monks from abroad in Sipsong Panna at least since the 1980s, and whereas some boys are novices for several years, others stay for only a few months.

14. From Sipsong Panna Prefecture Education Commission (ed.), *Xishuangbanna Zhou minzu jiaoyu qingkuang* (*The Educational Situation in Sipsong Panna Prefecture*) (Report, 1992), p. 2. Like in the rest of the country, elementary school education lasts for 6 years, but in the countryside of Sipsong Panna (and several other areas) it is often divided into 4 years of lower and 2 years of higher elementary school. Sometimes an examination after 4 years determines whether or not children can continue into higher elementary school.

15. Although I always tried to make clear the purpose of my interviews to the interviewees, it was inevitable that some Tai, especially in the villages, thought that I represented the Chinese school system and had come to criticize them for not sending their boys to school. Some people later told me that they had expected me, a university graduate, to regard their temple education as backward and useless.

16. An interview in Mengla 1994.

17. Sun Ruoqiong, Teng Xing and Wang Meifeng (eds.), *Zhongguo shaoshu minzu jiaoyuxue gailun (An Introduction to the Education of China's National Minorities)* (Beijing: Zhongguo loadong chubanshe, 1990), p. 266.

18. Ibid, p.268.

19. Although they would paraphrase the official policy when talking in their office with other cadres walking in and out, many of them were actually more radical in their opposition against the temple education when talking in private. A few (retired) cadres were, on the contrary, more in favor of it when talking privately.

20. It is very important to notice that national statistics concerning education of the Tai are useless because they concern not only the Tai in Sipsong Panna, but the various other Tai people in other parts of Yunnan especially who are officially part of the *Dai*. These statistics (which I have not included in this article) give a wrong picture of the situation among the Tai in Sipsong Panna, partly because Chinese education has a longer history and is much more widespread among the Tai in Dehong than among the Tai in Sipsong Panna.

21. Apart from some unpublished local statistics, figures have been derived from Zou Zhenxie, "Fazhanzhong de Xishuangbanna minzu jiaoyu" ("The Developing Minority Education of Sipsong Panna") in Yan Sanlong et al. (eds.), *Xishuangbanna minzu jiaoyu* (*Ethnic Minority Education in Sipsong Panna*) (Kunming: Yunnan minzu chubanshe, 1992); *Xishuangbanna Daizu Zizhizhou tongji nianjian* (*Statistical Yearbook of Sipsong Panna Dai*

Nationality Autonomous County) (Jinghong County, 1989); *Xishuangbanna Daizu Zizhizhou gaikuang* (*A Survey of Sipsong Panna Dai Nationality Autonomous Prefecture*) (Kunming: Yunnan minzu chubanshe, 1986).

22. Many researchers, teachers and cadres outside Sipsong Panna (and indeed some within) tend to believe that bilingual education (*shuangyu jiaoyu*) is more widespread among the Tai than it is in practice.

23. During fieldwork, I was only able to locate one such school. Teachers in this school claimed that the Tai students in the one experimental bilingual class performed better in all subjects than the other Tai in regular classes in this school. (All children in the school were Tai).

24. From an interview with a Han Chinese teacher and administrator.

25. See Mette H. Hansen, "Fostering 'Love of Learning': Naxi Responses to Ethnic Images in Chinese State Education," in Kjeld Erik Broedsgaard and David Strand (eds.), *Reconstructing Twentieth Century China: Social Control, Civil Society and National Identity* (Oxford: Oxford University Press, forthcoming) about the education of the Naxi minority for a more detailed discussion of the teaching of ethnic categories and social evolution in textbooks.

26. From an interview in November 1994, secondary school in Sipsong Panna.

27. From the compulsory teaching material for the 3 years of lower and upper secondary school, see *Sixiang zhengzhi* (*Ideology and Politics*) (Guangdong: gaodeng jiaoyu chubanshe, 1992), p.121.

28. Some of the different stages of the evolution of *minzu* are described in, for instance, *Sixiang zhengzhi* (*Ideology and Politics*) for third year of upper secondary school (1992, pp. 119-121.)

29. From an interview in October 1994, secondary school in Sipsong Panna.

30. *Sixiang zhengzhi* (*Ideology and Politics*), third year of upper secondary school (1992, p.127.)

31. Ibid, p. 123.

32. Ibid, p. 130.

33. *Sixiang zhengzhi* (*Ideology and Politics*), first year of lower secondary school (1993, p. 67.)

34. Ibid, p. 67.

35. *Sixiang zhengzhi* (*Ideology and Politics*), third year of upper secondary school (1992, p. 139.)

36. Ibid, pp. 147-148.

37. On blackboards outside the school buildings teachers, students and representatives of the Party's sub-organizations write short stories, political slogans, moral encouragement, etc. In 1995 the patriotic speech competitions were held in connection with China's National Day on October 1, and the 50 years, anniversary of the end of World War II, and therefore most blackboards during this time were dominated by patriotic themes. However, during the rest of the year as well, nationalism and patriotism are central topics on blackboards.

38. Aini is a local appellation for the Akha people officially classified as *Hanizu.*'

39. From participants' speeches in the competition for the best patriotic speech in Chinese, November, 1994.

40. From an interview in 1994, lower secondary school, Sipsong Panna.

41. See, for instance, Xie Benshu et al. (eds.), *Minzu diqu aiguozhuyi jiaoyu jianming duben* (*An Elementary Study of Patriotic Education in Minority Areas*) (Kunming: Yunnan renmin chubanshe, 1994) and Yunnan Province History Society et al. (eds.), *Aiguozhuyi yu lishi jiaoyu* (*Patriotism and History Education*) (Kunming: Yunnan daxue chubanshe, 1990).

42. From an interview in a lower secondary school in Sipsong Panna.

43. Hsieh Shih-Chung, "On the Dynamics of Tai/Dai-Lue Ethnicity" in Stevan Harrell (ed.), *Cultural Encounters on China's Ethnic Frontiers,* (Seattle: University of Washington Press, 1995.)

44. From an interview with Tai monk and student.

45. From an interview with Tai girls of a lower secondary school.

The Development of Modern School-Based Tibetan Language Education in the PRC[1]

Janet L. Upton

Although Tibetans occupy a prominent position in the "family" of China's nationalities, surprisingly little Western scholarly attention has been paid to the history of their recent development under the political regime of the People's Republic of China (PRC). This is largely due to the fact that Tibetan Studies as a discipline in Western countries remains strongly tied to its historical roots in philology and Buddhist studies, a situation which has undoubtedly been compounded by the relative lack of access scholars have had to Tibetan areas during recent decades.[2] One area of scholarship that has thus been sorely neglected until very recently by Western scholars is research on the education of Tibetans in the PRC in the modern era, particularly secular (i.e., non-monastic) education. Although the educational sector represents a prominent point of intersection between the Chinese state and Tibetan society, to date we know very little about how educational policies have been implemented at the local level, and even less about the effects of those policies and modern teaching methods on the development of Tibetan culture and society within the PRC.

In the Western literature on minority education in the PRC, the Tibetan case has only been dealt with cursorily, and references to the current state of education for Tibetans are by and large limited to the citation of a few official statistics, which often misrepresent the situation on the ground.[3] To date there are few Western-language-published essays and no monograph-length studies of either Tibetan-language education or the general education of Tibetans in the PRC.[4] Published Western-language Tibetan-language education have largely focused on studies of modern education in the Tibetan exile community[5] or on traditional monastic educational practices,[6] and while several studies of the history of modern Tibetan education have been published recently in Chinese[7], these remain focused on broader policy issues or educational history and thus contain little detailed information on specific regions or educational practice at the local level. Though general studies such as those described above are certainly valuable contributions to our knowledge of educational policy as it has been developed for minority regions, they do little to improve our understanding of how the state educational agenda has actually been implemented in minority communities. In particular, general historical surveys or policy-oriented analyses give the reader little sense of how the state education project has both collided with and colluded with the cultural agendas of Tibetan communities in the PRC.

The educational system that is and has been accessible to Tibetans in the PRC is incredibly complex, with huge variations in the educational infrastructure and degrees of access depending on geographical area, and thus such general surveys are of limited value to those interested in conditions on the ground. The division of so-called "ethnic Tibet" into separate political units both prior to and since the founding of the PRC has been the focus of much political and scholarly controversy, but it is generally accepted that this division is a reflection of the complex history of the Sino-Tibetan border regions.[8] In the educational field, this political and administrative division has had some striking consequences, the most important being that there has historically been no strictly unified policy for the education of Tibetans throughout the Tibetan cultural region. This is not to say that there is no general policy: certain features of educational policy for Tibetans are indeed shared across the political boundaries that divide the Tibetan population. Since the mid-1970s, for example, there has been a concerted effort to develop a standardized Tibetan-language curriculum that could be employed in Tibetan schools in all areas. This project has resulted in the publication of a series of textbooks under the rubric of the "Five Provinces and Regions Cooperatively Written Textbooks" (*Ljongs zhing lnga'i mnyam bsgrigs slob gzhi/Wu sheng-qu xiezuo jiaocai*). In addition, certain aspects of educational policy are delimited at the state level, and these features are therefore common not only among Tibetans but also among all the minorities of China. The provision in state education policies that demands that religious institutions refrain from getting involved in education at any level, for example, is one nationwide policy that has affected many minority communities in which education was traditionally the province of religious practitioners.[9]

But in spite of certain commonalties, other issues such as how schools are established, what is taught (and in what language or dialect), where one can go to study and where one is placed for work following graduation are all matters that vary widely from one Tibetan area to another. As pointed out in the introduction to this volume, room for variations in educational policy and practice at the local level is built into minority educational policy at the national level, and minority communities have a certain (but admittedly limited) degree of leeway in implementing educational policy under the rubric of "carrying out education in accordance with local conditions." Such variations in theory and practice in Tibetan-language education were perhaps greatest in the early years of the Chinese state's attempt to develop a modern educational infrastructure in Tibetan regions, but remain significant even 40 years later. These differences make it difficult to discuss the contemporary or historical practices of Tibetan-language pedagogy in general, and call on us instead to look at specific case studies. Only by examining in detail the history and current practices of education in local communities will we eventually be able to move beyond the often misleading statistics and develop a more nuanced understanding of how Tibetans engage with the Chinese educational system and construct their own vision of their cultural past, present and future.

In this essay, I will discuss the historical development and cultural significance of modern school-based Tibetan-language education in one Tibetan region.[10] Songpan County lies at the far northern boundary of Sichuan Province, and straddles the upper reaches of the Min River. As part of an important trade corridor between the Sichuan basin and China's northwest frontier, the Songpan region has long been an important point of intersection between the Tibetan and Chinese populations, and also between the Tibetan and Hui (Chinese Muslim) communities.[11] Incorporated into the Sichuan Province Tibetan Autonomous Region in 1953, Songpan County became a part of the Aba Tibetan Autonomous Prefecture upon its founding in 1956.[12]

According to 1990 census figures, Tibetans make up 37.27 percent of a total county population of 65,019.[13] Though described in official publications as a semi-agricultural, semi-nomadic area (e.g., *Aba Zangzu Qiangzu zizhizhou difang zhi bianzuan weiyuanhui* (AZZ),[14] the Tibetan parts of the county are inhabited primarily by sedentary agriculturalists. The high degree of cross-cultural contact in the Songpan region and the relatively settled nature of the Tibetan population have contributed to the rapid development of the educational system, both historically and in the present context, thus making the area worthy of further investigation.

A DIFFERENT KIND OF LIBERATION: TIBETAN-LANGUAGE EDUCATION UNDER EARLY COMMUNIST RULE

Though monastic-based Tibetan-language education has a history of many hundreds of years in the Songpan region, modern school-based education is a comparatively recent development.[15] The classical academies set up under Chinese administration (particularly during the late Qing) in the county town may have had a few Tibetan students, but attention was not generally paid to reaching the Tibetan population at large until the republican period, particularly after the Nationalist Party rose to power in 1927. From 1911 to 1949, several schools were established by the republican government in Songpan in an effort to reach the Tibetan population with its new nationalist message, including some schools set up in Tibetan communities.[16] But given the educational statistics available for the early communist period, these schools never seemed to have had very high enrollments: by late 1949, for example, the entire prefecture had a total of only 101 elementary schools and 3 secondary schools, with a total enrollment of only about 3,000 students, 0.8 percent of the total population (See Appendix 9.1-9.6).[17] Though a fair number of these schools were located in the Songpan administrative region, the limited number of institutions and students indicates that the general population of the region (much less the Tibetan population) was not being adequately served by the educational system. It was into this relatively open playing field that the communist government would march in the early 1950s, carrying with them a new political and social agenda that would transform the face of local Tibetan society.

The liberation of Songpan County in 1950 by the People's Liberation Army (PLA) was to bring about sweeping changes in local society. Though the more remote western regions of Songpan had witnessed the passing of the Long March in the 1930s, the rest of the county had seen little Communist influence and was at least nominally under nationalist control until it was liberated on February 9, 1950. But most of the Tibetan areas of Songpan County (especially those areas distant from the administrative center) had retained a great deal of social and political autonomy under this nominal nationalist rule, and were not to be brought into the Chinese communist fold without some convincing.[18] One of the primary means by which the new communist government thus tried to both convince the local population of its benevolence and spread its social and political messages was through the establishment of elementary schools, including schools offering Tibetan-language instruction.

The policy of setting up schools offering Tibetan-language education seems to have been at its high point locally in the early to mid-1950s, a historical period which included perhaps the greatest efforts at conciliating the local Tibetan population on the part of the new communist regime. Beginning in 1952, the local government established schools in several Tibetan communities (listed in temporal order): Mounigou, Shangniba, Hongtu, Yanyun, Hongzha, Daxing, Xiaoxing, Shanba, Qiming, Yuanba, Linpo and Dazhai.[19] Set up as so-called Minority Schools (*Minzu Xuexiao*) or Tibetan Schools (*Zangmin Xuexiao*), these new institutions had full-time Tibetan teachers, and used both Chinese and Tibetan as languages of instruction, at least in the early years of their operation.[20] At least one other institution offering Tibetan-language instruction-the Maoergai Minzu Xuexiao-was established in 1957.[21]

Although little documentary evidence remains from these early communist-era schools, many of the graduates (and even some of the former teachers) of the Zangmin Xuexiao and Minzu Xuexiao of the 1950s and 1960s are still living in Songpan, and through interviews with these individuals we can obtain a fairly good picture of what local educational practices were like during this period.[22] The following description of the Minzu Xuexiao in Mounigou is based on interviews I conducted in 1993 with two individuals who had been connected with the school: a man in his eighties who was the founder and former headmaster of the school (and who also taught Tibetan there through the mid-1960s) and a woman in her forties who was one of the first graduates of the school (and who went on to become a teacher in the local community herself).[23] In the remainder of this section of the essay, data obtained from these interviews is supplemented with information from additional informants who attended schools in different communities during the same time period, as well as by a limited amount of information gleaned from materials published in Chinese and Tibetan, to provide a general picture of educational policies and practices at the local level during the early 1950s.

The Mounigou Minzu Xuexiao was officially commissioned by the Songpan County government in 1951. The man who received the commission to establish the school (and later became its headmaster and chief Tibetan instructor) was a young resident of Mounigou. Born in 1923 to a wealthy and politically prominent local family, he studied Tibetan with a private tutor (a monk) for 4 years beginning at age 18. Following the liberation of Songpan in 1951, he went on a tour of the interior areas of Sichuan Province as the representative of the former local ruler (*tuguan*) in Mounigou. It was during this tour that the idea of founding a school in Mounigou was first proposed. The delegation had been studying land reform methods and theory, as well as some educational theory, when they were invited to meet with some provincial and national-level officials who were involved in setting up the Southwest Institute for Nationalities in Chengdu.[24] It was at that meeting that it was decided to open a Minzu Xuexiao in Mounigou, with the objective of teaching Tibetan, Chinese and political theory. As originally proposed, the school would have no limits on enrollment—classes were to be open to anyone who wanted to attend.

Upon returning to Songpan, the future headmaster was given the official commission to open the Mounigou Minzu Xuexiao by the Songpan County People's Government, but the school did not begin actually to receive students until 1953.[25] A primary reason for the delayed opening of the school seems to have been the lack of willing students. In the early 1950s, there was a great deal of concern in the local community with respect to what would happen to students sent to the school. Still uncertain about the new government's intentions, some parents worried that their children might be sent away to Beijing and not come back. As a result, many families left the local villages for the mountains when the school year was set to begin so that they could keep their children out of the school.

In order to try to calm people's fears and provide parents with some incentive to send their children to the school, the local government offered money and food to families who enrolled their children, and reportedly agreed to provide books, clothing and food for the students for the duration of their studies. In actuality, these incentives did not appear to be universally offered to all students, and most ceased to be offered at all after the first few years of the school's operation.[26] But in the initial years, at least, such incentives induced at least some families to send their children to the school. In addition to providing these more material incentives, local officials and intellectuals (including the headmaster) also made personal visits to families to try to convince them of the value of sending their children to school and assure parents that their children would be safe in the school environment. At first these efforts were of only limited success: the school opened in 1953 with an initial enrollment of only 17 or 18 students, mostly from the poorer families in the area or from the families of local officials, who were trying to set a good example. But the positive experiences of these initial students (as well as the material benefits granted to them and their families by the local government) soon brought the enrollment up to over 100 students.

The school was established in Shangzhai, which is one of the main Tibetan settlements in the Mounigou valley, an area settled primarily by Tibetans who belong to the Gelugpa sect. The school was set up in a traditional Tibetan two-story building that had once belonged to a prominent family but had been taken over first by the nationalists and later by the communist government.[27] The school remained in this building for 20 years before being moved to another village. The former school building no longer exists, though some of the classroom furnishings are still being used in the current school building. Most of the students at the school came from the local village or nearby areas.

When the school first opened, it was heavily subsidized by all levels of the government. Subsidies from the national government included supplies of rice, meat, butter and other food (which was prepared in the school's cafeteria and eaten jointly by the school's students and teachers), as well as a supply of coal for cooking and winter heating. The government also provided clothes for the students who were from poor families-one set for the winter and one set for the summer. The clothes were Han-style (rather than Tibetan), but not uniform-girls received "female" clothing and boys received "male" clothing.[28] According to the former headmaster, the students were very happy to receive these things, especially the new clothes, but the community response was not entirely positive. Some people felt that the government was up to some kind of trick, and a small number of local people felt that Tibetans shouldn't wear "Han" clothes and were especially critical of the headmaster for doing so.

Much of the local community's uneasiness can be linked to the drastic changes in social practice the school was attempting to instigate, sometimes at a very personal level. For the majority of students, enrollment in the school represented the first time spent away from their families and called for significant changes in their personal habits. Students lived at the school Monday through Saturday morning, and were only allowed to go home from Saturday afternoon to Sunday afternoon. All meals were eaten at the school. The former headmaster claimed that when students first arrived at the school, the teachers had to teach them how to take care of themselves-how to wash their clothes, brush their hair, and so on. In training students in matters of hygiene, in particular, the headmaster was careful to explain why the students had to do certain things, for example, telling them "if you don't wash your clothes, they will be ruined," "if you don't wash your face, it will be dirty," and so forth. The former student also vividly recalled the stringent requirements for students, especially regarding their sanitation. According to her, students would go home on Saturday, then wash when they came back to school on Sunday. On Monday morning they had to pass inspection by the teachers: if they failed to pass muster, they were punished.[29]

Eventually students learned more or less to care for themselves, a task that was necessitated by the lack of staff at the school: other than the teachers and the school cook, there were no other adults who monitored the students. In addition to his administrative and teaching duties, the headmaster acted as the school doctor, since he had received some training in Tibetan medicine. Using traditional methods, he would prepare medicines of his own to give to students. He was also given a medical kit every year by the government, which he would use in treating students' ailments.

The students slept in large dormitory rooms, one for the boys, and one for the girls: they slept on the floor, since there were no beds. When bedtime came, the students were all put to bed by the teachers, and were supposed to sleep whether they felt like it or not. Often the headmaster or one of the other staff members would go around at night with a flashlight to make sure that everyone was asleep and all right. Usually some students would stay up talking, and if they were caught they had to get up and stand outside in the cold.

Since the school was a new phenomenon in Mounigou, students were of a broad age range. During the first year of classes, the youngest students were only 6 or 7 years old, and the oldest were in their late teens. Since virtually all the students were starting to learn Tibetan from scratch, they were divided into three classes according to their ages: the older students in one class, the mid-range students in another and the youngest students in third class.[30] At year's end, those students who had failed to master the year's material were held back to repeat the class, a practice that may have changed the age breakdown of the classes somewhat over time.

The students attended six class periods per day, with 1 day per week being devoted to labor in the school's fields. Students had two class periods of Tibetan instruction per day, with one lesson devoted primarily to recitation of texts and one devoted primarily to learning new vocabulary. Four class periods per day were conducted in Chinese, the subject matter of which included Chinese language and literature as well as mathematics.

The school had only two teachers: one for Tibetan and one for the subjects taught in Chinese. The headmaster taught Tibetan to all of the classes at the school (and eventually to all six grades), and claimed that he used "modern" teaching methods. Instruction at the school was organized along the lines of a modern school rather than a monastery: students sat on chairs and at desks (rather than on the floor) and heard their lessons in the same room as the teacher.[31] For students in the youngest class, the school day began with the reading and recitation of religious texts. The students all gathered in one room and the headmaster would have them go over the text for the day. Each student would then have to stand and recite-those who could do so correctly could go off to the other classrooms for their daily lessons, while those who could not recite correctly had to stay and practice until they could do so.

When they first began classes in Mounigou, there were no standardized Tibetan textbooks. Later they used a textbook written by a monk from a nearby county, but the quality was not very good and it only taught the basics. The headmaster wrote a textbook himself that they used for a while, which used culturally relevant material to teach Tibetan.[32] After the school had been open for 2 years, they received a lot of books and teaching materials from Beijing, all provided by the government: these texts were most likely the first version of the standardized Tibetan-language curriculum used throughout China's Tibetan regions.

Tibetan lessons started from *ga ka*, the Tibetan equivalent of the ABCs. The Tibetan teacher would write the Tibetan letters on a blackboard and the students would copy them with pen and ink at their desks. Students had to mix their own ink, and it reportedly made quite a mess, with ink getting all over everyone's hands, faces, mouths and clothes.

Chinese lessons also comprised a major part of the curriculum. The first Chinese language teacher at the school was called Secretary Yang (Yang Shiye), since he had been the secretary of a local *tuguan* (local offical) prior to Songpan's liberation. Although he taught a modern curriculum, his teaching style was in the traditional Han method—he was easily angered and frequently hit and yelled at students. In the headmaster's assessment, he didn't like the students and they didn't like him. As a result, he was dismissed from his teaching position after the first year.

The second Chinese teacher was much more suitable, if a bit more regimented in terms of his pedagogical approach. His name was Xiao Shiming, and he was originally from Dayi County near Chengdu. He was a university graduate, and was apparently very serious about applying what he had learned about pedagogy once he arrived at the school: the headmaster claimed that while they had rules before he came, they became even more numerous after he arrived. Xiao remained at the school as the Chinese language teacher until 1963, when both he and the headmaster were sent to work in Maoergai. The former student recalled that Xiao learned to speak a little bit of Tibetan, which he used in his lessons, and according to the headmaster he eventually learned Tibetan very well.

Generally, students seemed to be willing to be at the school, and more or less abided by the school rules. Students seldom ran away: the headmaster could recall only one student who was in the habit of doing so (but only after classes and meals were over), and he was always returned to the school by his parents, who wanted him to receive an education. The former headmaster claimed that even when conditions at the school deteriorated following the famine of the early 1960s, only 4 or 5 of the students at the school left. Throughout the school's early years, the students were reportedly quite devoted to their studies, and many went on to become local leaders and government workers.[33]

How long Tibetan-language classes were conducted in Mounigou is unclear. The former headmaster claimed that he continued to teach Tibetan at the school up to the time he was sent to Maoergai to work in 1963, but his former student claimed that Tibetan-language instruction stopped in 1958. Whatever the particular circumstances may have been in Mounigou, it is clear that social upheaval and changes in local policy in the mid to late 1950s brought an end to the climate of conciliation that had led to the initial establishment of the *minzu xuexiao* (nationality school) and the widespread introduction of elementary level school-based Tibetan-language education in Songpan County. This initial period was to prove to be somewhat of a golden age in local educational history, an era whose achievements would not be surpassed for several decades to come.

In summary, the early 1950s represented a period of unprecedented development in Songpan's educational infrastructure, including the expansion of modern school-based Tibetan-language education. Throughout Aba Prefecture during the period between 1949 and 1957, the total number of schools increased by 2.8 times, and the total number of students enrolled in those schools increased by 8.6 times.[34] Although these raw figures do not necessarily reflect identical increases in education for Tibetans, the experiences of places such as Mounigou do serve to give us a good general idea of how educational policy was conceived of and implemented in Tibetan areas in these early years, more often than not by Tibetans and for Tibetans.

THE 10 (OR 20) BAD YEARS: POLITICAL TURMOIL AND EDUCATIONAL STAGNATION, 1958-1978

Though the rest of the country would not face major disruption of the educational system until the upheavals that accompanied the onset of the Cultural Revolution in 1966, formal Tibetan-language education in Songpan County virtually ground to a halt in the late 1950s. The primary reason given for the cessation of Tibetan-language teaching in Aba Prefecture's schools during this period is described in one official publication as follows:

> Corresponding with the beginning of the Democratic Reforms and the Cooperative Movement, villages in areas settled by minorities universalized the setting up of elementary schools. But people had many negative opinions because experience was lacking in the establishment of "bilingual" education, the students' course load was too heavy and the quality of education was poor. In 1958, *in order to strengthen Chinese language education*, Tibetan classes ceased to be offered at the minority schools. Thereafter, specially established minority schools ceased to exist.[35]

What this account fails to explain is why local and prefectural officials found it advantageous, if not necessary, to cease the operation of Tibetan classes at this particular point in time. Though official interpretations such as the one cited above may not draw the connection, it is reasonable to assume that the decision to abandon Tibetan-language education in the late 1950s in areas such as Songpan was intimately connected to broader political events at both the local and national levels. On the national level, salient events included a general shift of the political winds to the left, culminating in the onset of the anti-rightist campaign and a rapid push toward collectivization. At the local level the important events included the introduction of land reform in Tibetan areas, the subsequent outbreak and suppression of local rebellions, and the eventual completion of the Democratic Reforms. All of these events were to lead to great social changes affecting every aspect of life in Songpan County's Tibetan communities, including the newly developed educational system.

In December 1955, Aba Prefecture's first Multi-Nationality People's Congress (*Gezu Renmin Dahui*) decided to begin the land-reform movement in Aba Prefecture's agricultural areas,[36] which by definition included most of the Tibetan communities in Songpan. By November 1956, full-scale land reform was being carried out throughout Songpan, including the Tibetan herding areas.[37] The general goal of the initial land-reform movement was to redistribute property and personal wealth from the rich to the poor, and it resulted in the confiscation of the land of wealthy individuals and monasteries. In the redistribution process, each former landlord or slave holder was reportedly given the same amount of land as the average peasant, thereby ending an age-old system of institutionalized inequality. Although certain conciliatory policies purportedly existed which caused the wealthy members of these Tibetan communities to be treated less harshly than their counterparts in Chinese communities (at least in the early stages), the basic social upheaval caused by the reform movement led to a great deal of local anti-government sentiment and an active opposition movement developed. According to official accounts, Tibetan uprisings in Songpan lasted from May 1956 to September 1957,[38] though in fact there were scattered outbreaks of rebellion in Songpan throughout the late '1950s and into 1960.[39] Following the suppression of the majority of these local rebellions, the land-reform movement was completed, and the preliminary forms of collectivization were more or less in place throughout Songpan's Tibetan agricultural regions by early 1958.[40]

In this atmosphere, the continued official support of traditional Tibetan culture through institutions such as the educational system was called into question, and the general reversal of cultural policy that hit minority areas throughout China in the late 1950s began seriously to affect Tibetan-language education in Songpan and throughout Aba Prefecture. The anti-rightist campaign of 1957-1958, which focused primarily on intellectual circles in Han Chinese areas, took on a much broader scope as it was implemented in minority areas, primarily under the objective of eliminating "local ethnic chauvinism (*difang minzu zhuyi*)." One of the primary signs of such chauvinism was judged to be the overt support of the maintenance of traditional cultural practices, including the use of minority languages in the educational system. As local cultural leaders and those who had been instrumental in setting up the nascent Tibetan-language educational system fell before such rhetoric, support for the system was eroded and the general policy shift outlined in the paragraph quoted above took place. No longer would Tibetan-language instruction be a primary focus of the curriculum: education was instead to meet the goal of "strengthening Chinese-language education." Though practical necessity sometimes dictated the use of Tibetan in the classroom (through the employment of a Tibetan teacher who understood Chinese and could ease the cross-cultural or cross-linguistic communication barrier, for example, local educational practice saw little formal Tibetan-language pedagogy for the next two decades. [41]

It is important to note that this change in policy seems to have taken place at the prefectural level, and was not necessarily implemented in other Tibetan areas outside of Aba Prefecture. Even materials published by the prefecture itself in the intervening years seem to indicate it was an aberration that did not necessarily correspond with provincial- or national-level policy. For example, an article highlighting important dates in Chinese minority educational policy published under the auspices of the Prefectural Education Commission notes that in September and October 1959 a meeting was held by the Cultural Bureau, the Education Bureau and the Nationalities Affairs Commission in Beijing which determined the appropriate content for curriculum in minority regions to be a combination of the nationally approved Chinese language textbooks and/or translations of them into the local language, combined with locally produced native-language texts, Chinese-language textbooks and other supplementary texts.[42] The same account also describes a meeting held by the Education Bureau in Beijing in March 1963 that focused on issues related to the education of minorities in remote areas of Yunnan, Guizhou and Sichuan. This meeting determined that the general principal for organizing the curriculum should be to utilize the minority language for elementary level education, particularly in the early years, but to introduce Chinese language instruction in the upper years of the elementary curriculum. It was also pointed out at this meeting that the standard for Chinese language learning should not be too high, and that by no means should it be imposed in an attempt to emulate ethnic Chinese students.[43] In spite of such rhetoric at higher levels, however, local educators seem to have had little choice but to comply with the new county- and prefectural-level policies that took the maintenance of Tibetan-language education in local schools as a sign of political (if not social) backwardness.

It should be pointed out, however, that although mainstream Tibetan-language education fell into a period of serious decline in the late 1950s, it was not completely eliminated.[44] Tibetan-language education of a very limited scope continued to exist in the form of special classes that were introduced in Tibetan communities as a means of preparing young children to enter elementary school. An official account describes the development of these classes as follows:

> In 1958, during the Great Leap Forward, the [number of] elementary schools [in] the entire Prefecture increased sharply, [but] the Tibetan-language classes that had been started in each elementary school in areas settled by Tibetans were halted, [and] Chinese was mostly what

was studied. [When] Tibetan children study Chinese, it belongs to [the category of] studying a second language, and this carries with it great difficulties for the teachers' teaching and for the students' studying. When Tibetan children enter school, there exists a linguistic obstacle[. . .]. In order to wipe out the early linguistic obstacle, in actual educational practice there appeared "Pre-School Chinese Conversation Classes" (*Xueqian hanyu huihua jiaoxue ban*). These sorts of pre-school Chinese conversation class for Tibetan children were later termed preparatory classes (*yubei ban*). Early on teachers themselves compiled Chinese conversation texts adapted to the children's studies, [but] the length of such study was not fixed, [with some preparatory classes being] one month long, some three months or half a year, and some up to a year. This structure for running a school got good results, and received the support of the education bureaus and society. After 1959, most of the village elementary schools in every county in the Prefecture, especially those schools in areas settled by ethnic minorities, universalized such preparatory classes. At the same time, the writing of preparatory class teaching materials was begun, with mimeographs being sent to the teachers. In 1960, the Aba Prefecture Education Section, on the basis of the teaching materials which had been compiled in each county, produced the letterpress book *Conversation Teaching Materials (Huihua jiaocai)* for the use of preparatory classes.[45]

For the most part, these preparatory classes were taught by former monks, by Tibetans who were members of the County Political Consultative Conference (often former members of the upper classes who had been granted political posts as part of the so-called "united front" movement), or by individuals who had been trained by the county Education Bureau in specially designed short-term courses.[46] But there were several problems related to the implementation of these preparatory classes that detracted from their effectiveness, the most important of which was the impracticality of the general policy of expecting students to board at the school: whether due to parents' concerns about lack of facilities and supervisory staff, or sheer logistical difficulties such as distance from the school, many students were kept out of the preparatory classes.[47]

Political pressures and overt social upheaval eased off some following the suppression of the local rebellions and in the wake of implementation of the Democratic Reforms in the late 1950s, but the development of Tibetan-language education in the Songpan area was to more or less stagnate for the next 20 years. Widespread famine in the early 1960s made it difficult for educational institutions to continue operating normally, much less institute reforms or develop in any practical way. Although limited room for local maneuvering seemed to exist in educational policy up through 1966, the official onset of the Cultural Revolution brought all overt practice of Tibetan-language instruction (including the use of preparatory classes) in Songpan's schools to a halt.[48] For the most part, educational practice in Songpan during the early years of the Cultural Revolution mirrored that of other regions in China during this period, with excessive focus being placed on politics and the expression of a correct political attitude. This did not always signify a total disassociation from local cultural practices, however: one Songpan native who attended elementary school during the Cultural Revolution recalled that the manner in which he and his classmates recited the "three old essays" (*lao san pian*) every morning during that period differed little stylistically from the traditional method of reciting Buddhist scriptures.[49]

Whatever tactics local Tibetans may have employed to cope with the social and political upheavals that took place between the onset of the Democratic Reforms and the institution of more liberal minority policies in the late 1970s to early 1980s, it cannot be denied that this period represented a low point in cultural autonomy and cultural expression. Local monasteries were closed (and in many cases physically destroyed), religious and folk practices were banned (or at the very least not condoned) and even the use of the Tibetan language in local schools was severely restricted. As a result, many Songpan Tibetans who came of age during this period are either illiterate or literate only in Chinese, a point which has been a strong motivating factor in the recent resurgence of Tibetan-language education in the region: the parents of many of today's students are unwilling to see their children cut off from their cultural roots, and providing those children with an education in Tibetan is seen as a way of righting at least some of the wrongs of the past decades.

TENTATIVE STEPS: TIBETAN-LANGUAGE EDUCATION AND CULTURAL REVIVAL IN THE POST-MAO ERA

The death of Chairman Mao and the subsequent fall of the Gang of Four in 1976 was to herald a turn-around in educational policy throughout China, but perhaps nowhere was the change to be as striking as in minority areas. Particularly after the passage of various resolutions that dealt with minority cultural policy at the third plenary session of the eleventh Central Committee of the Communist Party of China in 1979, all levels of the government began to pay increased attention to the improvement of education in minority areas. At the national level, the Ministry of Education and the Nationalities Affairs Commission issued a joint directive on minority education in 1980 that was to become a guiding force in the development of minority education over the next decade. In this directive, entitled "Thoughts on Strengthening Minority Education Work (*Guanyu jiaqiang minzu jiaoyu gongzuo de yijian*)",[50] several points were stressed which were to have important effects on educational practice at the grassroots level throughout China's minority regions. It was admitted that although promising steps in the development of education for China's minorities had been made in the early 1950s, since 1958 (and especially during the Cultural Revolution) minority education had suffered from "leftist" policies, particularly the closing or consolidating of minority schools, the elimination of instruction in minority languages and the elimination or reduction of funding for minority students.[51] In order to deal with the resultant fallout (such as the prevalence of schools suffering from the "three lacks" (*san wu*)—lack of a school building, lack of desks and chairs and lack of a government-funded teacher (*wu xiaoshe, wu zhuoyi, wu gongban jiaoshi*)—in minority areas) changes in both policy and practice were to be implemented immediately. Of primary importance was the official recognition of the special character of minority areas and of the need to develop policy to fit particular local conditions rather than simply emulating the practices of Han Chinese areas: former policies which had followed a practice of "one cut of the knife" (*yi dao qie*) were to be eliminated, and the restructuring of a semiautonomous minority educational policy was to begin.

Given the decimated state of minority (and other) education in most areas, one of the first tasks in rebuilding the system was the centralization of resources. In minority areas as well as in their Han counterparts, the preceding two decades had witnessed a rapid expansion in the sheer number of schools, teachers and students, if not in the quality of the education available.[52] Since limited financial and personnel resources made it impossible to introduce minority-language teaching in every village school-or at least to do so in a way that would be an improvement on the existing system-a general policy of concentrating resources in centralized schools (particularly boarding schools) was adopted. The general attitude was that with the state "providing and managing residence, diet and attire (*guan zhu, guan chi, guan chuan*)," a more efficient and sufficient education could be provided.[53] Due to the lack of qualified Tibetan-language teachers in Songpan County, one of the early tasks facing the local Education Bureau was to concentrate the available resources in selected areas (usually at the township or district level) and to establish a small number of boarding schools and/or classes especially for Tibetan students, some of which offered limited Tibetan-language instruction.[54] In 1981, the county began key boarding elementary classes (*jisuzhi minzu zhongdian ban*) at the central/complete elementary schools (*zhongxin wanxiao*) in Zhangla and Rewugou. Later, minority boarding schools (*minzu jisuzhi xuexiao*) were started in Maoergai, Qingyun, Daxing and Xiaoxing. As of 1992, there were 11 elementary level institutions (including both entire schools and individual classes) offering a residential program for students studying Tibetan, with a total of 33 Tibetan-language classes (*ban*) and 1,036 students, 9.89 percent of the county's total student population.[55]

In addition to the establishment of boarding schools and classes, attention was also focused on gradually increasing the number of schools that offered Tibetan-language instruction in the village and township setting. Facing an initial severe shortage of teaching staff, and compounded by constant attrition in the teaching ranks due to increased professional and economic opportunities in other sectors, the expansion of Tibetan-language schooling continued relatively slowly until the late 1980s, but then began to improve more steadily.[56] As of September 1996, the number of elementary institutions offering the Tibetan language had increased to 15; 3 of them were village schools (*cunxiao*).[57]

Tibetan-language secondary education developed at a slower pace in terms of sheer numbers, partly due to the dire lack of qualified teachers. Though teacher training colleges in Aba Prefecture quickly expanded their recruitment of Tibetan speakers in the early 1980s, the output of new qualified teachers simply could not keep up with the demand for them at the local level. Still, in terms of percentages, it was the secondary level institutions that underwent the biggest leaps in terms of Tibetan-language instruction-simply because there were fewer such institutions in the county. By 1996, of the eight secondary level institutions in Songpan County, three were offering Tibetan-language instruction in some form or another. Of these institutions, the one with the most outstanding record in Tibetan-language education was the one with the shortest history: the Songpan County Tibetan-Language Secondary School (*Songpan xian zangwen zhongxuexiao*). Though founded only 8 years ago, this institution has had a remarkable success rate and has contributed greatly to the expansion and improvement of Tibetan-language education in Songpan County. As the primary upper-level institution offering Tibetan-language instruction in the county, it serves as the gateway for most local Tibetans seeking a higher-level education, and serves an important role in bringing together members of the local Tibetan community. Due to the amount of social support it receives and its role as a focal point for the Tibetan community, in addition to its considerable achievements, this institution merits close scholarly attention.

TOWARD A BRIGHTER FUTURE: ESTABLISHING THE SONGPAN COUNTY TIBETAN-LANGUAGE SECONDARY SCHOOL

The year 1988 witnessed a monumental step in the history of Tibetan-language education in Songpan County: the formal establishment of the Songpan County Tibetan-Language Secondary School.[58] Following many years of hard work on the part of educators concerned with the future of Tibetan-language education (and education in general) in Songpan County, the founding of the school in many ways represented the culmination of a period of cultural renaissance among the local Tibetan population that had been inspired by changes in minority policy and the comparatively rapid development of the local economy.[59]

By 1983, several local intellectuals and cultural workers had begun to work formally toward the establishment of a Tibetan-language secondary school in Songpan County. Over the course of several years, they wrote over 30 reports to various levels of the government and educational bureaucracy seeking support for their quest. The movement to establish such a school not only attracted the support of members of the local community and government officials at all levels, but was also in keeping with the central government's initiatives to "Do Education in a Big Way (*Da ban jiaoyu*)" and "Energetically Develop the Cultural Education Enterprise in Minority Areas (*Nuli fazhan shaoshu minzu diqu wenhua jiaoyu shiye*)."[60] After a long period of preparation, the Songpan County Tibetan-Language Secondary School (*Songpan xian zangwen zhongxuexiao*) received the official approval of the Aba Prefecture Government and was formally established on August 1, 1988.

Though the school had only "a bare patch of land, an official seal, and five teachers"[61] when it was commissioned, no delay was taken in seeking out the next important component: a student body. A scholarly report on the school describes the initial search for students as follows:

> On August 20-23, the principal of the Tibetan-Language Secondary School, according to arrangements made by the County Culture and Education Bureau (*Xian wenjiao ju*), posted announcements throughout the entire county seeking students. The conditions for entry were that students: (1) would not be restricted by nationality, but be fluent in spoken Tibetan; (2) be sound in mind and body; (3) have written Chinese proficiency to the elementary-graduate level, and written Tibetan proficiency to the fourth-grade level; (4) be under 17 years of age; and (5) those possessing the above qualifications must take tests in written Tibetan and Chinese in order to be admitted. In the space of 3 days, 149 people had registered. After the school had administered tests in written Tibetan and Chinese and oral tests in spoken Tibetan, 81 students were admitted: of those, 46 were male and 35 were female. Seventy-seven students were ethnic Tibetans (*Zangzu*), making up 95 percent, 2 were Hui and 2 were Han. The youngest student was 13, the oldest 18. The parents of many students who were not admitted asked that their children be allowed to come and listen to classes, with the parents providing desks. The school had no choice but to admit 20 of these students as auditors.[62]

The school thus began its history with over 150 students, but no school building, books, desks, benches or educational facilities. Since waiting for the government to provide such things "was not the character of the Tibetan people (*hai bu shi zangjia renmin de xingge*),"[63] the school's officials eventually arranged to borrow four old classrooms from the central school (*zhongxin wanxiao*) in Zhangla. Three of the four classrooms were used for teaching, and the remaining classroom became the joint office/living quarters for the five teachers. The teachers asked the parents of the students to supply their own desks and benches, and to furnish tents, daily living supplies and food for the students' use. After several weeks of such logistical preparation, the opening ceremony for the school was held on September 10, 1988.

Though the students' parents had worked hard to provide what they could, the number and quality of the desks and benches brought by the students did not meet the school's requirements. Moreover, the students still lacked beds, and were facing the prospect of sleeping on the ground in the dead of winter in an area where the temperatures frequently drop to −20°C and below.[64] The teachers were disturbed by this, and therefore went on a fund-raising campaign throughout the villages in the county to try to raise money to alleviate the problem. During the course of this campaign, the school's staff eventually raised over 80,000 yuan in bits and pieces: the largest amount given by a single individual was 2,000 yuan. Those who didn't have money donated building materials to the school, often from the supplies they had gathered to build their own houses.

In all, almost 1,000 people donated to the school in one way or another. The most moving case was that of an elderly Tibetan woman who was on a sort of public assistance, but nevertheless wanted to contribute to the school.[65] She walked over 30 kilometers from her village to the site of the temporary school at Zhangla and asked to see the principal. After he met with her and told her who he was, she didn't say anything but took a 5-mao note from inside her robe and offered it to him with both hands, saying "Principal, I don't have any more money than this, but this is from my heart. Please accept it." The tears welled up in his eyes and all the people around were so quiet you could hear them breathing. By the time they started to recover themselves, the old woman had already left their sight.[66]

After solving the problem of basic furnishings for the school, the teachers encountered another major problem—the required politics text, *Legal Knowledge (Falü zhishi)*, had no Tibetan edition, but only existed in Chinese. They eventually decided to translate the entire text themselves—all several tens of thousands of characters of it. The headmaster did the translation, two other teachers edited it, and two other did the mimeographing. After an entire week of overtime work like this, they gradually started to put out the translation for the students to use one section at a time.[67]

During the first year that the school was in operation, the five teachers taught all three grades, with a curriculum comprised of over 12 different subjects. Each teacher taught three or four different subjects, teaching over 30 class periods per week: this was the only way that the courses that needed to be taught could be taught.[68] As documents prepared by the school recall:

> The teachers didn't complain, but persevered, thinking of their students who came from the villages, bringing their own tents to sleep in, making their own tea and food, and using cold water to wash their faces and hands in the subfreezing weather of the Zhangla winter. What kind of school was this? But if you asked the students if they were having any troubles, they would smile and say "Nope!" and be off running before you knew it.[69]

Several of the students came from very poor families: they survived primarily on a diet of tsampa and were not able to eat meat more than once or twice a month, since they had only 3 to 5 yuan of spending money per month.

At the same time as they were dealing with all their regular responsibilities as teachers, the staff members were also working hard to get the new school building established. The headmaster was running between the county town, the prefectural government and the provincial government, trying to raise money and organize the construction. So busy was he fulfilling these responsibilities that he didn't return home to see his sick mother, his wife or his children for over half a year. He spent his life savings of 700 yuan on behalf of the school, and also went several thousand yuan into debt.

The building of the new school campus commenced on March 12, 1989 on the present site northeast of the county seat. The campus occupies an area of 4152 square meters , and was established with an investment of one million yuan from the county, prefectural and provincial governments. While working to get the school built, the teachers had to be sure that the graduating class was well-prepared for exams and also that the first and second-year classes were learning their lessons properly. Ordinarily, the teachers were teaching in Zhangla during the day and then going down to the county town in the evening to help with the building, covering a round trip distance of over 35 kilometers on bad roads with each trip. They had many sleepless nights and made countless numbers of trips between the two school sites.

In September, the school saw its first "harvest"—of the 41 students who took part in the entrance exams for professional schools within and outside the prefecture, 38 of them were admitted—a promotion rate of 92.7 percent, which took first place in the prefecture and received the praise of both the county and the prefectural governments, as well as that of the local people. In addition, the school construction was almost completed, and the students and teachers would soon be able to move to the new campus. That move was completed later in the fall of 1989, and the school's campus currently consists of a teaching building that can house a total of 12 classes, a teachers' residence building that can house 19 teachers, a student dormitory that can house 170 students; a cafeteria; a public outhouse; and a wall, guardhouse and gate.

In the now eight-year history of the Songpan County Tibetan-Language Secondary School, the number of staff has multiplied numerous times over, and the number of students enrolled each year has more than doubled. As of the 1995-1996 school year, the school had a total enrollment of 345 students. Ninety-one percent of the student body is Tibetan (313 students), with the remainder of the students coming from the other ethnic groups that reside in Songpan County: Qiang (20 students), Hui (7 students) and Han (5 students). Females make up 60 percent of the student body. As of 1996, the school had a total of 38 staff members: 7 primarily administrative personnel (including the party secretary, the principal, three vice-principals (all of whom also teach), an accountant and an administrative secretary), 26 full-time teachers, and 5 support staff (including security personnel and cafeteria staff). As of the summer of 1995, the school had graduated a total of 648 students, among whom over half have gone on to higher education (202 to professional schools and 128 to senior high schools). Of those graduates who have completed professional school and senior high school, 37 have gone on to pursue post-secondary education. The number of classes (*ban*) at the school has increased from the initial 3 to the current 6, with plans of offering an additional class in 1996-1997.[70]

In accordance with the stipulations of the State Education Commission regarding the composition of the junior-high level curriculum, the school requires that its students study 14 subjects: Tibetan language and literature, Chinese language and literature, English language, history, geography, math, physics, chemistry, biology, politics and ideology, music, physical education, art and physical labor. In keeping with local plans for economic development (which involve the expansion of the tourist industry), the school has taken the initiative of adding a course in conversational English to its curriculum.[71] The school thus takes two approaches to tri-lingual education, both of which are designed to meet the diverse needs of the entering student body: (1) "Take Tibetan as the focus, learn Chinese well, and add some English," or (2) "Take Chinese as the focus, learn Tibetan well and add some English."[72] In the first system, the majority of classes (with the exception of Chinese language and literature) in all 3 years of the junior high school program are taught primarily in Tibetan, with Chinese explanations being added if and when needed by the students: this is the system followed by the majority of students who have graduated from elementary institutions that offered Tibetan-language instruction. In the latter system, which is offered primarily to those students with little or no background in written or spoken Tibetan, the first year classes are taught mainly in Chinese, but with an intensive focus being placed on developing written and spoken Tibetan language skills. By the second year, most classes (other than Chinese language and literature) are being taught in Tibetan, though with more supplementary explanations being offered in Chinese than in the classes following the primarily Tibetan-language track. This two-tiered system, while complicated, is the only reasonable way the school has of facing the problems brought on by the lack of Tibetan-language education at the elementary level. It is a credit to the teachers at the school (most of whom are bilingual in Tibetan and Chinese) that they are able to make such a complicated system work efficiently.

At present the Songpan County Tibetan-Language Secondary School is unable to meet the demands of secondary level minority education in the Songpan region, because although there are over 600 graduates of Tibetan elementary schools every year, the school can only accept about 120 of them as students, or only about 20 percent of the entire graduating class. According to school officials, most of the remaining graduates from schools where Tibetan has been the medium of instruction drop out of school. In addition, a large number of students who have graduated from elementary schools where Chinese is the medium of instruction wish to continue their education in a Tibetan-language environment, and the school has had a hard time in turning them away. The demands on the school's resources are thus being stretched well beyond what the staff and facilities can handle. According to current plans, by the year 2000 the school will have produced close to 1,000 junior high school graduates and close to 100 graduates with professional training. But impressive as this achievement is, it falls far from meeting the needs of Songpan's development. In particular, there remain no opportunities within Songpan County for Tibetan-language education at the upper secondary level: the Songpan County High School (*Songpan xian zhongxuexiao*) is the only institution offering senior high school-level instruction in the county, and it lacks Tibetan-language instruction of any kind. Though the Songpan Country Tibetan-Language Secondary School continues to seek permission to expand its program to the senior high-school level, such requests have been repeatedly denied by the county and prefectural education bureaus.[73] It remains to be seen if the school will be able to build on its past and future successes and eventually overcome the practical and bureaucratic obstacles it faces, going on to develop to even greater heights.

Particularly in its first few years of operation, the Songpan County Tibetan-Language Secondary School had a tremendous impact on the local Tibetan community. Educational statistics have improved dramatically since the school was founded, a change that both school officials and officials in the local education bureau attribute largely to the presence of the school and its role as a conduit to higher levels of education. The school uniformly attracts more applicants than it can admit, and its graduates have consistently performed better than average on the entrance exams to institutions at the upper secondary level. Although the promotion rate (*shengxue lü*) for graduates from the school has fallen off in recent years—from an initial high of 92.7 percent in the first year to a current rate of 30.5 percent (for 1995 graduates; 1996 promotion statistics are not available at the time of writing)—this reflects not so much a decline in the standard of education or quality of the students (though teachers at the school have perceived a drop-off in the quality of the student body as the school has expanded its size), but rather the institution of a regional quota system at the upper secondary level. Under the current system, the higher level institutions are unwilling to have their classes dominated by students from any one area (since this would contribute to placement problems upon graduation), so in spite of the fact that large numbers of students attain marks that should qualify them for entry to the higher level institutions, they are not always accepted by those schools.[74] In spite of this, the Songpan County Tibetan-Language Secondary School remains the primary destination for Tibetan students interested in obtaining a secondary-level education, and especially for those who are interested in pursuing even higher levels of education in the future.

The Songpan County Tibetan-Language Secondary School therefore represents the primary training ground for what may well become Songpan County's future Tibetan elite: those individuals capable of functioning in both a Chinese and a Tibetan social context. These students remain tied to their cultural roots through their educational focus on the Tibetan language, yet they are also introduced to a broader state-oriented culture through the standardized curriculum. To be certain, there are disjunctures between these two worlds, some of which can be bridged more or less successfully and others which remain as more gaping chasms. In the next section of this chapter, I will focus on teaching practices I have witnessed in the course of my research, and illustrate with some concrete examples what can be achieved by Tibetan-language education in a Chinese-dominated society.

EDUCATION IN CULTURAL CONTEXT: TEACHING THE TIBETAN-LANGUAGE CURRICULUM IN SONGPAN COUNTY

One point that should be evident throughout this discussion of both historical and current practices of Tibetan-language education in Songpan County is the frequent disjuncture between the content of the formal, standardized curriculum and students' individual experiences and personal backgrounds. Whether one is discussing the practices employed in the minority schools of the 1950s or the teaching that takes place in a contemporary context, one of the major tasks teachers face is making the curriculum—which generally comes from above and often has an overtly political tone—relevant to and comprehensible by the students. Although this is a task that must be faced in all aspects of the curriculum, from mathematics to politics, one of the areas in which cultural interpretation forms an integral aspect of daily lessons is in the course in Tibetan language and literature (in Tibetan, *skad yig*). In this final section of the chapter, I will examine in some detail the content of this one facet of the Tibetan-language curriculum, and discuss the ways in which I have seen it taught and received during the course of my classroom observations in Songpan.[75]

Contrary to the rhetoric that often surfaces in Western and Tibetan exile reports about the Tibetan-language curriculum in the PRC, the textbooks currently in use do contain a fair amount of material drawn from Tibetan sources and relevant to Tibetan cultural life in the broad sense. Texts of direct Tibetan origin are drawn from both historical and contemporary sources. The second book of the junior secondary level Tibetan Language and Literature series (*Mtsho sngon mi rigs slob gzhi rtsom sgyur khang*),[76] for example, opens with a chapter-length text by the twelfth-century Tibetan author Po to wa rin chen gsal, and also includes additional short texts by Sum pa ye shes dpal 'byor (1704-1788), Gung thang dkon mchog bstan pa'i sgron me (1762-1823), and 'Phags pa'i lu sgrub (Nagarjuna).[77] In addition to these examples drawn from the historical literature, there are also numerous texts by contemporary Tibetan authors, many of which have appeared previously in one of several literary journals that have been published in Tibetan areas since the early 1980s. Contemporary Tibetan authors whose works appear in the text cited above, for example, include Don grub rgyal, Lha gyal tshe ring and Rang grol.[78]

Though the focus of both the historical and the contemporary texts certainly departs from a traditional monastic curriculum, and though the particular texts included may surely represent different choices than those that have been made in establishing the curriculum utilized in the Tibetan exile community, these lessons nonetheless play an important role in establishing a sense of unified Tibetan culture and identity among young Tibetans, for they represent the new "cultural capital" that educated youth are being encouraged to acquire. Perhaps even more important than the lessons derived from Tibetan literature in this respect are those lessons that refer to Tibetan history and/or cultural practices. While it must be admitted that the view of Tibetan history that is presented in the formal curriculum under the current political and cultural regime is far removed from the "real history" that so many Tibetans at home and abroad currently crave, the policy of allowing for the discussion of minority culture and history does allow for some creative imagining of Tibetan experience, past, present and future. In addition, the content of certain chapters in the standard curriculum lends itself directly to the discussion of the commonalities of Tibetan experience, thereby further establishing a sense of connectedness to other Tibetans who may live in distant places, speak different dialects and belong to different religious sects.

During the course of my fieldwork in 1996, this point was brought home in the very first class session that I observed, which happened to cover a text on the eight auspicious symbols (*bkra shis rtags brgyad*) of Tibetan Buddhism.[79] The instructor, a member of the Communist Party, offered the students a detailed explanation of the symbolism of each of the eight objects, and did not shy away from their connection to traditional religious doctrine, a connection that was brought out in the text itself through its explicit use of terms drawn from Tibetan religious philosophy to define the meaning of each of the symbols. The instructor went beyond the limited content of the text, however, and mapped out various issues central to Tibetan philosophy. He discussed the significance of the wheel (*'khor lo*) and how it represents the cyclical nature of existence. He discussed in detail the various classifications of sentient beings (*'gro ba*) – *lha* (gods), *lha min* (titans) and *mi* (people) – pointed out how all of them are trapped in a cycle of suffering and explained that the parasol (*'dugs*) represents that which shields those beings from the unbearable heat of that suffering. His explanations covered the entire series of symbols, and throughout the lesson he treated the religious nature of the symbolism in a level-headed manner, and sometimes downright enthusiastically. The students reacted equally enthusiastically, shouting out answers to his periodic questions and engaging with the text in an obvious way.

The instructor also used the text as a means of exploring the commonalities of Tibetan culture across regional and linguistic difference. He began by explaining that the symbols were commonly used throughout the Tibetan cultural area – that they appear painted on houses and on monasteries, and are often used in printed materials as well. Local experience attests to this universality: the symbols are indeed commonly painted conspicuously in local residents' houses. The symbols are thus an important unifying marker of Tibetan culture, relevant to Buddhists and Bonpos alike. Linguistic difference was another type of difference that the instructor was able to bridge in teaching this text, for although the local dialect terms for some of the symbols differed from the written terms given in the text, the instructor was able to build on students' familiarity with the symbols to introduce the students to those symbols' more standard written referents. Thus, in both cultural and linguistic senses, texts such as these provide a powerful tool for the construction of a notion of common Tibetan experience and identity.

If the construction of a unified sense of Tibetan identity is an implicit (and possibly somewhat subversive) goal of the Tibetan-language curriculum, an infinitely more explicit goal is the construction of a sense of unity with the Chinese nation. One of the ways in which this is attempted is through the inclusion of literature translated from Chinese sources that deal with what might be considered Chinese national themes, both in a contemporary and historical context. These include such issues as China's feudal and semicolonial past, revolutionary history, and the need for science and technology. A significant proportion of the lessons in the Tibetan language and literature textbooks are comprised of lessons related to these themes that have been translated from the standard Chinese language and literature textbooks used throughout the PRC. Though many of these texts are overtly political in nature (including extracts from the collected works of Mao Zedong in Tibetan translation), others represent important works by modern Chinese authors, works that form an important part of the education of any person in the PRC. Examples of the latter type that can be found in *Skad Yig* (Language and Literature), include the short stories "A Small Sparrow (Mchil ba chung chung)" by Lao She (Chapter 19) and "A Minor Incident (Don phran tshegs shig)" by Lu Xun (Chapter 22). [80]

One of the biggest challenges that Tibetan teachers in Songpan face is making the content of these lessons seem relevant to their students, most of whom have never left Songpan County and who are unfamiliar with much of the cultural context to which these lessons refer. Their work is complicated by the fact that these texts often have been translated awkwardly into Tibetan, and are expected to teach linguistic lessons that may have been appropriate to the Chinese original, but are not necessarily so in the Tibetan derivative. But what may come as a surprise to some readers, as it did to me, is that some of the most forceful lessons about the value of Tibetan culture can be taught to students through lessons that derive from works that are historically and culturally very distant.

During the course of my classroom observations, this became most evident as I witnessed a drawn out lesson on the text "A Final Lesson (Mjug mtha'i slob thun gcig)," a translation of the short story "The Final Lesson" by Alphonse Daudet.[81] The story's protagonist is a young boy from Alsace who is not very fond of his lessons. On his way to school one day, he contemplates all the things he could otherwise be doing, and almost decides to play the truant. Eventually, he makes his way to school, however, and finds himself in the French class, for which he is woefully under prepared. As the lesson begins, however, he is startled to hear his teacher announce that this will be the last French lesson—not just for that day, but for the near and possibly distant future. The boy's homeland has been invaded by the Germans, and from the next day on all instruction will be held in German. This announcement stuns the class and sets the protagonist to reflecting on the error of his non-scholarly ways.

When taught to the first-year class I was observing, this text served as a reminder of a very important moral and intellectual lesson that recent events had necessitated. Just before this text was covered in class, the students had taken their spring mid-term exam, and had generally done rather poorly. More than once, my presence (and the fact that, with generous grading and the liberal use of a dictionary, I did better than many of the students on the exam) was used to point out how disgraceful it was that they, as Tibetans, did not understand even the most basic things about their own language. With this as a backdrop, the instructor launched into "A Final Lesson," which over the course of the next few days was used repeatedly to drive home the message that one has a responsibility to learn one's own language, for one never knows when the window of opportunity to do so may (once again) be slammed shut.

In light of the experiences of Tibetans with modern education over the past several decades, the lesson this text seems designed to drive home is all the more poignant and dramatic. Most of the students at the Songpan County Tibetan-Language Secondary School are the children of Tibetan parents who were never permitted to learn their own language when they were in elementary and secondary school. Though the experiences of recent years are certainly an improvement over the sorry state of Tibetan-language education Songpan County witnessed in the 1960s, 1970s and early 1980s, constant threats to the status quo remain, and the likelihood of increased resources seems less and less likely. The county government is currently facing an operating deficit: meeting the demands of day-to-day government operation is difficult enough, and there is little if any money left for further investment in the educational infrastructure.

In addition, certain educational policy decisions at the local level are not necessarily conducive to the further expansion of Tibetan-language education, and sometimes even seem to threaten the maintenance of the current system. The policy on language use at the elementary level is a good example. Although over 31 percent of the student body in Songpan County is of Tibetan ethnicity,[82] at present the entire county has only 15 elementary schools and/or classes offering Tibetan-language instruction, and only one of them—the central elementary school in Maoergai—offers Tibetan-language instruction before the fourth grade. Though the general policy for education in minority areas in Sichuan and Aba Prefecture seems to support instruction in the mother tongue from entry in elementary school, educational policy as implemented in Songpan County does not.[83] This is, perhaps, a reflection of an attempt to deal with the complex ethnic makeup of Songpan as well as local wishes, but it goes against both common sense and educational research on bilingual education.[84]

Perhaps the largest obstacle the development of Tibetan-language education in Songpan (and in other Tibetan areas) faces is a practical one: in most areas other than the educational field, there is little demand for individuals literate in the Tibetan language. Though official policy may promote the use of minority languages in the so-called minority autonomous regions, practice is not usually so generous: the language of officialdom remains Chinese, and with the exception of formal translation work there is little opportunity for the use of Tibetan in the public sphere. Being able to take advantage of changes in the developing private sector also depends largely on Chinese, rather than Tibetan, skills—particularly in a place such as Songpan, which is so close to the major centers of Chinese population. Thus, even though Songpan Tibetans may feel a great emotional attachment to their own language, as a language of education it is not necessarily their first choice, since the "outlet" (*chulu*) it offers may be narrower than the road offered by a Chinese-language education.[85]

The challenge for Tibetan educators and their supporters is thus to prove the value of a Tibetan-language education in a sociopolitical context which is not always supportive of, and is sometimes downright hostile to, the maintenance and development of Tibetan language and culture. This is particularly important in regions such as Songpan, where bilingualism is already widespread and local linguistic and cultural traditions seem to be losing some of their power and relevance in the face of encroaching Chinese and global cultural forces. Unless the tide of these trends can be stemmed, the risk will remain that today's class, or tomorrow's, will be "The Final Lesson" for Tibetan-speakers in Songpan County.

Appendix 9.1. General Elementary-Level Educational Statistics for Aba Prefecture, 1949-1990

Calendar Year	Total Number of Elementary Schools	Total Number of Students Enrolled	Number of Minority Students Enrolled	Minority Students as % of Total Enrollment
1949	101	1,963	0	0.00
1950	125	4,414	2,032	46.04
1951	166	8,526	3,994	46.84
1952	225	12,638	5,956	47.13
1953	243	16,750	7,918	47.27
1954	258	20,862	9,880	47.36
1955	270	15,511	6,706	43.23
1956	301	18,618	7,861	42.22
1957	348	23,650	10,305	43.57
1958	513	35,560	18,447	51.88
1959	597	43,388	21,065	48.55
1960	662	44,530	24,449	54.90
1961	645	29,725	16,360	55.04
1962	601	25,019	13,145	52.54
1963	633	28,781	14,818	51.49
1964	754	37,730	19,892	52.72
1965	895	46,925	23,728	50.57
1966	955	51,535	25,348	49.19
1967	951	53,168	27,516	51.75
1968	981	52,029	27,330	52.53
1969	1,159	53,246	25,616	48.11
1970	1,261	59,560	27,946	46.92
1971	1,346	54,422	24,272	44.60
1972	1,492	67,939	33,078	48.69
1973	1,416	76,489	37,292	48.75
1974	1,591	85,782	41,889	48.83
1975	1,782	98,112	49,614	50.57
1976	1,788	102,507	53,510	52.20
1977	1,776	102,948	53,286	51.76
1978	1,735	104,148	53,316	51.19
1979	1,724	102,985	45,956	44.62
1980	1,697	102,619	54,391	53.00
1981	1,673	97,809	53,375	54.57
1982	1,593	95,319	56,233	58.99
1983	1,553	89,975	54,669	60.76
1984	1,549	95,769	59,413	62.04
1985	1,546	94,270	59,832	63.47
1986	1,483	93,560	61,120	65.33
1987	1,455	89,536	62,369	69.66
1988	1,430	86,349	61,888	71.67
1989	1,425	83,815	59,946	71.52
1990	1,401	83,529	61,843	74.04

Source: Aba Zhou Jiaoyu Weiyuanhui (AZJW) (Aba Prefecture Education Commission) 1992: 533-536

Appendix 9.2. General Junior High School-Level Educational Statistics for Aba Prefecture, 1949-1990

Calendar Year	Total Number of Junior High Schools	Total Number of Students Enrolled	Number of Minority Students Enrolled	Minority Students as % of Total Enrollment
1949	2	65	24	36.92
1950	2	101	56	55.45
1951	2	163	80	49.08
1952	2	204	164	80.39
1953	2	394	226	57.36
1954	2	461	269	58.35
1955	2	472	280	59.32
1956	3	575	324	56.35
1957	5	820	362	44.15
1958	8	2,128	667	31.34
1959	9	2,677	813	30.37
1960	10	2,320	761	32.80
1961	10	1,599	705	44.09
1962	10	1,259	502	39.87
1963	11	1,582	551	34.83
1964	11	1,890	661	34.97
1965	15	2,743	879	32.05
1966	17	2,719	863	31.74
1967	24	2,318	686	29.59
1968	24	1,743	644	36.95
1969	24	3,341	1,126	33.70
1970	66	3,820	1,096	28.69
1971	49	5,200	1,881	36.17
1972	41	6,224	2,277	36.58
1973	44	8,887	2,866	32.25
1974	54	11,950	4,131	34.57
1975	71	16,977	5,911	34.82
1976	112	19,681	7,431	37.76
1977	149	27,210	8,914	32.76
1978	109	27,082	8,791	32.46
1979	104	24,906	8,531	34.25
1980	88	26,274	10,519	40.04
1981	59	24,569	9,840	40.05
1982	54	23,511	9,962	42.37
1983	49	21,943	9,563	43.58
1984	48	20,134	9,393	46.65
1985	48	18,479	9,009	48.75
1986	46	17,486	8,568	49.00
1987	47	18,532	9,992	53.92
1988	46	19,388	10,971	56.59
1989	45	19,598	12,444	63.50
1990	46	20,151	12,780	63.42

Source: AZJW 1992: 533-536

Appendix 9.3. General Senior High School Level Educational Statistics for Aba Prefecture, 1949-1990

Calendar Year	Total Number of Senior High Schools	Total Number of Students Enrolled	Number of Minority Students Enrolled	Minority Students as % of Total Enrollment
1949	1	75	39	52.00
1950	1	68	29	42.65
1951	0	0	0	N/A
1952	0	0	0	N/A
1953	0	0	0	N/A
1954	0	0	0	N/A
1955	0	0	0	N/A
1956	0	0	0	N/A
1957	1	45	20	44.44
1958	1	315	141	44.76
1959	1	360	162	45.00
1960	1	395	177	44.81
1961	1	377	159	42.18
1962	1	275	100	36.36
1963	1	313	118	37.70
1964	1	309	117	37.86
1965	1	312	118	37.82
1966	2	354	117	33.05
1967	3	335	131	39.10
1968	3	274	101	36.86
1969	3	161	48	29.81
1970	3	195	47	24.10
1971	4	120	52	43.33
1972	7	469	128	27.29
1973	9	1,247	392	31.44
1974	10	2,049	661	32.26
1975	15	2,684	919	34.24
1976	19	4,369	1,208	27.65
1977	48	7,006	1,582	22.58
1978	46	7,542	1,741	23.08
1979	38	7,191	1,759	24.46
1980	35	6,145	1,585	25.79
1981	31	5,296	1,421	26.83
1982	30	4,884	1,713	35.07
1983	28	4,596	1,547	33.66
1984	28	4,445	1,702	38.29
1985	28	5,053	1,930	38.20
1986	27	4,982	2,307	46.31
1987	25	5,195	2,815	54.19
1988	26	5,268	2,331	44.25
1989	26	4,919	1,530	31.10
1990	26	4,831	2,422	50.13

Source: AZJW 1992: 533-536

**Appendix 9.4. Elementary-Level Graduation and Promotion Statistics for
Aba Prefecture, 1949-1990**

Calendar Year	Total Number of Graduates	Minority Students as % of Graduates	Min. Students as % of Students Promoted to Junior High	Min. Students Promoted as % of Min. Students Graduated	Students Promoted as % of Students Graduated
1949	6	83.33	83.33	100.00	100.00
1950	77	36.36	41.18	100.00	88.31
1951	114	46.49	54.64	100.00	85.09
1952	221	51.13	48.05	65.49	69.68
1953	1,005	27.36	58.33	33.00	15.52
1954	693	34.05	61.15	36.00	20.06
1955	1,069	35.36	65.69	23.81	12.82
1956	1,512	32.34	53.21	28.83	17.53
1957	2,287	24.31	38.79	32.37	20.29
1958	2,844	38.26	42.40	47.70	43.04
1959	3,464	36.03	33.33	21.07	22.78
1960	4,343	33.20	29.30	13.94	15.80
1961	4,117	38.64	43.58	10.25	9.08
1962	2,729	41.92	32.58	16.35	21.03
1963	2,710	42.73	32.35	17.01	22.47
1964	4,281	43.45	31.49	11.61	16.02
1965	4,735	39.85	26.28	13.30	20.17
1966	3,578	41.59	23.39	20.03	35.61
1967	2,991	38.65	27.51	8.30	11.67
1968	4,757	42.25	26.59	5.62	8.93
1969	4,489	49.16	24.93	7.61	15.01
1970	4,907	45.53	20.37	21.26	47.52
1971	4,535	37.00	28.46	46.96	61.06
1972	3,122	43.56	29.22	55.59	82.86
1973	4,945	42.02	27.86	49.28	74.34
1974	9,600	28.93	26.69	56.03	60.73
1975	9,236	37.75	30.09	67.48	84.67
1976	11,665	43.77	30.34	64.34	92.81
1977	14,674	35.62	38.71	95.71	88.08
1978	13,993	44.16	35.29	59.53	74.50
1979	11,796	46.90	38.29	65.00	79.61
1980	12,461	45.03	39.93	64.71	72.98
1981	12,411	49.03	42.93	59.13	67.54
1982	11,863	49.80	47.21	66.13	69.75
1983	10,614	53.52	45.92	58.83	68.57
1984	8,001	51.53	49.99	74.00	76.28
1985	7,177	57.22	52.46	74.48	81.25
1986	6,263	49.51	48.65	85.46	86.97
1987	8,690	54.66	55.43	81.94	80.81
1988	8,612	63.39	58.57	76.30	82.57
1989	8,798	65.31	63.35	76.58	78.94
1990	8,514	67.71	68.48	83.12	82.19

Source: AZJW 1992: 537-538

Appendix 9.5. Junior High Graduation and Promotion Statistics for Aba Prefecture, 1949-1990

Calendar Year	Total Number of Junior High School Graduates	Minority Students as % of Junior High Graduates	Minority Students as % of Students Promoted to Senior High	Minority Students as % of Students Promoted to *zhongzhuan*	Students Promoted to Upper-Secondary Level Education as % of Graduates	Minority Students Promoted to Upper Secondary as % of Minority Graduates
1949	0	N/A	N/A	N/A	N/A	N/A
1950	0	N/A	N/A	N/A	N/A	N/A
1951	5	60.00	N/A	N/A	0.00	0.00
1952	5	80.00	N/A	N/A	0.00	0.00
1953	42	38.10	N/A	N/A	0.00	0.00
1954	62	48.39	N/A	N/A	0.00	0.00
1955	35	60.00	N/A	N/A	0.00	0.00
1956	123	65.04	N/A	N/A	0.00	0.00
1957	141	60.99	80.00	N/A	31.91	41.86
1958	120	60.83	71.11	N/A	37.50	43.84
1959	336	30.65	66.67	N/A	13.39	29.13
1960	398	41.71	65.00	N/A	20.10	31.33
1961	434	35.02	52.94	N/A	23.50	35.53
1962	262	32.44	46.67	N/A	34.35	49.41
1963	266	33.08	51.72	N/A	32.71	51.14
1964	286	33.57	48.24	N/A	29.72	42.71

Appendix 9.5 (continued)

Calendar Year	Total Number of Junior High School Graduates	Minority Students as % of Junior High Graduates	Minority Students as % of Students Promoted to Senior High	Minority Students as % of Students Promoted to zhongzhuan	Students Promoted to Upper-Secondary Level Education as % of Graduates	Minority Students Promoted to Upper Secondary as % of Minority Graduates
1965	378	37.57	50.00	N/A	24.34	32.39
1966	604	37.25	40.59	N/A	28.15	30.67
1967	319	46.08	77.78	N/A	14.11	23.81
1968	702	24.22	N/A	N/A	0.00	0.00
1969	598	24.92	N/A	N/A	0.00	0.00
1970	455	26.59	11.25	N/A	17.58	7.44
1971	1097	40.29	13.51	N/A	6.75	2.26
1972	695	27.91	19.35	N/A	61.73	42.78
1973	1785	30.53	32.00	N/A	44.99	47.16
1974	2340	30.60	31.75	N/A	52.09	54.05
1975	2806	33.68	33.36	N/A	51.71	51.22
1976	5458	30.71	29.18	N/A	56.14	53.34
1977	6972	33.16	28.23	32.41	78.50	68.86
1978	8896	37.11	26.03	24.64	55.94	38.75
1979	8805	34.66	28.09	28.08	54.34	44.04
1980	5437	38.33	26.48	35.48	68.71	51.30

Appendix 9.5 (continued)

Calendar Year	Total Number of Junior High School Graduates	Minority Students as % of Junior High Graduates	Minority Students as % of Students Promoted to Senior High	Minority Students as % of Students Promoted to *zhongzhuan*	Students Promoted to Upper-Secondary Level Education as % of Graduates	Minority Students Promoted to Upper Secondary as % of Minority Graduates
1981	7375	39.21	33.04	28.81	47.32	38.66
1982	6563	43.01	36.27	42.18	46.64	41.02
1983	6125	43.17	33.54	45.88	47.35	40.36
1984	6074	61.80	40.05	42.12	43.84	28.85
1985	6257	40.37	39.18	45.12	45.17	45.68
1986	5649	43.05	28.02	43.51	103.61	72.99
1987	5421	46.32	41.69	47.41	49.79	46.83
1988	5042	47.14	45.94	47.99	55.32	54.65
1989	5164	50.95	46.10	49.40	52.19	48.46
1990	5699	51.54	48.25	48.93	48.69	45.83

Source: AZJW 1992: 537-538

Appendix 9.6. Senior High Graduation and Promotion Rates for Aba Prefecture, 1949-1990

Calendar Year	Total Number of Senior High Graduates	Number of Minority Graduates	Minority Students as % of Graduates	Minority Students as % of Students Promoted to *dazhuan*	Students Promoted to *dazhuan* as % of Students Graduated	Minority Students Promoted to *dazhuan* as % of Minority Students Graduated
1949	0	0	N/A	N/A	N/A	N/A
1950	0	0	N/A	N/A	N/A	N/A
1951	0	0	N/A	N/A	N/A	N/A
1952	0	0	N/A	N/A	N/A	N/A
1953	0	0	N/A	N/A	N/A	N/A
1954	0	0	N/A	N/A	N/A	N/A
1955	0	0	N/A	N/A	N/A	N/A
1956	0	0	N/A	N/A	N/A	N/A
1957	0	0	N/A	N/A	N/A	N/A
1958	0	0	N/A	N/A	N/A	N/A
1959	0	0	N/A	N/A	N/A	N/A
1960	45	23	51.11	N/A	0.00	0.00
1961	120	60	50.00	N/A	0.00	0.00
1962	44	22	50.00	N/A	0.00	0.00
1963	38	19	50.00	N/A	0.00	0.00
1964	72	27	37.50	N/A	0.00	0.00

Appendix 9.6 (continued)

Calendar Year	Total Number of Senior High Graduates	Number of Minority Graduates	Minority Students as % of Graduates	Minority Students as % of Students Promoted to *dazhuan*	Students Promoted to *dazhuan* as % of Students Graduated	Minority Students Promoted to *dazhuan* as % of Minority Students Graduated
1965	80	27	33.75	N/A	0.00	0.00
1966	112	47	41.96	N/A	0.00	0.00
1967	70	35	50.00	N/A	0.00	0.00
1968	50	25	50.00	N/A	0.00	0.00
1969	115	38	33.04	N/A	0.00	0.00
1970	173	56	32.37	N/A	0.00	0.00
1971	655	146	22.29	N/A	0.00	0.00
1972	114	8	7.02	N/A	0.00	0.00
1973	73	8	10.96	N/A	0.00	0.00
1974	481	122	25.36	N/A	0.00	0.00
1975	776	228	29.38	N/A	0.00	0.00
1976	1148	326	28.40	N/A	0.00	0.00
1977	1393	385	27.64	17.44	18.52	11.69
1978	2610	670	25.67	41.85	7.05	11.49
1979	3427	910	26.55	51.53	4.76	9.23
1980	3355	858	25.57	40.78	5.34	8.51

Appendix 9.6 (continued)

Calendar Year	Total Number of Senior High Graduates	Number of Minority Graduates	Minority Students as % of Graduates	Minority Students as % of Students Promoted to *dazhuan*	Students Promoted to *dazhuan* as % of Students Graduated	Minority Students Promoted to *dazhuan* as % of Minority Students Graduated
1981	3088	951	30.80	55.24	6.80	12.20
1982	2447	817	33.39	57.79	9.97	17.26
1983	2059	795	38.61	54.47	11.95	16.86
1984	1715	735	42.86	61.74	13.41	19.32
1985	1201	447	37.22	49.85	28.39	38.03
1986	1528	1311	85.80	53.79	25.92	16.25
1987	1410	473	33.55	45.57	28.01	38.05
1988	1732	733	42.32	47.41	27.89	31.24
1989	1775	680	38.31	49.76	23.32	30.29
1990	1590	728	45.79	54.30	21.19	25.14

Source: AZJW 1992: 537-538

NOTES

1. This essay is based primarily on data collected during several months of fieldwork in Songpan County over the past 3 years. Fieldwork methods have included formal and informal interviews, extensive observation and audio and visual documentation of classroom teaching and school and community life, and the collection and analysis of related documents. While conducting my research I have been affiliated with the Tibetan Department of the Southwest Institute for Nationalities in Chengdu, Sichuan, and I am particularly grateful to them for their long-term assistance and support. Research assistance in the field has been capably provided by Pad ma mtsho, a researcher in the Minority Languages and Literature Research Institute of the Southwest Institute for Nationalities. I am most indebted to her and to my many other Chinese and Tibetan colleagues in Songpan and Chengdu who have been instrumental in making my research possible. Different stages of the research have been supported by grants from the following institutions and organizations: the National Science Foundation for a NSF Graduate Fellowship, 1991-1994 and a Summer Fieldwork Training Grant (administered by the University of Washington's Department of Anthropology), 1993; the Chester Fritz Fund of the University of Washington Graduate School (for a grant for summer fieldwork expenses, 1993); the Luce Foundation (for an Inner-Asian Language Fellowship, 1993-1994); the Blakemore Foundation (for an Asian Language Training Fellowship, 1995-1996); the Pacific Cultural Foundation (for a Graduate Research Fellowship, #SC7016); and the National Security Education Program (for a NSEP Doctoral Dissertation Grant, 1996-1999). I am grateful to all of these institutions and individuals for their support of my research, but the opinions and interpretations expressed in this essay are, of course, my own.

2. Chinese- and Tibetan-language scholarship is, understandably, more abundant, but this scholarship remains largely inaccessible to the non-specialist due to the formidable language barrier. Scholarship produced within the PRC is also often tied to a political agenda that makes it unpalatable to many Western scholars, though it must be admitted that such scholarship can often contain data valuable to the Western scholar in spite of (and also perhaps because of) its overt political orientation.

3. Studies that refer to educational statistics for the Tibet Autonomous Region (TAR), which admittedly lags behind many other areas inhabited by Tibetans in the development of the educational infrastructure, often read as if such lack of development were the case for all Tibetan regions. A further problem lies in the treatment of literacy statistics, which are often based on

literacy in Chinese alone: thus, a Tibetan who cannot read Chinese but is literate in Tibetan is often registered as illiterate in Chinese survey and census materials (cf., Badeng Nima (Dpal ldan nyi ma), "Zangzu jiaoyu de chulu" ("The Outlet for Tibetan Education") in *Xizang yanjiu (Tibetan Studies (Chinese Edition))*, No. 3 (1994), p. 44). This leads to a distorted picture of cultural and educational levels which is difficult to remedy through analysis of official statistics alone.

4.   One valuable exception is an account by a Tibetan refugee of his experiences as a student in Beijing (Tsering Dorje Gashi 1980), but it is an autobiographical work rather than a scholarly analysis. A recently published monograph by Katrin Goldstein-Kyaga, *The Tibetans – School for Survival or Submission: An Investigation of Ethnicity and Education* (Stockholm: HLS Frlag, Department of Educational Research, The Center for Pacific Asia Studies, 1993) does include a chapter on the education of Tibetans in the PRC, but it does not appear to be very comprehensive, at only 29 pages. Unfortunately, this volume is unavailable to me at the time of writing. A forthcoming issue of the journal *Chinese Education and Society,* guest edited by Gerard Postiglione, will contain several essays on Tibetan education translated from Chinese sources, which should represent a welcome addition to the English-language scholarly literature.

5.   Margaret Nowak, *Tibetan Refugees: Youth and the New Generation of Meaning* (New Brunswick, NJ: Rutgers University Press, 1984).

6.   See for example, Dungkar Lobzang Tinley (Tib. Dung dkar blo bzang phrin las), "Development of the Monastic Education System in Tibet," trans. Sangye T. Naga, in *The Tibet Journal* Vol. 18, No.4 (1993), pp. 3-48.

7.   See for example, Duoji Caidan (Tib. Rdo rje tshe brtan), in *Xizang de jiaoyu (Education in Tibet)* (Beijing: Zhongguo zangxue chubanshe, 1991); Yang Ming and Wang Gang, *Zhongguo zangzu jiaoyu shilue (A Brief History of Education for China's Tibetans)* (Chengdu: Chengdu keji daxue chubanshe, 1993); Zu Jielin, *Zangzu jindai jiaoyu shilue (A Brief History of Modern Tibetan Education)* (Xining: Qinghai minzu chubanshe, 1990).

8.   The Tibetan cultural area includes not only the entire TAR, but also significant portions of the provinces of Qinghai, Gansu, Sichuan and Yunnan. For the most part, the parts of these provinces settled by Tibetans have historically had only weak political ties to the central Tibetan administration, and since the onset of their administration as Autonomous Prefectures in the 1950s, those political ties have become virtually non-existent. The administrative structure of the autonomous prefectures as subprovincial units has also led to a surprising amount of variation in the development and

implementation of official policy, making it dangerous to generalize from one region to another. For a detailed discussion of the complex nature of this situation and the importance of distinguishing between ethnic and political Tibet, see Melvyn C. Goldstein, "Change, Conflict and Continuity Among a Community of Nomadic Pastoralists: A Case Study from Western Tibet, 1950-1990," in Robert Barnett (ed.), *Resistance and Reform in Tibet* (Bloomington and Indianapolis, IN: Indiana University Press, 1994), pp. 76-90.

9. The most obvious comparison here is with the Hui (Chinese Muslim) nationality, who were traditionally schooled in the mosques (or in, more recent times, in schools attached to mosques) by traditional religious elders known in Chinese as ahong. It should be noted here that there is extensive anecdotal (and some published) evidence that certain schools in minority areas have been established in conjunction with religious institutions (both Tibetan monasteries and Hui mosques), though this is not officially sanctioned. This is a sensitive issue, one that I have not thus far dealt with in detail in my own research due to concerns I have about jeopardizing the future of these institutions.

10. Throughout this essay, my usage of the term "Tibetan-language education" refers to the general use of the Tibetan language as the primary language of instruction in the classroom, and is not therefore limited to the formal teaching of the Tibetan language per se. It should be noted that throughout the Tibetan cultural region there generally exists a two-track educational system, particularly at the secondary level and above: a Tibetan-language track, in which most or all subjects other than Chinese language and literature are taught in Tibetan; and a Chinese-language track, in which Chinese is the primary language of instruction and Tibetan language and literature may or may not be taught as a required or elective course. While both of these systems exist in Songpan County, I have elected to focus my research (and the content of this essay) primarily on the Tibetan-language track, since it attracts the majority of Tibetan students and represents more of a bridge between traditional cultural practices and modern educational methods.

11. For a discussion of the historical importance of this trade route and its relationship to local cultural practices, see Baimacou (Tib. Pad ma mtsho), "Shitan zangdong cha ma shangdao" ("An Exploration of the Tea/Horse Trade Route in Eastern Tibet"), in *Xizang yanjiu*, No. 3 (1994), pp. 35-49.

12. The name of the prefecture was changed to the Aba Tibetan-Qiang Autonomous Prefecture in 1987, thereby better reflecting the multiethnic nature of the prefecture's population.

13. Census figures for the population of Songpan County by ethnicity are as follows: 27,712 Han Chinese (42.6 percent); 24,230 Tibetans (37.3 percent);

8,487 Hui (13.2 percent); 4,554 Qiang (7 percent); and 36 other (0.1 percent). It should be noted that although Tibetans currently make up less than half of the total population of Songpan County, the vast majority of the county's physical area is occupied by Tibetans, who also tend to live in primarily Tibetan enclaves. The Han and Hui populations are concentrated mainly in the county town (which is the local administrative center) and in nearby villages in the central river valley, and the Qiang population is largely limited to a small area in the southern part of the county. Though Tibetan-Han and Tibetan-Hui interactions (and occasional conflicts) are an important aspect of local social life, I have not dealt with them explicitly in this essay. See also Songpan Xian Zangwen Zhongxuexiao (SXZZ)(Songpan County Tibetan-Language Secondary School), *Songpan xian zangwen zhongxuexiao chuangjian fazhan qingkuang de huibao caike* (*Materials for a Report on the Establishment and Development of the Songpan County Tibetan-Language Secondary School*), unpublished report, n.d.

14.   Aba zangzu qiangzu zizhi zhou difang zhi bianzuan weiyuanhui (AZZ)(Aba Tibetan-Qiang Autonomous Prefecture Local Annals Editorial Commission), *Aba Zhou Zhi (The Aba Prefecture Annals)* (Beijing: Minzu Chubanshe, 1994).

15.   Though materials exist regarding the history of Songpan's monasteries (e.g., Zing-chu-rdzong gi lo-rgyus deb-ther byed-sgo sgrig-mkhan gtso-wo) (ZCKC) (Songpan County Historical Annals Editorial Group), *Zing-chu-rdzong dgon-pa so-sogs dkar-chag* (*A Guide to the Various Monasteries of Songpan County*) (Songpan County: Zangzu yuyan chubanshe, 1993), little information is available regarding traditional monastic teaching practices, including such practices as private home-based tutoring of students by monks. Though it may be possible to generalize based on materials from other Tibetan areas, the specifics of the Songpan case (particularly its remoteness from the primary centers of monastic instruction and the fact that most of the local monasteries are Bonpo, not Buddhist) make such generalization hazardous. For a brief discussion of contemporary monastic educational practice in Songpan's Bonpo monasteries, see J. F. Marc Desjardins, "A Preliminary Field Report on the Bon Community of the Songpan Area of North Sichuan," unpublished Master's thesis, Macgill University, Montreal, Canada, 1993, pp. 58-61.

16.   Guo Fuyi, "Aba diqu minzu jiaoyu fazhan shilue (Ming, Qing, Minguo Buen)" ("A Brief History of the Development of Minority Education in the Aba Region (Ming, Qing and Republican Section),") in AZJW, *Minzu jiaoyu yanjiu wenji (Collected Essays on Minority Education)* (Chengdu: Sichuan Daxue Chubanshe (1992), p. 491, divides the implementation of educational policy in

Aba Prefecture under republican rule into five periods: (1) an initial stage of relatively slow development but significant reform in content and structure of the educational system (1911-1928); (2) a stage of rapid development which included the establishment of the first minority schools (1929-1935); (3) a stage which focused on compulsory education and short-term study (1936-1940); (4) a stage which focused on "national citizen education" (*guomin jiaoyu*) and represented the high point of republican educational development in Aba Prefecture (1941-1946); and (5) a final period of decline prior to communist liberation (1947-1949). The development of education in Songpan County, including education for Tibetans, seems to correspond with this historical framework. During the early republican era, several modern-style elementary schools were established in Songpan County: one in 1915, eight in 1916, four in 1917 and two in 1918 (including a girls' school in the Zhangla district) (Yang and Wang, *Zhongguo zangzu jiaoyu shilue (A Brief History of Education for China's Tibetans)* (Chengdu: Chengdu keji daxue chubanshe, 1993), p. 280) But the vast majority of these schools were located in the county town, which at that time had an extremely limited Tibetan population. It is therefore unlikely that Tibetan enrollment in these institutions was very extensive. After the ascendance of the Nationalist Party in 1927, the government began to focus on setting up elementary level institutions (especially the so-called "Border Peoples' Schools" ("Bianmin Xuexiao")) in or near Tibetan settlements, sometimes in conjunction with pre-existing Tibetan institutions. In 1929, for example, the county government set up the "Barbarian Border Peoples' School" (*Fanyi Bianmin Xuexiao*) at Rin-spungs (Chinese Linpo) Monastery, with the senior lama at Rin-spungs serving as the head of the school. (Xu Ming and Chen Xinfu, "songpan xian zangwen zhongxue xiankuang diaocha" ("An Investigation of the Current Situation at the Songpan County Tibetan-Language Secondary School,"), pp.124-125, in Li Weijun (ed.), *Sichuan Zangqu dianxing siyuan ji xuexiao xiankuang diaocha (An Investigation of the Current Situation at Representative Monasteries and Schools in Sichuan's Tibetan Regions)* (Chengdu: Sichuan Zangxue Yanjiusuo (Sichuan Tibetology Research Bureau), 1992) (For internal circulation), pp. 124-132). This was the first border peoples' school to be established in Aba Prefecture, and one of three such schools in the prefecture, which by 1934 had a combined enrollment of 159 students (AZZ 2001). In 1931, a private elementary school called the Western Sichuan Chinese and Barbarian Elementary School (*Chuanxi hanyi xiaoxuexiao*) was established in the northern part of the county town: the name indicates that this school was designed to serve the local Chinese population as well as Tibetans, and the school received some money from the local government each year to

help with operating costs (AZZ, *Aba Zhou Zhi (Aba Prefecture Annuals)*, pp.
2,001-2,002). In 1936, the local county government established an additional
school in Daxing Township called the Yunchang Monastery Barbarian
Elementary School (*Yunchangsi fanmin xiaoxuexiao*) (Xu and Chen, "Songpan
xian zangwen zhongxue xiankuang diaocha" ("An Investigation of the Current
Situation at the Songpan County Tibetan-Language Secondary School,"), p.
125), which given the name, most likely was set up at or near a Tibetan
monastery. In the same year, four "Barbarian Schools (*fanmin xuexiao*)" were
set up in Shangniba and other Tibetan villages (Xu and Chen, p. 125): Guo
Fuyi, "Aba diqu minzu jiaoyu fazhan shilue (Ming, Qing, Minguo Bufen)" ("A
Brief History of the Development of Minority Education in the Aba Region
(Ming, Qing and Republican Section),") p. 512, *in AZJW, Minzu jiaoyu yanjiu
wenji (Collected Essays on Minority Education)* (Chengdu: Sichuan Daxue
Chubanshe (Sichuan University Publishing House), 1992), pp. 479-520,)
indicates that 10 such schools were established in Songpan that year, but this
figure most likely includes schools that were set up in areas outside the present
county boundaries (since the area nominally under Songpan's administration at
that time was larger than the present territory, reaching all the way to the Golok
(Chinese Guoluo) region now incorporated into Qinghai Province). In addition
to studying the standard national Chinese-language curriculum, these schools
also offered instruction in Tibetan. (See Xu Ming and Chen Xinfu, "Songpan
xian zangwen zhongxue xiankuang diaocha ("An Investigation of the Current
Situation at the Songpan County Tibetan-Language Secondary School"), in Li
Weijun (ed.), *Sichuan Zangqu dianxing siyuan ji xuexiao xiankuang diaocha
(An Investigation of the Current Situation at Representative Monasteries and
Schools in Sichuan's Tibetan Regions)* (Chengdu: Sichuan zangxue yanjiusuo
(Sichuan Tibetology Research Bureau), for internal circulation, (1992), p. 125).
In 1946, a border people's school was established in Dazhai, which in 1948 was
offering 2 hours per week of instruction in written Tibetan in addition to the
standard Chinese curriculum. (See Guo, "Aba diqu minzu jiaoyu fazhan shilue
(Ming, Qing, Minguo Buen)" ("A Brief History of the Development of
Minority Education in the Aba Region (Ming, Qing and Republican Section),")
p. 517). A secondary level institution offering limited Tibetan-language
instruction was also established in Songpan in the late 1930s: for an account of
the history of this institution, see An Benqin and Ma Qiyang, "Ji guoli songpan
shiyong zhiye xuexiao" ("Remembering the Songpan National Practical
Vocational School") in *Sichuan wenshi ziliao xuanji (Selected Sichuan
Historical Materials)*, Vol. 27, (Chengdu: Sichuan renmin chubanshe, 1982),
pp. 130-137.

17. Chen Qiang, "Abazhou minzu jiaoyu fazhan zhanlue chusuo ("A Preliminary Exploration of the Struggle to Develop Minority Education in Aba Prefecture)," in AZJW, *Minzu jiaoyu yanjiu wenji* (*Collected Essays on Minority Education*) (Chengdu: Sichuan daxue chubanshe (Sichuan University Publishing House), 1992, pp. 7-38.

18. Up until the communist takeover, the majority of Songpan's Tibetan communities were controlled through a system of government-appointed local rulers known as *tuguan* in Chinese or *mgo-ba* in Tibetan: in most cases, these ethnic Tibetan local leaders were only nominally subordinate to the republican government, having a great deal of power and authority in their local communities. For a short (though somewhat idealized) description of the pre-liberation situation in one Tibetan community in Songpan, see Samten G. Karmay, "Mountain Cults and National Identity in Tibet," in Robert Barnett (ed.), *Resistance and Reform in Tibet* (London: Hurst and Company, 1994), pp. 116-117. A more detailed ethnohistorical account of pre-Liberation life in this community by Samten Karmey and Phillippe Sagant is forthcoming, but unavailable for referencing at this time.

19. Xu and Chen, "Songpan xian zangwen zhongxue xiankuang diaocha" ("An Investigation of the Current Situation at the Songpan County Tibetan-Language Secondary School,") pp. 124-132.

20. Ibid., p. 125, states that these schools offered Tibetan-language instruction up until the beginning of the Cultural Revolution, but other published accounts and my own research indicate that this was not the case in most communities. For example, Zhang Jianshi and Shi Suo, "Zangzu diqu siyuan yu suozai shequ guanxi de ge'an diaocha: songpan xian shanba cun yu shanbasi ji xuexiao jiaoyu de guanxi ("A Preliminary Investigation of the Relations Between Monasteries in Tibetan Areas and the Communities in Which They Are Located: Songpan County's Shanba Village, Shanba Monastery and Their Relationship to School-based Education," in *Xizang yanjiu* (*Tibetan Studies (Chinese Edition)*), No. 2 (1992), p. 106, indicate that the elementary school in Shanba was not built until 1958, and only offered Tibetan-language instruction for a few months; thereafter, it switched to monolingual Chinese instruction. For a more detailed discussion of educational practices during the late 1950s, please refer to the next section of this essay.

21. Xu and Chen, "Songpan xian zangwen zhongxue xiankuang diaocha" ("An Investigation of the Current Situation at the Songpan County Tibetan-Language Secondary School.")

22. Locally, virtually all documents and textual materials (including textbooks) from these early years have disappeared, either through general

processes of deterioration or more active destruction (such as during the Cultural Revolution). Though additional materials may exist in various archives, I have as yet been unable to investigate such sources in the course of my research.

23. Interviews were conducted in Tibetan and Chinese, with responses recorded in English paraphrases of the informants' answers. In addition, one informant consented to be tape-recorded, and the transcript from that interview has also been used as data here. In the interests of protecting their privacy, I have not used the names of these and other informants in this essay.

24. For an account of the history of this institution's development during this period, see Xinan minzu xueyaun bianji shi (The Editorial Office of the History of the Southwest Institute of Nationalities), *Xinan minzu xueyuan yuanshi 1951-1991(The History of Xinan Nationalities Institute 1951-1991)*, (Chengdu: Sichuan minzu chubanshe, 1991), pp. 2-5. For a discussion of the general role that the Nationalities Institutes played in early communist minority policy, see June Dreyer, *China's Forty Millions: Minority Nationalities and National Integration in the People's Republic of China* (Cambridge: Harvard University Press, 1976), pp.113-114.

25. The time lag between the commissioning of the school and its actual opening has led to a certain degree of local controversy over which community actually had the first post-liberation Minzu Xuexiao: Mounigou residents claim the honor of having had the first school (based on the date of the government's commission), while residents of Shangniba also claim that honor (since their school actually began to offer classes before the school in Mounigou). In both cases, a great deal of local pride seems to be attached to the school as a symbol of political and cultural advancement.

26. When the school in Mounigou first opened, for example, only the poorest students were given clothing, though in subsequent months all the students were supplied with clothing, books and food. As time went on, the local government first stopped offering books, food and clothing to all but the poorest students, and then later ceased to offer any material incentives at all. Partially as a result of this decline in material support, attendance at the school dropped off over time.

27. The appropriation of existing buildings for the establishment of local schools seems to have been a common practice, though the type of building appropriated (and perhaps the social and cultural significance of its appropriation) varied from community to community. In Dongbei (a village in the northwest part of Songpan County), the local school was also set up in the

residence of the former *tuguan,* while in Shangniba (a village near the county town), the *minzu xuexiao* was established in what had been a local temple.

28. In other Tibetan areas, including other parts of Songpan, male and female students were often given identical clothing, a practice which seriously challenged local gender boundaries. This practice often impeded the expansion of the educational enterprise, since females were reluctant to go to school if it meant having to wear "men's" clothes.

29. It is important to note how common the linkage is worldwide between the introduction of schooling and the introduction of formal public health and sanitation practices to traditional communities, the transformation of native peoples' personal hygiene practices often occupying a central position in both colonial and nationalist modernization projects. For example, Timothy Mitchell, *Colonizing Egypt* (Berkeley and Los Angeles: University of California Press, 1991), pp. 63, 99 demonstrates how schooling and sanitation were linked in multiple ways in the context of colonial Egypt; and K. Tsianina Lomawaima, "Domesticity in the Federal Indian Schools: The Power of Authority Over Mind and Body," in *American Ethnologhist*, Vol. 20, No. 2 (1993), pp. 1-14 shows how the cult of domesticity and attitudes about personal hygiene in the United States were transmitted to Indian populations through the federal boarding school system.

30. The practice of establishing classes by grouping students of a similar age does not seem to have been a standardized practice in Songpan, at least not in the initial years when schools were first being established. In at least one other school, classes were divided up by relative skill into three groups: a fast class (which was presumably made up of the brightest students), a middle class and a slow class.

31. Current teaching practice at local monasteries, which more or less resembles the traditional practices, has the instructor and students sit in separate rooms joined by a window: both the lama and the novices sit cross-legged on the floor, and engage in both recitation and a question-and-answer dialogue about the text under study.

32. His former student claimed that he used religious texts to teach Tibetan, which may be the "culturally relevant" material the former headmaster was referring to. It is also possible that he was using a modified form of the religiously oriented Tibetan materials he himself had used to learn Tibetan.

33. Many of the graduates of the *minzu xuexiao* were put to work in the land reform movement of the late 1950s, which provides evidence of the important role these schools played, both in introducing communist ideology

and in training a cadre of local Tibetan officials to implement policy on the ground.

34. Aba zangzu zizhizhou gaikuang bianxiezu (AZZG) ("The Survey of Aba Tibetan Autonomous Prefecture Editorial Collective"), in *Aba zangzu zizhizhou gaikuang (A Survey of Aba Tibetan Autonomous Prefecture)* (Chengdu: Sichuan minzu chubanshe, 1985), p. 256.

35. AZZ, *Aba Zhou Zhi (Aba Prefecture Annuals)*, 1994, p. 2,003; translated from the Chinese original , with emphasis added.

36. Ibid., p. 888.

37. Ibid., p. 1081.

38. Ibid., pp. 769-772

39. Evidence of the continued outbreaks of violence can be found in the final sections of the Prefecture Annals, where a list of local heroes is given. This list includes the names of over 90 individuals who died while suppressing the rebellions in the following areas of Songpan County: Maoergai (1956-1960), Rewugou (1956), Laoxionggou (1956, 1959), Huangshengguan (1952, 1957), Gagema (1956-1957), Lazishan (1953,1956, 1958-1959), Zhaerdong (1959), Kalonggou (1956-1957), Qilingayun (1956), Maladun (1956) Jigongzhai (1956, 1958), Lianghekou (1958), Shibazi (1956), Xiaobaosi (1956), Anhong (1956), and Longtousi (1956,1958).(AZZ, *Aba Zhou Zhi (Aba Prefecture Annuals)*, pp. 2,735-2,761)

40. In minority areas of Aba Prefecture, early forms of collectivization followed a policy of "small, simple and relaxed" collectivization, with collective units being made up primarily of village members, usually with no more than 20-30 households in a collective; See also ibid., p. 890.

41. AZZ, *Aba Zhou Zhi* AZZ *(Aba Prefecture Annuals)*, (1994), p. 2,006.

42. Se Lize, "Minzu jiaoyu shiliao zhaibian" ("Excerpts From Historical Materials on Minority Education,") in AZJW, *Minzu jiaoyu yanjiu wenji (Collected Essays on Minority Education)* (Chengdu: Sichuan Daxue Chubanshe, 1992), p. 527.

43. Ibid., pp. 527-528.

44. It is also important to note that the decline of Tibetan-language education did not necessarily mean the decline of education in the general sense, since the late 1950s represented a period of rapid development of the educational infrastructure and also saw large increases in the total number of minority students enrolled in elementary-level educational institutions: see Appendix 9.1-9.6 (appended to this chapter) for general educational statistics in Aba Prefecture during this period.

45. AZZ, *Aba Zhou Zhi (Aba Prefecture Annuals)*, (1994), p. 1,964.

46. Ibid., p. 2,003.

47. Ibid.

48. The Prefecture Annals do note that a few schools continued to operate the preparatory classes discussed above during the Cultural Revolution, but these were the exception rather than the rule. (Ibid., p. 1,964). In my documentary research and interviews, I have not yet found any evidence of Tibetan-language education being practiced in local schools during the period 1966-1969, although the reinstitution of Tibetan-language education in certain local schools seems to have begun in the early to mid-1970s. It should be noted that there is an important distinction to be made between educational policies and practices during the early years of the Cultural Revolution (especially 1966-1969) and the later years—which were only made part of the same historical era in official rhetoric and analysis after the death of Mao. Telling evidence of the effects of later historical rhetoric on the periodization of the Cultural Revolution can be see in one of the pioneering works of Chinese minority studies: Dreyer's *China's Forty Millions* (1976). Published before the historical revisionism of the post-Gang of Four era was in full swing, Dreyer's account treats the period between 1966 and 1970 as the Cultural Revolution, and rightly points out the very different policies that went into effect in minority areas in the early 1970s. Dreyer's account should serve to remind us of the need to carefully document cultural practices as they actually occurred, rather than simply accepting the dominant historical narrative.

49. The "three old essays" ("Serve the People," "The Foolish Old Man Who Moved Mountains," and "In Memory of Dr. Norman Bethune") are classic revolutionary texts that were used extensively during the Cultural Revolution to teach correct political thought and behavior. However ironic this statement may have been, it serves as a poignant reminder of the ways in which Tibetans have made and continue to make sense out of the extreme social upheavals they have confronted over the past half century, and also points out the necessity of moving beyond the official and unofficial rhetoric concerning educational practice during the Cultural Revolution so that we can examine in detail the practices of that period and their effects on local culture and social organization. That, however, is a task that exceeds the scope of this essay.

50. Sichuan sheng jiaoyu weiyuanhui minzu jiaoyuchu (SMJ) (Nationality Education Department of the Sichuan Provincial Education Commission), *Minzu jiaoyu wenjian cebian (A Collection of Documents on Nationality Education)* (Chengdu: Sichuan sheng jiaoyu qeiyuanhui minzu jiaoyuchu, no publication data given—for internal circulation, 1993), pp. 7-14.

51. Ibid., p. 7.

52. In Aba Prefecture, for example, the number of elementary schools had risen from 513 in 1958 (with a total enrollment of 35,560 and a minority student enrollment of 18,447) to 1,735 in 1978 (with a total enrollment of 104,148 and a minority student enrollment of 53,316)(See Table 10.1 for additional data).

53. This type of attitude has historically been very prevalent in practices of education for minority or indigenous peoples throughout the world, particularly when those practices involve the establishment of boarding institutions. In the Chinese case, the current focus on providing residential education for minority students needs to be viewed both in its practical and historical contexts: not only is it virtually the only practical solution to providing an education for children in China's remote mountain regions, it was also a system that achieved notable successes in the early 1950s and thereby set an important precedent.

54. From the 1950s until 1988, Songpan was divided into six administrative districts, and the seat of the district administration was most frequently where educational (and other) resources were concentrated. Though the district level administration was abolished in 1988, historical precedent still leads to the concentration of resources in those areas.

55. Xu and Chen,"Songpan xian zangwen zhongxue xiankuang diaocha" ("An Investigation of the Current Situation at the Songpan County Tibetan-Language,") p. 125.

56. As in other parts of China throughout the 1980s, the teaching profession lost much of its attractiveness to educated and skilled individuals in Songpan who could do more to enhance their status and/or make more money in the developing private sector and/or the local bureaucracy. One example is the village school in Dongbei: the two government-funded teachers assigned to the school in the early 1980s left the school soon after being posted there, one for a job in the county government and the other for the private sector. Following the departure of the second government-funded teacher, the school lost its funding for that post and the school was more or less with out any steady teachers until the completion of the new school building in 1995.

57. These and other statistics for 1996 were provided by the Songpan County Culture and Education Bureau (*Songpan xian wenjiao ju*).

58. For the most part, information found in this section of the chapter is taken either from my personal field notes or from an unpublished report issued by the *Songpan xian zangwen zhongxuexiao* (SXZZ) (Songpan County Tibetan-Language Secondary School), n.d.(a) application for Financial Support for Songpan County Tibetan High School; n.d. (b) materials for a Report on the Establishment and Development of the Songpan County Tibetan-Language

Secondary School (Songpan xian zangwen zhongxuexiao chuangjian fazhan qingkuang de huibao caike); unpublished report. In order to make the essay more readable, in many cases I have elected not to cite the latter source in the text unless I quote from it directly: detailed references can be provided on request.

59. For a discussion of the effects of this cultural renaissance on local Tibetan religious practice, see Toni Huber, "Modernity, Revival and Decline in Tibetan Mountain Pilgrimages: The Case of Northern Bird Bementery (Byang Bya Dur) and Eastern Conch Mountain (Shar Dung Ri) in A-mdo Shar-khog," paper presented at the Conference on Pilgrimage in Tibet, September 12-13, 1996, International Institute for Asian Studies, University of Leiden, Leiden, the Netherlands.

60. *Songpan xian zangwen zhongxuexiao* (SXZZ) (Songpan County Tibetan-Language Secondary School), unpublished report, p. 3.

61. Ibid.

62. Xu and Chen, "Songpan xian zangwen zhongxue xiankuang diaocha" ("An Investigation of the Current Situation at the Songpan County Tibetan-Language Secondary School") (1992), pp. 124-132.

63. Ibid.

64. c.f., Songpan xian diminglu lingdao xiaozu (SXD)(The Songpan County Place-names Guide Leadership Group), *Songpan xian diminglu* (*A Guide to Place-names in Songpan County*) (Songpan County, Sichuan, for internal circulation (*neibu*), 1983), p. 109.

65. This individual had been recognized as a "five guarantees household (*wubaohu*)" by the local government: this designation refers to childless and infirm old persons who are guaranteed food, clothing, medical care, housing and burial expenses. Individuals so designated often have little social support and are among the poorest of the poor in China's rural communities.

66. *Songpan xian zangwen zhongxuexiao* (SXZZ) (Songpan County Tibetan-Language Secondary School), unpublished report, pp. 4-5.

67. The lack of an adequate Tibetan-language curriculum used to be a major problem, especially at the secondary level, but is no longer so serious: entire elementary and secondary level curriculum has now more or less been published in a standardized Tibetan version under the title of the "Five Provinces and Regions Jointly Produced/Cooperatively Written Curriculum" (*Ljongs zhing lnga'i mnyam bsgrigs slob gzhi/Wu shengqu tongbian xiezuo jiaocai*). The secondary-level ideology and politics curriculum in China was significantly revised in the mid to late 1980s, and was among the last to be issued in Tibetan translation. An analysis of the current elementary and

secondary level Tibetan-language curriculum and its historical precedents will be included in my upcoming doctoral dissertation.

68. While this type of course load might seem average in a Western setting, it should be pointed out that the customary teaching load for secondary level instructors in this part of China is 12-15 class periods per week. By this standard, the teachers at the Tibetan-Language Secondary School were sorely overworked in their first year.

69. *Songpan xian zangwen zhongxuexiao* (SXZZ) (Songpan County Tibetan-Language Secondary School), unpublished report, p. 6.

70. The school has, for the past few years, offered 2 classes per grade, but the current plan is to expand that to 3 classes per grade, gradually developing to 9 classes with a total enrollment of around 450 students at the junior high school level. If expansion continues at the current rate, the school should reach this goal in the 1997-1998 school year. Additional plans for expansion have been proposed, including the addition of vocational courses and the possible reintroduction of a senior high school level class (which was provisionally introduced in 1993 but was closed down in 1995 after failing to get the requisite governmental approval). These plans have yet to be approved by the relevant official agencies, however, and the prospect for such future development seems grim given the fact that the school still lacks such basic resources as full dormitory housing for students and faculty.

71. English classes were only added to the curriculum in the 1995-1996 school year. They are being taught by the school's new headmaster, a local Tibetan who recently received a masters degree from Sichuan University as a member of a special class made up of Tibetan educators and officials from the Tibetan regions of Sichuan province.

72. *Songpan xian zangwen zhongxuexiao* (SXZZ) (Songpan County Tibetan-Language Secondary School), unpublished report, p. 12.

73. The Songpan County Tibetan-Language Secondary School initiated a senior high school class in the fall of 1993 prior to receiving official permission to do so. This class was closed down after 2 years and the students were not allowed to graduate, though many were subsequently placed in courses at other institutions of an equivalent level. Subsequent requests to start a senior high school level class have been denied, though the school still persists in attempting to expand its program (with the current goal being the addition of a senior high school level class in the fall of 1997). Until the serious infrastructural deficits the school currently faces have been resolved (see Note 43), however, it is unlikely that the school's application will be approved.

74.   In discussing the promotion prospects for the graduating class of 1996, for example, this new quota system was shown to have dramatic effects. Of 39 students from the Songpan County Tibetan-Language Secondary School who took the 1996 entrance exams for the next level of schooling, 35 obtained passing marks (roughly 90 percent). The main teacher training college in the prefecture was only willing to take 8 or 9 students, however, even though over 20 students scored above the minimum test score for that particular institution. Teachers in Songpan estimated that about 10 additional places should be available at other institutions. This would leave about 16 students with passing marks (over 45 percent) without a place in an institution of higher education, a dramatic decline from the rates of previous years.

75.   In this section of the chapter, I can only offer the briefest overview of selected aspects of the data I have collected to date. Those interested in a more detailed analysis of the curriculum and its transmission should refer to my forthcoming Ph.D. dissertation.

76.   Mtsho sngon mi rigs slob gzhi rtsom sgyur khang (MMS) (eds.), *Skad Yig, Deb Gnyis Pa* (*Language and Literature, Book Two*)*, Ljongs zhing lnga'i mnyam bsgrgs slob gzhi. Lo dgu'i 'gan babs slob gso'i dma' rim slob 'bring slob deb* (*Textbook for the Junior Secondary Level of [the] 9-year Compulsory Education [system], Five Provinces/Regions Jointly Produced Curriculum*) (Siling (Xining): Mtsho sngon mi rigs dpe skrun khang (Qinghai minzu chubanshe), 1993).

77.   Although the latter example is technically a Tibetan translation of a text that is Indian in origin, the particular text in question ("Letter to a Spiritual Friend") has become a well-established part of the Tibetan canon. It is therefore included here as an example of a historical Tibetan text. I would also like to note here that the textual examples cited in this section of the chapter are primarily drawn from the textbook cited above, since that is the text that was being used in many of the lessons I observed and I therefore have rich data about how the content was conveyed and received in a classroom setting. The remaining volumes of the Tibetan Language and Literature series at the junior secondary level also contain a similar distributions of textual materials, however, and I therefore feel that an analysis of one volume can serve as a representative sample of the entire series.

78.   Don grub rgyal's text "Ode to the Grasslands" (*Rtswa thang dran glu*) was previously published in a collection of his works entitled *Bol rtsom zhogs pa'i skya rengs (Dawn Pillow Writings)*. It is the basis for the fourth chapter of the second book of the junior secondary Tibetan Language and Literature series. Rang grol's short essay "A Small Footpath" (*Rkang lam phra mo*)

appeared in the literary journal *Sbrang char* (*Light Rain*), Vol. 3 (1984); Lha
rgyal tshe ring's poem "Phangs pa'i mchi ma dbang med bzhur" ("Tears of
Regret Flow Uncontrollably") appeared in a later issue of the same journal
(Vol. 2., 1986). The latter two texts comprise the main texts of Chapters 14 and
17, respectively, in the second volume of the junior secondary series.

79. This text can be found in Mtsho sngon mi rigs slob gzhi rtsom sgyur
khang (MMS) (eds.), *Skad Yig, Deb Gnyis Pa* (*Language and Literature, Book
Two*), 1994, p. 91

80. Mtsho sngon mi rigs slob gzhi rtsom sgyur khang (MMS) (eds.), *Skad
Yig, Deb Gnyis Pa* (*Language and Literature, Book Two*), *Ljongs zhing lnga'i
mnyam bsgrgs slob gzhi. Lo dgu'i 'gan babs slob gso'i dma' rim slob 'bring
slob deb* (*Textbook for the Junior Secondary Level of [the] 9-year Compulsory
Education [system], Five Provinces/Regions Jointly Produced Curriculum*)
(Siling (Xining): Mtsho sngon mi rigs dpe skrun khang (Qinghai minzu
chubanshe), 1993).

81. The Tibetan text can be found in Mtsho sngon mi rigs slob gzhi rtsom
sgyur khang MMS (eds.), *Skad Yig, Deb Gnyis Pa* (*Language and Literature,
Book Two*), 1993, pp. 130-142. An English translation of this story can be
found under the title "The Last Class: The Story of a Little Alsatian" in William
Allen Neilson, ed., *French Fiction: Honor de Balzac, George Sand, Aalfred de
Musset, Alphonse Daudet, Guy de Maupassant* (Harvard Classic Shelf of
Fiction, New York: P.F. Collier, 1917).

82. Xu and Chen, "Songpan xian zangwen zhongxue xiankuang diaocha"
("An Investigation of the Current Situation at the Songpan County Tibetan-
Language Secondary School"), p. 124.

83. See, for example, "Aba zangzu qiangzu zizhizhou shixing 'Sichuan
sheng yiwu jiaoyu shishi tiaoli' de buchong guiding" ("Aba Tibetan-Qiang
Autonomous Prefecture's Supplementary Stipulation on Carrying Out the
'Sichuan Province Regulation for the Implementation of Compulsory
Education'"), in AZZ, *Aba Zhou Zhi*, pp. 2,777-2,779), which states as its
eighth provision: "Elementary and secondary schools within the Prefecture that
enroll mainly Tibetan students should both allow them to study Tibetan
language and literature, and promote the common speech (*Putonghua*) used
throughout the country. These schools can (1) take Tibetan-language education
as the mainstay, while at the same time adding classes in Chinese language and
literature; (2) take Chinese as the mainstay, while at the same time adding
classes in Tibetan language and literature; or (3) implement an all-Tibetan-
language (system of) education." (AZZ, *Aba Zhou Zhi*, p. 2,778). Note that
there is no provision given for all-Chinese-language instruction at schools

enrolling a majority of minority students. The system currently being employed in most Tibetan areas in Songpan is thus not in line with higher level policy.

84.   When I was conducting fieldwork in the summer of 1993, I visited one elementary school that had begun offering Tibetan-language instruction from the first grade, but that experiment has since been discontinued. The attitude of parents in many parts of Songpan seems to be that it is important to be competent in Chinese, and that it is better to start learning the language from an early age, so the lack of Tibetan-language education in village schools does not always reflect simple bureaucratic insensitivity to local concerns. It must be admitted, however, that this policy has an extremely detrimental effect on the development of education in general, as well as Tibetan-language education in particular. Tibetan students often enter school with very little understanding of spoken Chinese, yet they are expected to complete an all-Chinese curriculum for at least the first 3 years of their schooling. For the most part, students not only fail to do well in Chinese, but their other subjects also suffer. Those students who begin Tibetan in the fourth grade graduate from elementary school having only completed half of the elementary level Tibetan curriculum: if they go on to study at the Tibetan-Language Secondary School, they are required to finish the elementary curriculum in addition to the standard junior high curriculum, a process which essentially crams 6 years of Tibetan-language course work into 3 years of study. And this is what happens to the lucky few who enter junior high school with some prior Tibetan schooling: the remainder begin their secondary level Tibetan-language education with the Tibetan equivalent of the ABCs, and it is a credit to them and their teachers if they are able to complete the required curriculum in the time allotted, much less advance to higher levels of education.

85.   For a more detailed discussion of the "outlet" problem as it relates to Tibetan-language education, see Badeng Nima (Tib. dPal-ldan Nyi-ma), "Zangzu jiaoyu de chulu" ("The Outlet for Tibetan Education"), in *Xizang Yanjiu (Tibetan Studies (Chinese Edition))* (1994), No.3, pp.44-50.

CHAPTER 10

Education among the Minhe Monguor[1]

Zhu Yongzhong and *Kevin Stuart*

The Minhe County Monguor are an enclave of the larger Monguor (Tu) minority in China. Their experience with schooling illustrates a number of factors related to education in the Chinese countryside for minorities living far from an urban center. Their educational experience confronts such difficulties as a woefully inadequate education infrastructure; minimal financial support by the local government; low-quality teaching; high levels of historical illiteracy and poverty; and being taught in Chinese, a Sinitic language that is very different from their own Altaic one, for which a written form has never been used in education. Furthermore, we will examine the Monguor historical experience with formal education, and make suggestions as to how the present situation might be improved. In accomplishing this, we examine a number of related written records, present interviews from informants, and periodically call on the knowledge of the first author, who has taught in Minhe Monguor regions since 1987.

"Monguor," as an ethnic appellation, may be understood as a collection of people who, while demonstrating considerable variation in language and cultural presentations,[2] are related in speaking dialects with numerous affinities to Mongol, are non-Islamic, are much influenced by Dge-lugs-pa[3] Buddhism, and dwell primarily in eastern Qinghai[4] and adjoining Gansu provinces. Brought to international attention by the studies of Francis Schram[5] and Dominik Schröder[6] and, more recently, by Stuart and his Qinghai colleagues,[7] the Monguor were designated as the "Tu" nationality by the Chinese government in the 1950s and, today, are one of China's 55 officially acknowledged minorities. Because *most* of the nationality refer to themselves as "Monguor,"[8] we employ this term.[9] As is the case for a number of China's minorities, this grouping is not without controversy.[10] A review of publications related to the Mongol language family notes that "Tu" is a contested term.[11] Not all residents of Nianduhu Village,[12] Tongren County, for example, are pleased with the designation "Tu," which they are classified as. The same people are dubbed "Baoan" by Chen Naixiong[13] of Inner Mongolia University's Mongol Language Study Center. One also cannot escape the conclusion that many of the nationality identify themselves, in order of importance, with a clan bearing a particular family name, a specific ancestral village, a region, a county, Monguor, and finally as "Tu." Table 10.1 depicts the 1994 population distribution of the Monguor in China.

HUZHU MONGUOR AS REPRESENTATIVE

Profound differences exist within certain peoples classified as a single member of China's 55 officially recognized minority nationalities. When a "model" group is recognized and its language used in educational instruction, difficulties may ensue for those outside the "model" group. The Monguor illustrate this predicament. Writings about the Monguor often presume that the Huzhu Monguor represent the entire nationality to the neglect of other, distinctively different Monguor groups. There are several reasons for this. First, Huzhu is closer to Xining than other Monguor areas; consequently, it is more accessible to tourists, researchers and government leaders on periodic inspection tours of minority areas. Secondly, Monguor language materials used by students of Mongol-related languages[14] have nearly always emanated from Huzhu. Third, of the three minority autonomous counties in China with "Monguor" in their names, only Huzhu is solely "Monguor." For Minhe and Datong counties, "Monguor" follows "Hui." This third factor, specially, has lent authority to representing Huzhu Monguor in terms of their language, clothing and customs as illustrative of all Monguor.[15]

Limited solidarity exists between different Monguor groups. A rare exception is the annual *Tuzu anzhao nadun jie*, or Monguor Dancing and Recreational Festival, held annually in Xining around the fifteenth day of the sixth lunar month. The 1992 meeting featured professional

Table 10.1. Distribution of China's Monguor Population in 1994

Location	Population
China	190,000
Qinghai Province	160,000
Xining City	36,800
Datong Hui and Monguor Autonomous County	34,650
Haidong District	103,600
Huzhu Monguor Autonomous County	57,000
Minhe Hui and Monguor Autonomous County	37,900
Ledu County	6,600
Other Counties	2,000
Huangnan Tibetan Autonomous Prefecture	7,971
Tongren County	7,471
Haibei Tibetan Autonomous Prefecture	7,579
Menyuan Hui Autonomous County	6,091
Hainan Tibetan Autonomous Prefecture	3,496
Guide County	1,289
Gonghe County	1,186
Haixi Mongol and Tibetan Autonomous Prefecture	2,800
Yushu and Guoluo Tibetan Autonomous Prefectures	—
Gansu Province	20,000*
Yunnan Province	2,000**

*Source:*Cunfu Li, "Tuzu pian" ("Monguor Section") in Muchi Yundeng Jiacuo et. al. (eds.), *Qinghai shaoshu minzu (Qinghai Minority Nationalities)* (Xining: Qinghai renmin chubanshe, 1995), p. 247.

* The Gansu Monguor population figure reported by Cunfu Li is significantly higher than the 2,567 listed by Xuewei Li and Kevin Stuart, " Population and Culture of the Mongols,Tu, Baoan, Dongxiang and Yugu in Gansu," in *Mongolian Studies,* Vol. 12 (1989), pp. 71-93, p. 75, who used Zhengliang Ma (compiler), *Gansu shaoshu minzu renkou (The Population of Gansu Minorities)* (Lanzhou: Keji chubanshe, 1986). In Li and Stuart's table, p. 76, Tianzhu Tibetan Autonomous County accounted for 10, 051 of Gansu's Monguor population.

** We know nothing about Yunnan residents classified as Monguor.

dancers in synthetic costumes only superficially resembling traditional Huzhu Monguor dress, performing stylized dances fit for general audience consumption. This style depends upon colorful costumes, attractive young females whose ethnicity is immaterial in roles that supersede those of males, and a good deal of arm-waving, all to the tune of loudly played pre-recorded music involving instruments unknown to the time-honored repertoire of the nationality and bearing little semblance to traditional melodies, accentuating how distant public representations of ethnic groups may be from the actual cultural mosaic of the concerned people.

ORIGINS

Monguor origins are disputed and obscure.[16] Mongol soldiers stationed in present Monguor areas during the era of Mongol power and influence beginning in the early thirteenth century undoubtedly affected the formation of the nationality.[17] Just what role ancestors of present-day Monguor played in the Yuan dynasty (1271-1368) remains unclear, as does the question of similarities in the early Ming dynasty (1368-1644). The influence of Chinese and Tibetan[18] on Monguor dialects demonstrates that the nationality is not static.

It is also important to point out how distant and irrelevant the Mongols and their written language and glorious Chinggis Khan history have been. This is particularly true for those not part of lamasery communities where Monguor, Mongols and certain Yugur undoubtedly did find similarities in their respective languages and customs. In the last Mongol hurrah in Qinghai, Luobuzangdanjin (1692-1755) met with 31 Mongol leaders in 1723 on the banks of Qinghai Lake, where they organized a rebellion against the Qing dynasty (1644-1911) government. After being defeated in 1724, Luobuzangdanjin fled to the Zhunge'er.[19] He was captured in Yili[20] in 1755, taken to Beijing and executed.[21] In a study of the function of Monguor *tusi*[22] during the Ming and Qing dynasties, Yong Qin[23] argues that several Monguor *tusi* each controlled troops numbering as many as 10,000 during the early days of the Ming dynasty and that they played a crucial role in subduing periodic Mongol attempts to reestablish the glory days of the Mongol empire. This did little to enhance Mongol-Monguor solidarity.

THE EDUCATION STATUS OF QINGHAI'S POPULATION

Tables 10.2-10.5 depict the educational attainments of Qinghai's population according to ethnic group. [24] Of all residents, irrespective of nationality, 54 percent have received some education. Of this number, 33 percent are male and 21 percent are female. The Han, who comprise a majority of the province's population, have the most education, with nearly 70 percent having received some schooling. This contrasts sharply with the Salar population, who receive the least-only 27 percent have some formal education. The Salar,[25] an Islamic, Turkic-speaking population living primarily in Xunhua Salar Autonomous County in eastern Qinghai, face similar problems as the Monguor by being educated in Chinese. Ninety-five percent of Salar females are illiterate. Four times the number of Salar males as Salar females receive some education, suggesting that traditional attitudes toward women diminish their opportunity to attend school. Other nationalities are ranged between the Han and Salar with regard to the amount of education received. The Monguor have the highest educational attainments of any Qinghai minority, with 45 percent of the population having received some education. The reasons why this is the case deserve further study. In part, it is because few Monguor are herdsmen, and therefore, have greater access to schooling than nomadic Tibetans living in southern Qinghai. This is particularly true for the 36,800 Monguor living in Xining City. Most Monguor students resident in Xining speak Monguor poorly, if at all, and do not experience the difficulties with Chinese-language education that countryside Monguor do. The Tibetanized Mongols of Henan Mongol Autonomous County, Huangnan Tibetan Autonomous Prefecture and the Mongols of Haixi Mongol and Tibetan Autonomous Prefecture have less access to schooling than the sinicized Mongols of Qinghai living in Xining and adjacent agricultural counties. The educational attainments of the latter might explain the status of Mongol education.

The term "having received some education" may mean little. Those who have spent some time studying at elementary school are the largest

Table 10.2. The Education Status of Qinghai's Population (1990)

Nationality	Population	% of Total Population	Nationality	Population Receiving Some Schooling*						
				Male + Female		Male		Female	
Total	4,456,946	100	Total	2,410,039	54.07%	1,487,117	33.37%	922,922	20.71%
Han	2,580,419	57.90	Han	1,781,663	69.05	1,045,457	40.52	727,206	28.18
Tibetan	911,860	20.46	Monguor	73,333	45.03	49,173	30.19	24,160	14.83
Hui	638,847	14.33	Mongol	20,179	40.97	17,430	24.48	11,749	16.56
Monguor	162,865	3.65	Hui	245,576	38.44	167,110	26.17	78,466	12.28
Salar	77,003	1.73	Tibetan	248,977	27.30	176,113	19.31	72,864	7.99
Mongol	71,215	1.60	Salar	20,291	26.35	16,790	21.80	3,501	4.55

* Percentages of those in each ethnic group at different levels of education are calculated against the figure for total population of each ethnic groups.

Table 10.3. University Graduates in Qinghai (1990)*

	University Graduates**				Institute Graduates**		
Nationality	Male + Female	Male	Female	Nationality	Male + Female	Male	Female
Total	28,406 .63%	20,235 .45%	8,171 .18%	Total	37,956 .85%	26,447 .59%	11,509 .26%
Han	22,685 .88	16,222 .63	6,463 .25	Han	31,691 1.23	21,571 .84	10,120 .39
Mongol	485 .68	308 .43	172 .24	Mongol	540 .76	367 .52	173 .24
Monguor	786 .48	586 .36	200 .12	Monguor	661 .41	544 .33	117 .07
Salar	219 .28	184 .24	35 .05	Tibetan	2,873 .32	2,338 .26	535 .06
Hui	1,550 .24	1,031 .16	519 .08	Salar	238 .31	204 .26	34 .04
Tibetan	2,129 .23	1,562 .17	567 .06	Hui	1,461 .23	1,132 .18	329 .05

* "University" is not an entirely accurate term. For example, graduates of Qinghai Junior Teachers' College, a three-year teacher training school, provides what is equivalent to the first 3 years of university education to its students. Qinghai Education Insstitute provides what is equivalent to the first 2 years of university education to its students. Graduates of both schools are likely counted in the "university" category.

** Percentages of those in each ethnic group at different levels of education are calculated against the figure for total population of each ethnic groups.

Table 10.4. Special/Secondary School Graduates in Qinghai (1990)

	Special/Technical Secondary School*							Upper Secondary School**					
Nationality	Male + Female		Male		Female		Nationality	Male + Female		Male		Female	
Total	97,243	2.18%	59,772	1.34%	37,471	.84%	Total	271,679	6.10%	150,928	3.39%	120,751	2.71%
Mongol	2,295	3.22	1,240	1.74	1,055	1.48	Han	237,504	9.20	130,148	5.04	107,356	4.16
Han	74,454	2.89	45,040	1.75	29,414	1.14	Mongol	2,437	3.42	1,255	1.76	1,182	1.66
Tibetan	12,873	1.41	8,492	.93	4,381	.48	Monguor	5,312	3.26	3,276	2.01	2,036	1.25
Monguor	1,996	1.23	1,313	.81	683	.42	Hui	12,462	1.95	7,492	1.17	4,971	.78
Salar	684	.89	555	.72	129	.17	Salar	1,016	1.32	727	.94	289	.38
Hui	4,167	.65	2,726	.42	1,441	.23	Tibetan	10,577	1.16	6,862	.75	3,715	.41

* Students who have graduated from lower secondary schools or upper secondary schools might be eligible to attend a *zhongzhuan* (specialized secondary school), which includes secondary schools devoted to, for example, the teaching of technical skills, accounting, the training of future teachers and the training of future policemen.

** Percentages of those in each ethnic group at different levels of education are calculated against the figure for total population of each ethnic groups.

Table 10.5. Secondary and Elementary School Education in Qinghai (1990)

Nationality	Elementary School*					
	Male + Female		Male		Female	
Total	1,182,463	26.54%	728,898	16.35%	453,565	10.18%
Han	773,162	29.96	446,681	17.31	326,481	12.65
Monguor	46,730	28.70	30,603	18.79	16,127	9.90
Hui	161,444	25.27	109,706	17.17	51,738	8.10
Mongol	15,949	22.40	9,717	13.64	6,232	8.75
Tibetan	168,674	18.50	119,262	13.08	49,412	5.42
Salar	13,659	17.74	11,352	14.74	2,307	3.00

Nationality	Lower Secondary School*					
	Male + Female		Male		Female	
Total	792,292	17.78%	500,837	11.24%	291,455	6.54%
Han	642,167	24.89	394,795	15.30	247,372	9.59
Monguor	17,848	10.96	12,851	7.89	4,997	3.07
Mongol	7,478	10.50	4,543	6.38	2,935	4.12
Hui	64,492	10.10	45,024	7.05	19,468	3.05
Salar	4,475	5.81	3,768	4.89	707	0.92
Tibetan	51,851	5.69	37,579	4.12	14,254	1.56

* Percentages of those in each ethnic group at different levels of education are calculated against the figure for total population of each ethnic groups.

category for each nationality, but the duration of study is not specified. For example, in the case of the approximately 5 percent of Salar females who have received some education, only 3 percent of this group attended elementary school for unspecified periods. Illiteracy among Qinghai females at rates of 95 percent for Salar, 92 percent for Tibetans, 88 percent for Hui, 85 percent for Monguor, 83 percent for Mongols and 72 percent for Han Chinese suggests that the basic education of females at the grassroots level has only just begun and is in urgent need of being strengthened.

THE MINHE MONGUOR

With the above as background, we now turn to Minhe County and examine the local geography and linguistic-ethnic environment, the economy, the history of education and several accounts by individuals of their personal experience with education.

Geography and Linguistic-Ethnic Environment

Qinghai Province is located in northwest China, south of the Xinjiang Uygur Autonomous Region, north of the Tibet Autonomous Region, and west and south of Gansu Province where most of China's Baoan, Dongxiang and Yugur[26] populations live, who speak Mongolic languages related to Minhe Monguor. Minhe Hui and Monguor Autonomous County, Haidong District is positioned in a complex multiethnic environment in the central eastern sector of Qinghai. Minhe Monguor speakers are concentrated in the southern part of the county near Gansu's western border, delineated by the Yellow River. Within the Minhe Monguor speaking area, Tibetans live in Xinger Tibetan Autonomous Township (*xiang*) and in northwest Gangou Township.[27] The Monguor area in southern Minhe County is generally known as Sanchuan, or "Three Plains." It consists of the plains of Zhaomu, Middle (*zhong*) and Gan Family (*ganjia*). In addition, Monguor live in the five valleys of Minzhu, Shidie,[28] Damajia, Wushi and Xing'er, in addition to the mountain villages around these plains and valleys such as Zhangjiaola, Badaola, Yangjiaola, Ximiaola, Zhujiaola and Anchaola. The Jishi, Yundong, Bieluo, Hulang, Wobo, and Badao mountains are positioned in an east-west direction across the wide valley area.

Tibetans living in Xing'er Township strongly retain the Tibetan language. In Tibetan areas of Gangou Township (*xiang*), however, Tibetan is used primarily by people over 70 years of age. Younger Tibetans generally cannot speak Tibetan. Most males in Minhe can speak local Mandarin-related dialects, regardless of ethnicity. Tibetan and Monguor females may be either unable to speak Chinese, or speak it only poorly. This is due to a lack of formal education and considerably less contact with the Chinese-speaking world. Zhu, a lifelong resident of southern Minhe, estimates that approximately 98 percent of Minhe Monguor are fluent in Monguor, which indicates the strength with which the dialect is preserved.[29] Furthermore, many Hui living near Minhe Monguor speak Monguor fluently. Unlike many other predominantly minority areas in China, Monguor is the language spoken by most workers in local shops, banks, post offices, police offices, courts and so on in Minhe Monguor regions.

Table 10.6 provides a detailed summary of where the Minhe Monguor population live. In Guanting Region (*zhen*)[30] and Zhongchuan and Xiakou townships, Monguor represent 71-89 percent of the total population. Monguor-speaking Hui merchants have occupied most business niches, presenting few entrepreneurial opportunities for "outsiders." Similarly, every bit of arable land is presently under cultivation; consequently, "immigrants" from other areas do not relocate here as farmers. In fact, land scarcity has induced a number of Minhe Monguor to move to newly opened agricultural land in Haixi Mongolian and Tibetan Autonomous Prefecture situated in northern Qinghai. This suggests that Monguor may be spoken for several more generations in Minhe, although it is increasingly being modified by the Chinese language. This linguistic modification is related to Chinese language education, improved transportation permitting greater access to the outside world, increased accessibility of printed materials in the Chinese language and greater availability of electricity that has brought Chinese language radio and television broadcasts into many Minhe Monguor homes.

Certain Monguor, especially female Monguor[31] in their sixties and seventies with bound feet, have never left this area. However, with the passage of time, it has become ever more convenient to go and come from this area. Completion of a dirt track in 1956 from Chuankou to Guanting that is sufficiently wide to accommodate trucks made this

Table 10.6. Population of Selected Minhe Areas in 1993*

Area Name**	Total	Han****		Hui		Monguor		Tibetan		Others***	
	Population	%	Population	%	Population	%	Population	%	Population	%	Population
Minhe County	344,273	100	159,709	46	133,367	39	38,872	11	11,601	4	724
Manpin	1,464	4	7,851	5/54	6,398	5/44	269	1/2	128	1/1	3
Qianhe	11,602	3	3,739	2/32	4,106	3/35	3,746	10/32	11	—/—	—
Gangou	13,238	4	4,582	3/35	4,703	4/36	2,581	7/19	1,372	12/10	—
Guanting Region	14,882	4	198	—/1	1,276	1/9	13,266	34/89	16	—/—	236
Zhongchuan	17,188	5	60	—/—	4,288	3/25	12,790	33/74	18	—/—	32
Xinger	3,605	1	388	—/11	—	—/—	781	2/22	2,436	21/68	—

* The information used to generate this table is taken from Zhu, Ojiyediin Chuluu, and Stuart, "'The Frog Boy': An Example of Minhe Monguor."

** Unless otherwise indicated, areas are townships.

*** This includes 34 Salar, 50 Mongols, 420 Dongxiang, 14 Koreans, 179 Manchu, 7 Zhuang, 3 Xibo, 8 Bai, 1 Miao, 6 Qiang, 1 Tujia and 1 Baoan.

**** All percentages were generated by the authors of this chapter. Their sums may not equal 100, owing to rounding to the nearest whole number. A "–" indicates either a value of "0" or a value of less than 1 percent.

easier. This was especially true after this track was laid with asphalt and after the 1990 construction of the Great Yellow River Bridge over the Yellow River. This bridge linked an area 3 kilometers west of Guanting to Dahejia Township, Jishi Mountain Baoan, Dongxiang and Salar Autonomous County, Gansu Province. Subsequently, bus and truck traffic dramatically increased, bringing a period of unheralded contact with "outsiders." Similar contact has also been encouraged by many young Monguor males engaged in construction work in the last decade. Since 1980, many Minhe Monguor have graduated from institutions of higher education in Xining, Gansu, Shaanxi and Beijing. Though only a minority have returned to work among the Minhe Monguor, regular visits during festival periods bring information about the outside world.

Economy

Although most families have some sheep, which are grazed on nearby mountainsides, agriculture is the main mode of livelihood. Monguor cultivate wheat, highland barley, corn, sesame, potatoes, beans and apples. Fieldwork continues to be done without mechanization. Consequently, many families own one or two head of cattle,[32] donkeys or mules. In addition to sheep, chickens and swine are also fed. Much local trade involves eggs, animal hair and young domestic livestock, as well as cash. In addition to agriculture and the raising of livestock, several private construction teams are based in the Minhe Monguor region. This has provided numerous jobs to local males. Furthermore, many males also search for gold in such areas as Urtmörön[33] in Haixi Mongol and Tibetan Autonomous Prefecture.

History of Education

There is little information about Monguor education prior to the beginning of the twentieth century. Information about the latter period is more abundant but, at times, contradictory. A. Doak Barnett (born 1921) is one of the few Westerners to have written about education in Qinghai based on personal experience. His observations on northwest China, published in 1993, include four pages on education on Qinghai. He writes that provincial officials told him in 1948 that there were 1,057 elementary schools with 94,000 students and 13 secondary schools with 4,500 students in Qinghai. However, in 1988, provincial officials stated to him that in 1949 there were only 109 elementary schools and eight secondary schools.[34]

One of the earliest observations involving formal education and the Monguor involves an observation recorded by Yong Qin:

Military schools appeared at the beginning of the Ming dynasty. . . . The doctrines of Confucius and Mencius were popularly taught and people began participating in imperial examinations. According to the known facts, Monguor of the Ming dynasty included Li Wan, who passed the *juren* examination;[35] Li Ji, who passed the *jinshi* examination;[36] Li Guangxian, who passed the *jinshi* martial examination; at the beginning of the Qing dynasty, Qi Zhongzhi passed the martial *jinshi* examination; and there were many *xiucai*.[37] Although most of those who participated in the imperial examinations were the children of ranking *tusi*, to a certain degree these people played an energetic role in the development of Monguor education.[38]

In 1428, *weixue* (city schools)[39] were established in Xining and *shexue* (town schools) were founded in certain *bu*, or villages, in contemporary Monguor areas. Some Monguor attended these schools and studied Confucianism, medicine and mathematics. A few students took the Chinese examination.[40] Nearly 300 years later in 1725, *weixue* were renamed *fuxue* (city[41] school) and *shexue* were widely established. The first *yixue*[42] in Minhe was established in Chuankou,[43] Nianbo County[44] in 1725. During the period 1781-1784, a *yixue* was established in Maying, situated in the present-day Minhe County.[45]

In the early twentieth century, modern *xuetang*[46] were founded in China, including several in the Minhe area. From 1909-1911, the Guanting Village Elementary School was established. Later, there were intermittently operated private schools in Guanting, Qianjin Village (located in the present Zhongchuan Township); and Qi Family Village (in today's Zhongchuan Township). Classes were held in temples and in teachers' and villagers' homes.[47] Students were taught *Sishu* (the four books),[48] *Wujing* (the five classics),[49] *Sanzi Jing*[50] (three characters primer), and *Baijia Xing*[51] (surnames of all families).[52] In private schools, teachers were annually given *shuxiu*[53] during the festivals of *Duanwu* (dragon boat festival), *Zhongqiu* (mid-autumn day), and *Dongzhi* (winter solstice). Students[54] also sent gifts of grain and silver to the teachers.[55]

In the first year of a student's study, his family was charged one *sheng*[56] of grain. The second year, two *sheng* were charged. Tuition increased as the student continued to study. Consequently, many students dropped out because their families did not have sufficient grain to pay. This grain was the sole source of teachers' "salaries." Students generally did not have textbooks, rather, they copied books by hand onto coarse paper.[57]

In 1930, when an independent Minhe County was carved out of Nianbo County, there were three complete (grades 1 through 6) elementary schools,[58] 42 lower level (grades 1 through 4) elementary schools and one girls' school in this new county. Of the 1,050 students in all these schools, only 30 were girls.[59]

Mention, during this time frame, needs to be made of the intriguing figure, Zhu Haishan (1894-1980), known more commonly as "Zhu Lama." He is the most widely recognized of any Minhe Monguor. His current hagiography is based on the half of his life spent in China—little is known about his decades in exile beginning in 1947, other than a predictable "he traveled in Nepal, Sri Lanka, India, and Myanmar practicing Buddhism" before dying in south Nepal at the age of 86.[60]

Zhu, known variously as Tiancilu, Funan Zhu, Haishan and Bsod-nams-lha-rgyas, was born in the present Jielong Village, Xianfeng Administrative Village, Guanting Township. He became a monk at the age of 13 and lived in the present Zhu Family Temple, Zhongchuan Township and the much more acclaimed Kumbum (Ta'er) Temple in today's Huangzhong County. His path to success seems to be based on the formula that other Monguor monks also applied: a winning personality plus fluency in Monguor, Mongol, Tibetan and Chinese that allowed them to facilitate between the different groups of Dge-lugs-pa devotees. Given the linguistic similarities between Monguor and Mongol, and the frequent contact between Mongols and Monguor at lamaseries, learning Mongol has been an easier proposition for Monguor than for Tibetans. Knowledge of these languages was surely a major factor when the ninth Panchen Lama[61] chose Zhu as his translator in 1923 while he was in Qinghai. Zhu was to be an important aide to the Panchen from that time until the death of the latter in 1937 in Yushu.

In 1934, Zhu returned from Nanjing to the land of his birth. Surely shocked by the poverty and illiteracy, especially in comparison to contemporary Nanjing, he resolved to strengthen local schooling. His authority as a powerful religious figure in intimate contact with the Panchen Lama meant that his insistence that schooling was important was heeded. In 1936, Zhu Haishan contributed 1,000 silver yuan to build Zhongchuan, Wushi, Meitian, Zhenbian, Hulangcheng and Zhaomuchuan lower elementary schools, all of which were under the administration of Guanting Elementary School. Zhu also collected funds from people, built Guanting Library, and stocked it with items that he financed himself. In sum, Zhu was a powerful progressive force in emphasizing the value of education.

In the period 1936-1943, there were 13 complete elementary schools and a number of lower level elementary schools in the county. By late 1948, there were more than 70 elementary schools, with 2,190 students and approximately 100 teachers in Minhe County. These schools had few students and minimal operating funds and equipment. At that time, poverty meant few children could attend school. Some so-called schools had no students. A general sense of instability in education was kindled by government officials periodically dismantling and merging schools.[62]

In order to provide a more intimate view of the reality of education at the village level, we provide the accounts below, which are germane to the time period under discussion.

Account One

In Erhuang[63] Village, located in today's Qianjin Administrative Village, Zhu Tingjun[64] conducted a private school in his home in the early decades of the twentieth century. Attendance depended on ability to pay tuition in grain. Students were not placed in grades. Rather, students asked the teacher, who typically sat on a *kang*,[65] to explain characters they did not know.

Observing rules of etiquette in dealing with the teacher was important. When entering the teacher's home, a student put his book down on the floor in front of his teacher, *zuoyi* (bowed at the waist to show respect) and picked up his book. After the teacher's explanation the student bowed again, walked backward three steps and exited the teacher's home.

A student pledged to read and recite a certain amount per day, which the teacher checked. If the student did not do what he had pledged, the teacher beat him on the palm with a ruler. Consequently, certain students whose families could afford tuition were afraid of being punished and therefore did not attend school.[66]

Grades did not exist. When students finished the books they were assigned, they traveled to larger towns and cities, such as Xining, to take higher education entrance examinations. Few students from Monguor areas passed these examinations.[67]

Account Two

Mr. Zhang (born 1925) began attending Zhezi School when he was 10. Most families had to obtain money by selling wheat to pay for their children's books, which cost about 1.5 yuan. Every year each student was required to pay five *maying shengzi*[68] of grain to the school's single teacher.

Zhang and his schoolmates brought lumber made from nearby villagers' trees, which was then used to repair the old school building and build classrooms, rooms for teachers and student dormitory rooms. The school had four grades in two classrooms and a total of 50 students. Grades one and two shared a classroom, and grades three and four shared a classroom.

Most students wore patched clothing. Some students were barefoot during warm weather. Poor families could not send their children to school; nevertheless, they were required periodically to give the teacher token gifts or invite him to a banquet. If they did not, the teacher might order older, regular students to catch such poor students and forcibly drag them to the school where they were given new Chinese names and officially enrolled. A student's family was subsequently obliged to pay his tuition. In order to avoid such scenarios, some families sent children to distant locations to herd livestock.

When a family wished to discontinue a child's education, a sheep or a piece of felt had to be given to the teacher. If the teacher still did not consent, the family might have invited the teacher to a meal. If a boy with a younger brother wished to stop attending school, one half of a butchered sheep, or its cash value, might have been given to the teacher and then the younger brother enrolled at the usual fee.

When Zhang attended school, about one-half of the local eligible boys also attended. They were routinely beaten by the teacher, some so severely that they were unable to walk afterward. If a student was absent one day, he dreaded attending classes the next, for he was sure of the punishment. The same was true for students who could not recite the lessons that they had pledged to memorize. The amount of gifts a student, whom the teacher deemed deserving of a beating, presented to the teacher determined the severity of the punishment.

When a student reached the school, he approached the teacher with his chin touching his chest, and then orally greeted the teacher. Next, he walked backward out of the teacher's home. Students were expected to memorize and be able to read at least one book per year of study. After the students graduated from elementary school, they were eligible to attend Jinghe[69] Complete Elementary School or Guanting Complete Elementary School. However, owing to poverty, most students did not continue studying beyond Zhezi School.

Account Three

Hu Youcheng (born 1929) began attending Zhu Family School when he was 10 years old. One teacher taught four grades, with more than 40 students in one classroom. When he began school, Youcheng Hu's grandfather tried to teach him using some of his personal books, but Youcheng Hu did not learn much.

Students paid for the books given to them at school and also paid a small tuition fee. Hu Youcheng and his schoolmates were not serious scholars. One of his classmates was from a family wealthy enough to provide him with a fried cake daily for his lunch. In the morning, the classmate left his home and played in the sun along a small, local river. Hu and his classmates were dispatched on a daily basis to apprehend him and bring him to school. Often, however, they could not find him. When he was found and brought to the school, the teacher beat him. In the beginning, the teacher beat the classmate on his palm. Later, two students held him while the teacher beat him cruelly on the buttocks.

After Hu finished his fourth year of school, he dropped out to work at home. Two years later, he enrolled in Guanting Elementary School in order to avoid being impressed into Ma Bufang's[70] army.

After liberation, the county government attempted to improve the school system in line with national directives. One effort to improve adult literacy was made in 1950 in Minhe County and involved basic literacy classes held during the winter. In late 1951, there were 123 such schools. Village leaders assembled local illiterates in homes and temples. They invited a literate person from a local village to teach. If a proper "teacher" could not be located, one or two lower secondary school students taught. During this time, 93 teachers taught 3,594 peasants.[71]

In 1954, there was a bid to reform elementary education, particularly in terms of school management and pedagogy. Following the formation of agricultural cooperatives in 1955, the need for peasants to become literate was emphasized. Subsequently, schools increased dramatically in number along with student enrollment. At that time, 6,198 (29.3 percent of) school-age children in Minhe County attended school.[72]

In August 1958, Minhe Lower Normal School[73] in Chuankou, which trained elementary school teachers, became Minhe Secondary School with both lower and upper sections-a first for Minhe County.[74] In the same year, the first lower secondary school in the Monguor area was established in Guanting with one class of 20 students.[75] During this time of the Great Leap Forward, student numbers increased sharply. The number of six-year elementary schools increased from 25 to 46, four-year elementary schools from 120 to 176, and student numbers more than doubled, from 10,842 in 1957 to 25,679 in 1958. This resulted in most young laborers going to school. Schools lacked desks and chairs, while farms lacked laborers. Consequently, schools nonchalantly stopped classes for students to work. Although a "great leap forward in education" was advocated, certain schools had their own factories and farms and ordered students to do related work. Some students had little time to study. In general, the quality of instruction was low.[76]

For several years after 1958, most peasants were impoverished and many people died of starvation. From 1960 to 1962, 16,000 students over the age of 16 from Minhe County were told to return home to work. In 1960, according to provincial documents, the only secondary school to be retained in the county was Minhe Secondary School. Guanting, Maying, Gushan and Xinmin lower secondary schools were to be terminated, owing to China's impoverished condition. When Monguor were informed, many contested this decision, for it effectively denied a post-elementary school education to most Minhe Monguor. The only alternative was for children to walk 60 kilometers to Chuankou, or the same distance to Hanjiaji in Gansu. Zhang Wengui, leader of Yellow River People's Township,[77] insisted on keeping the schools, despite strong opposition from the county government. Eventually, according to some reports, Premier Zhou Enlai interceded on behalf of the Monguor, and Guanting Lower Secondary School was retained. Although the government dispensed limited support, local residents provided classrooms, desks and chairs, and relocated the Guanting Lower Secondary School to the Zhu Family Temple in Zhu Family Village in the present-day Guangming Administrative Village, where it operated for 3 years.[78]

From 1962-1964, the number of lower secondary school students decreased. In 1964, following the central government's instruction, 50 schools were established in Minhe. Students spent a half day engaged in agricultural labor and a half day studying. There were 1,097 students and 57 teachers. In 1966, the inaugural year of the Cultural Revolution, contemporary education was criticized and ravaged. Teaching basic knowledge was disparaged and the quality of instruction decreased a great deal.[79]From 1966-1976, peasants' spare time education was discontinued. One consequence of all of this was a rapid rise in illiteracy.[80]

In 1967, the number of students increased to 114 in three classes at Guanting Lower Secondary School. In 1968, an upper secondary section was added to this school. In 1969, a three-year, lower secondary system and two-year, upper secondary system was initiated. Rules stipulating passage of an examination in order to be promoted to a higher grade were canceled. The content of what students learned was quite rudimentary, consisting primarily of politics. Schools paid little attention to students acquiring literacy.[81]

In 1971, lower secondary schools were established in Zhongchuan, Guanting and Xiakou townships. In the same year, a number of elementary schools were also established at the village level, and a five-year elementary school system was put into effect.[82] Generally, however, students only attended school for 2 to 3 years and then, when old enough to do production team work for their families, they dropped out. Other factors restricting continued attendance were poverty, which made the purchase of textbooks difficult; and living far from a school.

Accounts four, five, and six provide additional insights into personal education experience during the early 1960s and the period of the Cultural Revolution.

Account Four

Ma Xuelin[83] (born 1955) is an elementary school mathematics teacher in Zhongchuan Township and one of six children. Being the eldest son, Ma Xuelin's father stayed at home to do fieldwork, while his two younger brothers became monks. Ma Xuelin's elder sister never attended school. Like most unmarried young Monguor women, she collected wild plants for pigs and cooked in the home. A younger brother studied for 2 years in elementary school, a second younger brother and younger sister each studied for 5 years in elementary school. They had little interest in what the school had to offer. They were sure that, as the children of peasants, they too would be peasants. They believed "advanced" knowledge had little practical value. Furthermore, schooling was a heavy drain on the family's limited finances.

When Ma Xuelin was a first-year elementary school student in 1962, his educational expenses were several *jiao* [84] for books. Students ate lunch at the school (this was started in 1958). Most students attended school to eat rather than to study. If they stayed at home, the village dining room refused to serve them. Often, as soon as pupils received their allotment of barley cake, they ran to nearby fields to eat raw barley and wheat grain. Hunger was a frequent companion.

Ma and his schoolmates studied diligently while in grades two, three, and four. In second grade, 7 of the 40 students were female. In fourth grade, of the less than 30 students, only 3 were girls. These girls had well-off parents with government jobs.

When Ma was in fifth grade, the Cultural Revolution began. Many students stopped attending school because their parents thought that what they were being taught had little value. The government did pay several yuan to some poorer students in the ensuing years. Ma, for example, was given 3 yuan per month when he was a fifth-grade student at Meiyi Elementary School in Zhongchuan. At that time, students did not take competitive examinations to judge if they were fit to be promoted to the next grade. Instead, students voted for or against each student's promotion. About 60 percent of elementary school students went on to Zhongchuan Lower Secondary School.

There was only one girl in the first year of Ma's lower secondary school class. Several other students and Ma received 8 yuan each from the school per month. When they graduated, 37 of the 45 students in his class went to Guanting to attend upper secondary school. There was no opportunity for him to continue studying at a university after he finished upper secondary school. At that time, such opportunities depended largely upon personal relationships, and Ma lacked the necessary connections. Ma then worked in his parents' fields and, years later, he was chosen as a *minban*[85] teacher by a township education bureau official, who was also Ma's former teacher.

In the early 1960s, peasants were paid on the basis of field labor. Without at least two laborers in a home, it was difficult to earn a living. When Ma was in his teens, he planned to stop attending school to help his parents do fieldwork. However, his father persuaded him to continue his studies so that he could know and understand the amount of labor points, otherwise, he would be cheated by those who could read Chinese. Subsequently, Ma continued in school but, as was common, he was often absent from classes. The most students at that time aspired to was becoming accountants or dining room workers. These were considered desirable vocations because the work was not physically demanding and they could easily get good food and were also awarded work points.

Today, Ma is considered one of the best elementary school math teachers in Zhongchuan Township. He says he learned most of his math while teaching. Of Ma's generation in Wangjia Village, only 18 students attended school. Counting Ma, three obtained jobs. They all became teachers. The other 15 are peasants.

Account Five

Mr. Xie,[86] who is Ma's age, is a teacher in Xiakou Township. In 1968, 6 boys and 1 girl graduated from Mei'er Elementary School in Xiakou. Of the school's 50 students, 3 were girls. There was no local lower secondary school in Xiakou at that time; therefore, Xie and his 6 classmates went to Zhongchuan Secondary School to study, which required walking 8 or 9 kilometers daily. No tuition was required, and a great deal of class time was spent in copying and reciting the works of Mao Zedong. The first-year class of Xie's lower secondary school had 62 students, including 5 females. Of the school's approximately 120 students, only about 12 were female. In grade two, there were 44 students. In Xie's lower secondary school graduating class, there were 36 students, of which 4 were girls.

Account Six

Ms. Chen (born 1955) is presently an elementary school teacher. She began attending Wushi Elementary School in 1964. Her father was the village leader and his brother was a teacher in the school. Her two elder sisters both graduated from elementary school and continued their education in Chuankou. Wushi Elementary School had four or five teachers when she attended. When she was in the first grade, there were three girls. From the third grade on, she was the only girl in her class.

After graduating from Wushi Elementary School in 1971, she attended Guanting Secondary School while boarding in a classmate's home. In 1973, the school offered accommodations to students who needed to board. Such students had to pay tuition and grain. Boarding students received two yuan per month from the school. In her first term in lower secondary school, there were 5 female students in her class. When she graduated, her class had 3 girls and more than 40 boys. In 1973, she attended Minhe Normal School and, 3 years later, she was employed as a teacher.

During the period 1974-1976, the number of lower secondary schools, classes and students increased.[87] In 1977, there were 4 upper and lower secondary schools and 84 lower secondary schools in Minhe.[88] In 1977, peasants' spare time education was restarted. In 1985, 741 of the 3,547 students attending Minhe County's 222 night schools graduated.[89]

In 1978, there were 533 elementary schools in Minhe County. In 1981, there were 8 upper and lower secondary schools and 25 lower secondary schools. At this time, the county government managed the upper secondary schools, lower secondary schools were managed by the townships and villages managed most elementary schools.[90]

The following account is the most recent one that we present. It illustrates certain difficulties faced in the post-Cultural Revolution era.

Account Seven

Wu Haiping[91] (born 1970) is a teacher from a mountain village and one of five children. His elder sister (born 1965) is illiterate. His elder brother (born 1968) dropped out in his first year in lower secondary school to work in the family's fields after land division among families in 1981. Because his father was a *minban* (community school) teacher at a nearby elementary school, the family was somewhat financially better off. Consequently, Wu Haiping was able to finish lower secondary school. After successfully passing an examination, he attended Minhe Normal School for 3 years and became an upper and lower secondary school teacher in the Minhe Monguor area.

Our village elementary school was in a valley. Those of us who lived on the mountain had to climb down the steep mountain every morning and back every evening. We were often numb with cold in the winter and suffered much during rainy days in summer and autumn. Only a few students studied well, for no one could get a job on the basis of what they learned at school. The teachers were limited, for they were only elementary school graduates. My own family did not encourage me to study. For example, both my father and grandmother scolded me for "wasting lamp oil" when I used a kerosene lamp to study late at night. Such ideas were common. One of my friends burned his cap, because he covered the lamp with it in order not to be discovered "wasting oil" by his father late at night. Only 3 of any 21 classmates passed the entrance examination given by the local secondary school.

At that time, I was only 10 years old and had to walk more than 11 kilometers daily to attend school. I had the distinction of being the youngest and also the student from the longest distance from the school.

Because I am Monguor, I had a difficult time in secondary school. Schoolmates often laughed at my poor Chinese and low marks. I could not practice Chinese at home because my grandmother and my sisters knew only a little Chinese and I also was required to cut grass and tend our family's livestock for 2 hours each evening after I returned from school. Nevertheless, in observing how hard my parents and brother worked, I knew how difficult a peasant's life was. I was determined to learn as much as I could.

My family worried about the long distance I walked and the prejudice I suffered from at school. Consequently, the next year, I changed to Zhongchuan Secondary School. This school, in terms of instruction, was worse than the previous one because most teachers and students were Monguor and their level of Chinese-the language of instruction-was poor. Nevertheless, I could sleep and eat at this school and no longer had to suffer the taunts of other students for being "different" for they were nearly all Monguor.[92]

In 1981, there were 8 upper and lower secondary schools and 25 lower secondary schools.[93] In 1985, there were 318 elementary schools in the county with a total enrollment of 36,343. This represented 91.05 percent of elementary school-age students, of which 14,445 were girls. In 1985, there were 40 secondary schools with 11,800 students. Eight of these schools were complete secondary schools.[94]

In 1994, only Guanting Monguor Secondary School had both lower and upper grades. There were 3 lower secondary schools: Guanting Region Lower Secondary School, Zhongchuan Township Lower Secondary School and Xiakou Township Lower Secondary School; 31 elementary schools; and 10 lower level elementary schools (i.e., elementary schools with one to three grades). There were 164 secondary school teachers, 250 elementary school teachers, 1,821 Monguor secondary school students, and 4,257 Monguor elementary school students. From 1977 to 1993, more than 700 graduates of these secondary schools entered universities and *zhongzhuan.* [95]

Generally, one administrative village[96] has one school. If there are one or two remote mountainous villages in one large administrative village, the latter often have a two-year elementary school that typically has a *minban* teacher who is paid 100 yuan per month. In the event that such students continue their education in a five-year elementary school and graduate, they must take an entrance examination to their township's lower secondary school. Most examinees can attend a lower secondary school. Those who cannot may be limited by poverty, a fervent dislike of school, living too far away from the nearest non-boarding lower secondary school to be able to walk back and forth daily, the lower secondary school may be a boarding school but may lack an adequate number of classrooms and dormitories to accommodate all students desiring to attend and a lower secondary school may not have enough desks and stools to accommodate every student that wishes to attend.

Students from Guanting, Zhongchuan, Xiakou, Xing'er, Gangou and some from Qianhe Lower Secondary School come to study in the upper secondary school section at Guanting Secondary School. Recently, enrollment in the latter school has dramatically decreased from more than 1,600 students in 1990 to less than 900 in 1995. This decrease of approximately 50 percent may be explained by poor crop yields, increased tuition rates, a decline in the number of school-age children owing to national birth control policies, and poor teaching quality of the school. The last factor has led families who can afford it to send their children to Minhe First Secondary School to study.

Supporting a single student to study at this school costs more than 1,000 yuan per year and limits access.

Among the Monguor townships, Zhongchuan has the largest population and the largest number of students. Zhongchuan lacks classrooms, quarters for teachers and students, desks and chairs. As a result, students from Guangming, Qianjin, Hong'yi, Hong'er, Hexi, Hedong, Hulangcheng and Zhujialing Administrative Village must go to Guanting Secondary School to study, while students from Hulangcheng and Zhujialing attend school in Gangou Township.

Hulangcheng Elementary School has nine teachers. One is from a local village, and the others are from as much as 8 kilometers away. At present, because all the teachers' quarters have collapsed, the preschool class has been dismissed and its classroom appropriated as a communal dormitory for teachers.

In Zhongchuan Secondary School, 228 of 455 students live far from the school and, ideally, need to board at the school. However, the school has no students' quarters. Some students spend 3 hours daily walking to and from school. Furthermore, eight teachers live in rooms designated in danger of imminent collapse.

Table 10.7. Zhongchuan Township Elementary School Enrollment and Girls' Attendance

Date	Student Number	% Girls
September 1986	2,670	43.9
September 1987	2,530	43.1
September 1990	2,439	unavailable
September 1991	2,224	44.5
September 1994	1,854	42.6
September 1995	1,767	42.9

Source: Zhongchuan Schools Report Forms (1986, 1987, 1990, 1991, 1994, 1995).

Table 10.8. Zhongchuan Township School Enrollment and Percentage of Girls.

School Name	September 1987		September 1994		September 1995	
	Total Students	% Girls	Total Students	% Girls	Total Students	% Girls
Zhongchuan Lower Secondary School	not available		471	38.2	455	41.8
Zhujialing Elementary School	31	35.5	23	47.8	12	41.7
Hulangcheng Elementary School	165	40.0	179	39.1	141	33.3
Hedong Elementary School	210	30.0	152	25.0	122	20.5
Hexi Elementary School	140	43.6	33	27.3	44	27.3
Hongyi Elementary School	282	42.9	130	43.8	125	42.6
Hong'er Elementary School			61	42.6	53	49.1
Xiangyang Elementary School	76	35.5	60	36.7	60	45.0
Guangming Elementary School	260	46.2	171	50.9	164	46.3
Qingquan Elementary School	376	44.7	333	40.2	322	42.5
Qianjin Elementary School	192	43.8	174	46.0	164	48.8
Jiantian Elementary School	313	46	197	53.8	173	50.3
Meiyi Elementary School	476	46	323	45.5	303	48.8

Source: Zhongchuan School Reports Forms 1987, 1994, 1995.

OBSTACLES TO IMPROVING EDUCATION

A number of insights can be gained from the above accounts. In terms of gender, females are expected to sew and embroider; cook; do fieldwork; care for children; observe rules of etiquette governing "proper" interaction with family members, neighbors and kinsmen; and so on. Being literate, however, has historically been viewed as unimportant for them.[97] This is related to the Monguor world view with regard to women. Stuart inquired of a Monguor village woman in her eighties in 1988, for example, why she counted prayer beads. "Because," she answered immediately, "I wished to be a man in my next reincarnation." Although this is anecdotal, it resonates with Goa's[98] observation on the relationship between the nature of the social concept of Mongol women and Buddhism: "If a woman wished to enter Paradise, she must first purify herself through suffering. After such travails, she may aspire to be reincarnated as a man and thereby have the opportunity to enter Paradise." In fact, there is a sense among the Monguor that a woman is a woman because she did something wrong in her last life. Thus, the difficulties that she faces in her present life are deserved and, if she is docile, hardworking, and bears the suffering inherent in being a woman, she may be a man in her next incarnation. Another strike against girls is that nearly all marry into the homes of their husbands. Consequently, an impoverished family does not have the resources to "invest" in a girl who will soon "belong" to another family. Some parents reason that it is better to maximize the benefits a girl can bring the family by taking her out of school for house work and fieldwork. All of these factors help in understanding why "education" is mostly a study of male activity with very limited female participation, although this has recently begun to change, as depicted in the following tables.

Qingquan, Meiyi and Qianjin elementary schools are the major elementary schools in Zhongchuan Township with qualified teachers. The areas in which students live who attend these three schools enjoy better economic conditions than many other areas. In contrast, Zhujialing, Hulangcheng and Hedong elementary schools are in impoverished areas. Families, with more resources seem prone to provide for girls' schooling.

Education may be divided into two spheres-religious and secular. The importance of Tibetan Buddhism meant that historically, a knowledge of written Tibetan was seen as important for the many males who became Buddhist monks. The influence of Tibetan Buddhism continues today with, for example, death rituals[99] and death anniversary ceremonies requiring monks to read Tibetan scriptures. Many Monguor males were monks for the following reasons: they were generally able to obtain enough food from being part of the religious community to live, they were part of an undertaking that allowed them to earn money and they were not conscripted into the military. In addition, parents were relieved of the worry of providing for a son's marriage if he was sent to the monastery, and they did not have to divide their small amount of arable land. Typically, if a family had four sons, one stayed home to do fieldwork, while the other three became monks.

For a very long time in the secular sphere, Minhe Monguor have recognized the advantages that knowledge of the Chinese language brings in dealing with various government agents who, in the past, treated them with a general denigrating attitude; in the enhancement of employment opportunities; in the ease with which one can function outside the Monguor-speaking area; and in the generally higher status that being literate conveys in a community where most residents are illiterate. Being illiterate in Chinese means being vulnerable to chicanery, as the following vivid example demonstrates.[100]

Once there was a Monguor man who was strong as an ox. Eventually, he was caught by Ma Bufang's soldiers, who had come to conscript men for military duty. The officer in charge of conscription said to the Monguor man, "If you take this note to the Xiangtang[101] Army, you won't be drafted." The incredulous Monguor man then walked to Xiangtang and produced the note. He was promptly detained and made a new soldier. The Monguor man exclaimed, "Your representative said that if I gave you this note, I would not be a soldier." "Are you blind? The note orders us to keep the bearer of this note as a soldier," was the response.

The importance attached to schooling is visible in the banquets certain families held in the 1980s for children who had passed the higher education examinations that provided a government-paid education at a university. Some banquets were more expensive than weddings-normally the most lavish of all Minhe Monguor individual family-sponsored ceremonies. Passing this examination resonated with the passing of imperial examinations in that university-educated children were assured of a government job eventually leading to far more power and prestige than a peasant could ever hope to achieve. Moreover, to the extent that children are a reflection of their parents, it was a time for the concerned family to engage in self-congratulation.[102]

Families do not deny the value of a university education and the benefits it brings to their children; however, the barriers children face in successfully passing higher education examinations are momentous. For example, only four residents from Zhujialing have ever passed higher education entrance examinations. Prior to the more open economy of today, along with its employment opportunities, a job obtained through studying well in school and passing higher education examinations was one of the very few ways peasants could change their station in life. Today, however, parents may choose to remove a child from school if an economic opportunity beckons. This is particularly the case when the family is poor, school facilities are miserable, the nearest school is far away, teachers are of poor quality, the child is female and the child is not receiving good marks. Many parents reason that if there is little chance for children to pass the higher education entrance examination, the long-term investment needed to sustain a child through upper secondary school provides no more advantages in life than the basic literacy obtained through attending elementary school for a few years.

Teaching quality is another serious obstacle. In some single classrooms, there are 40-50 students spanning three grades. One teacher responsible for such a teaching situation is hard-pressed to provide individual attention to students. The appalling living conditions for many teachers at schools means that few qualified teachers would want to remain. Xiakou Lower Secondary School, for example, has minimal teaching equipment, such as reference materials, for teachers. Xiakou is 10 kilometers from Guanting. The rough road makes transportation inconvenient. Only one bus irregularly ventures to Xiakou. Winter snows and heavy summer and autumn rains mean the bus does not run at all because the road becomes a quagmire. Consequently, Xiakou teachers living in Guanting must walk 90 minutes one way. If they wish to bring a large piece of luggage, they must pay 15 yuan to rent a tractor. To make matters worse, teachers' dormitory rooms are in such danger of collapsing that some teachers have put poles inside their rooms, hoping that this will keep the roof from falling on them. Furthermore, many teachers are from local areas. They teach when assigned to do so, but frequently return home to do fieldwork. This limits the time they devote to class preparation and marking assigned homework.

Poverty, and the limitations it imposes on receiving an education, remain with the Minhe Monguor, although to a lesser extent than in the past. There are patterns of literacy that detailed analysis would likely tie to a history of family class, wealth and literacy among family members. The poorest and most remote of Minhe Monguor populations, for example, continue to have very meager levels of education. The future does not appear to hold much hope that this will improve. Although there have been calls from nearly every level of government for countryside areas to "get rich," it seems likely that residents of areas with very limited natural resources and access to transportation and a centuries-old history of poverty, though desirous of "getting rich," may not obtain wealth in the foreseeable future. As school fees continue to climb, it is likely that an increasing number of children from impoverished families will not have access to education—a haunting return to pre-1949 conditions. A related barrier to children being schooled is the persistent perception that formal education offers children little of value beyond basic literacy.

An example of how poverty limits access to education may be seen from Zhu Yongzhang's observations based on teaching in Minzhu Administrative Village Lower Secondary School, Xiakou Township from 1991-1992. In this instance, there were 60 students, 13 teachers and one cook. In terms of physical structure, the school was one of the worst lower secondary schools in Qinghai. The adobe-structure classrooms and teachers' quarters were of poor quality and had been classified as in imminent danger of collapse by township authorities. Subsequently, the school was closed in 1993 by township authorities, who had no funds to repair or rebuild the school, which was receiving only approximately 600 yuan per year for general upkeep and expenses[103] prior to its closure. Xiakou Lower Secondary School, the nearest lower secondary school for Minzhu children, is 6 or 7 kilometers away. Beginning in 1994, the inadequate number of dormitory rooms at Xiakou Lower Secondary School were in danger of collapsing and were closed; consequently, few students from Minzhu attend secondary school.[104]

Another theme in the above accounts is the artificiality of the educational experience. Although "schooling" may have taken place in the sense that the actors (students and teachers) were present and the necessary props (books, blackboards) were there, little was actually learned. This seems to be a common thing today, with many students in secondary schools complaining that they are unable to understand their teachers, who teach only in non-local Chinese dialects. Education in Mongolian, as far as we have been able to determine, has never been a topic of discussion for any group of Monguor, although it is a language much closer to Monguor than Chinese and easier to deal with as a language of instruction. Furthermore, *pinyin*ized Minhe Monguor has only been used in a few international research publications.[105] Students are generally taught in oral Chinese when they enter elementary school. All the texts are in Chinese. If the teachers are Monguor, they may speak Monguor to grades 1through 3, but later they speak only Chinese. Recently, many young Chinese teachers have been assigned to Monguor-speaking areas, thus the trend toward teaching in Chinese has intensified. The sense that Chinese-language instruction leads to gradual competence in Chinese is belied, however, by the fact that many third-year elementary school students are unable to make a sentence in correct Chinese. During the teaching process, the teacher writes a sentence on the blackboard, explains it and the students copy it and recite it after the teacher. Actually, many students are only copying and learning the meaning of certain Chinese characters. This is not the same as gaining overall competence in the Chinese language. This is particularly true in more remote, impoverished areas where few homes have televisions, access to printed Chinese materials is extremely limited and where everyone speaks Monguor.

Some years ago, a school in the area decreed that teachers and students must not speak Monguor, but were instead to speak only Chinese. To this end, teachers were routinely fined when they spoke Monguor on the school grounds. Less than one year later, it was realized that this had actually caused a decline in the quality of instruction, and the experiment was concluded. The position that teaching in Monguor conveys a better understanding of the subject at hand is substantiated by the comment of an elementary school Monguor teacher in an elementary school. He stated that in the 1980s, most elementary school classes were taught by teachers who explained subject content in Monguor and that the students so taught eventually entered higher education institutions. The reality today is that secondary students who understand Chinese poorly and who are taught in that language have little chance of furthering their education.

Monguor teachers note that owing to the rapidly increasing difficulty of school texts, it is challenging to teach many students in the first grade of lower secondary school, owing to a poor Chinese base from elementary school. Subsequently, these students soon fall behind students who do know Chinese well. Such students and their parents often concur that they are better off contributing to the family economy rather than being a drain on it when there is no hope of the student being able to enter an institution that will lead to guaranteed government employment.

Although there has been some effort to teach Monguor language using its *pinyin*-based alphabet in a few Huzhu schools,[106] as of 1996, there has been no discussion in Minhe about teaching Monguor. There are no current deliberations that would suggest that primary and secondary texts might appear in the near future in bilingual editions for either Huzhu or Minhe. In the event that such discussions do arise, it is likely that they would be based on the Huzhu dialect. Given the differences in the Huzhu and Minhe Monguor dialects, this would make such texts virtually unusable for Minhe Monguor children.

CONCLUSION

A basic problem calling for solution in remote, impoverished areas is the absence and very poor condition of elementary schools. A policy emphasizing local education by studying the present situation and implementing realistic solutions is required. Agreements between local regions stipulating local support in terms of labor and some measure of financial support in partnership with government assistance is one possible option. Good quality classrooms and teachers' quarters would produce an atmosphere conducive to teaching and learning. Understandably, few qualified teachers wish to teach in remote areas where basic living conditions are woeful. Furthermore, good quarters for teachers would allow teachers to live at the school. Presently, many teachers spend much of their free time walking to and from their homes every day, giving them little time to check students' homework assignments and prepare for the next teaching day. Certain schools urgently need students' quarters to allow students from distant village to sleep at the school. Time saved in walking to and from school could then be spent on study.

The two and three year elementary schools should be changed into full six year elementary schools. The former schools are primarily situated in remote valleys and mountain areas that are characterized by poverty and low levels of education. These areas would be immeasurably helped if they had good quality classrooms and teachers' quarters and competent teachers, and if students were not required to pay tuition.

Several schools discussed in this chapter are important sites for the reinforcement of Monguor ethnic identity because of the large enrollment of Monguor students. For example, children speak Monguor while at school, except when in the classroom and called upon to perform by their teachers, and associate with other Monguor students. This is not by conscious design on the part of any authority; rather, it merely reflects local demographic realities. As mentioned previously, however, there is nothing in the curricula that reinforces this sense of ethnic identity, for texts are the standard Chinese-language national curricula.

NOTES

1. We thank Margery Devlen for her helpful editorial remarks.

2. There is such difference in Monguor groups that, for example, Monguor from different areas of Tongren County may speak Tibetan when they meet, while Huzhu and Minhe Monguor speak Chinese as a mutually comprehensible language. Furthermore, Huzhu Monguor sing most wedding songs in Monguor, the Minhe Monguor sing most wedding songs in Chinese, and the Nianduhu Monguor sing all their weddings songs in Tibetan. The traditional costume of the nationality is also site-specific.

3. It is known as Gelupai and Huangjiao (literally "Yellow sect") in Chinese. This religious sect was established by Tsong-kha-pa (1357-1419), who was born in present-day Qinghai, and later greatly influenced various aspects of Tibetan, Mongolian and Monguor society. (We are grateful to Mr. Dpal-ldan-bkra-shis for writing the Tibetan used in this chapter.)

4. Qinghai is known in older literature by its Mongol name "Koko Nor" (literally "blue lake"), which is similar to what "Qinghai" (blue/green sea) translates as. This name derives from Qinghai Lake, China's largest inland saline lake, located in northeastern Qinghai Province.

5. Francis Schram, 1883-1971. A missionary of Scheut, Belgium, he came to Gansu/Qinghai in 1909 and left Qinghai in 1922. His publications

include Louis Schram, "Le mariage cez les T'ou-jen du Kan-sou," in *Variétés Sinologiques*, No. 58 (1932). [Available in an English translation (1962) by Jean H. Winchell, "Marriage Among the T'ou-jen of Kansu (Gansu)," in *Human Area Relations File*, AE9 (1962)]; LMJ Schram, "The Monguor of the Kansu-Tibetan Frontier, I: Their Origin, History, and Social Organization," in *Transactions of the American Philosophical Society*, No. 44 (1954), p. 44; LMJ Schram, "The Monguor of the Kansu-Tibetan Frontier, II: Their Religious Life," in *Transactions of the American Philosophical Society*, No. 44 (1957), p. 2; LMJ Schram, "The Monguor of the Kansu-Tibetan Frontier, III: Their Origin, History, and Social Organization," in *Transactions of the American Philosophical Society*, No. 44 (1961), p. 3.

6. Dominik Schröder, 1910-1974. A German missionary, he received a master's degree in anthropology at Furen University, Beijing. He came to Qinghai in 1946 and left in 1949. (I am indebted to Dr. Anton Quack for this biographical information, as well as the biographical information in the note above.) His publications include Dominik Schröder, "Zur Religion der Tujen des Sininggebietes (Kukunor)" (On the religion of the Tujen of the Xining Region [Kokonor]"), in *Anthropos*, No. 47, pp. 1-79, 620-658, 822-870; No. 48, pp. 202-249 (1952/1953). [Available in an English translation by Richard Neuse, "On the Religion of the Tujen of the Sining [Xining] Region (Koko Nor)," in *Human Area Relations File*, AE9, (1962)]; Dominik Schröder, *Aus der Volksdicntung der Monguor ([Selections] From the Popular Poetry of the Monguor)*; *1. Teil: Das weibe Glücksschaf (Mythen, Märchen, Lieder) (Part 1: The White Lucky-Sheep [Myths, Fairy Tales, Songs])*, Asiatsche Forschungen 6, (Wiesbaden: Otto Harrassowitz, 1959); Dominik Schröder, *Aus der Volksdichtung der Monguor ([Selections] From the Popular Poetry of the Monguor]); 2. Teil: In den Tagen der Urzeit (Ein Mythus vom Licht und vom Leben)* (Part 2: In the Days of Prehistory [A Myth of Light and Life]), Asiatische Forschungen 31, (Wiesbaden: Otto Harrassowitz, 1970). Weisbaden: Otto Harrassowitz.

7. Yizhi Bao (Jun Hu and Kevin Stuart, trans.), "Goddess Pool," in *China Today* (North American edition), Vol. 39, No. 8 (1990), pp. 57-59; Yizhi Bao (Lide Feng and Kevin Stuart, trans.), "Mill Valley's Last Mill," in *Chinese Literature*, Spring, (1991), pp. 18-30; Jun Hu and Kevin Stuart, "Illness Among the Minhe Tu, Qinghai Province: Prevention and Etiology," in *Mongolian Studies*, No. 15 (1992), pp. 111-135; Jun Hu and Kevin Stuart, "The Guanting Tu (Monguor) Wedding Ceremonies and Songs," in *Anthropos*, No. 87 (1992), pp. 109-132; Jun Hu and Kevin Stuart, "Review of Mongolian Family Language Materials," in *Mongolian Studies*, No. 17 (1994), pp. 142-146;

Deyuan Li (Limusishiden and Kevin Stuart, trans.), "My Monguor Father," in *The Mongolia Society Newsletter*, New Series No. 16, (1994), pp. 62-63; Limusishiden and Kevin Stuart, "'Caring for All the World': The Huzhu Monguor (Tu) *Pram*," in Edward H. Kaplan and Donald W. Whisenhunt (eds.), *Opuscula Altaica: Essays in Honor of Henry Schwarz* (Bellingham, WA: Western Washington University Press, 1994), pp. 408-426; Limusishiden and Kevin Stuart, "Larinbuda and Jiminsu: A Monguor Tragedy," in *Asian Theatre Journal*, Vol. 12, No. 2, (1995), pp. 221-263; Limusishiden and Kevin Stuart, *English-In-Mongghul: Mongghulla Yinyii* (Weiyuan *zhen* [Weiyuan Town], Huzhu Monguor Autonomous County: Huzhu *yinshuachang* [Huzhu Publishing Station], 1996); Limusishiden and Kevin Stuart, "Review of *Shilaode* (Dominik Schröder)," in *Anthropos*, No. 91, (1996), p. 297; Guangxing Ma (translated and with a commentary by Jun Hu and Kevin Stuart), "Wedding, Etiquette, and Traditional Songs of the Minhe Region Tu," in *Asian Folklore Studies*, Vol. 49, No. 2, (1990), pp. 197-222; Kevin Stuart and Jun Hu, "Death and Funerals Among the Minhe Tu (Monguor)," in *Asian Folklore Studies*, Vol. 51, No. 2, (1992), pp. 67-87; Kevin Stuart and Jun Hu, "The Monguor Kitchen Goddess," in *The Mongolian Society Newsletter*, New Series 12, (1992), pp. 52-53; Kevin Stuart and Jun Hu, "A Tu Nationality Harvest Festival," in *China Reconstructs* (North American edition), Vol. 38, No. 4, (1989), pp. 1-2, 29-31; Kevin Stuart and Jun Hu, "Stories of the Tu Nationality by Bao Yizhi," in *China Today* (North American edition), Vol.39, No. 8, (1990), pp. 56-57; Kevin Stuart and Jun Hu, "The Tu Nadun," in *China Pictorial*, June (1990), pp. 36-37; Kevin Stuart and Jun Hu, "Bao Yizhi—The Wailing Bullhorn," in *The Mongolian Society Newsletter*, New Series 9, (1991a), pp. 55-58; Kevin Stuart and Jun Hu, "The Tu Fala: Trance Mediums of Northwest China," in *Shaman's Drum*, No. 23 (1991), pp. 28-35; Kevin Stuart and Jun Hu, "Death and Funerals Among the Minhe Tu (Monguor)," in *Asian Folklore Studies*, Vol. 51, No. 2, (1992), pp. 67-87; Kevin Stuart and Jun Hu, "'That All May Prosper': The Monguor *Nadun* of the Guanting/Sanchuan Region," in *Anthropos*, Vol. 88, (1993), pp. 15-27; Kevin Stuart and Limusishiden (eds.), "China's Monguor Minority: Ethnography and Folktales," in *Sino-Platonic Papers*, No. 59 (1994); Kevin Stuart, "Young Scholar Explores Tu's Culture, Tradition," in *China Daily*, January 9, 1992, p. 6; Kevin Stuart, "Review of Huiyan Wang and Shenglin Chao, Editors, Hometown of the Rainbow: For the 40th Anniversary of the Founding of the Huzhu Tu Nationality Autonomous County," in *Mongolian Studies*, No. 18 (1995), p. 152; Xianzheng Wang and Kevin Stuart, "Blue Skies and Emoluments': Minhe Monguor Men Sing I," in *Chinese Music*, Vol. 18, No. 1, (1995), pp.13-18; Xianzheng Wang and Kevin Stuart, "'Blue Skies and

Emoluments': Minhe Monguor Men Sing II," *Chinese Music*, Vol.18, No. 2, (1995), pp. 28-33; Xianzheng Wang, Yongzhong Zhu, and Kevin Stuart, "The Brightness of the World": Minhe Monguor Women Sing," in *Mongolian Studies*, Vol. 18 (1995), pp.65-83; Yongzhong Zhu and Kevin Stuart, "A Minhe Monguor Drinking Song," in *Central Asiatic Journal*, Vol. 40, No. 2, (1996), pp.283-289; Yongzhong Zhu and Kevin Stuart, "'Happy Star Opens Heaven's Gate: Minhe Monguor Nadun Texts," in *CHIME* (forthcoming); Yongzhong Zhu and Kevin Stuart, "'Two Bodhisattvas From the East': Minhe Monguor Funeral Orations," in *Journal of Contemporary China* (forthcoming); Yongzhong Zhu, Üjiyediin Chuluu and Kevin Stuart, "'The Frog Boy': An Example of Minhe Monguor," in *Orientalia Suecana*, No. XLII-XLIV (1995), pp. 197-207.

8. It should be noted, however, that in the Huzhu Monguor written system, the name of the nationality is rendered "Mongghul."

9. Zhengde Yan and Yiwu Wang, *Qinghai baike dacidian (Qinghai Encyclopedic Dictionary)* (Beijing: Zhongguo caizhen jingji chubanshe [China Finance and Economic Press], 1994), p. 861 gives the following account of the Monguor:

> *The Tu are a minority nationality of our country. They are a main nationality in Qinghai. They call themselves "Chahan* Monguor," "Monguor Kun*," "Tukun," "Tuhujia"; Han and Hui refer to them as "Tumin" and "Turen"; Tibetans call them "Huo'er"; Mongols call them "Chahan Mongol" (White Mongol). In Chinese history books, they are called *"Xining zhou turen"* and "Tumin." After liberation, these names were unified as "Tuzu."

> **Chahan* is more correctly rendered *chighang* in Mongolic and means "white."

> **Kun* is Mongolic for "person."

10. There are several thousand Muslims living in Hualong Hui Autonomous County, Qinghai, for example, who speak Tibetan as a first language. They are classified as "Hui."

11. Hu Jun and Stuart, Kevin, "Review of Mongolian Family Language Materials," in *Mongolian Studies*, No. 17 (1994), pp. 142-146.

12. In Tibetan, *Gnyan-thog*. The same attitude is probably prevalent for nearby Sgo-dmar Village.

13. Naixiong Chen, *Baoanyu cihui (Baoan Vocabulary)* (Huhehaote: Neimenggu renmin chubanshe, 1985); Naixiong Chen, *Baoanyu huayu cailiao (Baoan Language Materials)* (Huhehaote: Neimenggu renmin chubanshe),

1986); Naixiong Chen, *Baoanyu he mengguyu* (*Baoan and Mongolian Languages Compared*) (Huhehaote: Neimenggu renmin chubanshe), 1986).

14. Examples of this include A. Rona-Tas, *Tibeto-Mongolica: The Tibetan Loanwords of Monguor and the Development of the Archaic Tibetan Dialects* (Budapest: Publishing House of the Academy of Sciences, 1966); Keyu Li, *Mongghul Qidar Merlong* (*Monguor-Chinese Dictionary*) (Xining: Qinghai renmin chubanshe, 1988); Kan Hua, "Tuzuyuzhongde zangyu jieci" ("Borrowed Tibetan Words in Monguor") in *Xibei minzu yanjiu* (*Northwest Nationalities Research*), No. 14 (1994), pp. 238-244. All use Huzhu as a source for Monguor lexical items.

15. The variance between Minhe and Huzhu Monguor underscores the blurry lines that often exist between officially designated nationalities in China. For example, in terms of language, Minhe, Tongren and Huzhu Monguor dialects are, for all practical purposes, mutually incomprehensible and thus at greater odds than Dagur and Mongol, speakers of which are classified as separate ethnic entities in China. Furthermore, in terms of religion, many Tibetan speakers of Hualong Hui Autonomous County in Qinghai are classified as "Hui" because they are Islamic.

16. See Keyu Li, *Tuzu (Mengguer) yuanliu kao* (*An Investigation of Tu [Monguor] Origins and Development*) (Xining: Qinghai renmin chubanshe, 1992), for example, who argues that the Monguor owe their origins to the Mongols. Conversely, Weizhou Zhou, *Tuyuhun ziliao jilu* (*Tuyuhun Material Compilation*) (Xining: Qinghai renmin chubanshe, 1991), argues for a Tuyuhun origin.

17. The archaeological record indicates that areas where Monguor live today have been inhabited for several thousand years. A basic question is whether these people spoke Mongolic before the arrival of Mongol soldiers in the thirteenth century.

18. For the influence of Tibetan on Huzhu Monguor, see Hua, "Tuzuyuzhongde zangyu jieci" ("Borrowed Tibetan Words in Monguor") and Rona-Tas, *Tibeto-Mongolica: The Tibetan Loanwords of Monguor and the Development of the Archaic Tibetan Dialects*.

19. Dzungar, Jungar, Zunghar, Zunggar, Zungar.

20. Ili.

21. Yan and Wang, *Qinghai baike dacidian* (*Qinghai Encyclopedic Dictionary*), p. 1,090.

22. The *tusi* system was an administrative system used in Mongol, Tibetan and other minority areas in northwest and southwest China during the Yuan, Ming and Qing dynasties. The government designated tribal government

officials and allowed them to govern their own ethnic peoples. Yuan dynasty tribal leaders were granted numerous titles. They were established as officials at the *fu* (government office), *zhou* (prefecture), and *xian* (county) levels. The Ming government had *xuanwei*, *xuanfu* and *anfu* positions in the military and *zhifu*, *zhizhou* and *zhixian* in the civil service. All these titles were hereditary. *Tusi* were not only responsible to the central government for contributions and requisition, but they also exercised traditional power in their respective local areas. During the Ming and Qing dynasties, Qinghai had in excess of 60 *tusi*. There were 40 *tusi* in the present Yushu Tibetan Autonomous Prefecture. The remaining *tusi* controlled the present Minhe, Ledu, Ping'an, Huzhu, Huangzhong, Xining, Datong and Xunhua counties. In 1931, the *tusi* system was abrogated in agricultural areas, and former officers became landlords. The *tusi* system in herding areas lasted until the period of democratic reformation in 1958 (Yan and Wang, *Qinghai baike dacidian* [*Qinghai Encyclopedic Dictionary*], p. 863). (We thank Dr. Qiang Chan for this translation.)

23. Yong Qin, "Mingqing tuzu diqu de tusi zai lishishangde zuoyong" ("The Ming-Qing dynasty Monguor area *Tusi*'s Function in History,") in *Qinghai shehui kexue bao* (*Qinghai Social Science Journal*), No. 31 (1985), pp. 87-83. Comments drawn from Qin Yong come from an unpublished English translation prepared by Wang Jianbin, Li Fang , He Jing and Chen Qiang.

24. Tables 10.2-10.5 were created using data from Wang Jianhua, Hai Shenggui, Lui Baomin and Yao Huimin, *Renkouxue duben* (*Population Studies Reader*) (Xining: Qinghai renmin chubanshe, 1993); Qinghaisheng renkou pucha bangongshi (Qinghai Province Population Census Office) (ed.), *Qinghaisheng 1990 nian renkou pucha ziliao* (*Qinghai Province 1990 Yearbook of Population Statistical Information*), (Beijing: Zhongguo tongji chubanshe, 1992).

25. For a recent introduction to the Salar, see Xuewei Li and Kevin Stuart, "The Xunhua Sala," in *Asian Folklore Studies*, Vol. 49, No. 1, (1990), pp. 39-52. For a comprehensive study of the origin and development of the Salar language and related literature, see Reinhard F. Hahn, "Notes on the Origin and Development of the Salar Language," in *Acta Orientalia Academiae Scientiarum Hung.*, Vol. XLII (No. 2-3) (1988), pp. 235-275.

26. For recent relevant language materials, see Chuluu Üjiyediin, "Introduction, Grammar, and Sample Sentences for Baoan," in *Sino-Platonic Papers* No. 58 (1994); Chuluu Üjiyediin, "Introduction, Grammar, and Sample Sentences for Dongxiang," in *Sino-Platonic Papers*, No. 55, (1994); Chuluu Üjiyediin, "Introduction, Grammar, and Sample Sentences for Jegün Yogur," in *Sino-Platonic Papers*, No. 54 (1994c); Chuluu Üjiyediin, "Introduction,

Grammar, and Sample Sentences for Monguor," in *Sino-Platonic Papers*, No. 57 (1994).

27. A description of this township may be found in Lide Feng and Kevin Stuart, "Interethnic Cultural Contact on the Inner Asian Frontier: The Gangou People of Minhe County, Qinghai," in *Sino-Platonic Papers*, No. 33 (1992).

28. A Monguor word.

29. This is the estimate of Zhu Yongzhong, one of the authors of this article.

30. Guanting Town is a trading center for Minhe Monguor 86 kilometers south of Chuankou, the county's administrative center and largest town.

31. The occasional statement to the effect Mongol women's feet were not bound is challenged by the practice among the Minhe Monguor.

32. "Cattle" also includes animals crossed with yaks.

33. In Chinese: Wutumeiren.

34. A. Doak Barnett. *China's Far West* (Boulder Co: Westview, 1993), p. 315.

35. *Juren* was a title for those who had passed the imperial examination at the provincial level during the Ming and Qing dynasties.

36. *Jinshi* was a title for those who had passed the highest imperial examination during the Ming and Qing dynasties.

37. *Xiucai* was a title for one who had passed the imperial examination at the county level during the Ming and Qing dynasties.

38. Yong Qin, "Mingqing tuzu diqu de tusi zai lishishangde zuoyong" ("The Ming-Qing Dynasty Monguor Area Tusi's Function in History,") in *Qinghai shehui kexue bao (Qinghai Social Science Journal)*, No. 31 (1985), pp. 87-63. Comments drawn from Qin Yong come from an unpublished English translation prepared by Wang Jianbin, Li Fang, He Jing and Chen Qiang.

39. *Wei* refers to an old administrative unit used during the Ming and Qing dynasties, roughly equivalent to today's "province."

40. Li Cunfu, "Tuzu pian" ("Monguor Section") in Muchi Yundeng Jiacuo (ed.), Qinghai shaoshu minzu (Qinghai Minority Nationalities), Xining: Qinghai renmin chubanshe (Qinghai People's Press) (1995), pp. 315-316.

41. *Fu* refers to an old administrative unit subordinate to a province. The term was used during the Ming and Qing dynasties when Xining was a *fu*.

42. A free private school funded primarily through land rent.

43. The township where today's Chuankou is located.

44. Nianbo County was established in 1724. The name became "Ledu County" in 1929 and, in 1930, the eastern part became Minhe County.

45. Binghui Wu (ed.), *"Jiaoyu" in Minhe xian zhi (Education in Annals of Minhe County)* (Xi'an: Shaanxi renmin chubanshe, 1993), p. 453.

46. In the late Qing dynasty, all sorts of schools were known as *xuetang (hall of study)*.

47. Huaizhi Xin, "Zhu haishan yu Minhe Sanchuan wenhua jiaoyu" ("Haishan Zhu and Education in Sanchuan, Minhe,") in *Minhe wenshi (Minhe Culture and History)* (Chuankou: Minhe yinshuachang, 1994), No. 3, p. 42.

48. *The Great Learning, The Doctrine of the Mean, The Analects of Confucius* and *Mencius*.

49. *The Book of Songs, The Book of History, The Book of Changes, The Book of Rites* and *The Spring and Autumn Annals*. Shufen Gao (ed.), *Datong huizu tuzu zizhixian gaikuang (General Conditions of Datong Hui and Monguor Autonomous County)* (Xining: Qinghai renmin chubanshe, 1986), p. 107.

50. A textbook for beginning Chinese language learners written during the Sung dynasty (960-1279) and rewritten in 1928.

51. A collection of Chinese surnames used by Chinese language students.

52. Huazhong Qin, personal interview conducted by Yongzhong Zhu, July 1996. Informants have been given fictitious names.

53. Gifts or salary provided by students.

54. At that time, students were called *tongshen (same birth place)*.

55. After 1949, teachers continued to be paid in grain. School headmasters and vice-headmasters received 150 kilograms monthly. Teachers received 125 kilograms for the same time period. In 1952, teachers began to be paid in hard currency at the rate of 26-45 yuan per month (Wu (ed.), *Minhe xian zhi (Annals of Minhe County)*, pp. 453, 484-485). In 1997, teachers salaries ranged from 420-1,000 yuan per month. Salaries averaged 600 yuan per month.

56. A volume unit equal to approximately 7.5 kilograms.

57. Qin Huazhong, personal interview conducted by Zhu Yongzhong, July 1996.

58. Six-year primary schools became five-year schools in 1971.

59. Wu (ed.), *Minhe xian zhi (Annals of Minhe County)*, p. 454.

60. Xin Huaizhi, "Tuzu zhiming renshi zhu haishan" ("The Well-known Monguor Personage Zhu Haishan"), in *Minhe wenshi (Minhe Culture and History)*, 1 (Minhe: Minhe yinshuachang, 1988), p. 139.

61. Choskyi Nyima (1883-1937).

62. Wu (ed.), *Minhe xian zhi (Annals of Minhe County)*, pp. 455-456.

63. In Chinese; Erfang.

64. His diminutive name was Hushouzi.

65. A heatable, raised platform made of bricks used as a place for sitting and sleeping.

66. Qin, personal interview conducted by Zhu Yongzhong, July 1996.

67. Ibid. Aged informants could only recall Zhang Tingshi and Lü Chunde having passed the examinations.

68. A unit of volume equaling 5 kilograms. Accounts attest that it was first used in today's Maying Region, hence the name.

69. The former name of Gangou.

70. Ma Bufang (1902-1973) was a member of the "Ma dynasty" that controlled a good deal of northwestern China (the present Qinghai, Gansu and Ningxia Hui Autonomous Region) beginning in the 1860s and lasting until 1949. A good deal more about the Mas can be learned from Gu Feng, *Xibei wang* (*Northwest Kings*) (Beijing: Zhongguo wenlian chubangongsi [China Literature Association Publishing Corporation], 1989); Wang Yasen and Yao Xiuchuan (compilers), *Qinghai sanma* (*Qinghai's Three Mas*) (Beijing: Zhongguo wenshi chubanshe [China Literature and History Press], 1988); and Hu Jun and Kevin Stuart, "Review of '*Xibei wang*' (*Northwest Kings*) and '*Qinghai sanma*' ('*Qinghai's Three Mas*')," in *Asian Profile*, Vol. 19, No. 4, (1991), pp. 379-380.

71. Wu (ed.), *Minhe xian zhi* (*Annals of Minhe County*), pp. 474-475.

72. Ibid., p. 456.

73. Founded in 1941 (*Ibid.*, p. 472).

74. Ibid. p. 463.

75. Lü Jianzhong and Lü Jianzhang, "Sanchuan tuzu diqu xuexiao jiaoyude lishi yu xianzhuang" ("Sanchuan Monguor Schooling History and the Present Situation") in *Zhongguo tuzu* (*China's Monguor Nationality*), No. 3 (1994), p. 40.

76. Wu (ed.), *Minhe xian zhi* (*Annals of Minhe County*), p. 456.

77. A temporary administrative division that included today's Guanting, Zhongchuan, Xiakou and Xinger townships, that is, an area where most of Minhe County's Monguor speakers live.

78. Li Quanming, personal interview conducted by ZhuYongzhong, July 1996; Wu (ed.), *Minhe xian zhi* (*Annals of Minhe County*), p. 464.

79. Wu (ed.), *Minhe xian zhi* (*Annals of Minhe County*), pp. 457, 464-465; Gao Shufen (ed.), *Minhe huizu tuzu zizhixian gaikuang* (*General Conditions of Minhe Hui and Monguor Autonomous County*) (Xining: Qinghai renmin chubanshe, 1986), p. 110.

80. Wu (ed.), *Minhe xian zhi* (*Annals of Minhe County*), pp. 474-475.

81. Ibid., pp. 464-465.

82. Jianzhong Lü and Jianzhang Lü, "Sanchuan tuzu diqu xuexiao jiaoyude lishi yu xianzhuang" ("Sanchuan Monguor Schooling History and Present Situation,") in *Zhongguo tuzu (China's Monguor Nationality)*, No. 3 (1994).

83. This information is taken from Ma Xuelin, personal interview conducted by Yongzhong Zhu, July 1996.

84. Ten *jiao* is equivalent to one *yuan*, or about two cents.

85. A teacher who is paid by local people and subsidized by the state.

86. This information is taken from Ma Xuelin, personal interview conducted by Zhu Yongzhong, July 1996.

87. Wu (ed.), *Minhe xian zhi (Annals of Minhe County)*, pp. 464-465.

88. Ibid., pp. 464-465.

89. Ibid., pp. 474-475.

90. Ibid., pp. 464-465.

91. This information is taken from Ma Xuelin, Personal interview conducted by Zhu Yongzhong, July 1996).

92. From an interview with Wu Haiping.

93. Ibid., pp. 464-465.

94. Gao (ed.), *Minhe huizu tuzu zhizhixian gaikuang (General Conditions of Minhe Hui and Monguor Autonomous County)*, p. 110.

95. Lü and Lü, "Sanchuan tuzu diqu xuexiao jiaoyude lishi yu xianzhuang" ("Sanchuan Monguor Schooling History and Present Situation"). This number is from the three townships just mentioned, and does not include Monguor students from such places as Gangou, Qianhe and Xinger.

96. This refers to a collection of several small villages that is given a single name and treated as a single administrative entity.

97. But not always useless, as in the case of an old woman in Xiakou Township who reads scriptures in Chinese when old women meet regularly to chant prayers. The others repeat what she reads.

98. Goa (Kevin Stuart, editor), "It Was a Great Misfortune to be Born a Woman," in *Journal of the Anglo-Mongolian Society*, Vol. 13, Nos. 1&2, (1991), pp. 85-92 and p. 86.

99. See Kevin Stuart and Hu Jun, "Death and Funerals Among the Minhe Tu (Monguor)," in *Asian Folklore Studies*, Vol. 51, No.2, (1992), pp. 67-87, for a lengthy treatment of the Minhe Monguor funeral.

100. Xin Cunwen, "Haishan Zhu," in *Zhongguo tuzu (China's Monguor Nationality)*, Vol. 1, 58-64 (1992), p. 60.

101. A village in the present-day Chuankou Region.

102. Xie Fuliang, personal interview conducted by Zhu Yongzhong, July 1996.

103. Teachers are paid by the county education bureau. Schools receiving only a few hundred yuan per year for operating expenses is the norm in eastern Qinghai. This is far from sufficient to meet the costs of repairs and new construction. This is particularly true of adobe structures requiring frequent repair.

104. It should be noted that in 1996, the Trace Foundation of New York donated approximately 500,000 yuan to Xiakou Lower Secondary School. These funds were used to build brick classrooms, teachers' quarters and dormitory rooms for schools. This significantly strengthened access to education on the part of local children—particularly those who needed to board at the school.

105. Zhu, Chuluu, and Stuart, "'The Frog Boy': An Example of Minhe Monguor.

106. The texts that we have seen are small, handwritten, mimeographed paperback versions.

Chinese Glossary*

Achang 阿昌
aiguozhuyi jiaoyu 爱国主义教育

Bai 白
Baijia xing 百家姓
ban 班
baocunxing 保存型
Beijinghua 北京话
bianjiang Hanzu 边疆汉族
bianti 变体
Blang (Bulang) 布朗
Bonan (Baoan) 保安
Bouyei (Buyi) 布依
bu shi zangjia renmin de xingge
不是藏家人民的性格

changyong Yiwen 常用彝文
chuanyi 穿衣
chulu 出路
chuzhong 初中
cun 村
cunxiao 村校

da ban jiaoyu 大办教育
Daur, Tahur (Dawoer) 达斡尔
dazhuan 大专
Deang 德昂
dianshi daxue 电视大学
dididaodao de Zhongguo ren
地地道道的中国人
difang minzu zhuyi 地方民族主义
Dong 侗
Dongxiang 东乡
Dongzhi 冬至
Drung (Delong) 独龙
Duanwujie 端午节

erduanshi 二段式
erlin 尔林
Ewenki (Ewenke) 鄂温克

Falü zhishi 法律知识
fangkuai Zhuang 方块壮
fengjian nongnu zhidu 封建农奴制度
fenshuxian 分数线
fuxue 府学

Ganjia 甘家
gaodeng xuexiao ruxue kaoshi (gaokao)
高等学校入学考试（高考）
Gaoshan 高山

gaozhong 高中
Gelo (Gelao) 仡佬
Gezu remin dahui 各族人民大会
gongtongxing 共同性
guan zhu, guan chi, guan chuan
管住，管吃，管穿
*Guanyu bangzhu wu wenzi de minzu chuangli
wenzi de baogao*
关于帮助无文字的民族创立文字的报告
Guanyu jiaqiang minzu jiaoyu gongzuo de yijian
关于加强民族教育工作的意见
gui 鬼
Guilinhua 桂林话
guoduxing 过渡型
Guyuan minzu shifan daxue 固原民族师范大学

halifa 哈里发
Han 汉
Hanhua 汉化
Hani 哈尼
Hanwen ban 汉文班
Hanyü 汉语
Hanyü pinyin 汉语拼音
Hanzu wenhua 汉族文化
Hezhen (Hezhe) 赫哲
Hongxing 红星
Huadong shifan daxue 华东师范大学
Hui 回
Huihua jiaocai 会话教材
Huimin Xueyuan 回民学院
Huiwen Daxue 回文大学
hukou 户口
huofo 活佛

jiafen 加分
jiao 角
Jiefang xiang 解放乡
Jing 京
jing tang jiaoyu 经堂教育
Jingpo 景颇
jingwen xiaoxue 经文小学
Jingxueyuan 经学院
jinshi 进士
Jinuo 基诺族
jisuzhi minzu zhongdian ban 寄宿制民族重点班
juren 举人

kaihua 开化
kang 炕
Kazak (Hasake) 哈萨克
kexue 科学
Kirgiz (Keerkezi) 柯尔克孜
Korean (Chaoxian) 朝鲜

Lahu 拉祜
lao san pian 老三篇

---
* This glossary does not include person names.

Lhoba (Luoba) 珞巴
Li 黎
li ke 理科
Lisu 傈僳
luohou 落后

Manchu (Man) 满
manla 满拉
Maonan 毛南
maying shengzi 卯子
Miao 苗
min kao han 民考汉
min kao min 民考民
minban 民办
minzu ban 民族班
minzu changshi 民族常识
minzu chengfen 民族成份
minzu daxue 民族大学
minzu huabao 民族画报
minzu jiaoyu 民族教育
minzu jiaoyu gu 民族教育股
minzu jiaoyu ke 民族教育科
minzu jiaoyu si 民族教育司
minzu jisuzhi xuexiao 民族寄宿制学校
Minzu quyu zizhi fa 民族区域自治法
Minzu sheng zhaogu zhengce 民族生照顾政策
minzu tuanjie 民族团结
minzu xiaoxue 民族小学
minzu xuexiao 民族学校
minzu xueyuan 民族学院
mixin 迷信
Moinba (Menba) 门巴
Mongol (Menggu) 蒙古
Muzi xuexiao 穆孜学校
Mulam (Mulao) 仫佬
Musilin zangli 穆斯林葬礼

Naxi 纳西
neidi 内地
nide wenhua chengdu duoshao
你的文化程度多少
Nu 怒
nü si 女寺
*nuli fazhan shaoshu minzu diqu wenhua jiaoyu
shiye* 努力发展少数民族地区文化教育事业

Oroqen (Elunqun) 鄂伦春

Pumi 普米
Putonghua 普通话

qian liu ming 前六名
Qiang 羌
qingzhen nüxue 清真女学
qiye fa 企业法

qu 区
quanyixing 权宜型

Russian (Elesi) 俄罗斯

Salar (Sala) 撒拉
san wu 三无
sanduanshi 三段式
Sanzi jing 三字经
shaoshu minzu 少数民族
She 畲
shen 神
sheng 升
sheng minwei 省民委
shengxue lü 升学率
shifan daxue 师范大学
shishi shang de pingdeng 事实上的平等
shixing shuangyu jiaoyu 实行双语教育
shuangyu xianxiang 双语现象
Shui 水
shuxiu 束脩
Sishu 四书
Songpan xian zangwen zhongxue xiao
松潘县藏文中学校

Tai (Dai) 傣
Tajik (Tajike) 塔吉克
Tatar (Tataer) 塔塔尔
Tibetan (Zang) 藏
tongbian jiaocai 统编教材
tongyi renshi 同意认识
tu 徒
Tu 土
tuguan 土官
Tujia 土家
tusi 土司

Uygur (Weiwuer) 维吾尔
Uzbek (Wuzibieke) 乌孜别克

Va (Wa) 佤

wanxiao 完小
weixue 卫学
wen 文
wen ke 文科
wenhua 文化
wenhua chengdu 文化程度
wenming 文明
wenming shidai 文明时代
wenyan 文言
wu gongban jiaoshi 无公办教师
Wu sheng-qu xiezuo jiaocai 五省区协作教材
wu xiaoshe 无校舍
wu zhuoyi 无桌椅
Wujing 五经

Wuminghua 武鸣话

xian shen bao guo 献身报国
xian wenjiao ju 县文教局
xiang 乡
xianjieshi 衔接式
xianjin 先进
xiansheng 先生
xiao qin bao guo 孝亲报国
Xibe (Xibo) 锡伯
Xibei minzu daxue 西北民族大学
xin Yiwen 新彝文
Xinan minzu daxue 西南民族大学
Xinjiang ban 新疆班
Xinjiang shifan daxue 新疆师范大学
xiongdi 兄弟
Xishuangbanna 西双版纳
Xishuangbanna dili 西双版纳地理
xiucai 秀才
Xizang ban 西藏班
Xizang daxue 西藏大学
Xizang minzu xueyuan 西藏民族学院
Xizang nongmu xueyuan 西藏农牧学院
xueqian Hanyu huihua jiaoyu ban
学前汉语会话教育班
xuetang 学堂

Yao 瑶
Yi 彝
yidao qie 一刀切
Yiwen ban 彝文班
yixue 义学
yixueyuan 伊学院
youhui zhengce 优惠政策
yuanshi shehui 原始社会
yuanshi zongjiao 原始宗教
yubei ban 预备班
Yugur (Yugu) 裕固
yuke ban 预科班

Zang yi xueyuan 藏医学院
Zangmin xuexiao 藏民学校
zhen 镇
zhijie guodu 直接过渡
zhong 中
Zhonga nüzi xuexiao 中阿女子学校
zhongdian 重点
Zhongguo Musilin 中国穆斯林
Zhonghua minzu 中华民族
Zhonghua minzu wenhua 中华民族文化
Zhongqiu 中秋
zhongxin wanxiao 中心完小
zhongxin xiaoxue 中心小学
Zhongyang minzu daxue 中央民族大学
zhongzhuan 中专
zhua haole 抓好了

Zhuang 壮
zhudao xitong 主导系统
zi xitong 子系统
zifei or zikaoban 自费，自靠班
zijue ziyuan 自决自愿
ziqiang 自强
zizhi difang 自治地方
zonghe 综合
zongjiao 宗教
zongjiao re 宗教热
zuoyi 作揖

Selected Reference Material

DOCUMENTS, STATISTICS AND YEARBOOKS IN CHINESE

Shaoshu minzu jiaoyu gongzuo wenjian xuanbian, 1949-1988 (National Minorities Education Work Document Selections, 1949-1988). Inner Mongolia jiaoyu chubanshe. 1991.

Shengshi zizhiqu shaoshu minzu jiaoyu gongzuo wenjian xuanbian, 1977-1990 (Province, City and Autonomous Region National Minorities Education Work Document Selections, 1977-1990). Sichuan minzu chubanshe. 1995.

Zhongguo jiaoyu chengjiu, 1949-1983 (Achievement of Education in China, 1949-1983). Beijing: Renmin jiaoyu chubanshe. 1984.

Zhongguo jiaoyu chengjiu, 1980-1985 (Achievement of Education in China, 1980-1985). Beijing: Renmin jiaoyu chubanshe. 1986.

Zhongguo jiaoyu nianjian, 1949-1984 (China Education Yearbook, 1949-1984). Beijing: Hunan jiaoyu chubanshe. 1986.

Zhongguo jiaoyu nianjian, 1949-1981 (China Education Yearbook, 1949-1981). Beijing: Zhongguo dabaike quanshu chubaushe. 1984.

Zhongguo jiaoyu nianjian, 1982-1984 (China Education Yearbook, 1982-1984). Beijing: Hunan jiaoyu chubanshe. 1986.

Zhongguo jiaoyu nianjian, 1985-1986 (China Education Yearbook, 1985-1986). Beijing: Hunan jiaoyu chubanshe. 1988.

Zhongguo jiaoyu nianjian, 1988. (China Education Yearbook, 1988). Beijing: Renmin jiaoyu chubanshe. 1989.

Zhongguo jiaoyu nianjian, 1989. (China Education Yearbook, 1989). Beijing: Renmin jiaoyu chubanshe. 1990.

Zhongguo jiaoyu nianjian, 1990. (China Education Yearbook, 1990). Beijing: Renmin jiaoyu chubanshe. 1991.

Zhongguo jiaoyu nianjian, 1991. (China Education Yearbook, 1991). Beijing: Renmin jiaoyu chubanshe. 1992.

Zhongguo jiaoyu nianjian, 1992. (China Education Yearbook, 1992). Beijing: Renmin jiaoyu chubanshe. 1993.

Zhongguo jiaoyu nianjian, 1993. (China Education Yearbook, 1993). Beijing: Renmin jiaoyu chubanshe. 1994.

Zhongguo jiaoyu nianjian, 1994. (China Education Yearbook, 1994). Beijing: Renmin jiaoyu chubanshe. 1995.

Zhongguo jiaoyu nianjian, 1995. (China Education Yearbook, 1995). Beijing: Renmin jiaoyu chubanshe. 1996.

Zhongguo jiaoyu tongji nianjian, 1987. (Educational Statistics Yearbook of China, 1987). Beijing: Beijing gongue daxue chubanshe. 1988.

Zhongguo jiaoyu tongji nianjian, 1989. (Educational Statistics Yearbook of China, 1989). Beijing: Renmin jiaoyu chubanshe. 1990.

Zhongguo jiaoyu tongji nianjian, 1990. (Educational Statistics Yearbook of China, 1990). Beijing: Renmin jiaoyu chubanshe. 1991.

Zhongguo jiaoyu tongji nianjian, 1991-1992. (Educational Statistics Yearbook of China, 1991-1992). Beijing: Renmin jiaoyu chubanshe. 1992.

Zhongguo jiaoyu tongji nianjian, 1993. (Educational Statistics Yearbook of China, 1993). Beijing: Renmin jiaoyu chubanshe. 1994.

Zhongguo jiaoyu tongji nianjian, 1994. (Educational Statistics Yearbook of China, 1994). Beijing: Renmin jiaoyu chubanshe. 1994.

Zhongguo jiaoyu tongji nianjian, 1995. (Educational Statistics Yearbook of China, 1995). Beijing: Renmin jiaoyu chubanshe. 1996.

Zhongguo minzu tongji, 1992 (Nationality Statistics of China, 1992). Beijing: Zhongguo tongji chubanshe. 1993.

Zhongguo minzu tongji nianjian, 1995 (Nationalities Statistical Yearbook of China, 1995). Beijing: Minzu chubanshe. 1995.

Zhongguo minzu tongji nianjian, 1996 (Nationalities Statistical Yearbook of China, 1996). Beijing: Minzu chubanshe. 1996.

Zhongguo shehui tongji ziliao (China Social Statistical Data). Beijing: Zhongguo tongji chubanshe. 1987.

Zhongguo tongji nianjian (China Statistics Yearbook). Beijing: Zhongguo tongji chubanshe. 1989, 1990.

BOOKS AND ARTICLES IN CHINESE

Anonymous. "Qieshi gaohao shaoshu minzu diqu dang de jianshe—qingzhu zhongguo gongchandang chengli qishi zhounian" ("Conscientiously Build the Ethnic Minority Areas—Celebrate the 70th Anniversary of the Founding of the Communist Party of China"), in *Minzu tuanjie*, No. 7 (November 10, 1991), 1990, p. 3.

Chen, H.T., ed. *Sichuan minzu jiaoyu yanjiu* (Research on Ethnic Education in Sichuan). Beijing: Zhongyang minzu xueyuan chubanshe (Central Institute of Nationalities Press). 1992.

Chen, H.T. *Zhongguo minzu jiaoyu fazhan tujing tantao* (An Examination of Ethnic Nationality Education Development in China). Beijing: Zhongyang minzu xueyuan chubanshe (Central Institute for Nationalities Press). 1990.

Chen, N.X. *Baoanyu cihui* (*Baoan Vocabulary*). Huhehaote: Neimenggu renmin chubanshe (Inner Mongolia People's Press). 1995.

Chen, N.X. *Baoanyu huayu cailiao* (*Baoan Language Materials*). Huhehaote: Neimenggu renmin chubanshe (Inner Mongolia People's Press). 1986.

Chen, N.X. *Baoanyu he mengguyu* (Baoan and Mongolian Languages Compared). Huhehaote: Neimenggu renmin chubanshe (Inner Mongolia People's Press). 1986.

Chen, Q. "Abazhou minzu jiaoyu fazhan zhanlüe chusuo" ("A Preliminary Exploration of the Struggle to Develop Minority Education in Aba Prefecture"). In AZJW, *Minzu jiaoyu yanjiu wenji* (Collected Essays on Minority Education). Chengdu: Sichuan daxue chubanshe (Sichuan University Publishing House). 1992.

Cheng, S.K. "Xinjiang jiaoyude fangxiang zhanxian shi tigao zhiliang", ("Raising Quality is the Orientation of the Front in Xinjiang's Education"). In *Xinjiang shehui kexue*, No. 3 (June 15, 1989), p. 38-62.

Gao, L.S. *Xishuangbanna Daizu de lishi yu wenhua* (*The History and Culture of the Tai Nationality in Sipsong Panna*). Kunming: Yunnan minzu chubanshe (Yunnan Nationalities Press). 1992.

Gao, S.F., ed. *Datong huizu tuzu zizhixian gaikuang* (*General Conditions of Datong Hui and Monguor Autonomous County*). Xining: Qinghai renmin chubanshe (Qinghai People's Press), 1986, p.107.

Gao, S.F., ed. *Minhe huizu tuzu zizhixian gaikuang* (*General Conditions of Minhe Hui and Monguor Autonomous County*). Xining: Qinghai renmin chubanshe (Qinghai People's Press), 1986, p.110.

Gele and X.S. Jin, eds. *Zhongguo qingkuang shu—bai xian shi jing shehui diaocha: Lasa juan* (*Book on China's National Condition: Economic and Social Investigation of One Hundred Counties and Cities: Lhasa Volume*). Beijing: Zhongguo da baikequanshu chubanshe (China Encyclopedia Press) 1995, p. 544.

Geng, J.S. and X.H. Wang, *Xizang jiaoyu yanjiu (Studies on Tibetan Education)*. Beijing: Zhongyang minzu xueyuan chubanshe (Central Institute of Nationalities Press), 1989.

Guo, F.Y. "Ba diqu minzu jiaoyu fazhan shilue (Ming, Qing, Minguo Bufen)" ("A Brief History of the Development of Minority Education in the Aba Region [Ming, Qing and Republican Section]") in *Minzu jiaoyu yanjiu wenji* (Collected Essays on Minority Education). Chengdu: Sichuan daxue chubanshe (Sichuan University Publishing House), 1992, pp. 479-520.

Huang, T.H. "Huizu wenhua shi" ("Hui Nationality Cultural History"), in Li Dezhu, ed., *Zhongguo shaoshu minzu wenhua shi* (A Cultural History of China's Ethnic Minorities). Shenyang: Liaoning renmin chubanshe (Liaoning People's Press), 1994, pp. 339, 344, 345.

Jiang, Y.L. *Daizu shi* (The History of the *Tai Nationality*). Chengdu: Sichuan minzu chubanshe (Sichuan People's Press), 1983.

Li, C.F. "Tuzu pian" ("Monguor Section"), in Muchi Yundeng Jiacuo, ed. *Qinghai shaoshu minzu* (Qinghai Minority Nationalities). Xining: Qinghai renmin chubanshe (Qinghai People's Press). 1995.

Li, D.H., ed. *Zhongguo shaoshu minzu wenhua shi* (A Cultural History of China's Ethnic Minorities). Shenyang: Liaoning renmin chubanshe. 1994.

Li, K.Y. *Tuzu (Mengguer) yuanliu kao (An Investigation of Tu [Monguor] Origins and Development)*. Xining: Qinghai renmin chubanshe (Qinghai People's Press). 1992.

Li, X.W. and K. Stuart. "Population and Culture of the Mongols, Tu, Baoan, Dongxiang, and Yugu." In Gansu, *Mongolian Studies*, Vol. 12 (1989), pp. 71-93: 75.

Liu, N.S., D. Zhang and X.Q. Liu, eds. *Xinjiang gailan (Xinjiang at a Glance)*. Shanghai: Xinjiang renmin chubanshe (Xinjiang People's Press). 1995.

Liu, Y.J. *Zhongguo jiaoyu da shi dian, 1949-1990 (Book of Great Events in Chinese Education, 1949-1990)* Vol. 2. Hangzhou: Zhejiang jiaoyu chubanshe (Zhejiang Education Press), 1993, p. 2,094.

Ma, X.L., ed. *Gansu shaoshu minzu renkou (The Population of Gansu Minorities)*. Lanzhou: Keji chubanshe (Science and Technology Press). 1986.

Ma, Z. "Tantan Qinghai Huizu nütong jiaoyu" ("On Girls' Education among the Hui of Qinghai"), in Jiang Huandong, ed., *Qinghai minzu nutong jiaoyu yanjiu* (Studies on Education for Girls among the Nationalities of Qinghai) Xining: Qinghai People's Press, 1994, pp. 183-184.

Minzu jiaoyu yanjiu wenji (Collected Essays on Minority Education). Chengdu: Sichuan daxue chubanshe (Sichuan University Publishing House). 1992.

Minzu Huabao (Nationality Pictorial). Beijing: Minzu Chubanshe (Nationalities Press), 1974.

Muchi Yundeng Jiacuo, ed. *Qinghai Shaoshu Minzu (Qinghai Minority Nationalities)*. Xining: Qinghai Renmin Chubanshe (Qinghai People's Press). 1995.

Ningxia huizu zizhiqu jiaoyu ting "Zai tansuo he gaige zhong fazhan minzu jiaoyu" ("Develop Minority Education in the Process of Exploration and Reform"). In *Minzu jiaoyu yanjiu (Nationalities Education Research)*, No. 1 (1990), pp. 7-11.

Qian, H.F., and T.C. Piao. "Jilin sheng bianjing qu minzu jiaoyu xianzhuang yu fazhan duice" ("The Current Situation and Policy for Development of Minority Education in Border Areas of Jilin Province"). In Wang Xihong, ed., *Zhongguo Bianjing Minzu Jiaoyu (Minority Education in Border Areas of China)*. Beijing: Zhongyang Minzu Xueyan Chubanshe, pp. 633-646.

Qin, Y. "Mingqing tuzu diqu de tusi zai lishishangde zuoyong" ("The Ming-Qing Dynasty Monguor Area *Tusi's* Function in History"). In *Qinghai shehui kexue bao* (Qinghai Social Science Journal), No.31 (1985), pp. 87-93.

Se, L. "Minzu jiaoyu shiliao zhaibian" ("Excerpts From Historical Materials on Minority Education"). In *Minzu jiaoyu yanjiu wenji (Collected Essays on Minority Education)*. Chengdu: Sichuan daxue chubanshe (Sichuan University Publishing House), 1992, pp. 521-532.

Shang, J.F. "Liangshan minzu jiaoyu zhanlue chutan" ("Preliminary Discussion of Strategy for Ethnic Education in Liangshan"). In Chen Hongtao, ed., *Sichuan minzu jiaoyu yanjiu (Research on Ethnic Education in Sichuan)*. Beijing: Zhongyang minzu xueyuan chubanshe (Central Institute of Nationalities Press), 1989.

Sixiang zhengzhi (Ideology and Politics). Guangdong gaodeng jiaoyu chubanshe (Higher Education Press). 1992.

Sun, R.Q., X. Teng and M.F. Wang. *Zhongguo shaoshu minzu jiaoyuxue gailun (An Introduction to the Study of China National Minority Education)*. Beijing: Zhongguo Laodong Press, p.116.

Wang, J.H., S.F. Hai, B.M. Liu and H.M. Yao. *Renkouxue duben* (Population Studies Reader). Xining: Qinghai renmin chubanshe (Qinghai People's Press). 1993.

Wang, T.Z. "Shaoshu minzu jiaoyu de xin fazhan" ("New Developments in Ethnic Minority Education"). In *Jiaoyu jianxun*, No. 4, (1987).

Wang, W. C. and Y.Y. Meng. *Shaoshu minzu diqu jingji fazhan jiegou moshi weilai, (The Future Structural Model of Economic Development in Ethnic Minority Regions).* Beijing: Minzu Press, 1990.

Weining Yizu Huizu Miaozu zizhi xian gaikuang (Survey of the Weining Yi, Hui and Miao Autonomous County). Guiyang: Guizhou minzu chubanshe (Guizhou People's Press), 1985.

Weiwu'er zu jian shi (A Brief Uyghur History). Urumqi: Xinjiang renmin chubanshe (Xinjiang People's Press). 1991.

Wu, B.H., ed. *Minhe xian zhi (Annals of Minhe County).* Xi'an: Shaanxi renmin chubanshe (Shaanxi People's Press), 1993, pp.453, 484-485.

Wu, Z.J. "Lun wo guo minzu guanxi fazhi tedian" ("On the Special Characteristics of the Legal System With Regard to our Country's Ethnic Relations"). In *Minzu yanjiu* (Nationalities Research) No. 1 (1992), pp. 8-14.

Xibu minzu diqu jingji kaifa tanshuo. (An Investigation into Economic Development in Ethnic Minority Regions of Western China), Beijing: Zhongyang minzuxueyuan chubanshe (Central Institute of Nationalities Press). 1986.

Xie, B.S. et al., eds. *Minzu diqu aiguozhuyi jiaoyu jianming duben (An Elementary Study of Patriotic Education in Minority Areas).* Kunming: Yunnan renmin chubanshe. 1994.

Xie, Q.H. *Zhongguo minzu jiaoyu shigang (China Nationality Education Historical Outline).* Guiyang: Guangxi Educational Press. 1987.

Xinan minzu xueyuan yuanshi bianji shi (The Editorial Office for *The History of the Southwest Institute for Nationalities*). *Xinan Minzu Xueyuan Yuanshi, 1951-1991 (The History of the Southwest Institute for Nationalities, 1951-1991)* Chengdu: Sichuan minzu chubanshe (Sichuan Nationalities Press) 1991.

Xishuangbanna daizu zizhizhou gaikuang (A Survey of Sipsong Panna Dai Nationality Autonomous Prefecture). Kunming: Yunnan minzu chubanshe (Yunnan Nationalities Press), 1986.

Yang, C.J. "Lizu xizang shiji; cujin gaojiao gaige" ("Gain a Foothold in Tibet's Reality; Promote the Reform and Development of Higher Education"). In *Zhongguo gaodeng jiaoyu* (Higher Education in China), October 1993, pp. 18-19.

Yang, C.P. "Wo guo shaoshu minzu wenhua shuiping da fudu tigao" ("Our country's minorities' cultural level is being raised to a great extent"). In *Minzu (Nationalities),* No. 6 (1994), pp. 40-41.

Yang, M. and G. Wang. *Zhongguo zangzu jiaoyu shilue (A Brief History of Education for China's Tibetans)*. Chengdu: Chengdu keji daxue chubanshe (Chengdu Science and Technology University Publishing House). 1993.

Ye, Z.Y. "Colleges Enrolling Students Throughout the Country Should Set a Unified Test Score Requirement and Practice Unified Admissions." In *Gaodeng jiaoyu zhanxian* (Higher Education Front) No. 10 (1984), pp. 13-14.

Yunnan Province History Society. *Aiguozhuyi yu lishi jiaoyu (Patriotism and History Education)*. Kunming: Yunnan daxue chubanshe (Yunnan University Press). 1990.

Zhang, J.S. and S. Shi. "Zangzu diqu siyuan yu suozai shequ guanxi de gen diaocha: songpan xian shanba cun yu shanbasi ji xuexiao jiaoyu de guanxi" ("A Preliminary Investigation of the Relations Between Monasteries in Tibetan Areas and the Communities in which They Are Located: Songpan County's Shanba Village, Shanba Monastery and Their Relationship to School-Based Education"). In *Xizang yanjiu (Tibetan Studies [Chinese Edition])* No. 2 (1992), pp. 102-110.

Zhang, T.L. *Zhongguo minzu renkoude yanjiang (Lectures on China's Minority Population)*. Beijing: Haiyang chubanshe (Haiyang Press) 1983, pp. 131, 199.

Zhang, Y., ed. *Zhongguo gaodeng yuanxiao* (China's Higher Institutes and Schools). Beijing: Kexue puji chubanshe (Popular Science Press), 1991, p. 384.

Zhongguo Minzu Jingji (The Economy of China's Ethnic Nationalities). Beijing: Zhongguo tongji chubanshe, 1994.

Zhou, C.H. "Shehui zhuyi chuji jieduan Sichuan minzu jiaoyu de sikao" ("A Consideration of Ethnic Education in Sichuan During the Early Stages of Socialism"). In Chen Hongtao, ed., *Sichuan minzu jiaoyu yanjiu (Research on Ethnic Education in Sichuan)*. Beijing: Zhongyang minzu xueyuan chubanshe (Central Institute of Nationalities Press), 1992.

Zhou, R.N. "Chuyi Xizang minzu jiaoyu fazhang" ("My Humble Opinion on Developing Minority Education in Tibet"), *Minzu yanjiu* (Nationalities Research) No. 5 (1988), pp. 46-55.

Zhou, W.Z. *Tuyuhun ziliao jilu (Tuyuhun Material Compilation)*. Xining: Qinghai renmin chubanshen (Qinghai People's Press). 1991.

Zhu, J.L., comp., *Zangzu jinxiandai jiaoyu shi (The History of Modern Tibetan Education)*. Xining: Qinghai renmin chubanshe (Qinghai People's Press), 1990.

Zou, Z.X. Fazhanzhong de Xishuangbanna minzu jiaoyu (The Developing Minority Education of Sipsong Panna). In Yan Sanlong ed., *Xishuangbanna minzu jiaoyu* (The Education of Ethnic Groups in Xishuang Banna). Kunming: Yunnan minzu chubanshe (Yunnan Nationalities Press), 1992.

Zu, J.L. *Zangzu jindai jiaoyu shilue (A Brief History of Modern Tibetan Education)*. Xining: Qinghai minzu chubanshe (Qinghai Nationalities Publishing House), 1990.

SELECTED NEWSPAPERS AND JOURNALS IN CHINESE

Gaodeng jiaoyu zhanxian (Higher Education Front, replaced by *Zhongguo gaodeng jiaoyu)*

Jiaoyu jianxun (Education News Briefs)

Jiaoyu Yanjiu (Educational Research),

Minzu (Nationalities)

Minzu jiaoyu yanjiu (Nationalities Education Research)

Minzu Tuanjie (Ethnic Unity, formerly *Nationalities Unity)*

Minhe wenshi (Minhe Culture and History)

Minzu yanjiu (Nationalities Research)

Qinghai shehui kexue bao (Qinghai Social Science Journal)

Xinjiang shehui kexue (Xinjiang Social Sciences)

Xizang de jiaoyu (Education in Tibet)

Xizang yanjiu (Tibetan Studies)

Zhongguo gaodeng jiaoyu (China Higher Education)

Zhongguo jiaoyu bao (China Education News)

Zhongguo minzu jingji (China's Natioanlities' Education)

MATERIALS IN TIBETAN

Mtsho sngon mi rigs slob gzhi rtsom sgyur khang (MMS), eds. *Skad Yig, Deb Gnyis Pa (Language and Literature, Book Two)*. Ljongs zhing lnga mnyam bsgrgs slob gzhi. Lo dgu an babs slob gso dma' rim slob ring slob deb. (Textbook for the Junior Secondary Level of [the] 9-year Compulsory Education (System), Five Provinces/Regions Jointly Produced Curriculum). Siling (Xining): Mtsho sngon mi rigs dpe skrun khang (Qinghai Nationalities Publishing House). 1993.

Mtsho sngon mi rigs slob gzhi rtsom sgyur khang (MMS) eds. *Skad Yig, Deb Bzhi Pa (Language and Literature, Book Four)*. Ljongs zhing lnga mnyam bsgrgs slob gzhi. Lo dgu an babs slob gso dma' rim slob ring slob deb.

(Textbook for the junior secondary level of (the) 9-year compulsory education (system), Five Provinces/Regions jointly produced curriculum). Siling (Xining): Mtsho sngon mi rigs dpe skrun khang (Qinghai Nationalities Publishing House). 1994.

Zing chu rdzong gi lo rgyus deb ther byed sgo sgrig mkhan gtso wo (ZCKC) (Songpan County Historical Annals Editorial Group) *Zing-chu-rdzong dgon-pa so-sogs dkar-chag (A Guide to the Various Monasteries of Songpan County)*. Songpan County: Tibetan Language Printing Press. 1993.

SELECTED BOOKS AND ARTICLES

Anagnost, A.S. "The Politics of Displacement." In Charles Keyes, Laurel Kendal and Helen Hardacre, eds., *State and Religion in East and Southeast Asia*. Honolulu: University of Hawaii Press.1994.

Barnett, R. and S. Akiner, eds. *Resistance and Reform in Tibet*. London: Hurst and Company. 1994.

Bauer, J., F. Wang, N.E. Riley and X.H. Zhao. "Gender Inequality in Urban China: Education and Employment." In *Modern China*, Vol. 18, No. 3 (July 1992), pp. 333-370.

Berberoglu, B. (ed.) *The National Question*, Philadelphia: Temple University Press, 1995, pp. 259-279.

Borchigud, W. "The Impact of Urban Ethnic Education on Modern Mongolian Ethnicity, 1949-1966," in Stevan Harrell, ed., *Cultural Encounters on China's Ethnic Frontiers*. Seattle: University of Washington Press, 1995, pp. 278-300.

Bowen, J. "The Forms Culture Takes: A State-of-the-field Essay on the Anthroplogy of Southeast Asia." In *Journal of Asian Studies*. Vol. 54, No. 4 (1995), pp. 1,004-1,068.

Bowen, J. *Muslims Through Discourse: Religion and Ritual in Gayo Society*. Princeton: Princeton University Press. 1993.

Bray, M. and R.M. Thomas. "Levels of Comparison in Educational Studies: Different Insights from Different Literatures and the Value of Multilevel Analyses." In *Harvard Educational Review*, Vol. 65, No.3 (1995), pp. 472-490.

Broedsgaard, K.E., and D. Strand, eds. *Reconstructing Twentieth Century China: Social Control, Civil Society and National Identity*. Oxford: Oxford University Press, forthcoming.

Brugger, B. and S. Reglar. *Politics, Economy and Society in Contemporary China*. Stanford: Stanford University Press. 1994, p. 337.

Chaliand, G., ed. *Minority Peoples in the Age of Nation-States*. London: Pluto Press. 1989.

Chan, W.T. *Religious Trends in Modern China*. New York: Columbia University Press, 1953; New York : Octagon Books, 1969, pp. 199-201.

Chang, A. *Painting in the People's Republic of China: The Politics of Style*, Boulder Co: Westview Press. 1980.

Chen, H.S. *Frontier Land Systems in Southernmost China*. New York: Institute of Pacific Relations. 1949.

Clifford, J. and G.E. Marcus, eds. *Writing Culture: The Poetics and Politics of Ethnography*. Berkeley: University of California Press. 1986.

Cohen, J.L. *The New Chinese Painting 1949-1986*. New York: Harry N. Abrams, Inc. 1987.

Cohen, M.J. "Being Chinese: The Peripheralization of Traditional Identity," In *Daedalus*. Vol. 120, No.2 (1991), pp.113-34.

Crossley, P.K. "Thinking about Ethnicity in Early Modern China." In *Late Imperial China*. Vol. 11, No.1 (1990), pp.1-35.

Dankoff, R. (trans.) *Wisdom of Royal Glory, A Turco-Islamic Mirror for Princes*. Chicago and London: University of Chicago Press. 1993.

Diamond, N. "The Miao and Poison: Interactions on China's Southwest Frontier." In *Ethnology*. Vol. 27, No.1 (1988), pp.1-25.

Donnet, P. *Tibet: Survival in Question*. London: Zen. 1993

Dreyer, J. *China's Political System: Modernization and Tradition*. New York: Paragon House. 1993, p. 364-365.

Dreyer, J. "Ethnic Minorities in Mainland China Under Teng Hsiao-p'ing," in Bih-Jaw Lin and James Myers ed., *Forces for Change in Contemporary China*. Columbia: University of South Carolina Press. 1993.

Dreyer, J. T. *China's Forty Millions: Minority Nationalities and National Integration in the People's Republic of China*. Cambridge and London: Harvard University Press. 1976.

Engels, F. *The Origin of the Family, Private Property, and the State*. New York: International Publishers. 1883, 1972.

Erickson, F. "Transformation and School Success: The Politics and Culture of Educational Achievement." In *Anthropology and Education Quarterly*. No. 18 (1987), pp. 335-356.

Fei, X.T. "Ethnic Identification in China." In *Toward a People's Anthropology*. Beijing: New World Press. 1981.

Foley, D.E. "Reconsidering Anthropological Explanations of Ethnic School Failure." In *Anthropology and Education Quarterly*. No. 22 (1991), pp. 60-86.

Forbes, A.D.W. *Warlords and Muslims in Chinese Central Asia, A Political History of Republican Sinkiang 1911-1949*. Cambridge: Cambridge University Press 1986, p. 18.

Gittelman, Z. "The Politics of Ethnicity and Affirmative Action in the Soviet Union." In M. Wyzan, ed., *The Political Economy of Ethnic Discrimination and Affirmative Action*. New York: Praeger, 1990, pp. 167-196.

Gladney, D.C. "Masculinity and Alterity: Other Definition of Maleness among Minorities in China." In Jeffrey Wasserstrom and Susan Brownell, eds., *Chinese Femininities/Chinese Masculinities*. Berkeley: University of California Press, forthcoming.

Gladney, D.C. *Muslim Chinese, Ethnic Nationalism in the People's Republic*. Cambridge: Council on East Asian Studies. Harvard University. Harvard University Press. 1991.

Gladney, D.C. "Representing Nationality in China: Refiguring Majority/Minority Identities." In *The Journal of Asian Studies*. Vol. 53, No. 1 (1994), pp.92-123.

Gladney, D.C. "Salman Rushdie in China: Religion, Ethnicity, and State Definition in the People's Republic." In Charles F. Keyes, Laurel Kendall, and Helen Hardacre, eds., *Religion and the Modern States of East and Southeast Asia*. Honolulu: University of Hawaii Press. 1994.

Gladney, D.C. "Transnational Islam and Uighur National Identity: Salman Rushdie, Sino-Muslim Missile Deals and the Trans-Eurasian Railway." In *Central Asian Survey*, Vol. 11, No. 3 (1992), pp.1-18.

Goa (Kevin Stuart, editor). "It Was a Great Misfortune to be Born a Woman." In *Journal of the Anglo-Mongolian Society*, Vol.13, No.1&2 (1991), pp.85-92.

Goldscheider, C. ed. *Population, Ethnicity and Nation Building*. Boulder Co: Westview. 1995.

Goldstein, M. C. "Change, Conflict and Continuity Among a Community of Nomadic Pastoralists: A Case Study From Western Tibet, 1950-1990." In Robert Barnett, ed. *Resistance and Reform in Tibet*. Bloomington and Indianapolis, IN: Indiana University Press. 1994, pp. 76-111.

Goldstein-Kyaga, Katrin. *The Tibetans—School for Survival or Submission: An Investigation of Ethnicity and Education*. Stockholm: HLS Flag,

Department of Educational Research. The Center for Pacific Asia Studies. 1993.

Hahn, R.F. Notes on the Origin and Development of the Salar Language. In *Acta Orientalia Academiae Scientiarum Hung.*, Vol. XLII (2-3) (1988), pp. 235-275.

Hansen, M.H. *Lessons in Being Chinese: Minority Education and Ethnic Identity in Southwest China* (Seattle: University of Washington Press, in press).

Hansen, M.H. *Lessons in Patriotism: Ethnic Education in Southwest China.* Ph.D. dissertation. Asian Studies. University of Aarhus, Denmark. 1996.

Hansen, M.H. "Forstering Love of Learning: Naxi Responses to Ethnic Images in Chinese State Education." In Kjeld Erik Broedsgaard and David Strand, eds., *Reconstructing Twentieth Century China: Social Control, Civil Society and National Identity.* Oxford: Oxford University Press, forthcoming.

Harper, P. GSU. "China Schools Share Similar Goal." In *Chicago Tribune,* July 26, 1995, p. 3.

Harrell, S. *Cultural Encounters on China's Ethnic Frontiers.* Seattle and London: University of Washington Press. 1995.

Harrell, S. "Ethnicity, Local Interests, and the State: Yi Communities in Southwest China." In *Comparative Studies in Society and History,* Vol. 32, No. 3 (1990), pp. 515-548.

Harrell, S. "Introduction: Civilizing Projects and the Reaction to Them." In Stevan Harrell, ed., *Cultural Encounters on China's Ethnic Frontiers.* Seattle and London: University of Washington Press. 1995.

Harrell, S. "The Nationalities Question and the Prmi Problem." In Melissa J. Brown, ed., *Negotiating Ethnicities in China and Taiwan,* Berkeley: University of California Institute for East Asian Studies. 1996.

Havnevik, H. "The Role of Nuns in Contemporary Tibet." In Robert Barnett and Shirin Akiner, eds., *Resistance and Reform in Tibet.* London: Hurst and Company, 1994, pp. 259-266.

Hawkins, J.N. *Education and Social Change in the People's Republic of China.* New York: Praeger Press. 1983.

Hawkins, J.N. "The Politics of Intergroup Relations: Minority Education in the People's Republic of China." In Murray Thomas, ed., *Politics and Education.* New York: Pergamon Press. 1973.

Hayhoe, R., ed. *Education and Modernization: The Chinese Experience.* Oxford: Pergamon Press. 1992.

Hobsbawm, E. *Nations and Nationalism since 1780.* Cambridge: Cambridge University Press. 1991.

Jan-Ingvar, Lofstedt. *Education in Multi-Ethnic and Disadvantaged Areas: The Case of Gansu in China.* Stockholm: Institute of International Education. 1994.

Kaplan, E.H., and D.W. Whisenhunt, eds. *Opuscula Altaica, Essays Presented in Honor of Henry Schwarz.* Bellingham, Washington: Center for East Asian Studies, Western Washington University. 1994.

Karklins, R. "Ethnic Politics and Access to Higher Education: the Soviet Case." In *Comparative Politics,* Vol.16, No. 3 (April 1984), pp. 277-294.

Karmey, S. G. "Mountain Cults and National Identity in Tibet." In R. Barnett, ed., *Resistance and Reform in Tibet,* Bloomington, IN: University of Indiana Press. 1994, pp. 112-120.

Keyes, C.F. "State Schools in Rural Communities: Reflections on Rural Education and Cultural Change in Southeast Asia." In Charles F. Keyes, ed., *Reshaping Local Worlds: Formal Education and Cultural Change in Rural Southeast Asia.* Monograph 36/Yale Southeast Asia Studies. New Haven: Yale Center for International and Area Studies. 1991.

Keyes, C.F. "Who are the Tai? Reflections on the Invention of Identities, Lola Romanucci-Ross and George A. De Vos." In *Ethnic Identity.* Walnut Creek/London/New Delhi: Alta Mira Press. 1996.

Keyes, C.F., L. Kendal and H. Hardacre, eds. *State and Religion in East and Southeast Asia.* Honolulu: University of Hawaii Press. 1994.

Klitgaard, R. *Elitism and Meritocracy in Developing Countries.* Baltimore: Johns Hopkins University Press. 1986, p. 26.

Kormondy, E. "Observations on Minority Education, Cultural Preservation and Economic Development in China." In *Compare.* Vol. 25, No. 2 (1995), pp. 161-178.

Kwong, J. and X. Hong. "Educational Equality Among China's Minorities." In *Comparative Education.* Vol. 25, No. 2 (1989), pp. 229-243.

LaBelle, T. and E.V. Robert. "Education, Social Change, and Social Stratification." In *Harvard Education Review.* No. 45 (1975), pp.3-71.

Laing, E.J. *The Winking Owl: Art in the People's Republic of China.* Berkeley: University of California Press. 1988.

Lamontagne, J. "Educational Disparities in Mainland China: Characteristics and Trends." In Bih-jaw Lin and Li-min Fan, eds., *Education in Mainland China: Review and Evaluation.* Taipei: Institute of International Relations, National Chengchi University. (1990). pp. 130-151.

Lamontagne, J. "Improving the Education of China's National Minorities." In D. Ray and D. Poonwassie, eds., *Education and Cultural Differences: New Perspectives*. New York: Garland Publishing, Inc. 1992, pp. 183-209.

Lamontagne, J. and R. Ma. "The Development of Education in China's Cities and Counties," in G. A. Postiglione and Lee W.O., eds., *Social Change and Educational Development: Mainland China, Taiwan and Hong Kong*. Hong Kong: Centre of Asian Studies, The University of Hong Kong. 1995, pp. 153-173.

Latourette, K.S. *A History of Christian Missions in China*. London: Society for Promoting Christian Knowledge. 1929.

Lavely, W., Z.Y. Xiao, B.H. Li and R. Freedman. "The Rise in Female Education in China: National and Regional Patterns." In *The China Quarterly*. No. 121 (1990), pp. 61-93.

Law of the People's Republic of China on Regional National Autonomy. In Legislative Affairs Commission, National People's Congress, *The Laws of the People's Republic of China, 1983-1986*, Vol. 2. Beijing: Foreign Language Press. 1987, pp. 87-101.

Lê Thh Khoî. *L'education compare*. Paris: Armand Colin. 1981.

Ledlow, S. "Is Cultural Discontinuity an Adequate Explanation for Dropping Out?" *Journal of American Indian Education*, Vol. 31, No.3 (1992), pp. 21-36.

Lee, C.J. *China's Korean Minority: the Politics of Ethnic Education*. Boulder Co: Westview. 1986.

Lenthal, R. "The Mohammedan Press in China." In *The Religious Periodical Press in China*. Peking: Synodal Committee on China. 1940.

Lewin, K.M. and Y.J. Wang. *Implementing Basic Education in China: Progress and Prospects in Rich, Poor and National Minority Areas*. Paris: International Institute for Educational Planning, UNESCO. 1994.

Li, X.W. and K. Stuart. "The Xunhua Sala." In *Asian Folklore Studies*. Vol. 49, No.1 (1990), pp. 39-52.

Lin, B.J. and J. Myers. *Forces for Change in Contemporary China*. Columbia: University of South Carolina Press. 1993.

Lin, B.J. and L.M. Fan, eds. *Education in Mainland China: Review and Evaluation*. Taipei: Institute of International Relations. National Chengchi University. 1990.

Lola, R.R. and G.A. De Vos. *Ethnic Identity*. Walnut/Creek/London/New Delhi: Alta Mira Press. 1996.

Lomawaima, K. T. Domesticity in the Federal Indian Schools: The Power of Authority Over Mind and Body. *American Ethnologist,* Vol. 20, No. 2 (1993), pp. 1-14.

Lubin, N. *Labour and Nationality in Soviet Central Asia: an Uneasy Compromise.* London: Macmillan. 1984.

Lufkin, F. *Images of Minorities in the Art of the Peoples Republic of China.* Unpublished M.A. Thesis. University of California. Berkeley. 1990.

Ma, R. "Economic Patterns, Migration and Ethnic Relationships in the Tibet Autonomous Region, China." In Calvin Goldscheider, ed., *Population, Ethnicity and Nation Building.* Boulder: Westview, Co. 1995, pp. 37-75.

Ma, R. "Han and Tibetan Residential Patterns in Lhasa." In *The China Quarterly,* No. 128 (1992), pp. 814-835.

MacInnis, D.E., ed. *Religious Policy and Practice in Communist China, A Documentary History.* New York: Macmillan. 1972.

Mackerras, C. "Education in the Guomindang Period, 1928-1949." In David Pong and Edmund S.K. Fung, eds., *Ideal and Reality, Social and Political Change in Modern China, 1860-1949.* Lanham, New York, London: University Press of America, 1985, pp.164-165, 182.

Mackerras, C. *China's Minority Cultures: Identities and Integration Since 1912.* Melbourne: Longman Australia, New York: St Martin's Press. 1995, pp. 28-31, 40-43, 45-46, 116, 208-210.

Mackerras, C. *China's Minorities: Integration and Modernization in the Twentieth Century.* Hong Kong: Oxford University Press. 1994, pp. 173-176, 186-190.

Mackerras, C. "Religion, Politics and the Economy in Inner Mongolia and Ningxia." In Edward H. Kaplan and Donald W. Whisenhunt, eds., *Opuscula Altaica, Essays Presented in Honor of Henry Schwarz.* Bellingham, Washington: Center for East Asian Studies, Western Washington University. 1994, pp. 447-450.

Mandel, W. *Soviet But Not Russian: the Other Peoples of the Soviet Union.* Edmonton: Alberta. 1985. pp. 312-215.

McKhann, C. F. "The Naxi and the Nationalities Question." In Stevan Harrell, ed., *Cultural Encounters on China's Ethnic Frontiers.* Seattle and London: University of Washington Press. 1995.

Mitchell, E. R. *Diffusion of Innovations.* Third Edition. New York: Free Press, 1989.

Mitchell, T. *Colonising Egypt.* Berkeley and Los Angeles: University of California Press. 1991.

Morgan, L.H. *Ancient Society.* Tuscon: University of Arizona Press. 1877, 1985.

Niu, X. D. *Policy Education and Inequalities in Communist China Since 1949.* Lanham: University Press of America. 1992, Chap. 5.

Nowak, M. *Tibetan Refugees: Youth and the New Generation of Meaning.* New Brunswick, NJ: Rutgers University Press. 1984.

Ogbu, J. "Cultural Discontinuities and Schooling: A Problem in Search of an Explanation." In *Anthropology and Education Quarterly* No. 13 (1982), pp. 290-307.

Ogbu, J. "Variability in Minority School Performance." In *Anthropology and Education Quarterly* No. 18 (1987), pp. 312-334.

Olivier, B. *The Implementation of China's Nationality Policy in the Northeastern Provinces* San Francisco: Mellen Research University Press. 1993. p. 242.

Panchen Lama. "Address to the TAR Standing Committee Meeting of the National People's Congress held in Peking on 28 March 1987." In Pierre Donnet, *Tibet: Survival in Question.* London: Zed. 1993, p. 231.

Pas, J.F., ed. *The Turning of the Tide, Religion in China Today.* Hong Kong: Hong Kong Branch of the Royal Asiatic Society and Oxford University Press. 1989.

Pepper, S. *China's Education Reform in the 1980s.* Institute of East Asian Studies, University of California, Berkeley, China Research Monograph Series, no. 36, 1990. pp. 75-92.

Pepper, S. *China's Universities.* Ann Arbor: University of Michigan, Center for Chinese Studies. 1989.

Pepper, S. *Radicalism and Educational Reform in 20th Century China,* Cambridge: Cambridge University Press. 1996.

Pieke, F.N. "Chinese Educational Achievement and 'Folk Theories of Success.'" In *Anthropology and Education Quarterly* No. 22 (1992), pp.162-180.

Platero, P.R., E.A. Brandt, G. Witherspoon and P. Wong. *Navajo Students at Risk: Final Report for the Navajo Area Dropout Study.* Window Rock: Navajo Division of Education. 1986.

Pong, D. and E.S.K. Fung, eds. *Ideal and Reality, Social and Political Change in Modern China, 1860-1949.* Lanham, New York, London: University Press of America. 1985.

Postiglione, G.A. "Studying National Minority Education, in J. Liu, eds., *The Ethnographic Eye: Ethnographic Research on Education in China,* New York: Garland Publishing Inc., 1998.

Postiglione, G.A. "National Minorities and Nationalities Policy in China, in Berch Berberoglu (ed.) *The National Question,* Philadelphia: Temple University Press, 1995, pp. 259-279.

Postiglione, G.A. and W.O. Lee, eds. *Social Change and Educational Development: Mainland China, Taiwan and Hong Kong.* Hong Kong: Centre of Asian Studies, The University of Hong Kong. 1995.

Postiglione, G.A., X. Teng and Y.P. Ai. "Basic Education and School Discontinuation in National Minority Border Regions of China. In Gerard A. Postiglione and Lee Wing On, eds., *Social Change and Educational Development in Mainland China, Taiwan, and Hong Kong.* Hong Kong: University of Hong Kong Press. 1995.

Postiglione, G.A. "China's National Minorities and Educational Change," in *Journal of Contemporary Asia.* Vol. 22, No. 1 (1992), p. 39.

Postiglione, G.A. "The Implications of Modernization for the Education of China's National Minorities." In R. Hayhoe, ed. *Education and Modernization: The Chinese Experience.* Oxford: Pergamon Press. 1992.

Pyong, G.M. "A Comparison of the Korean Minorities in China and Japan." In *International Migration Review.* Vol. 26, No. 1 (1990), pp. 4-21.

Rabinow, P. "Representations are Social Facts: Modernity and Post-Modernity in Anthropology." In James Clifford and George E. Marcus., eds. *Writing Culture: The Poetics and Politics of Ethnography.* Berkeley: University of California Press. 1996. pp. 234-261.

Rosett, A. "Legal Structures for Special Treatment of Minorities in the People's Republic of China." In *Notre Dame Law Review.* Vol.66, No. 5 (1991), pp. 1,503-1,529.

Sautman, B. "Myths of Descent, Racial Nationalism and Ethnic Minorities in the People's Republic of China." In Frank Dikotter, ed., *Racial Identities in China and Japan.* London: Hurst; Honolulu: University of Hawaii Press, forthcoming, 1997.

Skinner, G.W. "Mobility Strategies in Late Imperial China: A Regional Systems Analysis." In Carol Smith, ed., *Regional Systems,* Vol. 1: Economic Systems. New York: Academic Press, 1976, pp.327-364.

Smith, C., ed. *Regional System.* New York: Academic Press. 1976.

Stafford, C. "Chinese Nationalism and the Family." Man. Vol. 27, No. 2 (1992), pp. 362-74.

Strassberg, R.E. *Inscribed Landscapes: Travel Writing From Imperial China.* Berkeley: University of California Berkeley Press. 1994.

Tefft, S. "Ethnicity Stirs in a China Set on Wealth." In *Christian Science Monitor,* June 27, 1995. p. 1.

Thierry, F. "Empire and Minority in China." In Chaliand, G., ed., *Minority Peoples in the Age of Nation-States*. London: Pluto Press, pp. 76-99.

Thomas, M., ed. *Politics and Education*. New York: Pergamon Press.

Tsering Dorje Gashi. *New Tibet: Memoirs of a Graduate of the Peking Institute of National Minorities*. Dharamsala: Information Office of H.H. the Dalai Lama. 1980.

Wang, J.P. "Concord and Conflict: The Hui Communities of Yunnan Society in Historical Perspective." In *Lund Studies in African and Asian Religions*. *Vol. 11*. 1996.

Woodside, A. and B.A. Elman. "Introduction." In Alexander Woodside and Benjamin A. Elman, eds., *Education and Society in Late Imperial China. 1600-1900*. Berkeley: University of California Press. 1994. pp. 1-15.

Wyzan, M., ed. *The Political Economy of Ethnic Discrimination and Affirmative Action*. New York: Praeger. 1990.

Yan, R.X. "Marriage, Family and Social Progress of China's Minority Nationalities." In Chien C. and N. Tapp, eds., *Ethnicity and Ethnic Groups in China*. Hong Kong: Chinese University of Hong Kong, New Asia College. 1989, pp. 79-88.

SELECTED NEWSPAPER AND JOURNALS

American Ethnologist
Anthropology and Education Quarterly
Asian Folklore Studies
Beijing Review
Central Asian Survey
China Daily
China News Digest—Europe/Pacific Section (CND-EP)
China Quarterly
Chinese Exchange News
Comparative Education
Comparative Education Review
Comparative Politics
Comparative Studies in Society and History
Compare
Daedalus
Harvard Educational Review
International Migration Review
Journal of American Indian Education

Journal of the Anglo-Mongolian Society
Journal of Asian Studies
Journal of Contemporary Asia
Journal of Negro Education
Late Imperial China
Lund Studies in African and Asian Religions
Man
Mongolian Studies
Modern China
Notre Dame Law Review
South China Morning Post
Tibet Press Watch
Tibet Journal
Tibetan Bulletin
Xinhua News

Contributors

Gerard A. Postiglione is associate professor in comparative sociology of education and director of advanced studies in education and national development at the University of Hong Kong. He is series general editor of *Hong Kong Becoming China*, a multi-volume series published by M.E. Sharpe, New York, and editor of a number of volumes including: *Higher Education in Asia* (Greenwood Press, 1997); *Hong Kong's Reunion With China: The Global Dimensions* (M.E. Sharpe, 1997); *Schooling in Hong Kong: Organization, Teaching and Social Context* (Hong Kong University Press), *Social Change and Educational Development: Mainland China, Taiwan, and Hong Kong* (Center of Asian Studies, 1996); *The Hong Kong Reader: Passage to Chinese Sovereignty* (M.E. Sharpe, 1996); and *Education and Society in Hong Kong* (M.E. Sharpe, 1991). He is associate editor of the journal *Chinese Education and Society*, and has been an international consultant to the United Nations Development Programme and the Asian Development Bank on ethnic minority education in China. He is currently conducting a three year study of Tibetan education for the Research Grants Council of Hong Kong.

Dru C. Gladney is the dean of academics, Asia-Pacific Center in Honolulu, currently on leave from his positions as senior research fellow at the East-West Center and professor of Asian Studies and Anthropology at the University of Hawai'i at Manoa. He is author of the award-winning book, *Muslim Chinese: Ethnic Nationalism in the People's Republic* (Harvard University Press, 1996, 1st edition 1991) as well as three new books: *Ethnic Identity in China: The Making of a Muslim Minority Nationality* (Harcourt Brace, 1998); *Making*

Majorities: Composing the Nation in Japan, China, Korea, Malaysia, Fiji, Turkey, and the U.S. (Editor, Stanford University Press, in press 1998); and *Dislocating China: Muslims, Minorities, and Other Sub-Altern Subjects* (London, C. Hurst, forthcoming). His articles have appeared in *The Journal of Asian Studies, Current History, Public Culture, Cultural Survival Quarterly, Central Asian Survey, History and Anthropology, The Fletcher Forum of World Affairs, The International Journal of Middle Eastern Studies,* and *China Exchange News.*

Mette Halskov Hansen received her Ph.D. (1996) from the University of Aarhus, Denmark. She currently holds a grant from the University of Oslo, working mainly on the topic of Han Chinese migrants in minority areas of China and representations of Han. She has published a number of articles concerning ethnic minorities and minority education in China, as well as the monograph *Lessons in Being Chinese: Minority Education and Ethnic Identity in Southwest China* (University of Washington Press, 1999).

Stevan Harrell is professor and chair of the Department of Anthropology at the University of Washington. His recent work involves ethnic identity and ethnic relations in Southwest China. His monograph, *Ways of Being Ethnic In Southwest China*, is nearing completion, and he is also the author (with Bamo Ayi) of "Combining Ethnic Heritage and National Unity: a Paradox of Nuosu (Yi) language textbooks in China," *in Bulletin of the Concerned Asian Scholars,* 1998. He is now preparing, with Ma Erzi and Bamo Qubumo, a museum exhibit on Nuosu Arts and Ethnic Identity. He is also editor of *Cultural Encounters on China's Ethnic Frontiers*, Seattle and London: University of Washington Press, 1995.

Jacques Lamontagne is professor of comparative education and sociology of education in the Faculty of Education, University of Montreal (Quebec, Canada). He is presently conducting a Sino-Canadian research project on Educational Development in China. He is guest editor (with Ma Rong) of two issues of *Chinese Education & Society* (Armonk, New York : M.E. Sharpe, May-June 1998 and July-August 1998) on Rural Education Surveys in China, and co-editor (with

Ma Rong) of *Regional Variations of Rural Educational Development in China* (Fuzhou : Fujian Educational Press, 1998. In Chinese).

Ma Erzi (Mgebbu Lunze) grew up in Yangjuan Village, Baiwu Township, Liangshan Prefecture, Sichuan Province, and is now Associate Researcher and Associate Director of the Liangshan Prefecture Nationalities Research Institute. He is the responsible editor of the journal *Liangshan Nationalities Studies*, and is the author of a series of works on Nuosu history and society. He is currently preparing, with Stevan Harrell and Bamo Qubumo, a museum exhibit on Nuosu Arts and Ethnic Identity.

Colin Mackerras is professor and head of the School of Modern Asian Studies, Griffith University, Brisbane, Australia. He has published many books and articles on China's history, politics, culture and minorities. His main books on minorities are *China's Minorities: Integration and Modernization in the Twentieth Century*, Oxford University Press, Hong Kong, 1994 and *China's Minority Cultures: Identities and Integration Since 1912*, Longman, Melbourne, St Martin's Press, New York, 1995. He is also chief editor of *Dictionary of the Politics of the People's Republic of China*, Routledge, London, 1998.

Barry Sautman holds law degrees from the University of California at Los Angeles and New York University and a Ph.D. in political science from Columbia University. An Assistant Professor in the Division of Social Science, Hong Kong University of Science & Technology, his research focuses on ethnicity and nationalism in China.

Regie Stites is a researcher in the Center for Education and Human Services at SRI International (formerly Stanford Research Institute) in Menlo Park, California, USA. Dr. Stites was formerly a Research Associate in the National Center on Adult Literacy, Graduate School of Education, University of Pennsylvania and a senior researcher at the International Literacy Institute, also at the University of Pennsylvania. He has also been employed as a Research Associate in the National Center for Research on Evaluation, Standards, and Student Testing and as an instructor in the UCLA Graduate School of Education. Dr. Stites specializes in research on literacy and assessment.

Kevin Stuart has lived in China (the Inner Mongolia Autonomous Region and Qinghai Province) and Mongolia (Ulaanbaatar and Erdenet) since 1984. A folklorist, ethnographer, small scale development specialist, and teacher of English, his interests include northern China minorities and the Qinghai Han Chinese. He currently resides in Xining, Qinghai.

Janet L. Upton is a candidate for the Ph.D. in anthropology from the University of Washington. She is currently completing a dissertation on Tibetan education in the PRC, entitled "Schooling Shar-khog: Education, Modernity and Culture in 'China's Tibet'."

Zhu Yongzhong is a graduate of Qinghai Education College. He has been an instructor since 1987 and has taught at Guanting, Xiakou, and Zhongchuan middle schools in Minhe Hui and Monguor Autonomous County, where nearly all students are Monguor. Fluent in Monguor, several local Sinitic dialects, Modern Standard Chinese, and English he presently teaches at Zhongchuan Middle School while engaging in Monguor linguistic and folklore research and community development.

Index

REFERENCE BOOKS IN INTERNATIONAL EDUCATION
EDWARD R. BEAUCHAMP, *Series Editor*